Understanding Employment Discrimination Law

Carolina Academic Press Understanding Series

Understanding Administrative Law, Sixth Edition
William Fox, Jr.

Understanding Alternative Dispute Resolution
Kristen M. Blankley and Maureen A. Weston

Understanding Animal Law
Adam Karp

Understanding Antitrust and Its Economic Implications, Seventh Edition
E. Thomas Sullivan and Jeffrey L. Harrison

Understanding Bankruptcy, Fourth Edition
Jeffrey Ferriell and Edward J. Janger

Understanding California Community Property Law
Jo Carrillo

Understanding Capital Punishment Law, Fourth Edition
Linda E. Carter, Ellen S. Kreitzberg, and Scott W. Howe

Understanding Civil Procedure, Sixth Edition
Gene R. Shreve, Peter Raven-Hansen, and Charles Gardner Geyh

Understanding Civil Procedure: The California Edition
Walter W. Heiser, Gene R. Shreve, Peter Raven-Hansen, and Charles Geyh

Understanding Civil Rights Litigation, Second Edition
Howard M. Wasserman

Understanding Conflict of Laws, Fourth Edition
William M. Richman, William L. Reynolds, and Chris A. Whytock

Understanding Constitutional Law, Fifth Edition
William D. Araiza

Understanding Contracts, Fourth Edition
Jeffrey Ferriell

Understanding Copyright Law, Seventh Edition
Marshall A. Leaffer

Understanding Corporate Law, Fifth Edition
Arthur R. Pinto and Douglas M. Branson

Understanding Corporate Taxation, Fourth Edition
Leandra Lederman and Michelle Kwon

Understanding Criminal Law, Eighth Edition
Joshua Dressler

Understanding Criminal Procedure: Vol. 1: Investigation, Seventh Edition
Joshua Dressler, Alan C. Michaels, and Ric Simmons

Understanding Criminal Procedure: Vol. 2: Adjudication, Fourth Edition
Joshua Dressler and Alan C. Michaels

Understanding Disability Law, Third Edition-
Mark C. Weber

Understanding Election Law and Voting Rights
Michael R. Dimino, Bradley A. Smith, and Michael E. Solimine

Understanding Employee Benefits Law Second Edition
Kathryn L. Moore

Understanding Employment Discrimination Law, Third Edition
Thomas R. Haggard and Bruce N. Cameron

Understanding Employment Law, Third Edition
Paul M. Secunda, Richard A. Bales, and Jeffrey M. Hirsch

Understanding Environmental Law, Third Edition
Philip Weinberg and Kevin A. Reilly

Understanding Estate and Gift Taxation, Second Edition
Brant J. Hellwig and Robert T. Danforth

Understanding Evidence, Fifth Edition
Paul C. Giannelli

Understanding Family Law, Fourth Edition
John Gregory, Peter N. Swisher, and Robin Wilson

Understanding Federal and California Evidence
Paul C. Giannelli

Understanding Federal Courts and Jurisdiction, Second Edition
Linda Mullenix, Martin H. Redish, and Georgene Vairo

Understanding Federal Income Taxation, Sixth Edition
J. Martin Burke and Michael K. Friel

Understanding the First Amendment, Seventh Edition
Russell L. Weaver

Understanding Immigration Law, Third Edition
Kevin R. Johnson, Raquel Aldana, Bill Ong Hing, Leticia M. Saucedo, and Enid Trucios-Haynes

Understanding Insurance Law, Sixth Edition Robert H. Jerry, II and Douglas Richmond

Understanding Intellectual Property Law, Fourth Edition
Tyler T. Ochoa, Shubha Ghosh, and Mary LaFrance

Understanding International Business and Financial Transactions, Fourth Edition
Jerold A. Friedland

Understanding International Criminal Law, Third Edition
Ellen S. Podgor and Roger S. Clark

Understanding International Law, Second Edition
Stephen C. McCaffrey

Understanding Jewish Law, Second Edition
Steven H. Resnicoff

Understanding Juvenile Law, Fifth Edition
Martin Gardner

Understanding Labor Law, Fifth Edition
Douglas E. Ray, Calvin William Sharpe, and Robert N. Strassfeld

Understanding the Law of Terrorism, Second Edition
Erik Luna and Wayne McCormack

Understanding the Law of Zoning and Land Use Controls, Third Edition
Barlow Burke

Understanding Lawyers' Ethics, Fifth Edition
Monroe H. Freedman and Abbe Smith

Understanding Local Government, Second Edition
Sandra Stevenson

Understanding Modern Real Estate Transactions, Fourth Edition
Alex M. Johnson, Jr.

Understanding Negotiable Instruments and Payment Systems, Second Edition
William H. Lawrence

Understanding Nonprofit and Tax Exempt Organizations, Second Edition
Nicholas P. Cafardi and Jaclyn Fabean Cherry

Understanding Partnership and LLC Taxation, Fourth Edition
Jerold A. Friedland

Understanding Patent Law, Third Edition
Amy L. Landers

Understanding Products Liability Law, Second Edition
Bruce L. Ottley, Rogelio A. Lasso, and Terrence F. Kiely

Understanding Property Law, Fourth Edition
John G. Sprankling

Understanding Remedies, Third Edition
James M. Fischer

Understanding Sales and Leases of Goods, Third Edition
William H. Henning, William H. Lawrence, and Henry Deeb Gabriel

Understanding Secured Transactions, Fifth Edition
William H. Lawrence, William H. Henning, and R. Wilson Freyermuth

Understanding Securities Law, Seventh Edition
Marc I. Steinberg

Understanding Taxation of Business Entities
Walter D. Schwidetzky and Fred B. Brown

Understanding Torts, Sixth Edition
John L. Diamond, Lawrence C. Levine, and Anita Bernstein

Understanding Trade Secret Law
John G. Sprankling, Thomas G. Sprankling

Understanding Trademark Law, Fourth Edition
Mary LaFrance

Understanding Trusts and Estates, Sixth Edition Roger W. Andersen and Susan Gary

Understanding White Collar Crime, Fourth Edition
J. Kelly Strader

Understanding Employment Discrimination Law

THIRD EDITION

Thomas R. Haggard
Distinguished Professor Emeritus of Law
University of South Carolina School of Law

Bruce N. Cameron
Reed Larson Professor of Labor Law
Regent University School of Law

Carolina Academic Press
Durham, North Carolina

Library of Congress Cataloging-in-Publication Data

Names: Haggard, Thomas R., author. | Cameron, Bruce N., author.
Title: Understanding employment discrimination law / by Thomas R. Haggard, Bruce N. Cameron.
Description: Third edition. | Durham, North Carolina : Carolina Academic Press, LLC, [2020] | Series: Understanding Series.
Identifiers: LCCN 2020026644 (print) | LCCN 2020026645 (ebook) | ISBN 9781531011772 (paperback) | ISBN 9781531011789 (ebook)
Subjects: LCSH: Discrimination in employment--Law and legislation--United States.
Classification: LCC KF3464 .H34 2020 (print) | LCC KF3464 (ebook) | DDC 344.7301/133--dc23
LC record available at https://lccn.loc.gov/2020026644
LC ebook record available at https://lccn.loc.gov/2020026645

Carolina Academic Press
700 Kent Street
Durham, North Carolina 27701
Telephone (919) 489-7486
Fax (919) 493-5668
www.cap-press.com

Printed in the United States of America

Professor Haggard dedicates this edition to his wife of 58 years, Nell; his daughters Kathrine Hudgins and Julie Crowley; his grandchildren Danielle Crowley, Sarah Hudgins, Laura Nell Hudgins, and Ross Crowley; and our family's newest addition, his great granddaughter Luna Gray Crowley.

Professor Cameron dedicates this edition to the wife of his youth, Margaret Brennan Cameron, his two children, Christian Blake Cameron and Courtney Blair Cameron, and his three grandchildren, Elizabeth Ann Cameron, Alexandra Cameron Xifos, and William Harrison Cameron.

Contents

Preface to the Second Edition

The operative word in the title of this book, Understanding, may promise more than it can deliver. It would be a presumptuous author indeed to claim to fully understand this area of the law—if that is taken to mean knowing all of the literally thousands of highly technical statutory and decisional rules, comprehending what they mean in their individual capacities; reconciling them into a coherent whole; and appreciating their practical consequences in both the workplace and in the practice of employment discrimination law.

The reasons for this obstacle to full understanding are manifold.

- First, employment discrimination law flows not from a single statutory source, but from many statutes (federal and state), constitutional provisions, administrative regulations, and cases construing these primary sources.
- Second, these sources of law, particularly the statutes and regulations, are complex and lengthy documents that do not yield easily to paraphrase. The cases construing them are similarly prolix and difficult to untangle.
- Third, many of the statutes and administrative regulations are not adroitly drafted, leaving enormous gaps and ambiguities.
- Fourth, in attempting to fill the gaps and resolve the ambiguities, the lower courts often reach conflicting decisions. Significant differences exist between each federal circuit, between panels on each circuit, between the districts within each federal circuit, and even between the individual judges within the districts and circuits. These differences account for the proportionately large number of Supreme Court decisions devoted to employment discrimination law. But the Supreme Court cannot resolve every conflict, and so employment discrimination law remains highly federal circuit/district specific.
- Fifth, when the Supreme Court does purport to resolve the differences and clarify the law, its decisions are often beset with concurring and dissenting opinions. The precise holding of many Supreme Court cases and the significance of these decisions are fertile areas of even further disagreement among the scholars and lower courts. And it is not uncommon for the Court to revisit an issue several years later, to explain what they really meant in a prior decision.
- Sixth, Congress has not been hesitant to legislatively overrule the Supreme Court decisions it disagrees with. And from a purely drafting perspective, its handiwork often leaves much to be desired. These legislative overrulings then take the courts back to the drawing board to begin anew the case-by-case process of working out the details of the law.
- Seventh, even when some degree of precision and certainty is attained on a particular issue, the result is an onion-like body of law, with layer upon layer of

rules, subordinate rules, exceptions to the rules, and exceptions to the exceptions.

- Eighth, the language of employment discrimination law is ripe with terms of art, jargon, acronyms, and case-name substitutes for the more descriptive names of various doctrines, theories, and methods of proof. Although this book has tried to minimize the confusing impact of this — with terms of art, for example, often being printed in italics— the practitioner of this art must, perforce, learn its language.
- And ninth, whatever the law is today, it is likely to be different tomorrow.

In sum, employment discrimination law is like a huge jigsaw puzzle—albeit one with many missing, mismatched, and constantly changing pieces. It can also be put together in a variety of ways at any given time, depending on one's vision—and even then the total picture is a matter of interpretation.

What can the student and beginning practitioner do? First, there are some fundamental concepts, principles, doctrines, and theories that do endure from season to season. They are the relatively stable foundation upon which the superstructure of employment discrimination law is being built—and constantly rebuilt. The primary purpose of this book is to help with the achievement of that level of understanding. Second, anyone studying or working in this field should also have at least a general grasp of what the superstructure looks like at the moment. A knowledge of the major legal rules, and of the fact that differences exist with respect to their specific details, is necessary in order to understand the significance and meaning of the changes as they occur. Although writing at that level is like shooting at a rapidly moving target, the second purpose of this book is to summarize those rules as they currently exist —as I understand them, and this too may be subject to disagreement by others also well-versed in the field. I extend my thanks to the many people who contributed, directly or indirectly, to this undertaking My students over the last 25 years, who expected me to provide them with some degree of understanding rather than leaving them in a state of puzzlement, forced me to grapple with legal issues that would have been easier to gloss over or ignore. And the honest give-and-take of our classroom discussions enriched my appreciation for the diversity of legal conclusions that might flow from a common set of premises. The practicing lawyers who I worked with as Of Counsel to several law firms provided me with invaluable insights about how the law can be used effectively to resolve or forestall actual discrimination disputes in the workplace. And they taught me to appreciate the difference between matters that are of practical significance and those that are purely academic interest, causing me to focus this book on the former rather than the latter.

The authors of the many fine casebooks and treatises have significantly enhanced my understanding of the law, have been instructive on the various ways in which the materials can be organized, and have provided enlightenment of which cases and topics deserve coverage in this book—which is intended to supplement, not supplant, those more comprehensive sources of information.

Finally, two former students, who are now enormously successful practitioners, have contributed in a more literal and significant sense. Tracey C. Green is Special Counsel with Willoughby and Hoefer, P.A., of Columbia, South Carolina. His expertise in the procedural device through which the constitutional protections are enforced, Section 1893, and knowledge of the confusing limitations of the Eleventh Amendment have provided an enormous depth to this book. Leigh Nason, Shareholder with Ogletree, Deakins, Nash, Smoak & Stewart, PC, in the Columbia, South Carolina office, has likewise provided an in-depth coverage of the special nondiscrimination duties of government contractors, Executive Order 11246, and of the atypical nondiscrimination precepts of the Americans With Disabilities Act. I am proud to have worked with them on the book.

To all the readers of this book: I wish you success, happiness, and a fulfilling career in the law. And as you continue your reading and study of the law, remember...

Of making many books, there is no end, and much study is a weariness of the flesh.

Ecclesiastes 12:12
Thomas R. Haggard
Columbia, South Carolina
May 2008

Preface to the Third Edition

Even as the ink was still wet on copies of the prior edition of this book, the seeds of a need for a third edition were beginning to germinate. In the time between manuscript submission and publication, judicial decisions and legislative changes had already begun nibbling at the edges of the text's currency. And so it has continued, unabated, for the past 12 years.

The new publisher, Carolina Academic Press, thus decided that it was past time for a new edition to come out. But entreaties to Professor Haggard were unavailing. He had long since turned his attentions from the hoary pursuits of the law toward the more pleasant, to him, endeavors of gardening, chess, photography, leisure reading, and the study of theology. He indicated a willingness, however, to work as a *senior advisor* of sorts with someone willing to undertake the massive task of updating and revising the book while leaving its general structure and approach mostly intact. Professor Cameron, who was already using the book in his employment discrimination course, indicated an interest in doing this. And Professor Haggard was delighted and honored when he learned of this, for he had known Professor Cameron by reputation for several years. The joint venture was thus undertaken, and it has been completed. We have become dear friends.

The observations made in the preface to the second edition concerning the nature of the law of employment discrimination warrant consideration by the readers of this edition as well. Professors Haggard and Cameron, however, would like to add this final observation to the points made there: We fear that when teachers, students, and even judges deal with legal cases, whether it is to study or decide them, the people in these cases (sometimes even without the honor of having a name) become mere objects, like stick figures drawn on the blackboard to illustrate some professor's far-fetched hypothetical—merely pieces in a complex puzzle we are all trying to fit together.

This is wrong. We must all remember that these are stories about real flesh-and-blood people like you and me. What happened to them may be "interesting" to us or considered a "critical fact" to a judge. But to them it is often a tale of hurt, disappointment, hopes dashed, fears materialized, jobs and income lost, families broken, work-related friendships shattered, and lives permanently altered. In addition, whether these people win or lose their cases, they experience what is to them an intimidating, incomprehensible, lengthy, and expensive ordeal of meetings with lawyers, depositions, trials, and interminable appeals. Months and even years of their lives are invested in that cold, impersonal *Statement of Facts* with which we start a brief.

As professors and students, we are not directly involved with this harsh reality; and for now, there may be little or nothing we can do to change it. But we should also never forget it, become hardened to it, or fail to be saddened by it. We must always allow the intellectual joy and challenge we find in the law to be tempered by a sensitivity to the human element.

Finally, the authors would like to thank Elisabeth (Biz) Ebben, our editor, Susan Trimble, our production associate, at Carolina Academic Press, and Kaitlyn Shepherd and Melissa Terrell, students at Regent University School of Law, for all their work in reviewing our submissions and their careful attention to the page proofs.

Thomas R. Haggard
Columbia, South Carolina

Bruce N. Cameron
Virginia Beach, Virginia

Part I

Introduction

Chapter 1

An Overview

Synopsis

§ 1.01 The Sources of Employment Discrimination Law

[A] The United States Constitution[1]

As the fundamental law of the land, the United States Constitution imposes on public employers duties that limit their ability to make employment choices on the basis of certain characteristics—race, sex, national origin, religion, age, disability, citizenship, and others. In evaluating the constitutionality of a statute, regulation,

1. *See* Part II.

policy, or action that involves distinctions based on those characteristics, the courts follow an equal protection mode of analysis, as dictated by the Fifth and Fourteenth Amendments. The strength of this limitation on state power varies, however, depending on which *level of scrutiny* the courts decide to use when reviewing a particular governmental decision. The prohibition against race discrimination is perhaps the strongest, because the courts apply a *strict scrutiny* test to distinctions that are made on this basis. At the other extreme are distinctions made on the basis of disability, which are unconstitutional only if they lack a *rational basis.* In between these two approaches lies the *intermediate scrutiny* approach, which is used in cases of gender discrimination. The First Amendment and a few other constitutional provisions are occasionally implemented in employment discrimination cases.

[B] The Civil Rights Act of 1964[2]

This is the flagship of federal employment discrimination law. It applies to most public agencies and private employers, employment agencies, and labor unions. Title VII encompasses virtually every aspect of the employment relationship. It prohibits discrimination on the basis of race, color, religion, national origin, and sex. It also includes an anti-retaliation provision that protects individuals who oppose illegal employment practices or who exercise their rights under the Act.

A person claiming a Title VII violation must first file a charge with the federal Equal Employment Opportunity Commission, which will notify the appropriate state agency. Exhaustion of these administrative procedures is mandatory. Once they are exhausted, however, Title VII may be enforced in court by either the person claiming discrimination or the EEOC on that person's behalf. As a result of amendments adopted in the Civil Rights Act of 1991, a full range of remedies are now available to the victims of illegal Title VII discrimination—including injunctive relief requiring that the plaintiff be hired, reinstated, promoted, or transferred, together with an award of retroactive seniority, back pay, compensatory damages, punitive damages in some situations, and attorney's fees.

[C] The Age Discrimination in Employment Act[3]

In the year following enactment of the Civil Rights Act of 1964, Congress decided to also prohibit discrimination on the basis of age. But rather than simply adding this to the Title VII list, Congress chose to enact a separate statute. The ADEA applies to public and private employers, employment agencies, and labor unions. The protection, however, extends only to individuals who are age 40 or older. Thus, age discrimination against younger workers is not illegal.

Like Title VII, the ADEA covers most employment decisions. Because the substantive prohibitions of the ADEA and Title VII are so similar, many of the theories

2. 42 U.S.C. §§ 2000e to 2000e-17. *See* Part III.
3. 29 U.S.C. §§ 621 to 634. *See* Part IV.

of discrimination and of proof that were developed under one statute have been readily transposed into the other. Nevertheless, important substantive differences do exist. The enforcement procedures for Title VII and the ADEA are almost identical.

[D] The Civil Rights Act of 1866, Section 1981[4]

In terms of time-of-enactment, Section 1981 is the earliest of the current federal anti-discrimination statutes. Section 1981, however, was not recognized as creating a private cause of action until 1975.[5] As construed by the courts and as amended by the Civil Rights Act of 1991, Section 1981 now prohibits race discrimination in the formation, terms, administration, and enforcement of all contracts. This includes employment contracts, but the section also applies to independent contractor relationships, making Section 1981 unique in that regard among the other discrimination statutes.

Although limited to intentional discrimination on the basis of race, the concept of *race* has been broadly construed to include certain ethnic characteristics that are closely related to national origin. Historically, the advantages of bringing a Section 1981 action have been that this law does not require the exhaustion of any administrative remedies, it applies to employers regardless of the number of employees, plaintiffs are entitled to a trial by jury, and a prevailing plaintiff can recover compensatory and punitive damages. Since 1991, however, a jury trial and a limited amount of compensatory and punitive damages have also been available under Title VII,[6] thus blunting the advantages of a Section 1981 action somewhat. Nevertheless, a Section 1981 cause of action is commonly added to an otherwise predominantly Title VII lawsuit, because Section 1981 allows for the recovery of damages in excess of those allowed by Title VII.

[E] Civil Rights Act of 1871, Section 1983[7]

Suits alleging a violation of a constitutional right are usually brought under Section 1983 of the Civil Rights Act of 1866. Apart from the difficulty defining precisely what types of discrimination are constitutionally prohibited, this area of the law is also complicated by the existence of certain judicially created immunities that are available to public officials and, when the defendant is a state or state agency, by the Eleventh Amendment, which deprives federal courts of jurisdiction over some of these lawsuits.

[F] The Civil Rights Act of 1871, Section 1985(3)[8]

This section of the Act prohibits conspiracies among state officials and private individuals if some state connection exists to deprive other persons of their constitutional

4. 42 U.S.C. § 1981. *See* Chapter 22.
5. Johnson v. Ry. Express Agency, 421 U.S. 454 (1975).
6. 42 U.S.C. § 1981a.
7. 42 U.S.C. § 1983. *See* Chapter 23.
8. 42 U.S.C. § 1985(3). *See* Chapter 24.

rights. Although rarely used in the employment context, it is available if a particular need for it arises.

[G] The Equal Pay Act of 1963[9] & Lilly Ledbetter Fair Pay Act of 2009[10]

The Equal Pay Act, which was enacted in 1963 as an amendment to the Fair Labor Standards Act of 1938, requires the payment of equal wages to male and female employees within the same establishment who are performing "equal work on jobs the performance of which requires equal skill, effort, and responsibility, and which are performed under similar working conditions." Coverage extends to all individuals employed in an enterprise engaged in interstate commerce, which includes virtually everyone. The Act also prohibits unions from attempting to cause an EPA violation.

The linchpin of an EPA claim is proof that the jobs in question are substantially *equal*, not merely *comparable*. EPA cases thus tend to involve a great deal of complex, industry-specific, factual, and statistical analysis, but rather uncomplicated legal analysis.

In 2009, the Lilly Ledbetter Fair Pay Act was enacted to clarify when the statute of limitations begins to run for employees filing equal pay claims.

[H] Executive Order 11246[11]

Employers who do business with the federal government and their employees have an additional source of employment discrimination duties and rights. Under Executive Order 11246, as a condition of contacting with the government, employers are required to agree to assume anti-discrimination obligations that go significantly beyond those imposed by statutes of general application. In large part, these additional obligations involve gathering information about the racial, ethnic, and sexual composition of the workforce and the population from which the workforce is drawn; identifying disparities between the workforce and population statistics; and creating programs to eliminate any existing disparities. The Executive Order is administered by the Office of Federal Contract Compliance Programs, a part of the Department of Labor.

[I] The Americans with Disabilities Act[12]

Prior to 1990, disability discrimination in employment was dealt with primarily by several limited-coverage federal statutes[13] and state laws. In 1990, Congress enacted the comprehensive Americans with Disabilities Act, which covers public and private

---

9. 29 U.S.C. § 206(d) (part of the Fair Labor Standards Act). *See* Part VI.

10. 42 U.S.C. § 2000e-5(e)(3).

11. Executive Order 11,246, 30 Fed. Reg. 12,319 (1965). See Part VII.

12. 42 U.S.C. §§ 12101 *et seq. See* Part VIII.

13. The Rehabilitation Act of 1973, 29 U.S.C. § 701; The Veterans' Readjustment Assistance Act of 1974, 38 U.S.C. §§ 4211–14.

employers (with 15 or more employees), employment agencies, and labor unions. In 2008, Congress passed the ADA Amendments Act of 2008 to counter Supreme Court interpretations of the ADA that narrowed disability coverage.

The ADA bears few similarities to the other federal anti-discrimination statutes. For example, under Title VII, the EPA, and the ADEA, few questions ever arise over who is protected by the prohibition against discrimination on a particular basis. Everyone has a race and sex and is either age 40 or older or not. The ADA, on the other hand, only protects a "qualified individual with a disability," and whether one falls within this category is an issue in a large percentage of the litigated cases. While the other statutes operate mainly by way of prohibition of conduct, the ADA also imposes an affirmative duty of "reasonable accommodation"—the meaning of which is also extensively litigated.

Rather than attempting to create its own set of procedures and remedies, the ADA simply incorporates the relevant provisions of Title VII in this regard.

[J] Administrative Regulations

It is unclear whether the EEOC has authority to exercise any true delegated legislative power by issuing substantive rules that have the force of law and are binding on the courts. Title VII only empowers the EEOC to adopt "procedural regulations." On the other hand, the ADEA and the ADA both authorize the EEOC to "issue such rules and regulations as it may consider necessary or appropriate for carrying out of this Act, and may establish such reasonable exemptions to and from any or all provisions of this Act as it may find necessary and proper in the public interest." It is unclear what binding force such regulations might have.

[K] State and Local Anti-Discrimination Laws

The states were the first to enact employment discrimination statutes, with New York's law being a particularly influential example. When Congress enacted the Civil Rights Act of 1964, it recognized the role state and local government should play in dealing with this social problem. Thus, Congress not only waived the normal preemption effect that a federal law has on a state law dealing with the same matter, it required that a complainant resort to state law when it was available.

Although the duplicate prohibition aspect of federal/state law has been resolved almost totally in favor of the federal prohibition, with few state-law cases on the books, the additional discrimination prohibitions of state and local law continue to be of significance. For example, Title VII's prohibition against discrimination on the basis of sex was generally not considered to include discrimination on the basis of sexual orientation until the Supreme Court decided *Bostick v. Clayton County* in 2020.[14]

---

14. 590 U.S.___(2020).

Yet, for many years prior to that it was a proscribed basis of discrimination under some state and local laws. Similarly, apparel, grooming, physical appearance, tobacco use, and domestic arrangement discrimination is banned in other jurisdictions, in a manner that goes quite beyond the prohibitions of Title VII. Some state constitutions also contain prohibitions against various forms of discrimination in employment and other contexts.

[L] Contract and Tort Theories

Collective bargaining agreements between an employer and a union, which provide the substantive terms of each employee's contract, often contain provisions prohibiting discrimination on all the bases covered by federal statutory law. Individual contracts sometimes contain similar provisions. Collective bargaining agreements are nearly always enforced through arbitration, and this is also true of some individual contacts. Depending on the wording of these contractual enforcement mechanisms, they can entirely displace statutory provisions. In *14 Penn Plaza v. Pyett*,[15] the Supreme Court held that employees claiming age discrimination would have their civil rights claims determined by an arbitrator and not by a federal court judge. Another potential source of employee rights are employer manuals and handbooks containing assurances of nondiscriminatory treatment, which are often construed as legally binding contracts.

In addition to the various contract remedies, in some jurisdictions a discriminatory discharge has been found to be in violation of public policy, which is a tort entitling a successful plaintiff to punitive as well as compensatory damages. Finally, the manner in which a discriminatory termination is handled may give rise to a cause of action for the intentional infliction of emotional distress. Title VII race and sexual harassment cases also frequently include this as a claim.

§ 1.02 Reconciling the Various Sources of Law

Whenever the same activity is subject to regulation from multiple sources, jurisdictional priorities must sometimes be established and conflicts resolved. This is clearly true of employment discrimination.

As the fundamental law of the land, the United States Constitution trumps anything that is inconsistent with its provisions. Thus, a federal employment discrimination law that exceeded the congressional power to legislate would simply be invalid—such as a statute that goes beyond even the far reach of the Commerce Clause. A federal anti-discrimination statute imposing monetary damages on states and state agencies is constrained by the various limits that lurk within the Eleventh Amendment. To the extent that a prohibition against sex discrimination encompasses a prohibition

15. 556 U.S. 247 (2009).

against the creation of a sexually hostile environment, and to the extent that this is construed as prohibiting certain forms of speech, the prohibition may be a violation of the First Amendment and thus invalid. To the extent that the Constitution prohibits certain forms of racially or sexually sensitive *affirmative action*, any statutory or regulatory requirements to the contrary must be disregarded.

When state and federal law directly conflict, federal law prevails under the Supremacy Clause of the Constitution. State laws prohibiting women from working in certain occupations or at specified times of day or that mandate certain job-related benefits to women are thus invalid because of the federal prohibition against sex discrimination. The *conflict* variant of the preemption doctrine remains a viable theory for attacking state laws that affirmatively require discrimination, but the same cannot be said of the *occupancy-of-the-field* theory. Although Title VII provides a pervasive scheme of regulation, to the extent that it would normally be construed as totally preempting all state regulation in the area, the statute itself disclaims having such an effect. The Civil Rights Act of 1964 expressly states that it shall not be construed "as indicating an intent on the part of Congress to occupy the field in which any ... title operates to the exclusion of State laws on the same subject matter, nor shall any provision of this Act be construed as invalidating any provision of State law unless such provision in inconsistent with any of the purposes of this Act, or any provision thereof."[16]

Some federal statutes seem to mandate or affirmatively allow what other federal statutes may prohibit. The federal statutes themselves sometimes recognize and attempt to ameliorate the overlap and potential conflict that they are creating. Title VII, for example, declares that it is not a violation of Title VII for an employer to "differentiate upon the basis of sex in determining the amount of wages or compensation ... to be paid to employees of such employer if such differentiation is authorized by the [Equal Pay Act.]."[17] Unfortunately, it required a Supreme Court decision to resolve the meaning of that cryptic legislative command. Similarly, when the Civil Rights Act of 1991 added compensatory and punitive damages to the available Title VII remedies, it specifically excluded the possibility of double recovery of these damages under a parallel Section 1981 lawsuit. Unfortunately, the wording of the statute left it open to the interpretation that if these damages were even legally available under Section 1981, then an individual had to recover them under that section, or not at all—an interpretation ultimately rejected by the courts. In sum, the ad hoc congressional attempts at reconciliation of the various federal statutes have not been particularly successful—in the sense of avoiding litigation, at least.

§ 1.03 Statutory Interpretation

Since most employment discrimination law has a statutory source, the rules and techniques of statutory interpretation have played an important role in discrimination

16. 42 U.S.C. § 2000h-4.
17. 42 U.S.C. § 2000e-2.

litigation. The majority and dissenting opinions of many Supreme Court cases illustrate, however, that the so-called canons of statutory interpretation can produce divergent results. How the approach or principle of interpretation that the Court takes can be determinative of the result is clearly evident in the Court's recent decision in *Bostock v. Clayton County*.[18] The substantive issue in that case is discussed in § 9.04, where Justice Gorsuch for the majority and Justice Alito in dissent disagreed radically over what the original meaning or textualism doctrine means and how it applied to the facts of that case.

[A] Legislative Intent

The ultimate objective, of course, is to determine the intent of Congress. The perceived intent of the 1866 Congress heavily influenced the Supreme Court's determination that Section 1981 did not prohibit the non-intentional or *disparate impact* form of racial discrimination. In contrast, the perceived intent of the 1964 Congress to address all the consequences of discrimination, intended or otherwise, led the Court to recognize this as a form of prohibited conduct under Title VII. On the ever-controversial affirmative action issue, the Court went beyond the normal indicia of intent and purported to divine the motivating "spirit" of the legislation. However, in nearly all these and the other cases in which deference to congressional intent appeared to play a pivotal role in the decision, dissenting opinions marshaled evidence of congressional intent that pointed in the diametrically opposite direction.

Perhaps the most radically different expressions of congressional intent occurred during the enactment of the Civil Rights Act of 1991, especially in regard to the meaning of the *business necessity* defense to disparate impact discrimination. Congress, thus, finally took the unprecedented step of identifying the legislative history that the courts could rely and limiting it to one fairly innocuous but inconclusive interpretive memoranda.[19]

[B] Interpretive Guidelines

One canon of interpretation that has played an important role in employment discrimination litigation is that, within limits, a court should defer to the interpretation given that statute by the administrative agency charged with its enforcement. Although they lack the force of law that a true administrative regulation possesses, the EEOC's *Interpretive Guidelines* provide extensive discussion of almost every aspect of federal anti-discrimination law. Whether the ADEA and ADA *carrying out* regulations truly have the force or law or not, they at least have the same weight as the EEOC's Title VII *Guidelines*. Although the Supreme Court has given these *Guidelines* almost statute-

18. 590 U.S. __ (2020).

19. 42 U.S.C. § 2000e-2(k)(1)(A).

like deference in some cases, it has treated them as merely persuasive authority in others. Nevertheless, these agency interpretations do play an important role in the day-to-day practice of advising clients in employment discrimination matters.

§ 1.04 Chapter Highlights

1. The employment discrimination lawyer must be familiar with the following legal authorities: The United States Constitution, the Civil Rights Act of 1964, the Age Discrimination in Employment Act, Section 1981, Section 1983, Section 1985(3), the Equal Pay Act, Executive Order 11246, the Americans with Disabilities Act, administrative regulations, state constitutions, state and local anti-discrimination laws, and various contract and tort law theories. (§ 1.01)

2. Among these sources of law, the United States Constitution, of course, controls. It provides and limits the authority of Congress to act. It also guarantees to individuals certain substantive and procedural rights that neither Congress nor the states may encroach upon. Although in the normal case extensive federal legislation would have a preemptive effect on state laws dealing with the same matter, federal employment discrimination law expressly contemplates resort to state laws and disclaims having a preemptive effect unless the state law requires conduct the federal law prohibits or prohibits conduct the federal law requires. (§ 1.02)

3. Statutory interpretation plays an important role in employment discrimination litigation. Because they are complex and sometimes poorly drafted, employment discrimination statutes can often be interpreted in several ways, thus forcing the courts to attempt to determine congressional intent from the legislative history. The legislative history, however, is also sometimes obscure and conflicting. Another resource that the courts often consult are the interpretive guidelines promulgated by the administrative agencies charged with the responsibility for enforcing these laws. (§ 1.03)

Part II
Constitutional Prohibitions

Chapter 2

The Proscribed Bases

Synopsis

---

§ 2.01 Constitutional Sources

[A] The Equal Protection Clause

The primary vehicle for challenging employment discrimination on constitutional grounds is the Equal Protection Clause of the Fourteenth Amendment, which provides that no state may "deny to any person within its jurisdiction the equal protection of the laws." Although the Fifth Amendment, applicable to the federal government, does not contain an express *equal protection* provision, the Fifth Amendment's Due Process Clause has been construed as containing an implied equal protection component that is identical to that of the Fourteenth Amendment.[1]

The Equal Protection Clause does not mandate treatment that is literally equal in all respects among all individuals. Rather, whether a particular differential treatment, or *discrimination*, is unconstitutional or not depends on the basis of the distinction, the context, and the asserted justification. This translates into levels of scrutiny analysis, of which there are basically three.

At the highest level, the courts undertake a *strict scrutiny* of the government action. This test is applied whenever a classification is *inherently suspect*. Under this test, the classification will be upheld only if it is *narrowly tailored* to further some *compelling state interest*.[2] Next is the so-called *intermediate level of scrutiny*. Although the verbal formula for this approach is less well entrenched and often simply applied rather than declared, it basically means that the challenged classification must serve *important* objectives and bear a *substantial relationship* to the achievement of those objectives.[3] Finally, there is the *rational basis* test, which merely requires a *rational relationship* to a *legitimate* state interest.[4] Obviously, those verbal formulae do not create bright-line tests, and the difference between them is a fuzzy one at best. Nevertheless, the test that a court applies to a particular form of discrimination will often be outcome determinative.

Even if a particular form or act of alleged discrimination fails to meet the appropriate Equal Protection standard, to establish unconstitutionality a plaintiff must still prove that the act was intentional. Some forms of non-intentional discrimination that are prohibited by statute cannot, thus, be the basis of a constitutional claim. Indeed, to the extent that the Fourteenth Amendment is the constitutional predicate of the statute, the statute may be unenforceable if its substance goes beyond the constitutional prohibition or its remedial reach. Thus, in *Washington v. Davis*[5] the Supreme Court held that Section 1981, which was adopted pursuant to the Fourteenth Amendment, did not extend to disparate impact discrimination, which does not involve an element of intent. The scope of this limitation remains unclear, however.[6]

Finally, although most equal protection challenges are to broad governmental policies and practices, this constitutional guarantee can also be used to challenge individual employment decisions that are alleged to be discriminatory.[7] The right of an individual

---

1. Buckley v. Valeo, 424 U.S. 1 (1976).
2. Adarand Constructors, Inc. v. Pena, 515 U.S. 200 (1995).
3. Craig v. Boren, 429 U.S. 190 (1976).
4. Pennell v. City of San Jose, 485 U.S. 1 (1988).
5. 426 U.S. 229 (1976).
6. A related but less rigorous limitation exists with respect to the question of whether Congress has effectively waived a state's immunity under the Eleventh Amendment. *See* Chapter 3, § 3.05.
7. Sims v. Mulcahy, 902 F.2d 524 (7th Cir. 1990).

to challenge an employment decision was greatly narrowed in *Engquist v. Oregon Dept. of Agriculture*,[8] which eliminated "class of one" equal protection claims. It is no longer sufficient merely to claim that the different treatment was "arbitrary"; rather, the claim must assert that the differentiation was based on membership in a protected class.

[B] Other Constitutional Provisions

In addition to the Equal Protection Clause, other provisions of the Constitution have been used to challenge alleged discrimination by government employers. Religious discrimination, for example, is litigated almost exclusively under the Free Exercise Clause of the First Amendment. Adverse employment actions on the basis of the advocacy or practice of homosexuality have been challenged under both the Free Speech Clause of the First Amendment and the Due Process Clause of the Fourteenth Amendment—specifically, the substantive due process right of privacy. The Privileges and Immunities Clause of the Fifth Amendment has also been used to challenge discrimination on the basis of state citizenship. And the First Amendment right of association has been asserted in a number of employment discrimination contexts. In addition to these substantive protections, government employees often enjoy the right to fair procedures when employers take adverse action against them.

§ 2.02 Discrimination on the Basis of Race

[A] The General Rule

Under the Equal Protection Clause, the *strict scrutiny* test was first articulated, by name at least, in the context of a racial or national origin classification.[9] Very little racial discrimination, on a class-wide or individual basis, has survived this test. The possible exceptions are rare indeed. Supreme Court Justice Hugo Justice Black, for example, once suggested that prison authorities could separate inmates by race to stop an outbreak of disorder based on racial conflict.[10] And, indeed, the Seventh Circuit has found that an express preference for a black officer in a prison boot camp where most of the inmates were also black satisfied this test, since the success of the program depended on the presence of a black male in one of the available slots.[11] Other than that, almost all public employment discrimination *against* racial minorities has been found to be unconstitutional. The issue, rather, has been whether the *strict*

---

8. 553 U.S 591 (2008).

9. Korematsu v. United States, 323 U.S. 214 (1944).

10. Lee v. Washington, 390 U.S. 333, 334 (1968) (Black, J., concurring).

11. Wittmer v. Peters, 87 F.3d 916 (7th Cir. 1996) (but rejecting the so-called *role model* justification for the preference).

scrutiny standard even applied when the discrimination inures to the benefit of racial minorities and, if so, what policies meet its stringent requirement.

[B] Affirmative Action

[1] Introduction

Whether it is a matter of public policy, philosophy, statutory interpretation, or constitutional law, few issues have divided this country—and the United States Supreme Court—more deeply than the issue of affirmative action.

[2] The Test

In *City of Richmond v. J.A. Croson Co.*,[12] a majority of the justices concluded that the *strict scrutiny* test should be applied to the city's plan to increase the number of minority-owned businesses who were awarded city construction contracts.[13] The dissenters contended that the *intermediate level of scrutiny* was appropriate. Subsequently, in *Metro Broadcasting, Inc. v. Federal Communications Commission*,[14] the four dissenters in *Croson* were now joined by Justice White in holding that the *intermediate level of scrutiny* test applied to affirmative action by the federal government. The state/federal distinction was predicated on the theory that Congress has an affirmative duty to ensure equal protection and that its remedial decisions in that regard were entitled to greater judicial deference than those of the states. Following Justice Brennan's retirement, the Court in *Adarand Constructors, Inc. v. Pena*[15] lost little time in overruling *Metro Broadcasting*, holding that the *strict scrutiny* test applied regardless of whether the government actor was state or federal. That view still prevails, with the focus now on what constitutes a *compelling state interest* and whether the means chosen are *narrowly tailored* to serve that interest.[16]

[3] Compelling *State Interests*

The only Supreme Court decision to deal directly with affirmative action in the public employment context is *Wygant v. Jackson Board of Education*,[17] which involved the constitutionality of the use of racial-minority preferences in determining which teachers would be laid off. Justice Powell's plurality opinion adhered to the *strict scrutiny* test. He indicated that remedying societal discrimination by creating "role models" for students was not a compelling interest insofar as this particular employer was concerned. And he further suggested that remedying that particular employer's

---

12. 488 U.S. 469 (1989).

13. In *Wygant v. Jackson Bd. of Ed.*, 476 U.S. 267 (1986), the plurality opinion of Justice Powell opined that *strict scrutiny* was the proper test to apply in affirmative action cases, but *Croson* was the first case in which that view garnered a majority of the justices.

14. 497 U.S. 547 (1990).

15. 515 U.S. 200 (1995).

16. Fisher v. Univ. of Tex., 136 S. Ct. 2198 (2016).

17. 476 U.S. 267 (1986).

own discrimination was possibly the only legitimate justification, which would further also require that the public employer "have sufficient evidence to justify the conclusion that there has been prior discrimination."[18] In her concurring opinion, Justice O'Connor agreed that *strict scrutiny* of the policy was required, that remedying "societal discrimination" was inadequate justification, and that the employer must have a "firm basis" for believing that it had engaged in the prior discrimination it was now allegedly remediating. But she left the door open for the Court's recognition of other *compelling state interests* in the employment context.

In other affirmative action contexts that the Court might look to in this regard, the other *interest* that is most frequently discussed is that of maintaining diversity. In *Petit v. City of Chicago*,[19] the Seventh Circuit accepted the "operational need for a diverse police department" as a sufficient compelling interest for modest affirmative action promotions. However, the "educational benefits" of acceptance, tolerance, or increased camaraderie that ostensibly arise from diversity do not constitute a compelling interest for firefighters.[20] The desire to create a "rainbow" is not a compelling interest.[21]

Even if an affirmative action plan is unconstitutional under the strict scrutiny test, a government action involving a specific individual may still be upheld under the *same decision* defense. As the Supreme Court put it, "[W]here a plaintiff challenges a discrete governmental decision as being based on an impermissible criterion and it is undisputed that the government would have made the same decision regardless, there is no cognizable injury warranting relief under § 1983."[22] Thus, a non-minority applicant who is not hired pursuant to what proves to be an unconstitutional affirmative action plan would not be entitled to relief if the public employer establishes that this person also lacked the minimal qualifications for the job.

[4] Relationship with Title VII

The difference between the meaning and application constitutional test and the Title VII test has never been clear. Certainly, the wording is different. The Title VII test[23] derives from *United Steelworkers of America v. Weber*,[24] and was most recently applied by the Court in *Johnson v. Transportation Agency, Santa Clara County*.[25] In *Johnson*, the Court noted that "we do not regard as identical the constraints of Title VII and the Federal Constitution on voluntarily adopted affirmative action plans."[26] Specifically, the difference seems to be that the Constitution requires proof that the

18. Wygant, 476 U.S. at 277; *see also* J.A. Croson Co., 488 U.S. at 497–98; Adarand, 515 U.S. 200.
19. 352 F.3d 1111, 1114 (7th Cir. 2003).
20. Lomack v. City of Newark, 463 F.3d 303, 310 (3d Cir. 2006).
21. *Lomack*, 463 F.3d at 311.
22. Texas v. Lesage, 528 U.S. 18, 21 (1999).
23. The Title VII test is discussed in Chapter 5, § 5.11.
24. 443 U.S. 193 (1979).
25. 480 U.S. 616 (1987).
26. Johnson, 480 U.S. at 632.

affirmative action plan was designed to remedy prior racial discrimination by the agency adopting the plan, while the Title VII test merely requires proof of a "conspicuous ... imbalance in traditionally segregated job categories,"[27] regardless of whether the *imbalance* was caused by the employer's own prior discrimination. Significantly, in *Johnson*, Justice O'Connor disagreed with the majority's asserted lack of congruence between the statutory and constitutional tests, but in doing so she also created some uncertainty over what she thought the unified test really meant.

§ 2.03 Discrimination on the Basis of National Origin

In *Hernandez v. Texas*,[28] the Supreme Court held that national origin discrimination is, like race discrimination, subject to the *strict scrutiny* test. It is unclear whether a national origin discriminatory classification that would qualify as a BFOQ under Title VII would also qualify as a *compelling state interest* under the Equal Protection analysis.

§ 2.04 Discrimination on the Basis of Sex

Sex-based classifications and decisions by public employers have usually been evaluated under what is termed an *intermediate level of scrutiny* test, as articulated by the Court in *Craig v. Boren*.[29] Prior to the crystallization of that test, the Court had invalidated laws that entitled women to fewer benefits for their families than were provided to male employees.[30] Presumably, those decisions survive *Craig*. For example, in *Frontiero v. Richardson*,[31] the Court invalidated federal statutes that allowed men in the military service to claim their wives as dependents but required women to submit proof that their husbands qualified. The Court later said that the statute in *Frontiero* was based on stereotypical notions about the respective roles of married men and women.[32]

Challenges to laws that provide greater benefits for women than men have met with mixed results. In *Wengler v. Druggists Mutual Insurance Co.*,[33] the Court extended

27. Johnson, 480 U.S. at 630 (quoting *Weber*, 443 U.S. at 209).
28. 347 U.S. 475 (1954); *see also* Korematsu v. United States, 323 U.S. 214 (1944).
29. 429 U.S. 190 (1976).
30. Weinberger v. Wiesenfeld, 420 U.S. 636 (1975); Frontiero v. Richardson, 411 U.S. 677 (1973).
31. 411 U.S. 677 (1973).
32. Schlesinger v. Ballard, 419 U.S. 498 (1975).
33. 446 U.S. 142 (1977).

the protection to men, invalidating a workers' compensation law that allowed death benefits to a widower under less favorable conditions that those allowed to a widow.[34] But many *benign discrimination* statutes have been upheld under the *intermediate level of scrutiny* test. Thus, in *Califano v. Webster*,[35] the Court upheld a provision in the Social Security law that enabled women to compute benefits based on past earnings under a more favorable formula that male employees used, on the theory that this was a necessary remedy for prior employment discrimination against women as a class. Similarly, in *Schlesinger v. Ballard*,[36] the Court upheld a mandatory discharge (for lack of promotion) policy that was more favorable to women than to men. This was justified on the grounds that women did not enjoy equal career opportunities, due in part to their ineligibility to work in combat roles.

In sum, both before and after *Craig* and the formal adoption of the *intermediate level of scrutiny test*, employment-related laws that disadvantage women have been struck down in much the same fashion as they would have been under *strict scrutiny*, while laws that advantage women because of past or existing discrimination are upheld more readily.

The requirement that constitutional violations be established with proof of discriminatory intent caused the Supreme Court to uphold a state veterans' preference statute in *Personnel Administrator of Massachusetts v. Feeney*.[37] Under the statute, the state was required to consider qualified veterans for civil service jobs before it could consider qualified non-veterans. Since most veterans are male, this obviously disadvantaged women as a class. However, the Court held that the statute was facially neutral, since it purported only to distinguish between veterans and non-veterans. Moreover, although the Court conceded that the legislature may have been aware of the impact the preference would have on women, it held that the *discriminatory intent* element requires proof that the legislature acted "because of, not merely in spite of" the adverse impact consequences a particular law might have.[38] The plaintiff had failed to make that proof.

§ 2.05 Discrimination on the Basis of Sexual Orientation

In *Bostock v. Clayton Cty.*[39] the Supreme Court held that sexual orientation is included as a part of the Title VII ban on sex discrimination. Prior to *Bostock*, plaintiffs

---

34. *See also* Califano v. Goldfarb, 430 U.S. 199 (1977) (striking down a provision of the Social Security law that required male, but not female, spouses of deceased wage earners to prove dependency as a condition of receiving benefits).

35. 430 U.S. 313 (1977).

36. 419 U.S. 498 (1975).

37. 442 U.S. 256 (1979).

38. Feeney, 442 U.S. at 258.

39. 590 U.S. __ (2020).

complaining of governmental employment treatment on this basis have relied on the Constitution. In *Bowers v. Hardwick*,[40] the Supreme Court first held that engaging in homosexual activity was not a fundamental right and that the *rational basis* test applied. Applying this test, most courts have thus found that state and federal laws prohibiting homosexual conduct and employment decisions on that basis are not unconstitutional.[41]

The challenges based on the First Amendment freedom of speech have fared only slightly better. In one case, for example, a court held that a statute allowing teachers to be terminated for advocating homosexuality violated the speech clause of the First Amendment.[42] But the court also noted that a termination for practicing homosexuality would not violate the constitutional right of privacy. On the other hand, another court upheld an Army regulation requiring the discharge and prohibiting the re-enlistment of a service member who admitted to being a homosexual.[43] The court reasoned that although this was putative *speech*, it implied a desire and propensity to engage in homosexual acts—*conduct* that the military could constitutionally prohibit. Similarly, another court upheld the military's former "don't ask, don't tell" policy on the grounds that an individual who admitted homosexuality still had the opportunity to demonstrate that he or she did not intend to engage in homosexual acts.[44]

These early lower court decisions, which generally deny constitutional employment rights to those with a homosexual orientation, are now subject to renewed challenges on the basis of two more recent Supreme Court decisions.

In *Romer v. Evans*,[45] the Court considered an Equal Protection challenge to an amendment to the Colorado constitution that forbad state and local governments from prohibiting discrimination on the basis of sexual orientation—which included at laws prohibiting employment discrimination on that basis.[46] The Court concluded that this amendment did not satisfy even the minimal requirements of the *rational basis* test and carefully avoided deciding whether a *strict scrutiny* standard might apply. The Court simply stated that "the amendment has the peculiar property of

40. 478 U.S. 186 (1986).

41. *See, e.g.*, Padula v. Webster, 822 F.2d 97 (D.C. Cir. 1987) (upholding FBI's policy of refusing to hire "practicing homosexuals"). *But see* SmithKline Beecham Corp. v. Abbott Labs, 740 F.3d 471, 481 (9th Cir. 2014) (heightened scrutiny); Cammermeyer v. Aspin, 850 F. Supp. 910 (W.D. Wash. 1994) (holding that the policy of barring individuals from military service because of homosexuality had no rational basis).

42. National Gay Task Force v. Board of Educ. of Oklahoma City, (10th Cir. 1984), *aff'd*, 470 U.S. 903 (1985) (per curiam, by equally divided court).

43. Shalom v. Marsh, 881 F.2d 454 (7th Cir. 1989).

44. Able v. United States, 155 F.3d 628 (2d Cir. 1998).

45. 517 U.S. 620 (1996).

46. Although the primary impact of the Amendment was, apparently, on local laws prohibiting discrimination by "providers of public accommodations," the Court also cited an Executive Order covering all state employees and several statutory provisions covering employees at state colleges.

imposing a broad and undifferentiated disability on a single named group, an exceptional and ... invalid form of legislation.... [which] lacks a rational relationship to legitimate state interests."[47]

Then, in *Lawrence v. Texas*,[48] the Court revisited the *Bowers* issue of the constitutionality of a state statute making "sodomy" a criminal offense. But instead of proceeding on an Equal Protection basis, the Court invalidated the statute on the grounds of the broader Due Process Clause—namely, the substantive Due Process right of privacy. Quoting from Justice Stevens dissent in *Bowers*, the Court held that "individual decisions ... by married as well as unmarried persons ... concerning the intimacies of their physical relationship ... are a form of 'liberty' protected by the Due Process Clause of the Fourteenth Amendment."[49] And the Court further added that the "statute furthers no legitimate state interest which can justify its intrusion into the personal and private life of the individual"[50]—which also has obvious relevance to an Equal Protection analysis.

In *Obergefell v. Hodges*,[51] the Supreme Court held in a 5–4 decision that the Due Process and Equal Protection Clauses require that same sex couples have a right to marry. Although the decision is premised on the right to marry, it noted "the interlocking nature of these constitutional safeguards in the context of the legal treatment of gays and lesbians."[52]

After *Bostick*, employees challenging discrimination on the basis of sexual orientation will likely rely on Title VII rather than constitutionally based arguments.

§ 2.06 Discrimination on the Basis of Age

Governmental classifications and decisions that are predicated on the age of an individual are subject only to the *rational basis* test. Thus, in *Massachusetts Board of Retirement v. Murgia*,[53] the Court upheld the mandatory retirement of state police officers at age 50. Similarly, in *Vance v. Bradley*,[54] the Court upheld the mandatory retirement of foreign service employees at age 60. Although the government articulated a rational basis for its policy and the facts seemed to support it, the Court emphasized

47. Romer, 517 U.S. at 632.
48. 539 U.S. 558 (2003).
49. Lawrence, 539 U.S. at 578.
50. Lawrence, 539 U.S. at 578.
51. 135 S. Ct. 2584 (2015).
52. *Obergefell*, 135 S. Ct. at 2590.
53. 427 U.S. 307 (1976).
54. 440 U.S. 93 (1979).

that it was not the government's burden to justify the classification. Rather, consistent with the *rational basis* test, it is the plaintiff who must "convince the court that the legislative facts on which the classification is apparently based could not reasonably be conceived to be true by the government decisionmaker."[55]

§ 2.07 Discrimination on the Basis of Disability

In *City of Cleburne v. Cleburne Living Center*,[56] the Supreme Court held persons with an intellectual disability did not constitute a suspect or quasi-suspect class and that differentiation need only be "rationally related to a legitimate governmental purpose"—a standard, however, that was not satisfied in that case. Subsequently, the Court applied an even less stringent test in a case also involving persons with an intellectual disability. In *Heller v. Doe*,[57] the court said that a classification on this basis "must be upheld against equal protection challenge if there is any reasonably conceivable state of facts that could provide a rational basis for the classification."[58]

The lower courts have thus expanded the coverage of the *rational basis* test to include persons with other disabilities and medical conditions.[59] Indeed, the Supreme Court has bluntly stated that special accommodations for the disabled must come through legislation, not the Equal Protection Clause of the Constitution.[60]

§ 2.08 Discrimination on the Basis of State Residence

States frequently attempt to favor residents over non-residents in the allocation of a variety of benefits, including employment. Although this distinction is subject to *rational basis* scrutiny under the Equal Protection Clause,[61] these cases are more likely to be litigated under the Privileges and Immunities Clause of Article IV, which pro-

55. Vance, 440 U.S. at 111.

56. 473 U.S. 432 (1985).

57. 509 U.S. 312 (1993).

58. Heller, 509 U.S. at 320 (quoting FCC v. Beach Communications, Inc., 508 U.S. 307, 313 (1970)).

59. *See, e.g.*, Leckelt v. Board of Comm'rs, 909 F.2d 820 (5th Cir. 1990) (persons with HIV infection working in a medical center); Costner v. United States, 720 F.2d 539 (8th Cir. 1983) (persons with epilepsy in a truck driver position).

60. University of Alabama v. Garrett, 531 U.S. 356 (2001).

61. Zobel v. Williams, 457 U.S. 55 (1982) (striking down, on equal protection grounds, Alaska's preference for long-term over short-term residents in the distribution of the state's oil-boom wealth).

vides: "The Citizens of each State shall be entitled to all the Privileges and Immunities of Citizens in the several States."[62]

The Supreme Court has articulated a two-step test for analyzing Privileges and Immunities Clause claims.[63] First, the activity in question must be one that the Privileges and Immunities Clause was intended to protect. The test the Court often states is taken from an early nineteenth-century decision by Justice Washington, sitting as a circuit court judge. He said that the clause protects only "those privileges and immunities which are, in their nature, fundamental; which belong, of right, to the citizens of all free governments; and which have, at all times, been enjoyed by the citizens of the several states which compose this Union."[64] Second, however, the non-resident restriction may still be justified if the discrimination promotes a significant state interest.

In *Hicklin v. Orbeck*,[65] the Supreme Court struck down an "Alaska hire" statute that imposed a state-residence preference on all employment related to the State's development of its oil and gas resources. The Court noted that the State's ownership of these resources was a factor to consider, but it was not conclusive of the Privileges and Immunities issue. Regarding employment directly with a governmental employer, the Court in *United Building & Construction Trades Council v. Mayor of Camden*,[66] stated that this principle also applied to a 40% City-resident hiring quota imposed on contractors and subcontractors doing work on City projects. The Court further stated: "Public employment, however, is qualitatively different from employment in the private sector; it is a subspecies of the broader opportunity to pursue a common calling"[67]—noting that public employment was not a fundamental right for Equal Protection purposes either.

§ 2.09 Discrimination on the Basis of Citizenship

The test for determining the constitutionality of citizenship or alienage employment discrimination depends on whether the discrimination is by the federal or a state government. In evaluating such discrimination under state law, the Court generally applies a *strict scrutiny* test. The Court has thus invalidated laws that bar aliens from

62. The Fourteenth Amendment also contains a Privileges and Immunities Clause, but one that is not limited to residents of other states and which, thus, has played no role in the cases involving discrimination against non-residents—or any other type of case, since it has been so narrowly construed.

63. United Building & Constr. Trades Council v. Mayor & Council of Camden, 465 U.S. 208 (1984).

64. Corfield v. Coryell, 6 F. Cas. 546, 551 (C.C.E.D. Pa. 1823) (No. 3,230).

65. 437 U.S. 518 (1978).

66. 465 U.S. 208 (1984).

67. United Building & Construction, 465 U.S. at 219.

all classes of state civil service jobs.[68] An exception exists, however, for "laws that exclude aliens from positions intimately related to the process of democratic self-government."[69] This applies "only to 'persons holding state elective or important nonelective executive, legislative, and judicial positions,' those officers who 'participate directly in the formulation, execution, or review of broad public policy' and hence 'perform functions that go to the heart of representative government.' "[70] The Court has thus upheld laws that require citizenship of police officers,[71] probation officers,[72] and teachers.[73]

On the other hand, the Court purports to review citizenship discrimination by the federal government on a more relaxed standard, on the theory that the federal government has express constitutional power over matters relating to immigration and naturalization. Nevertheless, the Court has struck down legislation barring aliens from all federal civil service laws.[74] However, if the President or Congress makes a determination that an alienage classification is necessary to or promotes the foreign policy of the United States, then the Court will normally defer to that determination.[75]

§ 2.10 Discrimination on the Basis of Religion

Article VI specifically prohibits the use of any religious test as a condition of employment with the federal government.[76] The First Amendment's Free Exercise Clause, which also applies to state and local governments, has been construed as containing a similar virtually absolute prohibition against discrimination on the basis of religious belief. Thus, in *Torcaso v. Watkins*,[77] the Supreme Court invalidated a state constitutional provision that made a belief in God a prerequisite to holding public office. Presumably, any employment discrimination by a public employer purely on the basis of an individual's religious beliefs or affiliations would be similarly unconstitutional.

Discrimination on the basis of religious practices has been treated somewhat differently. This derives from the Supreme Court's decision in *Reynolds v. United States*,[78] which held that while religious *beliefs* are entitled to absolute protection, religious

68. Sugarman v. Dougall, 413 U.S. 634 (1973).

69. Bernal v. Fainter, 467 U.S. 216, 220 (1984).

70. Cabell v. Chavez-Salido, 454 U.S. 432, 440 (1982) (quoting *Sugarman*, 413 U.S. 634, 647 (1973)).

71. Foley v. Connelie, 435 U.S. 291 (1978).

72. *Cabell*, 454 U.S. 432 (1982).

73. Ambach v. Norwick, 441 U.S. 68 (1979).

74. Hampton v. Mow Sun Wong, 426 U.S. 88 (1976).

75. Mathews v. Diaz, 426 U.S. 67 (1976); Vergara v. Hampton, 581 F.2d 1281 (7th Cir. 1978) (excluding resident aliens from federal competitive civil service).

76. U.S. Const. art. VI.

77. 367 U.S. 488 (1961).

78. 98 U.S. 145 (1879).

practices that are "in violation of social duties or subversive of good order"[79] receive virtually no protection. However, Supreme Court decisions later applied a more rigorous test for laws that burden the free exercise of religion. Some of these arose in the context of work or employment. For example, in *Sherbert v. Verner*,[80] the Court held that it was unconstitutional to deny unemployment compensation to an individual who was unemployed because of her religiously based refusal to work on Saturday. Once an individual establishes that a law creates a substantial burden on free exercise, then the state must justify the law by reference to a compelling state interest and show that the law was the least restrictive way to serve that interest. The state was unable to satisfy that test in *Sherbert*,[81] while in the earlier case of *Braunfeld v. Brown*,[82] the Court had upheld a Sunday closing law, despite the burden it placed on merchants whose religious beliefs required that they close on Saturday, because of the state's interest in providing a uniform day of rest for citizens. Similarly, in *Goldman v. Weinberger*,[83] the Court upheld a military regulation forbidding an Orthodox Jew from wearing his yarmulke while on duty, although this was premised in part on the high degree of deference the court are expected to afford military regulations.[84]

During this era, however, whatever protection the *Sherbert* test afforded to the free exercise of religion by employees, employers generally did not enjoy the same liberty. For example, in *EEOC v. Townley Engineering & Mfg. Co.*,[85] the Ninth Circuit Court of Appeals held that prohibiting an employer from requiring employees to attend a devotional service that the employer believed was required by his Christian obligation to "share the Gospel" simply did not have the requisite impact on religious beliefs to satisfy the *Sherbert* test.

Whatever promise *Sherbert* might have held for employment-related free exercise claims was ultimately dashed, however, by the Supreme Court's decision in *Employment Division, Department of Human Resources of Oregon v. Smith*.[86] Several members of the Native American Church were terminated from their jobs at a private drug rehabilitation center when it was discovered that they ingested peyote as part of a sacramental ritual. They were later denied unemployment benefits because they had been

79. Reynolds, 98 U.S. at 164.

80. 374 U.S. 398 (1963).

81. *See also* Thomas v. Review Bd. of the Indiana Employment Security Div., 450 U.S. 707 (1981) (individual who quit his job because of his religious beliefs preventing him from helping to produce war materials held to be entitled to unemployment compensation).

82. 366 U.S. 599 (1961).

83. 475 U.S. 503 (1986).

84. *But see* United States v. Board of Educ. for Sch. Dist. of Philadelphia, 911 F.2d 882 (3d Cir. 1990) (requiring Title VII accommodation of a female Muslim public school teacher who wanted to wear a head scarf and a long, loose dress despite state law prohibiting public school teachers from wearing clothes indicating membership in a religion); Brown v. Polk County, Iowa, 61 F.3d 650 (8th Cir. 1995) (en banc) (holding that any employee religious activities that can be accommodated under Title VII without undue hardship are also protected by the Free Exercise Clause when a public employer is involved).

85. 859 F.2d 610 (9th Cir. 1988).

86. 494 U.S. 872 (1990).

terminated for work-related misconduct; the use of peyote was a criminal act under the state's controlled substance laws. The Court noted that the only government action that had ever been invalidated by the Court under the Free Exercise Clause was the denial of unemployment benefits, but none of those cases involved the violation of a criminal statute and all required individualized governmental assessment of the employees religious claim. That was not the case here. Moreover, the Court went beyond that and said, albeit without overruling *Sherbert* on its facts, that it would not apply the compelling state interest test to religiously motivated objections to any other neutral, generally applicable laws. Thus, in *Ryan v. United States Dept. of Justice*,[87] the Seventh Circuit Court of Appeals upheld the discharge of an FBI agent who refused to investigate antiwar groups because of his religious beliefs. The Court held that the FBI insubordination rules satisfied the neutral rule of general application requirement of *Smith*.

Congress responded to the *Smith* case by enacting the Religious Freedom Restoration Act,[88] which restored the *Sherbert* compelling state interest test. The Supreme Court, however, had the last word and declared that Congress had exceeded its powers when it attempted to change the Court-articulated substance of constitutional law by legislation.[89]

More recently, the Court deviated from the *Smith* rule in *Hosanna-Tabor Evangelical Lutheran Church and School v. EEOC*.[90] It held that a religious school lawfully discharged a teacher who claimed rights under the Americans with Disabilities Act. Although the ADA is both neutral and generally applicable, the school's authority, pursuant to the Free Exercise and Establishment Clauses, to choose who would promote its religious teachings was determined to be paramount.

In sum, by virtue of *Smith*, both employees and employers have generally greater rights under the *reasonable accommodation* and *undue hardship* tests of Title VII[91] than they do under the Constitution.

§ 2.11 Discrimination on the Basis of the Exercise of Other First Amendment Rights

[A] Speech

Although termination of public employment can be a form of "abridgement" under the First Amendment, most speech by public employees is not protected. The Supreme

87. 950 F.2d 458 (7th Cir. 1991).
88. 42 U.S.C. § 2000bb (1988).
89. City of Boerne v. Flores, 521 U.S. 507 (1997).
90. 132 S. Ct. 694 (2012).
91. *See* Chapter 11, § 11.04.

Court articulated the controlling test in *Connick v. Myers.*[92] First, the subject of the speech must be one of "public concern." This has been held to include opposition to President Reagan's policies, even though it was expressed in the form of a hope that the next assassination attempt would be successful;[93] a questionnaire distributed to assistant district attorneys enquiring if they felt pressured to work in political campaigns on behalf of candidates the office supported;[94] and criticism of a clerk's use of public resources to make repairs on his home and the mayor's reappointment of that clerk.[95] On the other hand, matters that are not of "public concern" include matters relating to the confidence and trust other employees have in their supervisors, the level of office morale, the need for a grievance procedure, and speech relating to the employee's official duties.[96] Likewise, it does not include matters of purely individual concern, such as an employee's perceived salary disparity between himself and other employees.[97]

Second, even if the subject of the speech is a matter of "public concern," a court must balance that against the public employer's legitimate interests in preserving workplace discipline and efficiency. The burden is on the employer to establish such interference, although the courts are generally reluctant to question the wisdom of these employment decisions.

[B] Association

Most of the freedom-of-association cases involving public employees have involved discrimination on the basis of political affiliation or activity. Such discrimination is generally unconstitutional, subject to two exceptions.

First, public employers may terminate employees whose political associations pose serious loyalty or security risks. The employer, however, must prove: (1) that the employee is a member of a subversive organization; (2) that the employee is aware of the illegal aims of the organization; and (3) that the employee has a specific intent to advance those illegal aims.[98]

Second, political affiliation may be a legitimate job qualification when such affiliation is truly relevant to the public office involved. Low level public employees rarely occupy such positions. The Court, however, has indicated that the exception might apply to the position of an election judge, where a statute required one from each of the major political parties.[99] Similarly, the Court has said that the governor of a state

92. 461 U.S. 138 (1983).

93. Rankin v. McPherson, 483 U.S. 378 (1987).

94. *Connick*, 461 U.S. 138 (1983).

95. Casey v. City of Cabool, 12 F.3d 799 (8th Cir. 1993).

96. Garcetti v. Ceballos, 547 U.S. 410 (2006); *Connick*, 461 U.S. 138.

97. Ayoub v. Texas A & M University, 927 F.2d 834 (5th Cir. 1991).

98. United States v. Robel, 389 U.S. 258 (1967); Keyishian v. Board of Regents, 385 U.S. 589 (1967).

99. Branti v. Finkel, 445 U.S. 507, 518 (1980).

may have a legitimate interest in the political beliefs and loyalty of assistants who help write speeches, deal with the press, and communicate with the legislature.[100]

§ 2.12 Chapter Highlights

1. The principal provision in the Constitution is the Equal Protection Clause of the Fourteenth and, by construction, Fifth Amendments to the Constitution. The First Amendment and the Privileges and Immunities Clause of the Fifth Amendment have also been construed as prohibiting discrimination in certain contexts. Under the Equal Protection Clause, whether a form of governmental discrimination is unconstitutional or not depends in large part on how closely the courts will scrutinize the decision. The *strict scrutiny*, *intermediate scrutiny*, and *rational basis* tests will produce divergent results. (§ 2.01)

2. The Supreme Court has generally applied a *strict scrutiny* test to discrimination on the basis of race and national origin. (§§ 2.02 & 2.03) Discrimination on the basis of sex is generally reviewed under an *intermediate* level of scrutiny. (§ 2.04) Discrimination on the basis of sexual orientation, while ostensibly subject to the *rational basis* test, in recent application appears more rigorous. Discrimination on the basis of age, disability, and state residency are also subject only to the *rational basis* test. (§§ 2.06, 2.07, & 2.08) State residence discrimination is also subject to the Privileges and Immunities Clause of the Fifth Amendment. (§ 2.08) Discrimination on the basis of citizenship is subject to the *strict scrutiny* test when the discrimination is practiced by the states, but to a lesser level of scrutiny when the federal government is the discriminator. (§ 2.09)

3. Discrimination on the basis of religion is almost totally prohibited with respect to religious belief, but religious practice enjoys very little protection, apart from protection for religious institutions, when the prohibition is part of a statute of general application. (§ 2.10)

4. Discrimination on the basis of the exercise of other First Amendment rights is evaluated under specially formulated tests. To be protected, a public employee's work-related speech must address a matter of *public concern* and not otherwise interfere with workplace functions. (§ 2.11[A]) Discrimination on the basis of political or ideological associations is justified only if the association poses serious loyalty or security risks or involves a situation where political views are a legitimate job qualification. (§ 2.11[B])

100. Branti, 445 U.S. 507.

Chapter 3

The Eleventh Amendment[1]

Synopsis

§ 3.01 Introduction

A lawsuit against a state entity or official alleging discrimination in violation of either the Constitution or a federal statute must comply with the Eleventh Amendment. This Constitutional Amendment was ratified in 1795 to overrule a 1793 Supreme Court decision allowing a citizen of one state to sue another state in federal court,[2] and provides as follows:

> The Judicial power of the United States shall not be construed to extend to any suit in law or equity, commenced or prosecuted against one of the United States by Citizens of another State, or by Citizens or Subjects of any Foreign State.

In other words, the Eleventh Amendment by its express language prohibits a citizen of South Carolina from suing the State of Georgia in federal court. States, however, have even more protection from lawsuits in federal court than that given by the Amendment's simple language. "The ultimate guarantee of the Eleventh Amendment is that nonconsenting states may not be sued by private individuals in federal court."[3]

1. This chapter was written by Tracey C. Green, Shareholder, Willoughby and Hoefer, P.A., Columbia, South Carolina.
2. Chisholm v. Georgia, 2 U.S. (2 Dall.) 419 (1793).
3. Bd. of Trs. of the Univ. of Ala. v. Garrett, 531 U.S. 356, 363 (2001) (citing Kimel v. Fla. Bd. of Regents, 528 U.S. 62, 73 (2000)); *see also* Hans v. Louisiana, 134 U.S. 1 (1890) (holding that a state may not be sued in federal court by citizens resident in that state).

Although the Eleventh Amendment substantially limits the lawsuits that may be filed against states in federal court, this limitation is not absolute. The federal government is authorized to sue states in federal court by a number of statutes, especially in the employment discrimination context, and private citizens may be able to intervene in that lawsuit.[4] Private citizens also may sue state officials for a violation of federal law so long as the lawsuit seeks only prospective relief, such as injunctive or declaratory relief, rather than retrospective or compensatory relief.[5] Although state agencies also generally are immune from federal lawsuits by private citizens, counties, municipalities, and other government entities are not immune from suit unless they are an "arm of the state" or the state is the "real party in interest." A state may waive its Eleventh Amendment immunity or Congress may affirmatively abrogate that immunity by the proper exercise of congressional authority.[6]

A private citizen seeking to sue a state, state official, or other governmental entity in federal court therefore must resolve a series of issues before filing the lawsuit:

- Is there a pending federal action against the state in which the citizen can intervene?
- Is the entity an "arm of the state" or is the state the "real party in interest"?
- Does the lawsuit seek only prospective relief from a state official rather than retrospective relief?
- Has the state waived its Eleventh Amendment immunity?
- Has Congress abrogated the state's Eleventh Amendment immunity through a valid exercise of congressional power?

§ 3.02 The State for Eleventh Amendment Purposes

Although the Eleventh Amendment, as written, expressly protects only "one of the United States" from lawsuits in federal court, the protection extends to state agencies and instrumentalities, otherwise known as "arms of the state,"[7] but does not encompass politically independent subdivisions, such as counties and municipalities.[8]

4. Fed. R. Civ. P. 24; Arizona v. California, 460 U.S. 605 (1983); *see also* United States v. Mississippi, 380 U.S. 128 (1965).

5. Garrett, 531 U.S. at 374 n.9; *see* Ex parte Young, 209 U.S. 123 (1908).

6. Congress lacks the power to waive a state's sovereign immunity in the state's own courts. Alden v. Maine, 527 U.S. 706 (1999) ("[T]he sovereign immunity of the States neither derives from, nor is limited by, the terms of the Eleventh Amendment."). And a state cannot be sued in the courts of another state. Franchise Tax Bd. v. Hyatt, 139 S. Ct. 1485 (2019).

7. Mt. Healthy City Sch. Dist. Bd. of Educ. v. Doyle, 429 U.S. 274 (1977). A discussion of when state officials are protected by sovereign immunity is set forth in Chapter 23, § 23.06[A].

8. Northern Ins. Co. of N.Y. v. Chatham Cty., 547 U.S. 189 (2006); *see also* Mt. Healthy, 429 U.S. 274.

In between these outer parameters lie numerous other governmental entities with the characteristics of both state and local entities, such as commissions and interstate compacts. As one court expressly recognized, "[i]t is often difficult to determine whether a government entity with both state and local characteristics constitutes an arm of the state for Eleventh Amendment purposes."[9]

Nevertheless, there are some basic principles that can be identified with reference to the "arm of the state" analysis that should be considered when evaluating a lawsuit against a governmental entity whose status is uncertain. The primary focus is the impact a lawsuit would have on the state treasury and, thus, any "suit by private parties seeking to impose a liability which must be paid from public funds in the state treasury is barred by the Eleventh Amendment."[10] Similarly, if the state would be legally liable for a judgment, the state is immune under the Eleventh Amendment even if it would be indemnified against payment of that judgment by a third party.[11] This protection afforded to states from a judgment against the state treasury is so broad that, although counties and municipalities generally are not immune from lawsuit under the Eleventh Amendment,[12] a lawsuit against these entities may be barred if any judgment would be paid by the state pursuant to an insurance policy issued and funded by the state.[13]

Even if a judgment will not be paid from the state treasury, the Eleventh Amendment nonetheless will preclude a lawsuit against a governmental entity if other factors suggest that the entity is an arm of the state.[14] In rendering this analysis, courts consider some or all of the following factors: the status of the entity under state law,[15] the entity's level of autonomy from state control,[16] the source of funding,[17] whether it has the power to raise funds through bonds, taxation, or otherwise,[18] and whether the entity focuses on local or statewide concerns.[19]

---

9. Gray v. Laws, 51 F.3d 426, 431 (4th Cir. 1995). This difficulty is reflected in decisions of the various federal courts of appeal, which apply a variety of different factors in determining whether an entity is an arm of the state and, in addition, weigh and interpret those factors differently.

10. Edelman v. Jordan, 415 U.S. 651, 663 (1974); *see also* Hess v. Port Auth. Trans-Hudson Corp. 513 U.S. 30 (1994); Pennhurst State Sch. & Hosp. v. Halderman, 465 U.S. 89, 107 (1984) ("[T]he general criterion for determining when a suit is in fact against the sovereign is the effect of the relief sought.").

11. Regents of Univ. of Calif. v. Doe, 519 U.S. 425 (1997).

12. *Mt. Healthy*, 429 U.S. 274.

13. Bockes v. Fields, 999 F.2d 788 (4th Cir. 1993).

14. *Hess*, 513 U.S. 30 (1994).

15. *Mt. Healthy*, 429 U.S. 274. Although the determination whether a particular entity is an "arm of the state" is a question of federal law, that determination nevertheless must in part be made by reference to the entity's status under the relevant state law. Regents of Univ. of Calif. v. Doe, 519 U.S. 425 (1997).

16. *Mt. Healthy*, 429 U.S. 274; *see also* Cash v. Granville Cty. Bd. of Educ., 242 F.3d 219 (4th Cir. 2001).

17. *Mt. Healthy*, 429 U.S. 274.

18. *Mt. Healthy*, 429 U.S. 274.

19. *See, e.g.*, *Cash*, 242 F.3d 219 (4th Cir. 2001).

§ 3.03 State Officials and *Ex parte Young*

The Eleventh Amendment protects not only states and "arms of the state," but also state officials. "[W]hen the action is in essence one for the recovery of money from the state, the state is the real, substantial party in interest and is entitled to invoke its sovereign immunity from suit even though individual officials are nominal defendants."[20] Therefore, if a lawsuit seeks to recover retroactive monetary relief that the state will be required to satisfy, such as backpay or compensatory damages, the Eleventh Amendment prohibits maintaining that lawsuit in federal court.

The Supreme Court, however, held in *Ex parte Young*[21] that if a lawsuit seeks to have the federal court order a state official to comply with the law in the future, the Eleventh Amendment does not bar that suit even if compliance with the court order will require the expenditure of state funds. This exception rests upon the theory that "a suit challenging the constitutionality of a state official's action is not one against the State."[22] Stated another way, the primary purpose of prospective relief is ordering these officials to comply with federal law and any expenditure of funds resulting from efforts to comply with the Court's order is ancillary to that purpose, whereas the primary purpose of retrospective relief is ordering the payment of funds directly out of the state treasury.[23] Unfortunately, this theory does not provide a clear framework of analysis and "the difference between the type of relief barred by the Eleventh Amendment and that permitted under *Ex parte Young* will not in many instances be that between day and night."[24] The Eleventh Amendment therefore does not preclude a successful plaintiff in a wage discrimination case from obtaining an order requiring a state official to make equal payment in the future. The federal Courts of Appeal have held that an order reinstating an employee falls within the parameters of *Ex parte Young*.[25]

20. Ford Motor Co. v. Dep't of Treasury, 323 U.S. 459 (1945), overruled on other grounds by Lapides v. Bd. of Regents of Univ. Sys. of Ga., 535 U.S. 613 (2002)).

21. Ex parte Young, 209 U.S. 123 (1908); *see also Papasan v. Allain, 478 U.S. 265 (1986); Edelman*, 415 U.S. at 663–65.

22. *Pennhurst*, 465 U.S. at 102.

23. Frew v. Hawkins, 540 U.S. 431 (2004); *Edelman*, 415 U.S. at 663–65; Ex parte Young, 209 U.S. at 151–52.

24. *Edelman*, 415 U.S. at 667.

25. Mahn v. Jefferson Cty., 891 F.3d 1093, 1099 (8th Cir. 2018) (noting that the Second, Third, Fourth, Sixth, Seventh, Eighth, Ninth, and Tenth Circuits have held that claims for reinstatement seek prospective relief as allowed by *Ex parte Young*); Nelson v. University of Texas, 535 F.3d 318 (5th Cir. 2008) (holding that claim for reinstatement pursuant to the FMLA constituted prospective relief as allowed by *Ex parte Young*). But if the claim for reinstatement hinges upon an allegation of past conduct, *Ex parte Young* may not apply. Sonnleitner v. York, 304 F.3d 704, 717–19 (7th Cir. 2002) (holding that Plaintiff's allegation of a prior procedural due process claim was not a claim for prospective relief and, thus, *Ex parte Young* would not permit reinstatement of the employee). There, for a time, was some uncertainty regarding the nature of a claim for reinstatement as prospective in nature. *Compare, e.g.*, Doe v. Lawrence Livermore Nat'l Lab., 817 F. Supp. 77 (N.D. Cal. 1993), *with* Mackey v. Cleveland State Univ., 837 F. Supp. 1396 (N.D. Ohio 1993).

§ 3.04 State Waiver of Immunity

A "[s]tate's sovereign immunity is a 'personal privilege which it may waive at pleasure.'"[26] The federal courts rarely conclude that a state has waived its Eleventh Amendment immunity because any waiver must constitute "a clear declaration of the state's intention to submit its fiscal problems to other courts than those of its own creation...."[27] Consequently, state statutes generally waiving the state's sovereign immunity from suits in state court ordinarily do not waive the state's Eleventh Amendment immunity absent express language to that effect.[28] Nor is there a waiver of Eleventh Amendment immunity if the state merely consents to suits "'in any court of competent jurisdiction.'"[29]

Waiver generally cannot be inferred from actions taken by the state. Thus, the state's operation of a federally funded and regulated program does not waive its Eleventh Amendment immunity with respect to that general program unless Congress expressly required a waiver as a condition of receiving the grant.[30] The state's mere appearance in federal court does not constitute a waiver unless the state affirmatively and voluntarily invokes the jurisdiction of the federal court.[31] Even the failure to plead the Eleventh Amendment in the trial court as an affirmative defense does not prevent the state from raising it later on appeal as a jurisdictional bar.[32]

§ 3.05 Congressional Abrogation of State Immunity

Although a state rarely intends to waive its own immunity from suit in federal court and, thus, rarely is found to have done so, Congress may abrogate that immunity and often does so in the employment discrimination context. This is done in an effort to subject states to lawsuits in federal court for engaging in conduct generally prohibited by the statute. But a successful congressional abrogation of state immunity must satisfy two general requirements. First, congressional intent in this regard must be unequivocally expressed and unmistakably clear.[33] Second, Congress must act

---

26. Coll. Sav. Bank v. Fla. Prepaid Postsecondary Educ. Expense Bd., 527 U.S. 666, 675 (1999) (quoting Clark v. Barnard, 108 U.S. 436, 447 (1883)).

27. *Edelman*, 415 U.S. at 673 (1974) (quoting Great N. Life Ins. Co. v. Read, 322 U.S. 47 (1944)).

28. Welch v. Tex. Dep't of Highways & Pub. Transp., 483 U.S. 468 (1987); Ford Motor Co. v. Dep't of the Treasury of Ind., 323 U.S. 459 (1945).

29. *Coll. Sav. Bank*, 527 U.S. at 676 (quoting Kennecott Copper Corp. v. State Tax Comm'n, 327 U.S. 573 (1946)).

30. Sossamon v. Texas, 563 U.S. 277 (2011); Emps. of the Dep't of Pub. Health & Welfare v. Mo. Dep't of Pub. Health & Welfare, 411 U.S. 279 (1973).

31. *Coll. Sav. Bank*, 527 U.S. at 675–76. Thus, a state's voluntary removal of an action to federal court generally results in a waiver of its Eleventh Amendment immunity. Lapides v. Board of Regents, 535 U.S. 613 (2002).

32. *Edelman*, 415 U.S. at 677–78.

33. *Sossaman*, 563 U.S. at 284–85; Dellmuth v. Muth, 491 U.S. 223 (1989).

"pursuant to a valid grant of constitutional authority."[34] In recent history, Congress most often has accomplished the first requirement through the use of fairly express language, but has met with mixed success in achieving the second requirement. It is important to remember that, with respect to the various employment discrimination statutes discussed below, the United States may enforce the statute against the states, and private individuals may intervene in that lawsuit or may institute an action against a state official for prospective relief under *Ex parte Young* even if a state cannot be sued directly for a violation of the statute.[35]

The first requirement regarding the unequivocal and unmistakable expression requires the statute to contain language abrogating state immunity.[36] Legislative history suggesting a congressional intent to abrogate state immunity is insufficient,[37] as is language generally authorizing suits in federal court to enforce rights under the statute.[38] There is no specific language required, however, so long as the statute contains language making it clear that Congress intends to abrogate the state's immunity to suit under that statute.[39] Statutes containing language expressly referencing the Eleventh Amendment[40] or including numerous references to the state in the statute vesting federal courts with jurisdiction over lawsuits alleging violations of that statute[41] generally contain the "unmistakably clear language" necessary to abrogate the state's immunity against lawsuits in federal court. It seems likely that this aspect of the analysis will become less significant in the future because presumably Congress will take account of the Supreme Court's rulings in this regard and will expressly reference the Eleventh Amendment in abrogating the states' immunity.

But even if Congress unequivocally expresses its intent to abrogate state sovereign immunity in federal court, it also must act pursuant to a valid constitutional power to abrogate immunity, which for employment discrimination statutes is Section 5 of the Fourteenth Amendment.[42] Congress is not, however, restricted to "mere legislative repetition of [the Supreme Court's] constitutional jurisprudence," and may both "remedy and ... deter [the] violation of rights guaranteed [under the Fourteenth Amendment] by prohibiting a somewhat broader swath of conduct, including that

34. Kimel v. Fla. Bd. of Regents, 528 U.S. 62, 73 (2000) (citing Seminole Tribe of Fla. v. Florida, 517 U.S. 44, 55 (1996)).

35. *Garrett*, 531 U.S. 356 (2001).

36. *Kimel*, 528 U.S. 62; *see also Sossaman*, 563 U.S. at 287 ("[W]here a statute is susceptible of multiple interpretations, including one preserving immunity, we will not consider a State to have waived sovereign immunity.").

37. *Kimel*, 528 U.S. 62.

38. Atascadero State Hosp. Sys. v. Scanlon, 473 U.S. 234 (1985).

39. *Seminole Tribe*, 517 U.S. at 55–56.

40. Tennessee v. Lane, 541 U.S. 509 (2004).

41. *Seminole Tribe*, 517 U.S. at 56–57.

42. *Seminole Tribe*, 517 U.S. at 64–66. The Commerce Clause does not authorize Congress to abrogate state sovereign immunity. Although some commentators suggest that the Thirteenth and Fifteenth Amendments would permit abrogation of Eleventh Amendment immunities, it is unlikely that either of these constitutional amendments would serve as the basis for enacting a federal employment discrimination statute.

which is not itself forbidden by the Amendment's text."[43] Because Congress has authority to enforce the protections of the Fourteenth Amendment but not to define those protections, legislation that exceeds the scope of the rights protected by the Fourteenth Amendment "must exhibit 'congruence and proportionality between the injury to be prevented or remedied and the means adopted to that end.' "[44] This is the aspect of the analysis that likely will continue to present analytical uncertainty because of the tension between Congress's power and duty to enforce the Fourteenth Amendment and the Supreme Court's power and duty to determine the substance of a Fourteenth Amendment violation.[45]

The Supreme Court's first direct application of the "congruence and proportionality" test in an employment discrimination context occurred in *Kimel v. Florida Board of Regents*.[46] At issue were the 1974 amendments to the Age Discrimination in Employment Act, which extended the prohibition against age discrimination to the states. The Court concluded that the Act's authorization of backpay lawsuits "against any employer (including a public agency) in any Federal or State court of competent jurisdiction" indicated congressional intent to abrogate the states' Eleventh Amendment immunity. However, applying the *congruence and proportionality* test, the Court held that the ADEA was not appropriate legislation under Section 5. First, the Court noted that age discrimination under the Equal Protection Clause, which is the constitutional source of authority for most employment discrimination statutes, was subject only to the *rational relationship* test and that all of the Court's prior decisions had upheld state law differential treatment under that test. The Court held that, in contrast, the ADEA "prohibits substantially more state employment decisions and practices than would likely be held unconstitutional under the applicable equal protection, rational basis standard."[47] The Court acknowledged that the reach of the ADEA is limited somewhat by the availability of the *bona fide occupational qualification* defense, but noted that because this defense requires proof that age discrimination is *reasonably necessary* to the operation of the enterprise and not merely proof that the discrimination is *reasonable*, standards under the ADEA were "significantly different" than the applicable constitutional standards were and the ADEA therefore was not a valid exercise of Congressional authority.[48]

Since the *Kimel* decision, the Supreme Court has applied the same analysis to determine whether Congress abrogated state sovereign immunity in other employment statutes. It should be noted, however, that the waiver depends upon the language of the statutory provision at issue, and there may be a different result based on the provision of the statute that is at issue. In *Board of Trustees of the University of Alabama v. Garrett*, the Court held that express congressional language was insufficient to ab-

43. *Garrett*, 531 U.S. at 365 (2001) (internal quotation marks omitted).
44. *Garrett*, 531 U.S. at 365 (quoting City of Boerne v. Flores, 521 U.S. 507 (1997)).
45. *See Kimel*, 528 U.S. at 81–82.
46. *Kimel*, 528 U.S. at 62.
47. *Kimel*, 528 U.S. at 64.
48. *Kimel*, 528 U.S. at 82–83.

rogate state sovereign immunity with respect to Title I of the ADA, which prohibits discrimination in the employment of persons with disabilities, because the statute exceeds Congress's authority under Section 5 of the Fourteenth Amendment.[49] However, the Supreme Court held in *United States v. Georgia* that Congress validly abrogated state sovereign immunity for Title II of the ADA, which prohibits discrimination by a public entity in the provision of "services, programs, or activities" to qualified individuals with disabilities.[50] A similar apparent dichotomy has occurred regarding the FMLA. In *Nevada Dep't of Human Resources v. Hibbs*,[51] the Supreme Court held that the FMLA included a valid congressional abrogation of state sovereign immunity and allowed damage actions against states for not complying with the family-care provisions of the Act. But a few years later, in *Coleman v. Court of Appeals of Md.*, the Supreme Court refused to expand the ruling of *Hibbs*, holding that the FMLA did not contain a valid waiver of state sovereign immunity with respect to its requirements for allowing employees to take self-care leave and, thus, did not permit a suit for damages against a state employer regarding the self-care requirement.[52]

Application to the states of other statutes generally applicable in the federal employment discrimination context also has been challenged on Eleventh Amendment grounds, albeit with mixed results. For example, Title VII has been held to be a valid abrogation of state sovereign immunity with respect to disparate treatment[53] and disparate impact lawsuits even though the applicable constitutional command that "no state shall deny to any person the Equal Protection of the laws" requires a higher showing of discriminatory intent.[54] The Supreme Court has held that Section 1983 does not constitute a valid abrogation of state sovereign immunity,[55] and the lower courts generally have reached the same conclusion with respect to 42 U.S.C. § 1981.[56] Similarly, 42 U.S.C. § 1985 does not abrogate a state's Eleventh Amendment immu-

---

49. *Garrett*, 531 U.S. at 364 ("'A state shall not be immune under the Eleventh Amendment to the Constitution of the United States from an action in [a] federal or State court of competent jurisdiction for a violation of this chapter.'") (quoting 42 U.S.C. § 12202).

50. United States v. Georgia, 546 U.S. 151, 153, 159–60 (2006).

51. 538 U.S. 721 (2003).

52. *Coleman*, 566 U.S. 30 (2012). Although the Supreme Court affirmed the Fourth Circuit's conclusion that the FMLA does not validly waive sovereign immunity, the opinion of the Court was by a plurality. Justice Scalia agreed with the result but did not join the plurality because of his disagreement with the "congruence and proportionality" test. 566 U.S. at 45. *See also* Constantine v. Rectors & Visitors of George Mason Univ., 411 F.3d 474 (4th Cir. 2005) (holding that law student could seek damages for alleged disability discrimination under Title II of the ADA).

53. In *EEOC v. Abercrombie & Fitch*, 135 S. Ct. 2028 (2015), the Supreme Court clarified that religious accommodation claims should be considered disparate treatment claims.

54. Fitzpatrick v. Bitzer, 427 U.S. 445 (1976) (Congress validly abrogated state sovereign immunity in Title VII with respect to disparate treatment lawsuits); Crum v. Alabama (In re Emp't Discrimination Litig.), 198 F.3d 1305 (11th Cir. 1999) (prohibition against disparate impact discrimination by the states a proper exercise of § 5 remedial power, despite the fact that the Constitution requires proof of intent).

55. Quern v. Jordan, 440 U.S. 332 (1979).

56. *See, e.g.*, Demuren v. Old Dominion Univ., 33 F. Supp. 2d 469 (E.D. Va. 1999).

nity.[57] The federal Courts of Appeal to address the issue have uniformly held that the Equal Pay Act is a valid abrogation of state sovereign immunity.[58]

§ 3.06 Chapter Highlights

1. The Eleventh Amendment deprives federal courts of jurisdiction over suits brought by private parties against states. (§§ 3.01 & 3.02)

2. The Eleventh Amendment affords immunity to states and "arms of the state," but not to counties and municipalities. (§ 3.02)

3. The Eleventh Amendment generally precludes lawsuits against state officials if the state is the "real party in interest," unless the lawsuit seeks only declaratory or injunctive relief. (§ 3.03)

4. Any waiver of Eleventh Amendment immunity by a state must be clear and unequivocal. (§ 3.04)

5. Although Congress may abrogate the states' Eleventh Amendment immunity, it must do so using unequivocal language pursuant to Section 5 of the Fourteenth Amendment. The employment discrimination statutes or portions of statutes dealing with employment discrimination that have been found to satisfy those requirements, by the Supreme Court or lower courts, are as follows:

- Title VII of the Civil Rights Act of 1964
- The Equal Pay Act

Employment discrimination statutes (or the relevant portions thereof) that have been found not to satisfy those requirements are as follows:

- Age Discrimination in Employment Act
- Americans with Disabilities Act
- 42 U.S.C. § 1981
- 42 U.S.C. § 1983
- 42 U.S.C. § 1985

(§ 3.05)

---

57. *See, e.g.*, Ellis v. Univ. of Kan. Med. Ctr., 163 F.3d 1186 (10th Cir. 1998); Fincher v. Fla. Dep't of Labor & Emp't Sec. Unemp't Appeals Comm'n, 798 F.2d 1371 (11th Cir. 1986); Lawrence v. Acree, 665 F.2d 1319 (D.C. Cir. 1981).

58. *See, e.g.*, Hundertmark v. Fla. Dep't of Transp., 205 F.3d 1272 (11th Cir. 2000) (holding that the Equal Pay Act sufficiently abrogates Eleventh Amendment immunity and noting that "[e]very other circuit to have considered this issue has reached the same conclusion").

Part III
The Civil Rights Act of 1964

Chapter 4

The Civil Rights Act—An Overview

Synopsis

§ 4.01 Introduction

A Title VII claim consists of six basic elements:

(1) Certain forms of conduct;

(2) Engaged in for reasons relating to race, color, religion, national origin, and sex;[1]

(3) By an entity that is subject to the prohibitions of the statute;

(4) Directed at someone who is a member of a protected class;

(5) For which some form of relief is available;

(6) And which is brought in a forum having jurisdiction over the claim.

Most of these elements will be discussed more fully in the chapters that follow. But a brief preview of these elements, although not necessarily in the order listed above, may prove useful.

§ 4.02 The Prohibited Bases of the Conduct

This is the most basic element of all. Title VII prohibits discrimination only because of an individual's race, color, national origin, religion, or sex. The statute was not intended to impose a universal requirement of *fair treatment* in the workplace. It thus modified the older employment-at-will doctrine only in a limited respect—although within the scope of its coverage the statute effected a significant modification of the underlying employment relationship in many of its aspects.

[A] The Limited Statutory Definitions

The statute provides partial definitions of *religion* and *sex*. They will be discussed in later chapters. Suffice it to say that these limited definitions focus more on the scope of the prohibited conduct than the identity of the protected class. The other three bases are left undefined, with the courts resolving the coverage issues that have arisen. The specific scope of each of these bases will also be discussed elsewhere in the text.

1. In addition to its anti-discrimination provisions, the statute also protects covered individuals who oppose illegal actions or participate in the enforcement of the statute. *See* Chapter 12.

[B] Proxy Analysis

There is, however, a concept that applies to several of them—and to age discrimination as well. It involves discrimination on the basis of what is asserted to be a *proxy* for one of the listed bases. Under a *proxy by operation of law* theory, the plaintiff will argue that a facially neutral characteristic is nevertheless the equivalent of a protected characteristic and that an employer, therefore, violates the statute when it makes an employment decision *because of* that neutral characteristic whether the employer actually intended to do so or not. For example, plaintiffs have argued that particular hairstyles, clothing, accent, non-fluency in English, and speaking a non-English language are an integral part of their racial or ethnic identity. Prohibiting these hairstyles, clothing, and language characteristics is, therefore, a form of racial or national origin discrimination. Although the courts have reached mixed results in these cases, the courts seem generally disinclined to treat discrimination on one of these bases as an automatic proxy for bases of discrimination that are proscribed.[2]

The Supreme Court, however, has recognized another form of proxy analysis that may be used to show that a particular decision was related to an individual's protected characteristic rather than for some legitimate reason. This is the *proxy by intent* theory. Although it arose in the context of age discrimination, the Supreme Court's discussion of proxy analysis in *Hazen Paper Co. v. Biggins*[3] is illuminating. There, the employer had terminated an employee just a few weeks before the employee's pension would have vested. The plaintiff argued that since pension status correlated with age, the decision necessarily represented impermissible age discrimination. The Supreme Court held that a mere correlation between a neutral criterion and a proscribed criterion is not enough,[4] but recognized that a violation could be established with additional proof, as follows:

> We do not preclude the possibility that an employer who targets employees with a particular pension status on the assumption that these employees are likely to be older thereby engages in age discrimination. Pension status may be a proxy for age, not in the sense that the ADEA makes the two factors equivalent, ... but in the sense that the employer may suppose a correlation between the two factors and act accordingly.[5]

---

2. Garcia v. Spun Steak Co., 998 F.2d 1480 (9th Cir. 1993) (rejecting the EEOC position that English-only rules are presumptively a form of national origin discrimination); Rogers v. American Airlines, Inc., 27 FEP Cases 694 (S.D.N.Y. 1981) (expressions of cultural pride or identification, such as wearing a "corn row" hair style, are not covered by the prohibition against race discrimination). On the other hand, by disallowing accent discrimination in situations where it is not relevant to job performance, the courts may be implicitly treating accent as a proxy for national origin. Arzate v. City of Topeka, 884 F. Supp. 1494 (D. Kan. 1995).

3. 507 U.S. 604 (1993).

4. Although the repudiated correlation theory is conceptually different in some respects from the *proxy by operation of law* theory discussed above, *Hazen* certainly casts additional doubts on the validity of that theory.

5. Hazen, 507 U.S. at 612–13; *see also* EEOC v. Joe's Stone Crab, Inc., 220 F.3d 1263 (11th Cir. 2000).

When a neutral characteristic does correlate with a protected characteristic, but the plaintiff cannot prove that the employer knew of the correlation and thus used the neutral characteristic as a smokescreen for what was actually intentional discrimination, then the plaintiff may still rely on the disparate impact theory of discrimination—which dispenses with the requirement of subjective motivation. Proof of that form of discrimination will be discussed in Chapter 7.

§ 4.03 Entities Subject to the Prohibition

[A] Employers

Title VII defines an employer as "a person engaged in an industry affecting commerce who has fifteen or more employees for each working day in each of twenty or more calendar weeks in the current or preceding calendar year, and any agent of such a person." The *affecting commerce* requirement is easily satisfied in most cases. Although difficult issues arise over who qualifies as an *employee*,[6] the counting requirement itself is fairly mechanical.[7] The Supreme Court has also held that the employee-numerosity requirement is not jurisdictional but merely relates to the substantive adequacy of the plaintiff's claim. An employer, thus, waives the defect unless it is raised in timely fashion prior to the close of trial.[8]

Establishing the identity of the employer is extremely important for several reasons. First, this will determine whether the employee-numerosity requirement is met. If *hiring entity X* has nine employees and *hiring entity Y* has seven employees, viewed individually neither qualifies as a statutory *employer*. But if the two hiring entities are treated as one employer, then the employee-numerosity requirement is met. Second, the number of employees that the hiring entity has will also determine what cap applies to compensatory and punitive damages. Third, and most important, the identity of the statutory employer of the complaining employee determines who may be named as a defendant and, potentially, found liable for any discrimination. The most common problems that have arisen with respect to the identity of the statutory *employer* relate to (1) the liability status of supervisors, managers, corporate officers, and stockholders; (2) the status of the nominal employer's corporate parent, subsidiaries, and other affiliated business entities; (3) the status of an entity that qualifies as a statutory employer, but who is not the employer of the complaining employee; and (4) the status of provider and client employers of leased or contingent employees. These will be taken up in turn.

---

6. *See* § 4.04[A].

7. In *Walters v. Metro. Educ. Enters.*, 519 U.S. 202 (1997), the Supreme Court resolved a nagging controversy and held that individuals count as *employees* if they were on the payroll the requisite number of days, regardless of whether they were physically present at work.

8. Arbaugh v. Y & H Corp., 546 U.S. 500 (2006).

[1] Liability of Supervisors and Other Corporate-Related Individuals

At one time the courts were in conflict on whether supervisors and others up the corporate chain have personal liability under the *agent of* clause of the statutory *employer* definition or whether this merely serves to establish the vicarious liability of the corporate entity.[9] The issue has now been resolved among the circuits, with all rejecting the idea that Title VII creates personal liability for supervisors.[10]

The plaintiff's incentive to include the supervisor as a party defendant for liability purposes is also blunted somewhat by the Supreme Court's decisions that impose strict liability on an employer for supervisory hostile environment discrimination, even though it is subject to an affirmative defense.[11]

[2] The Aggregation of Nominally Separate Entities

A number of different theories and tests have been formulated by the courts for determining when nominally separate business entities can be aggregated and treated as one for both employee-numerosity and liability purposes. For example, the *single employer theory* is most often used in the context of parent-subsidiary relationships. Usually, the nominal employer is the subsidiary. But if the subsidiary has less than 15 employees or is essentially judgment proof, the complaining employee will need to also sue the parent by alleging that the subsidiary and its parent are a *single employer* entity. The following criteria are relevant in determining whether a subsidiary and its parent will be considered a *single employer*:

i. the degree of interrelation of their operations,

ii. centralized control of employment relations,

iii. common management, and

iv. common ownership or financial control.[12]

On the other hand, the *joint employer* theory is most often invoked in the context of contractor-subcontractor and franchisor-franchisee relationships, where the nominal employer is the subcontractor or franchisee. The contractor or franchisor, however, will also be liable (and its employees will be counted in satisfying the 15-employee requirement) if they are regarded as joint employers. In determining whether this status exists, the courts consider a variety of factors, such as:

---

9. Another issue that frequently arises in the context of sex harassment cases is whether the corporate employer is liable for the misconduct of a supervisor. This is discussed in the chapter on sex discrimination, Chapter 9, §9.03[E].

10. Fantini v. Salem State Coll., 557 F.3d 22, 28–31 (1st Cir. 2009).

11. Vance v. Ball State Univ., 133 S. Ct. 2434 (2013); Faragher v. City of Boca Raton, 524 U.S. 775 (1998); Burlington Indus., Inc. v. Ellerth, 524 U.S. 742 (1998). *See* Chapter 9, §9.03[B].

12. Baker v. Stuart Broadcasting Co., 560 F.2d 389 (8th Cir. 1977).

i. the dominant entity's control over the hiring, discipline, or discharge of the employees of the subordinate entity;
ii. control over work assignments and schedules; and
iii. the existence of a duty to train or pay these employees.[13]

[3] Employers Who Discriminate against Employees of Other Employers

Under the literal words of the statute, if an entity that otherwise qualifies as an *employer* discriminates against *an individual* (though not necessarily an employee of that employer) *in any way which would deprive ... [that] individual of employment opportunities* (even if these opportunities are with another entity, whether a statutory *employer* or not), then that first entity may be liable. For example, in *Sibley Memorial Hospital v. Wilson*,[14] the hospital had refused to assign a male private-duty nurse to care for female patients, who would technically be the employer. The Court held that the hospital was liable, despite the lack of a direct employer-employee relationship between the plaintiff and the defendant. Subsequent decisions, however, reveal a division among the courts concerning the scope of the *Sibley* principle.[15]

[4] Provider and Client Employers of Leased or Contingent Employees

When one employer entity (the *provider*) supplies employees to another employer entity (the *client*), either or both of these employers might qualify as the statutory *employer* for liability purposes. This depends on the details and nature of the contractual relationship between the provider and the client regarding pay and supervision, the nature and circumstances of the work that is being performed, the knowledge of the respective parties concerned the discrimination of the other, and other case-specific factors—some borrowed from the *joint employer* test, some borrowed from the *independent contractor* test, and some created for this particular purpose. Although not always followed by the courts, the EEOC policy statement on this complex and complicated issue at least identifies the salient issues and relevant considerations.[16]

---

13. Butler v. Drive Auto. Indus. of Am., 793 F.3d 404, 414 (4th Cir. 2015) (listing 12 factors, of which control is the most important).

14. 488 F.2d 1338 (D.C. Cir. 1973).

15. Circuits that adopted *Sibly* early on are the Eleventh Circuit in *Zaklama v. Mt. Sinai Med. Ctr.*, 842 F.2d 291, 294 (11th Cir. 1988), and the Ninth Circuit in *Gomez v. Alexian Bros. Hosp.*, 698 F.2d 1019, 1021–22 (9th Cir. 1983). However, more recent decisions have rejected *Sibly*, noting even that it conflicts with opinions of the U.S. Supreme Court. *See* Lopez v. Massachusetts, 588 F.3d 69, 83–88 (1st Cir. 2009); Gulino v. New York State Educ. Dep't, 460 F.3d 361, 373–75 (2d Cir. 2006).

16. *See generally* Enforcement Guidance: Application of EEO Laws to Contingent Workers Placed by Temporary Employment Agencies and Other Staffing Firms (1997), BNA FEPM 405:7551.

[5] Employer Exclusions

The statute expressly excludes certain entities either from the definition of *employer* or from being subject to the prohibitions of the Act, in whole or in part. These include:

(1) The federal government, which is subject to the same prohibitions, although the enforcement mechanisms differ.

(2) Indian tribes.

(3) Bona fide membership clubs that are both tax exempt under the Internal Revenue Code and meet other requirements.[17]

(4) Foreign companies doing business in the United States that are covered by a treaty authorizing discrimination otherwise prohibited by Title VII.[18]

(5) American employers doing business in a foreign country with respect to the employment there of aliens and, with respect American employees if compliance with Title VII would violate local law.

In addition, employers engaged in certain types of businesses are exempt from specific forms of otherwise prohibited discrimination. For example, businesses on or near an Indian reservation may grant preferential treatment to Indians living on or near the reservation.[19] This, however, does not extend to discrimination in favor of one tribe over another.[20] Likewise, a business that qualifies as being "religious" under the statute may discriminate on the basis of religion.[21]

[B] Labor Organizations

Title VII's definition of a *labor organization* is essentially the same as the one used under the National Labor Relations Act, which includes any organization whose purpose is "dealing with employers concerning grievances, labor disputes, wages, rates of pay, hours, or other terms or conditions of employment." In addition, the organization must either (a) operate a hiring hall or (b) have at least 15 members and be certified by the NLRB or recognized by at least one statutory "employer" as the representative of employees of that employer. If a particular local does not qualify under either test, it may still be subject to the Act if affiliated with a larger national or international union that exercises "substantial control" over the local.[22] Conversely, the Title VII liability of the national or international for the discriminatory acts of affiliated

17. Quijano v. Univ. Fed. Credit Union, 617 F.2d 129 (5th Cir. 1980).

18. Sumitomo Shoji America, Inc. v. Avagliano, 457 U.S. 176 (1982).

19. Section 703(i).

20. Dawavendewa v. Salt River Project, 154 F.3d 1117 (9th Cir. 1998).

21. Sections 702(a) & 703(e). *See* Chapter 11, § 11.06. The Constitution also provides a "ministerial exception" that applies to discrimination on bases other than religion. *See* Hosanna-Tabor Evangelical Lutheran Church & School v. EEOC, 565 U.S. 171 (2012).

22. United States v. Jacksonville Terminal Co., 351 F. Supp. 452 (M.D. Fla. 1972).

locals is determined by the common law of agency.[23] In addition to its potential liability as a union for discrimination against members, a union may also be liable as an employer for discrimination against its own employees.

[C] Employment Agencies

Title VII broadly defines an employment agency as "any person regularly undertaking without compensation to procure employees for an employer or to procure for employees opportunities to work for an employer...." Unlike statutory *employers*, employment agencies are subject to no size or volume-of-business requirements, and thus even an individual may qualify.[24] Two things are required. First, a person or entity must procure employees or employment opportunities for prospective employees on a *regular* basis, as a primary and not merely as an ancillary activity.[25] Second, at least one person or entity to whom job applicants are referred or from whom job opportunities are sought must qualify as a statutory *employer* (having 15 or more employees)—which then subjects the agency to coverage, even with respect to its referrals to other non-*employers*.[26]

Various entities, thus, have been found to qualify, including state employment services,[27] law school placement offices,[28] and various athletic and professional associations.[29] On the other hand, entities performing licensing and certification functions generally do not qualify.[30]

§ 4.04 Protected Persons

First, Title VII applies only to someone who is a member of a class as defined by one or more of the bases of discrimination. And here, the question of who is protected overlaps with the question of what the specific bases of discrimination really mean.

---

23. Berger v. Iron Workers Reinforced Rodmen, Local 201, 843 F.2d 1395 (D.C. Cir. 1988).

24. City Comm'n v. Boll, 8 Fair Empl. Prac. Cas. (BNA) 1139 (N.Y. Sup. Ct. Aug. 6, 1974) (applying an analogous state-law provision, court held that a person who regularly counseled graduates of a business school and supplied them with job leads was an "employment agency").

25. Brush v. San Francisco Newspaper Printing Co., 315 F. Supp. 577 (N.D. Cal. 1970), aff'd per curiam, 469 F.2d 89 (9th Cir. 1972) (holding that a newspaper did not qualify because publishing employment advertisements was not its primary function).

26. *EEOC, Policy Guidance: What Constitutes an Employment Agency Under Title VII, How Should Charges Against Employment Agencies Be Investigated, and What Remedies Can Be Obtained for Employment Agency Violations of the Act?* (Sept. 20, 1991), https://www.eeoc.gov/laws/guidance/employment_agency.cfm#_ftnref1.

27. Peques v. Mississippi State Employment Serv., 699 F.2d 760 (5th Cir. 1983).

28. Kaplowitz v. University of Chicago, 387 F. Supp. 42 (N.D. Ill. 1974).

29. Naismith v. Professional Golfers' Ass'n, 85 F.R.D. 552 (N.D. Ga. 1979); Jones v. Local 3, Operating Eng'rs, 20 Fair Empl. Prac. Cas. (BNA) 1068 (N.D. Cal. Oct. 5, 1976).

30. Tyler v. Vickery, 517 F.2d 1089 (5th Cir. 1975) (state board of bar examiners).

Are witches and warlocks protected because witchcraft is a "religion"? Are Gypsies protected under "national origin"? These matters will be addressed in chapters dealing specifically with those kinds of discrimination.

But second, only certain people within the generally protected class are protected under Title VII, as follows:

[A] Employees

To be entitled to the employment-related protections of the various employment discrimination statutes (Section 1981 excepted), the courts consistently require the existence of an employee/employer relationship—past, present, or future. If a person performs work for another, that person will normally qualify as an *employee*. But that is not true if the person who performs this work can be classified as an independent contractor—an issue over which there has been an enormous amount of litigation. Questions have also arisen over whether members of a partnership and stockholder-directors in a professional corporation can nevertheless be treated as statutory employees.

[1] Employee versus Independent Contractor

Few of the hundreds of state and federal statutes regulating one facet or another of the employment relationship deign to provide a useful definition of *employee*,[31] thus leaving it up to the courts to produce a workable definition. In distinguishing *employees* from *independent contractors*, the courts have taken a variety of approaches. For example, the *economic realities* test, which was developed under the Fair Labor Standards Act, focuses on the degree of worker/principal dependency that exists. Some courts have used this test in connection with the various employment discrimination statutes, including Title VII. The Supreme Court, however, seems to favor the common law *right of control* test to differentiate between an independent contractor and an employee. This is the test that it applied in *Nationwide Mutual Insurance Co. v. Darden*,[32] construing the Employee Retirement Income Security Act. More recently, in *Clackamas Gastroenterology Associates v. Wells*,[33] the Court suggested that this test was also appropriate in an Americans With Disabilities Act case—and, implicitly, in other employment discrimination cases as well.

In *Darden*, the Court articulated the relevant factors for determining whether, under the common law right of control test, the hired party is a statutory employee or an independent contractor. The touchstone is "the hiring party's right to control

31. The Title VII § 701(f) definition is totally circular: "The term 'employee' means an individual employed by an employer."

32. 503 U.S. 318 (1992).

33. 538 U.S. 440 (2003) (citing *Darden* and the Restatement (Second) of Agency, §§ 2(2) & 220(1) (1957)).

the manner and means by which the product is accomplished." Among other factors that might be relevant to this determination, the Court listed the following:

(1) the skill required;
(2) the source of the instrumentalities and tools;
(3) the location of the work;
(4) the duration of the relationship between the parties;
(5) whether the hiring party has the right to assign additional work to the hired party;
(6) the extent of the hired party's discretion over when and how long to work;
(7) the method of payment;
(8) the hired party's role in hiring and paying assistants;
(9) whether the work is part of the regular business of the hiring party;
(10) whether the hiring party is in business;
(11) the provision of employee benefits; and
(12) the tax treatment of the hired party.

[2] Partners as Employees *of the Partnership*

In *Hishon v. King & Spalding*,[34] the Supreme Court held that if being eligible for consideration for partnership has become a term, condition, or privilege of employment for an associate (who, at this point, is clearly an employee), then that consideration must be done on a non-discriminatory basis. Although the Court did not say so expressly, the decision has been construed as indicating that the partnership relationship itself does not make a partner an employee of the partnership.

That assumption is now open to question. In *Clackamas*,[35] the Court noted that "[t]oday there are partnerships that include hundreds of members, some of whom may well qualify as 'employees' because control is concentrated in a small number of managing partners." The Court quoted from Justice Powell's concurring opinion in *Hishon*,[36] to the effect that "an employer may not evade the strictures of Title VII simply by labeling its employees as 'partners' " and cited some other cases that had *pierced the partnership veil*, as it were—all suggesting that the Court is sympathetic to this approach. Presumably, the right of control test would be applied in that situation as well.

[3] Directors and Stockholders as Employees *of a Professional Corporation*

This was the specific issue that was before the Court in *Clackamas*. It involved four physicians actively engaged in medical practice as shareholders and directors of a

34. 467 U.S. 69 (1984).
35. 538 U.S. 440 (2003).
36. 467 U.S. 69 (1984).

professional corporation. Unless these physicians were counted as "employees," the employee-numerosity requirement of the Americans With Disabilities Act would not be satisfied.

The Court unequivocally adopted the common law right of control test, noting that this was the position advocated by the EEOC. Its Compliance Manual lists the *Darden* factors for applying that general test of employee status. In addition, the Manual articulates six additional factors for the narrower and more specific question of when partners, officers, members of boards of directors, and major shareholders qualify as statutory employees. The Court adopted these six factors as being controlling, while also agreeing with the EEOC that this list was not "exhaustive" and that the issue had to be resolved on a case-by-case basis. Nevertheless, the factors the Court endorsed are as follows:

(1) whether the organization can hire or fire the individual or set the rules and regulations of the individual's work;

(2) whether and to what extent the organization supervises the individual's work;

(3) whether the individual reports to someone higher in the organization;

(4) whether and to what extent the individual is able to influence the organization;

(5) whether the parties intended that the individual be an employee, as expressed in written agreements or contracts; and

(6) whether the individual shares in the profits, losses, and liabilities of the organization.

The Court then noted that some of the facts weighed in favor of the conclusion that the physicians were not employees, while others suggested a contrary conclusion. The Court thus remanded the case for further consideration by the District Court. Although the case involved the ADA, the *Clackamas* test has subsequently been applied to close corporations being sued under Title VII.[37]

[4] Elected Officials, Personal Staff, and Policy Advisors

The 1972 amendments to Title VII excluded from the definition of *employee* persons elected to public office and "any person chosen by such officer to be on such officer's personal staff, or an appointee on the policy making level or an immediate adviser with respect to the exercise of the constitutional or legal powers of the office."[38] Exactly who qualifies as being a member of the *personal staff* is an extremely fact-specific determination.[39] Under the 1991 amendments, personal staff are no longer totally exempt from coverage. They are, however, subject to a unique enforcement procedure. The other exemptions were unaffected by the 1991 amendments.

37. DeJesus v. LTT Card Servs., Inc., 474 F.3d 16 (1st Cir. 2007).

38. 42 U.S.C. §2000e(f).

39. Teneyuca v. Bexar County, 767 F.2d 148 (5th Cir. 1985).

[5] Miscellaneous

In addition, the courts have sometimes excluded from the *employee* class persons who are volunteers, students, interns, prisoners, uniformed officers, "testers," and non-Indians living near reservations.[40]

[B] Union Members, Applicants, and Others with a Union Connection

The statutory prohibition against discrimination by labor organizations essentially defines the protected class.[41] It includes union members, applicants for membership, candidates for union office, the employees the union represents in collective bargaining, persons who use union hiring halls and referral services, and participants in union apprenticeship and training programs.

[C] Employment Agency Clients

Anyone who actually uses an employment agency is protected against discriminatory treatment in the application process and in being referred for jobs. In addition, even potential applicants are protected in the sense that the Act prohibits agencies from accepting discriminatory job orders from employers and from publishing discriminatory advertising.

§ 4.05 The Prohibited Conduct

[A] The Basic Terms of the Statute

Sections 701(j), 703, and 704 identify the prohibited conduct. It includes the following when the conduct is *because of* a protected characteristic.

[1] Employer Conduct

An employer may not:

i. refuse to hire;

ii. discharge;

iii. act *against* a person with respect to that person's

- compensation;
- terms;

---

40. Kyles v. J.K. Guardian Security Services, Inc., 222 F.3d 289 (7th Cir. 2000) (persons not actually seeking employment, "testers," have standing to allege illegal discrimination); Haavistola v. Community Fire Co., 6 F.3d 211 (4th Cir. 1993) (volunteer services); Vanskike v. Peters, 974 F.2d 806 (7th Cir. 1992) (prison inmates claiming FLSA violations); Pollack v. Rice University, 28 FEP Cases 1273 (S.D. Tex. 1982), aff'd mem., 690 F.2d 903 (5th Cir. 1982) (graduate assistants).

41. 42 U.S.C. § 2000e-2(c) & (d).

- conditions; or
- privileges of employment.

iv. limit;

- segregate; or
- classify in a way that would
- deprive a person of employment opportunities, or
- adversely affect that person's status as an employee.

v. refuse to accommodate a person's religious observance or practice, or

vi. publish a notice or advertisement indicating any

- preference;
- limitation;
- specification; or
- other differentiation on an impermissible basis.

[2] Employment Agency Conduct

An employment agency may not:

i. refuse to refer for employment;

ii. otherwise act *against* a person; or

iii. publish a notice or advertisement indicating any

- preference;
- limitation;
- specification; or
- other differentiation on an impermissible basis.

[3] Labor Organization Conduct

A labor organization may not:

i. exclude or expel from membership;

ii. otherwise act *against* a person, to

- limit;
- segregate;
- classify; or
- refuse to refer for employment in a way which would
- deprive a person of employment opportunities,
- limit employment opportunities, or
- otherwise adversely affect that person's status as an employee or applicant,

iii. cause an employer to engage in prohibited conduct, or

iv. publish a notice or advertisement indicating any
- preference;
- limitation;
- specification; or
- other differentiation on an impermissible basis.

These terms are fairly comprehensive with respect to a person's employment, union, and employment agency relationships. The terms are, however, also very broad generalities that have required some degree of judicial clarification. Congress apparently felt that in resolving the far-reaching problems of discrimination in this country, a broadly worded identification of the prohibited conduct and then a case-by-case judicial delineation of the specifics was more sensible than any attempt to foresee all the facets of the problem and deal with them accordingly.

Nevertheless, as is readily apparent, everything that is prohibited involves conduct having a negative effect on a member of the protected class. This has crystallized into what some courts call a "threshold issue" in all employment discrimination cases. Has the plaintiff suffered a so-called *adverse employment action*? This has been defined as a "materially adverse change in the terms or conditions of ... employment."[42] It usually comes up in the context of an allegedly discriminatory or retaliatory transfer or change in job duties. But, if the employment decision involves no change in salary, benefits, title, responsibilities, or work hours,[43] it will generally not be considered *adverse*, no matter how subjectively unhappy the employee is with the employer's decision.

[B] The *Discriminatory* Nature of the Conduct

Title VII does not prohibit all of the listed forms of conduct, even if it does adversely affect a member of the protected class. Rather, the conduct must in some sense also be *discriminatory*. Oddly enough, the statute itself does not define the term. The common dictionary meaning of "discriminate" is, however, fairly straightforward:

Discriminate: to recognize a distinction; differentiate.

It would thus appear that the principal prohibition of Title VII, Section 703, applies to all differentiation on the basis of certain characteristics (sex, race, and so forth)—subject, of course, to certain specific statutory exceptions.[44] Conversely, it would also appear that the Section 703 prohibitions do not apply any differentiation on the basis

---

42. Kocsis v. Multi-Care Mgmt., Inc. 97 F.3d 876 (6th Cir. 1996).

43. Yates v. Avco Corp., 819 F.2d 630 (6th Cir. 1987). Chapter 12 discusses the specific, and different, adverse action standard for retaliation.

44. Section 703(e), for example, provides an exception where the differentiation is based on a characteristic that is a "bona fide occupational qualification."

of other characteristics—although the differentiation may be prohibited elsewhere in the statute.[45]

Title VII law, however, is not quite that simple. Some things that appear to be differentiation on the basis of a protected characteristic have been found not to be illegal. And some things that appear to be a differentiation on the basis of something other than a protected characteristic have nevertheless been found to be illegal under the core provision of the statute—Section 703. This is because the courts tend to go beyond the literal words of the statute and often determine whether conduct is prohibited or not based on the perceived purpose of the statute and the intent of Congress. Examples of this will be readily apparent in subsequent chapters.

[C] The State-of-Mind and Causation Requirements

The *because of* language of the statute seems to require a subjective intent on the part of the employer, union, or employment agency. This is certainly true with respect to individual disparate treatment discrimination, discussed in Chapter 5. This intent becomes something of a legal fiction in systemic disparate treatment cases, discussed in Chapter 6. And the requirement is dispensed with entirely in the disparate impact cases, discussed in Chapter 7.

In those kinds of cases where the *because of* element does require proof of subjective motivation, a plaintiff must prove that the employer not only had a negative bias against the plaintiff because of his or her class (race, religion,[46] and so on), but also establish a causal connection of some kind between that negative bias and the adverse employment action being challenged. In disparate impact cases, where proof of subjective motive is not required, the perceived negative impact on members of the protected class must be causally related to the employment practice being challenged.

These two subsidiary components of the *because of* element constitute an enormous amount of the complex and often confusing Title VII case law. They will be dealt with in painful detail in subsequent chapters.

45. Section 704, for example, prohibits differentiation on the basis of an employee's participation in certain activities protected by the statute.

46. In the context of a religion case, the Supreme Court explained that motivation does not include knowledge. An employer may violate Title VII if it wants to avoid making a religious accommodation, even if it has nothing more "than an unsubstantiated suspicion that accommodation would be needed." EEOC v. Abercrombie & Fitch, 135 S. Ct. 2028, 2032–33 (2014).

§ 4.06 Remedies and Enforcement Mechanisms

These two matters are of obvious importance to the practicing lawyer. Indeed, what the client is most interested in is the bottom line: What kind of relief will I being entitled to, for plaintiffs, or what kind of relief will I be ordered to give, for defendants? The practicing lawyer, thus, must be well-versed in these matters.[47]

Questions of procedure and the jurisdictional prerequisites, while they seem arcane to most clients, are truly *lawyer's law*—a delight to some and misery to others. But in the early years of Title VII, a large percentage of the reported cases dealt with procedural issues. Although the dust has now settled considerably, the lawyer who is ignorant of these matters can still easily be precluded from prevailing on a substantively meritorious claim or defense.[48]

§ 4.07 A Bird's-Eye View of the Materials

Like all complex areas of the law, Title VII is best understood in terms of various broad categories of case types. And within each category, major subcategories exist—and below them a myriad of legal pigeon-holes—each containing context-specific principles, doctrines, tests, and rules. To understand one category, however, requires at least some familiarity with the other categories. The limited purpose of this section is to provide that understanding. In pure outline form, the first levels of the breakdown are as follows.

- I. Disparate Treatment
  - A. Individual
    - 1. Single Motive
    - 2. Mixed Motive
  - B. Systemic
- II. Disparate Impact

Disparate treatment discrimination comports most closely with the common and literal understanding of the concept of discrimination. A person or a group of people of a certain protected class is treated differently from a person or a group of persons outside that class.

47. *See* Chapter 18.
48. *See* Chapters 15, 16, and 17.

Today, the most common Title VII claim is of the *individual* disparate treatment variety. A male got the promotion; a female did not. The disappointed candidate claims it was because she is female. As in that example, some disparate treatment discrimination is *singularly motivated.* Corporate employment decisions, however, are often the result of a *mixture of motives* by those who contribute to the decision. There may be compelling evidence of impermissible motives by one or more of those in the decisional process, but equally compelling evidence of legitimate motives by others. Indeed, a single decisionmaker may also act on the basis of a mixture of motives. In either case, the employer may be able to show that the disappointed candidate would not have gotten the promotion anyway.

Historically, the methods of proof differed radically, depending on whether it was a *single* or *mixed motive* type of case. Currently, the distinction is blurred and confusing, with the courts wrestling with competing standards of causation, schemes of proof, and the nature of the required evidence.[49]

In a sense, all discrimination is systemic rather than individual. If an employer has a bias against Hispanics, it is likely that this will manifest itself with respect to everyone in that class. In Title VII law, however, the term *systemic discrimination* has a different meaning. Originally, it was used to refer to statutory *pattern or practice* cases brought by the EEOC or by individuals in class actions. Rather than focusing on proof that a specific individual was discriminated against on an impermissible basis, the theory of these cases is that discrimination is the "standard operating procedure" of the defendant employer, affecting everyone in the protected class. The scheme of proof and the evidence used to satisfy it are radically different from those used in individual disparate treatment cases.[50]

Finally, adopting a broad reading of Title VII, in 1971 the Supreme Court defined what came to be known as *disparate impact discrimination.*[51] The theory was that if a facially neutral employment practice had the *consequence* of disadvantaging members of a protected class, this is a form of discrimination prohibited by the statute, regardless of whether the employer was aware of this consequence or motivated by a desire to achieve it. For many years, disparate impact discrimination was a major player in Title VII law. It is less often relied on today, for two reasons. First, most of the employment practices or requirements that have a disparate impact have been identified and are thus avoided. But second, thanks in large part to some later Supreme Court decisions and the congressional response to them, the theory of disparate impact discrimination is simply too complex and confusing to be of much practical use in combating discrimination.

---

49. *See* Chapter 5.
50. *See* Chapter 6.
51. *See* Chapter 7.

§ 4.08 Chapter Highlights

1. Title VII prohibits discrimination on the basis of race, color, religion, national origin, and sex. Religion and sex have partial statutory definitions, but the meaning of these terms is mostly a matter of case law. (§ 4.02[A])

2. Although plaintiffs have occasionally argued that some facially neutral characteristic is actually a proxy for one of the characteristics expressly protected by the statute, the courts are generally disinclined to accept the theory. On the other hand, if an employer intentionally relies on a facially neutral characteristic *because* it correlates with a protected characteristic, then this is illegal intentional discrimination. (§ 4.02[B])

3. Employers who are engaged in interstate commerce with 15 or more employees are covered. (§ 4.03[A])

4. Supervisors have no personal liability under Title VII. (§ 4.03[A][1])

5. Nominally separate business entities may nevertheless be treated as one under either the *single employer* theory (parent-subsidiary situations, for example) or the *joint employer* theory (most often used in contractor-subcontractor situations). (§ 4.03[A][2])

6. In a few situations, a qualified employer may be found guilty of discrimination against the employees of another employing entity. The circuits are divided on this issue. (§ 4.03[A][3])

7. Either or both the company that provides them and the company that uses leased or contingent employees may be regarded as the statutory employer, depending on a number of complex factors. (§ 4.03[A][4])

8. The major employer exclusions from coverage include the federal government, Indian tribes, bona fide membership clubs, foreign companies covered by a treaty, certain religious institutions, and American companies doing business abroad if Title VII compliance would violate local law. (§ 4.03[A][5])

9. Title VII's definition of a covered labor organization is essentially the same as that used under the Labor-Management Relations Act, which broadly applies to any kind of organization that represents employees in dealing with an employer. In addition, the labor organization must either operate a hiring hall or have at least 15 members. Labor unions may also be liable in their capacity as employers. (§ 4.03[B])

10. Employment agencies are defined broadly in terms of any kind of organization that regularly procures employees for at least one statutory employer. (§ 4.03[C])

11. At the most basic level, Title VII only covers individuals who fall within one of the protected classes—meaning members of a particular race, color, national origin, religion, or sex. (§ 4.04)

12. Beyond that, the critical distinction is between *employees* and *independent contractors*. This is determined by the *right of control* test, with the relevant *control* being determined from a long, factually oriented list of relevant factors. (§4.04[A][1])

13. An associate in a partnership is an employee and is entitled to non-discriminatory consideration for partnership. But the partners in a business enterprise have traditionally been thought of as owners, not employees. This has recently changed. If a small, select group of partners actually controls the enterprise, then the other partners will be treated as employees for Title VII purposes. (§4.04[A][2])

14. Whether or not certain directors and stockholders qualify as employees is also determined by the *right of control* test, supplemented by some additional factors listed in the EEOC Compliance Manual. (§4.04[A][3])

15. The statute expressly excludes elected officials from the employee category, as well as their immediate advisors and people they appoint to policy-making positions. Staff members are covered but are subject to a unique enforcement procedure. (§4.04[A][4])

16. Virtually anyone affected by any of the *conduct* that a labor organization is prohibited from engaging in will be considered a *union member* for the purposes of being protected against that conduct. (§4.04[B])

17. Anyone using the services of a statutory *employment agency* will be protected against the proscribed discrimination by that agency. (§4.04[C])

18. The statute enumerates the prohibited conduct in broad terms, many of which have required further judicial clarification. But one thing they have in common is that they represent an *adverse employment action*—that is, something that objectively disadvantages the affected member of the protected class (§4.05[A])

19. In addition, the conduct must *discriminate* on the basis of a protected characteristic. The term is not defined by the statute, and as construed by the courts, its Title VII meaning is broader in some respects than a literal dictionary definition might be and narrower than others. (§4.05[B])

20. The prohibited conduct must be subjectively motivated by negative bias in the disparate treatment cases, but not those involving disparate impact. And a wide variety types of causation are involved in Title VII proof. (§4.05[C])

21. The basic types of Title VII cases can be cataloged as follows, with the details being elaborated upon in subsequent chapters.

- I. Disparate Treatment
  - A. Individual
    - 1. Single Motive
    - 2. Mixed Motive
  - B. Systemic
- II. Disparate Impact

(§4.07)

Chapter 5

Individual Disparate Treatment

Synopsis

§ 5.01 Introduction

Individual disparate treatment cases constitute the bulk of the employment discrimination lawyer's litigation practice. While systemic disparate treatment and disparate impact theories still play an important role in dealing with large-scale issues, most counseling and litigation involve a single or a discrete number of individuals who claim that an employer, labor union, or employment agency has discriminated against them personally.

Unfortunately, the law of individual disparate treatment discrimination does not yield easily to analysis. Its individual components are enormously complex in their own right. Understanding one component presupposes some degree of understanding of the others. It continues to be unclear how the varied forms and doctrines of individual disparate treatment law fit together into a coherent whole. And the material can be cabined into any one of several possible organizational schemes. This chapter merely presents one way of getting a handle on the matter.

§ 5.02 The Discriminatory State-of-Mind Requirement

In the context of individual disparate treatment discrimination, the *because of* element of a violation requires proof of subjective bias. As the Supreme Court recently put it, Title VII "prohibits certain *motives*, regardless of the state of the actor's knowledge."[1] The kinds of evidence that are relevant to such proof and who has the burden of producing that evidence constitute a significant portion of individual disparate treatment law. This will be discussed more fully in the sections that follow.

The Supreme Court recently brought more clarity to the issue of intent and employer liability. Historically, only the intent of the ultimate decisionmaker was relevant to the enquiry. However, *Vance v. Ball State Univ.*,[2] created strict liability for employers in harassment cases involving a supervisor and "tangible employment actions."[3] When no tangible employment action is taken, the employer has an available affirmative defense that it took reasonable care to prevent harassing behavior and the employee failed to take advantage of what the employer provided. Outside of harassment cases, the bias of someone without the power or authority to make the ultimate decision who was nevertheless involved in the adverse employment decision will sometimes be attributed to the one who did make the decision, even if this person was unaware of the contributing person's taint.

The courts that are willing to impute the unknown bias of a subordinate to the ultimate decisionmaker, and hence to the employer itself, often characterize their theory in terms of a "cat's paw"[4] or "rubber stamp." Except as a matter of degree and

1. *Abercrombie & Fitch*, 135 S. Ct. 2028, 2033 (2015).

2. 570 U.S. 421 (2013).

3. Tangible employment actions include the authority to hire, fire, promote, demote, transfer, or discipline.

4. This term, first used in the mid-1600s in Britain to identify someone who uses other people to achieve his or her ends, is derived from an Aesop fable about a monkey who, through flattery, convinced a cat to snatch chestnuts out of the fire with its paws. While the cat was engaged in this

the subtlety of the pernicious influence, they seem to amount to about the same thing. The "rubber stamp" label most obviously applies when the ultimate decision-maker simply accepts the bottom-line recommendation of a subordinate without further examination of the merits of the termination (or other adverse action) decision. But when the biased subordinate has influenced the decision through recommendations/suggestions, false information, or unfair evaluations, this more aptly fits the notion of the subordinate using the ultimate decider as a "cat's paw" to accomplish his or her illegal objectives. In the leading case of *Shager v. Upjohn Co.*,[5] the court used both terms, treating not being a "rubber stamp" as being the logical converse of being a "cat's paw." The plaintiff had been terminated by a committee on the recommendation of a biased supervisor. The court indicated that if the committee "acted as the conduit [for the supervisor's] prejudice—his cat's paw—the innocence of its members would not spare the company from liability." On the other hand, the court added that if the committee "was not a mere rubber stamp, but made an independent decision to fire" the employee for legitimate reasons, then the company had no liability.

These colorful but imprecise labels aside, it basically boils down to a question of what kind of evidence is sufficient to satisfy what type of causation requirement. The Supreme Court recently resolved this in *Staub v. Proctor Hospital*.[6] It determined that when a biased supervisor's report is taken into account in the employer's ultimate adverse action, that biased report becomes "a motivating factor" creating employer liability. This is true even the employer does its own independent investigation. However, if the employer's independent investigation results in an adverse action for reasons unrelated to the actions of the biased supervisor, the employer is not liable.

Intent is a question of fact and the factfinder's determination in that regard can be set aside on appeal only if it is clearly erroneous.[7] This standard is satisfied only when, "although there is evidence to support it, the reviewing court on the entire evidence is left with the definite and firm conviction that a mistake has been committed."[8] Factual error satisfying that standard is rare.

§ 5.03 Proof of Causation

The *because of* element also entails proof of causation. The type of causation that is required and what evidence is relevant to proving it has provided a lively source of Title VII litigation that remains in a somewhat confused state. The various theories

---

painful process, the monkey was quickly cracking and eating the chestnuts that the cat tossed out. Nigel Rees, Dictionary of Phrase & Fable 64 (1991).

5. 913 F.2d 398 (7th Cir. 1990).

6. 562 U.S. 411 (2011).

7. Rule 52, FRCP; Pullman-Standard v. Swint, 456 U.S. 273 (1982); *see also* Anderson v. City of Bessemer, 470 U.S. 564 (1985).

8. United States v. United States Gypsum Co., 333 U.S. 364 (1948).

of legal causation become somewhat clearer, however, when they are viewed against the more firmly established theories of logical causation.

[A] Logical Theories of Causation

Classical logicians posit three possible types of relationships between a *causal event* and its *consequent event.* These are expressed in terms of *conditions,* and each has its own method of proof. Although the technical and sometimes arcane meanings of certain *logical* terms or concepts rarely translate perfectly in what are said to be their *legal* counterparts, they do provide a useful point of departure for determining the meaning and application of the legal term.

First, a causal event might be a *necessary condition* of the consequent event. What this means is that the absence of the causal event ensures the absence of the consequent event. Translating that negative test into a positive assertion, one can thus say that the presence of air is a necessary condition of the continuation of human life. Proof consists of showing that the consequent event (the continuation of human life) has never occurred or cannot occur in the absence of the causal event (the presence of air). In legal terms, this is known as "but for" causation. If, *but for* the defective brakes the car would not have crashed into the telephone pole, then the defective brakes are the legal cause of the crash.

Second, a causal event might be a *sufficient condition* of the consequent event. What this means is that the consequent event will always occur whenever the causal event is present. In this sense, the presence of a sufficient amount of arsenic in food is a sufficient condition of death. Proof consists of numerous instances where both the causal and the consequent event were present, compared with numerous instances where neither is present. Proof of the existence of a *sufficient condition* is often used to disprove an asserted *but for* causation. One thing cannot be a *necessary* condition of an event if something else is shown to be a *sufficient* condition. If the presence of ice on the road was itself sufficient to cause the car to crash into the telephone pole, then the defective brakes could not possibly have been necessary to that result. In law, the *motivating factor* test may be thought of as referring to something akin to the logical notion of a *sufficient condition.*

Third, a causal event might be both a *necessary* and a *sufficient condition* of the consequent event. Whenever the causal event is absent, the consequent event will also be absent; and whenever the causal event is present, the consequent will also be present. Thus, in theory at least, studying hard is both a necessary and a sufficient condition of receiving high grades. The closest legal counterpart to this kind of causation is probably the so-called *sole causation*—thus satisfying the requisite causal relationship.

[B] Title VII Causation

Causation has become enormously important in Title VII law in recent years. Until the early 1990s, the conventional wisdom was that Title VII—and the other employment discrimination statutes—required proof of *but for* causation.[9] That is, if *but for* the plaintiff's race or sex the employer would not have taken the adverse employment action in question, then the action was *because of* race or sex, and thus illegal. This suggests that impermissible motivation had to be shown as at least a *necessary condition* of the adverse employment action.

How Title VII *but for* causation differs from both *sole* causation and *sufficient-condition* causation is illustrated by the *characteristic-plus* form of discrimination. In *Phillips v. Martin Marietta Corp.*,[10] the employer made it a policy not to hire women with preschool-age children. Men were not similarly treated. Clearly, sex was not the *sole* reason Ms. Phillips was not hired nor was being a woman itself *sufficient* to cause her disqualification. Rather, her sex *plus* the possession of an otherwise unprotected characteristic combined to prevent her from being hired. And one can say that *but for* her sex, she would have been hired—thus satisfying the requisite causal relationship. Although it arose in the sex discrimination context, *characteristic-plus* discrimination can occur with respect to any of the Title VII bases of discrimination.

Despite what was for many years the virtually unanimous view that Title VII required proof of *but for* causation, for the most part this is no longer true. In the Civil Rights Act of 1991 Congress decreed that "an unlawful employment practice is established if an impermissible intent was "a *motivating factor* for any employment practice, even though other factors also motivated the practice." Since the *legal* term *motivating factor*—unlike *but for*—has no established meaning within the *logical* world of necessary and sufficient conditions, it is impossible to determine what the term means by reference to logical rules of inference. Indeed, it is yet unclear how the statutory change in the standard of causation is going to affect both how Title VII cases are litigated and how outcomes might now be different from what they would have been under the *but for* test. All of this is discussed more fully in §5.09 below. To fully understand this ongoing evolution of Title VII law, however, one must start with an understanding of what the law was, and continues to be to a large extent, before the statutory change.

§5.04 Single versus Mixed-Motive Decisions

In the past, the difference between a single motive and a mixed-motive employment decision has been of enormous importance in individual disparate treatment law. It affected the nature of the burdens of proof that the parties must produce, if and

9. Newport News Shipbuilding & Dry Dock Co. v. EEOC, 462 U.S. 669, 683 (1983).
10. 400 U.S. 542 (1971).

when these burdens shifted, the kind of evidence that was necessary to satisfy those burdens, and how the court instructed the jury. It was a rare but happy era of relatively certain legal rules. The relevance of the distinction has since been blunted, if not obliterated altogether—for reasons that will be discussed later. Nevertheless, the distinction is still useful for understanding what the law currently is and where it might be going.

The claim of *single motive* discrimination presents the trier of facts with an *either/or* proposition. The employer's treatment of one individual in a manner different from the treatment of another individual was *either* motivated by the adversely treated employee's membership in a protected class *or* it was motivated by something else. The proof of one constitutes disproof of the other.

The earliest forms of proof of individual disparate treatment discrimination were all based on this either/or assumption. However, the fact that both individuals and institutional decision processes often act on the basis of a mixture of motives was recognized earlier, in both constitutional law involving public employment and the law against discrimination on the basis of union activity under the Labor-Management Relations Act. The courts thus fashioned a mode of analysis to deal with those so-called *mixed-motive* employment decisions—that is, decisions in which there is evidence of both legitimate and illegitimate motivation. Eventually, the Title VII and ADEA courts were also forced to deal with it.

The most literal and clearest form of mixed-motive discrimination occurs when a particular employment decision is the joint effort of more than one individual. Assume, for example, that a termination requires the concurrence of three supervisors. Supervisor # 1 votes to terminate because the employee has not performed satisfactorily. Supervisor # 2 votes to terminate because the employee is a fan of the Dallas Cowboys, a team the supervisor detests. And Supervisor # 3 votes to terminate because the employee is Hispanic. Here, we have a legal and legitimate motive, a not-illegal but economically irrelevant motive, and an illegal motive. And the situation is further complicated if the concurrence of only two of the three supervisors is necessary to effectuate a termination. Or what if the supervisor writes in the termination report: "Ann Esthetic did not meet the production quota for six consecutive weeks, and I am sick and tired up putting up with these women anyway." Are these legal or illegal terminations? Who has the burden of proving what? And what if the evidence of illegal motivation were less compelling and more a matter of inference? These matters will be discussed next.

§ 5.05 Some Simple Paradigms of Proof

Individual disparate treatment law encompasses three simple paradigms of proof. As used below, *proof* means the production of evidence that, if accepted as true by the finder of fact, would be legally sufficient to establish what it purports to establish.

A = facts constituting the essential elements of a cause of action.
B = facts that raise an inference or presumption of A.
C = facts that neutralize the inference or presumption of A.
D = facts that constitute a legal justification for A or that limit the remedy.

Plaintiff's Case	Defendant's Case
I. Proof of A	Disproof of A.
II. 1. Proof of B	Articulation of C.
2. Disproof of C/proof of A	Proof of C/disproof of A.
III. Proof of A	Proof of D 1. Proof of an affirmative defense, 2. Proof that the same decision would have been made anyway, **or** 3. Proof of facts that the defendant obtained knowledge of after the decision was made but which have motivated and justified the decision if they had been known at the time.

[A] Model I

Model I is basically the same as any civil case. Plaintiff has the burden of producing evidence that would be legally sufficient to convince the finder of fact that all the necessary elements of the cause of action exist and of then so persuading the trier of fact. In the past, in employment discrimination cases, this was usually done with various kinds of strong or *direct* evidence. Under current law, some form of *circumstantial* evidence may also be sufficient. In any event, the burdens of production and persuasion always remain on the plaintiff.

The defendant's objective is merely to produce evidence that refutes the plaintiff's offered proof. This can be done by discrediting the plaintiff's evidence, by producing directly contrary evidence, or by producing evidence that casts doubt on the inferences the plaintiff derives from its evidence.

The normal rules of evidence control what is relevant and probative, as in any other kind of case. But in the Title VII context, specific questions arise concerning the type of evidence that is necessary and what kinds of evidence are even relevant.

[B] Model II

Model II is virtually unique to the Title VII proof process. It probably arose out of the difficulty plaintiffs have in proving the *because of* element of the violation. It is a rare case indeed where the plaintiff has *smoking gun* evidence of motivation. Evidence that would produce a conclusive or even strong inference also may not exist. And even if there is evidence from which one can draw an inference of illicit motive, as a practical matter the plaintiff is in the unenviable position of also proving a negative—namely, that no other possible explanation for the discrepancy of treatment exists.

Thus, in *McDonnell Douglas v. Green*,[11] the Supreme Court created a scheme of proof that made it easier for a plaintiff to at least get the issue of discrimination to the trier of facts. The plaintiff's initial burden is to prove a set of facts from which some inference of illegal motivation might be drawn. These facts, though weak, constitute the so-called *prima facie* case. All this does is create a rebuttable presumption of illegal motivation. A burden of production (only) then shifts to the defendant employer to articulate a legitimate, nondiscriminatory reason for its conduct. This then fully activates the plaintiff's burden of proving that the articulated reason is merely a pretext for discrimination—that is, producing evidence that establishes the elements of a Title VII cause of action, directly or inferentially, and convincing the trier of facts to accept the truth of the plaintiff's evidence.

Although the *McDonnell Douglas* prima facie case scheme of proof has been around for many years and is indeed relied on in a large percentage of individual disparate treatment cases, difficult questions still exist with respect to the specific facts that are sufficient to constitute a prima facie case with respect to a particular kind of discrimination, how that differs from other types of inferential evidence that might be produced in a Model I case, and the meaning of *pretext* and the kinds of evidence that are required to establish it.

[C] Model III

Unlike Model I, where the employer has no true burden at all, and Model II, where the employer initially has only a mandatory burden of producing evidence, under all three variants of Model III, once the plaintiff has met the burden of proving illegal motivation (and the other elements of the cause of action), a true burden of production and persuasion shifts onto the employer. The Model III scheme of proof certainly has analogs in other areas of the law, particularly under Defendant's Case A. In Title VII law, this particular variation arises most often when the discrimination is freely admitted, but the employer asserts (and has the burden of proving) some legal justification for it. Most commonly, this involves a claim that national origin, religion, or sex is a so-called *bona fide occupational qualification* for the job from which the plaintiff was excluded.

The Defendant's Case B is also not unique to Title VII law. It arises in the context of the *mixed-motive* employment decision discussed above. Here, once the plaintiff has proved illegal motivation, the defendant's burden is then to establish that the decision was also motivated by legitimate, nondiscriminatory reasons—and thus would have been made anyway. While this does not exonerate the employer from all liability, it does limit the remedies available to the plaintiff. While this accurately represents the law prior to the statutory change from *but for* to *motivating factor*, that change has radically affected this area of the law. The details of this will be discussed in § 5.09.

11. 411 U.S. 792 (1973).

Defendant's Case C presupposes that the employer actually had in mind and was motivated by an illegitimate reason at the time the adverse employment decision was made. But if the defendant can prove that it subsequently acquired evidence that would have justified the adverse employment decision at the time it was made, then this operates to limit the remedy available to the plaintiff-employee.

§ 5.06 Model I — Evidentiary Issues

The Model I form of individual disparate treatment is relatively uncomplicated in the structure of the proof. The pleading and evidentiary requirements are subject to the rules of procedure and evidence, as in any other civil case. Nevertheless, some Title VII-specific evidentiary issues do exist — even in this simplest model of litigation.

[A] Statements and Documents Admitting Discriminatory Intent

This is perhaps the strongest kind of evidence, often referred to as a *smoking gun*. This evidence leaves little, if anything, to inference. If believed by the trier of fact, it is virtually conclusive with respect to motive. In an early case,[12] for example, a supervisor told some black women that they were required to do some onerous, after-hours cleaning; a similarly situated white female was not required to do this. The black women objected, claiming this was not within their job description. They were ultimately terminated. The supervisor candidly explained the reason for his action in these terms: "Colored folks ... clean better." Likewise, in an age case, the employer had included in the notes on a rejected applicant: "Too old."[13]

Evidence of this kind, which is *direct* in every sense of the word is, however, also relatively rare today and usually appears in the case law only when the employer intends to assert some kind of affirmative defense, such as the BFOQ or a valid affirmative action plan. For example, in *Chambers v. Omaha Girls Club*,[14] the employer openly admitted that it had terminated the plaintiff because she was unmarried and pregnant but justified this as a BFOQ.

[B] Evidence Comparing the Treatment of Specific Individuals

Title VII discrimination is often thought of in terms of two identifiable individuals who are similar in all respects except for their race, color, national origin, religion, or sex who are treated differently, one favorably and the other unfavorably. Often,

---

12. Slack v. Havens, 522 F.2d 1091 (9th Cir. 1975).

13. Hodgson v. First Fed. Savings & Loan Ass'n of Broward Cty., Fla., 455 F.2d 818 (5th Cir. 1972).

14. 834 F.2d 697 (9th Cir. 1987).

such comparative evidence is the centerpiece of the plaintiff's case. The defendant will then attempt to justify the disparate treatment by establishing the dissimilarity of the two individuals. But if that defense fails and the essential similarity established, then impermissible motive can often be inferred from the disparity of treatment itself.

Of course, the strength of the inference varies, depending on the factual circumstances.

For example, in *McDonald v. Santa Fe Trail Transp. Co.*,[15] three employees were charged with stealing antifreeze from a boxcar. Two were white, and they were terminated; the third was black, and he was not terminated. After determining that the anti-discrimination laws protected non-minorities as well as minorities, the Court had no difficulty in concluding that this was a proscribed form of discrimination. Nor was it relevant, the Court indicated, that the offense was cause for discharge. The essence of the violation was not the termination itself; it was the unequal application of the for-cause criteria. That this unequal treatment was *because of* the race of the respective employees was so obvious the Court did not even feel compelled to discuss it.

This case involves the proof of impermissibly motivated differential treatment through the use of a *comparator*.[16] This is a very common form of proof and a suitable comparator is the first thing a plaintiff looks for when amassing evidence. Comparators, however, are rarely as perfect as the one in *McDonnell*, in the sense of being virtually identical in every respect except race. The greater the dissimilarity, the less likely it is that this alone will be sufficient to prove impermissible motive. And the courts disagree over which points of similarity are truly critical to the proof. For example, the courts have disagreed over the relevance and admissibility of testimony of nonparty employees alleging discrimination by supervisors other than the one charged with the discrimination in question. In *Sprint/United Management Co. v. Mendelsohn*,[17] the Supreme Court held that such testimony is neither *per se* admissible nor *per se* inadmissible and that a district must weigh the probative value of the evidence against its possible prejudice, giving due consideration to the particular circumstances of the case. Defendants, moreover, will frequently produce their own counter-comparators—that is, persons not members of the plaintiff's protected class but who are otherwise similar and who have been treated in the same fashion.[18] The courts, however, are divided over whether an employer's proof of a counter-comparator provides a total defense in Model I single-motive cases or a limited defense in the Model III mixed-motive cases.[19]

---

15. 427 U.S. 273 (1976).

16. Employment discrimination law hijacked this term from the scientific community and changed its meaning. In science, a *comparator* is a device for comparing a measurable property in a sample with a fixed reference or standard.

17. 552 U.S. 379 (2008).

18. Comparators and counter-comparators also play a role in the Model II method of proof. *See* § 5.06.

19. *Compare* Stella v. Mineta, 284 F.3d 135 (D.C. Cir. 2002), *and* Perry v. Woodward, 199 F.3d 1126 (10th Cir. 1999), *with* Brown v. McLean, 159 F.3d 898 (4th Cir. 1998).

[C] Epithets, Derogatory Remarks, Demeaning Jokes and Comments, and Expressions of Stereotypical Views

The case law is, unfortunately, rife with examples of language that would be grossly offensive to any reasonable person within a protected class. Although much of it arises in the context of hostile environment claims, it is also relevant to the establishment of motive in a straightforward disparate treatment case.

Some words or expressions are virtually derogatory per se. Others, however, may or may not reflect negative and motivating bias against a protected class. For example, in *Ash v. Tyson Foods*,[20] the Supreme Court held that the term "boy," unmodified by any indication of race or color, was not necessarily insufficient as a matter of law to establish discriminatory intent. "Although it is true the disputed word will not always be evidence of racial animus, it does not follow that the term, standing alone, is always benign. The speaker's meaning may depend on various factors including context, inflection, tone of voice, local custom, and historical usage."[21] In harassment cases, at least, the test is both subjective and objective. The plaintiff must be personally offended and the reasonable person in his or her position would also have to be similarly offended.[22] The specter of the *thin-skinned* litigant, however, often leads employers to adopt broadly encompassing work rules regarding even potentially offensive language.

Another common form of evidence consists of expression of stereotypical views about members of a protected class. This may consist of statements about how the speaker thinks members of the protection class actually *do act*—that is, usually derogatory assertions attributing to the class certain skills, work habits, and physical capabilities. In the case discussed earlier, the statement that "colored folks ... clean better" was probably intended as a positive statement, of sorts—without regard to the negative inference. But more common are the openly derogatory assertions, attributing to the class the lack of critical skills, work habits, and physical capabilities.

Another form of stereotyping manifests itself in statements reflecting the speaker's view about how a member of this class *ought to act*. For example, in *Price Waterhouse v. Hopkins*,[23] the Supreme Court concluded that expressions of stereotypical views about the *proper* demeanor or appearance of women could be admitted as evidence that an adverse employment decision was impermissibly motivated. In that case, an associate in an accounting firm was denied a partnership. In concluding that this was illegal sex discrimination, the Court relied on numerous comments suggesting that her evaluation was tainted by views relating to her aggressiveness and use of profanity, traits apparently acceptable in a man but not a woman. But the coup de grace was a comment by a principal decisionmaker that to improve her chances for promotion

20. 546 U.S. 454 (2006).
21. *Id.* at 456.
22. Harris v. Forklift Systems, Inc., 510 U.S. 17 (1993).
23. 490 U.S. 228 (1989).

in the future, Hopkins should "walk more femininely, talk more femininely, dress more femininely, wear make-up, have her hair styled, and wear jewelry."[24]

None of these comments, of any of the varieties listed in the heading, no matter how egregious, are necessarily conclusive proof that a subsequent adverse treatment of a member of this class was motivated by that individual's class membership, for we still have the matter of causation. The *stray comments* doctrine comes into play here.

Justice O'Connor's concurring opinion in *Price Waterhouse* is often quoted as authority for this doctrine. With respect to whether a particular individual had not been promoted because she was a woman, Justice O'Conner said this:

> [S]tray remarks in the workplace, while perhaps probative of sexual harassment, cannot justify requiring the employer to prove that its hiring or promotion decisions were based on legitimate criteria. Nor can ... statements by decisionmakers unrelated to the decisional process itself suffice to satisfy the plaintiff's burden in this regard.[25]

Another court cataloged the O'Connor criteria as follows: The comments must be "(1) related [to the protected class of which the plaintiff is a member]; (2) proximate in time to the [adverse employment decision]; (3) made by an individual with authority over the employment decision at issue; and (4) related to the employment decision at issue."[26] For example, the comment, "We'll burn his black ass," made by a co-worker two and a half years before he was made supervisor and eventually terminated the other employee, was found not to satisfy the test.[27]

The *stray comments* doctrine arose, however, in context of the then-critical distinction between direct and inferential evidence. Most courts required some form of direct evidence in order for the burden of proof to shift onto the defendant employer under the *Price-Waterhouse* mixed-motive formula, and *stray comments* did not constitute direct evidence. The Court in *Desert Palace*, however, held that direct evidence was not required in order for the burden to shift. Among the other uncertainties caused by the decision is the question of the continued relevance and function of the *stray comments* doctrine.

[D] Evidence Relating to the *Same Actor* Defense

If a plaintiff-employee has presented evidence from which the trier of facts could conclude that a particular employment decision was made *because of* a protected characteristic of the employee, the defendant-employer may attempt to neutralize or refute the evidence by showing that the employer-agent who made the unfavorable employment decision previously treated that employee in a favorable way. For example, if the person who terminated the female plaintiff is the same person who

24. *Id.* at 235 (quoting Hopkins v. Price Waterhouse, 618 F. Supp. 1109, 1117 (D.D.C. 1985).
25. *Id.* at 277 (O'Connor, J., concurring) (citation omitted).
26. Brown v. CSC Logic, Inc., 82 F.3d 651 (5th Cir. 1996).
27. Scott v. Suncoast Beverage Sales, Ltd., 295 F.3d 1223 (11th Cir. 2000).

hired her in the first place, then some courts will conclude that it is unlikely that the termination was *because of* her sex.[28] Other courts, however, say that the inference is weak, especially if at the time of hire the decisionmaker had racial or gender-based stereotypical expectations of the employee—expectations that were not met, resulting in discriminatory termination.[29]

§ 5.07 Model II—The Prima Facie Case Method of Proof

During the last half century, this has undoubtedly been the most popular method for establishing individual disparate treatment. It was first established by the Supreme Court *McDonnell Douglas Corp. v. Green*,[30] and refined and clarified by the Court in many subsequent decisions. Among the various forms of single-motive discrimination, this is undoubtedly the most inferential and thus weakest form of proof. For this reason, if the plaintiff satisfies its burden of proving the elements of a prima facie case, then this does not shift a true burden of proof onto the defendant; it merely shifts the burden of going forward with the evidence.

In the *McDonnell Douglas* proof scheme, the evidentiary dance-steps are as follows:

[A] Plaintiff Proves the Elements of the Prima Facie Case

First, the plaintiff must prove by a preponderance of the evidence the elements of a prima facie case. The prima facie case consists of a set of facts, including the unfavorable employment decision itself, that raise "an inference of discrimination ... because we presume these acts, if otherwise unexplained, are more likely than not based on the consideration of impermissible factors."[31]

For example, in *McDonnell Douglas*, the Court said that a plaintiff who is alleging racial discrimination in hiring may establish a prima facie case by showing

> (i) that he belongs to a racial minority; (ii) that he applied and was qualified for a job for which the employer was seeking applicants; (iii) that, despite his qualifications, he was rejected; and (iv) that, after his rejection, the position remained open and the employer continued to seek applications from persons of complainant's qualifications.[32]

---

28. Antonio v. Sygma Network, Inc., 458 F.3d 1177, 1183 (10th Cir. 2006) (citing cases from other circuits).

29. Stalter v. Wal-Mart Stores, 195 F.3d 285 (7th Cir. 1999); Johnson v. Zema Systems Corp., 170 F.3d 734 (7th Cir. 1999). *Same actor* evidence may also be presented in an attempt to rebut the presumption of illegal motivation created by the prima facie case under the Model II method of proof.

30. 411 U.S. 792 (1973).

31. Furnco Constr. Corp. v. Waters, 438 U.S. 567, 577 (1978).

32. *McDonnell Douglas*, 411 U.S. at 802.

The Court later explained that what this prima facie case does is to eliminate the most common reasons for an applicant's rejection, thus leaving race as the most likely explanation.[33]

Although some litigants and district courts seem to lose sight of this from time to time, a prima facie case is merely a set of inferential facts, not the fixed elements of a cause of action that must necessarily be pleaded or proved in every case.[34] The facts that will support a prima facie case will vary, depending on the employment context of the alleged discrimination (hiring, promotion, termination), the basis (race, sex, national origin), and the specific circumstances of the action. In other words, the prima facie case can be tailored for each circumstance. Consider the following examples:

Termination on any proscribed basis:[35]

- Plaintiff is a member of a protected class.
- Plaintiff was qualified for the job and was performing satisfactorily.
- In spite of these qualifications and performance, plaintiff was terminated.
- The position remained open to similarly qualified applicants after the termination.

Note how closely that prima facie case tracks the *McDonnell Douglas v. Green* refusal-to-hire prima facie case.

Discharge because of pregnancy:[36]

- Plaintiff was pregnant and employer knew she was pregnant.
- She was performing her duties satisfactorily.
- She was terminated.
- Similarly situated employees not in the protected class were treated more favorably.

Note that here the presence of comparators is included as a part of the prima facie case. Many courts, however, do not make that a necessary element of many prima facie cases.[37]

Refusal to promote because of sex:[38]

- Plaintiff is a member of a protected class.

---

33. Teamsters v. United States, 431 U.S. 324, 358 n.44 (1977). This is a simple principle of inductive logic, frequently used by Sherlock Holmes, who once explained, "When you have excluded the impossible [the usual grounds for adverse employment decisions], whatever remains [the employee's membership in a protected class], however improbable, must be the truth." ARTHUR CONAN DOYLE, THE SIGN OF FOUR, ch. 6 (1889).

34. Swierkiewicz v. Sorema N.A., 534 U.S. 506 (2002).

35. Benton v. ARA Food Servs., Inc., No. 93-1002, 8 F.3d 816 (Table), 1993 WL 425183 (4th Cir. Oct. 21, 1993).

36. Notter v. N. Hand Prot., No. 95-1087, 89 F.3d 829 (Table), 1996 WL 342008 (4th Cir. June 21, 1996).

37. Pivirotto v. Innovative Systems, Inc., 191 F.3d 344 (3d Cir. 1999).

38. Evans v. Technologies Applications & Serv. Co., 80 F.3d 954 (4th Cir. 1996).

- Her employer had an open position for which she applied or sought to apply.
- She was qualified for the position.
- She was rejected for the position "under circumstances giving rise to an inference of unlawful discrimination."

The interesting thing about that prima facie case is its tautological quality. What the proven facts of the prima facie case do in their totality is to present a set of circumstances from which one can draw an inference of discrimination. The fourth element listed above is like saying "one proves a prima facie case by proving a prima facie case."

The *qualified* element, which is present in many of the variations of the prima facie case, has been the source of considerable dispute. In *Patterson v. McLean Credit Union*,[39] the Supreme Court held that a plaintiff is not required to prove, as a part of the prima facie case or ultimately, that he or she was better qualified than the person who was hired instead. The plaintiff is not even required to prove that he or she was as qualified as the person hired or promoted.[40] Rather, most courts hold that the plaintiff needs only to establish that he or she was qualified in the sense of meeting the minimal, objective criteria for the job.[41]

If, however, the employer's articulated reason relates to the superior qualifications of the other party, then the plaintiff may still be able to prevail by showing that the asserted reason is pretextual—which entails proof of relative qualifications. The standard for determining whether the plaintiff has established sufficiently superior qualifications to suggest pretext is still an open question.[42] And the situation is particularly confusing when the employer advances purely subjective factors as its legitimate, nondiscriminatory reason.[43]

Similarly, in a termination case, some courts have held that the plaintiff need only prove that he or she met the minimal qualifications for the job, with deficient performance being a part of the defendant's articulation burden.[44] Other courts have held that a necessary element of the prima facie case is proof that the plaintiff was meeting the employer's "legitimate expections."[45] Or, this may come in as the employer's articulated legitimate, nondiscriminatory reason,[46] in which case the plaintiff will have to prove that it is pretextual.

Finally, if the employer has no published qualifications for a job, then a plaintiff obviously cannot be expected to prove the *qualification* element of the standard

39. 491 U.S. 164 (1989).

40. Walker v. Mortham, 158 F.3d 1177 (11th Cir. 1998).

41. Warch v. Ohio Casualty Ins. Co., 435 F.3d 510 (4th Cir. 2006) (ADEA case).

42. *Ash*, 546 U.S. 454 (2006) (rejecting the "slap you in the face" test but otherwise declining to define the standard more precisely). The Court in both *Hicks* and *Reeves* quoted, without any express disapproval, prima facie case tests in which nothing more than proof of "qualification" was required.

43. Medina v. Ramsey Steel, 238 F.3d 674 (5th Cir. 2001).

44. Arnold v. Nursing & Rehab. Center at Good Shepherd, LCC, 471 F.3d 843 (8th Cir. 2006).

45. Coco v. Elmwood Care, Inc., 128 F.3d 1177 (7th Cir. 1997).

46. Robin v. Espo Eng'g Corp., 200 F.3d 1081 (7th Cir. 2000).

prima facie case.[47] And a plaintiff may also be able to omit this element by showing, instead, that the employer does not actually apply the qualifications.[48] Statistical evidence may also be used to bolster the standard prima facie case or, if the statistics are compelling, satisfy the prima facie proof requirement without need to resort to the standard elements.[49]

Another problem with the prima facie case has arisen in the reverse discrimination cases. Although the original *McDonnell Douglas* formula referred to being a member of "a racial minority," after it was recognized that non-minorities (whites and men) were also protected against discrimination, this element was usually worded in terms of being a member of a "protected class," as in some of the above examples. Many courts, however, have concluded that the inference fails when the elements of prima facie case are changed in only that respect. That is, being a member of a historically discriminated class is critical to the original inference. Many courts have thus required proof of additional "background circumstances" when the alleged discrimination is against a white person or a male.[50] Such background circumstances might include the fact that the employer is black or female, that the job is stereotypically viewed as being more appropriate for blacks or women, that the workforce has a disproportionate number of minorities, that the employer has a non-qualifying affirmative action plan, or that a relevant comparator exists.[51]

The legal consequence that flows from proof of the elements of a prima facie case is that this creates a presumption of discrimination that, if left unanswered by the defendant, requires a judgment for the plaintiff. Thus, proof of a prima facie case shifts a burden onto the defendant.

[B] Defendant Articulates a "Legitimate Nondiscriminatory Reason"

In *McDonnell Douglas*, the Supreme Court explained that once the plaintiff proves the elements of the prima facie case, "[t]he burden then must shift to the employer to articulate some legitimate, nondiscriminatory reason for the" adverse employment

---

47. Shannon v. Ford Motor Co., 72 F.3d 678 (8th Cir. 1996).

48. Brummett v. Lee Enters., 284 F.3d 742 (7th Cir. 2002) (noting that when a plaintiff makes this proof, it may simultaneously establish both the prima facie case and pretext).

49. *Compare* Kadas v. MCI Systemhouse Corp., 255 F.3d 359 (7th Cir. 2001) (Judge Posner suggesting this might be sufficient in extreme cases), *with* Lowery v. Circuit City Stores, Inc., 158 F.3d 742 (4th Cir. 1998) (plaintiff in an individual disparate treatment case cannot rely on systemic disparate treatment statistics).

50. Notari v. Denver Water Dep't, 971 F.2d 585, 589 (10th Cir. 1992) ("The *McDonnell Douglas* presumption—that is, the presumption that unless otherwise explained, discrimination is more likely than not the reason for the challenged decision—is valid for a reverse discrimination claimant only when the requisite background circumstances exist"). *Contra* Iadimarco v. Runyon, 190 F.3d 151 (3d Cir. 1999) (purporting to reject the "background circumstances" test, although the prima facie case in question did include comparative qualifications evidence and the employer's expression of desire for "diversity"—which are simply specific forms of "background circumstances").

51. Gilbert v. Penn-Wheeling Closure Corp., 917 F. Supp. 1119 (N.D. W. Va. 1996).

action.[52] In a later case, the Court explained that what shifted was merely a burden of producing admissible evidence (something more than a pleading) that would, if believed, be legally sufficient to justify a judgment for the defendant.[53] The employer, however, does not have the burden of persuading the court that it was actually motivated by the proffered reason.[54]

Although it was relatively clear that *nondiscriminatory* referred to a basis for decision other than those proscribed by Title VII, it was initially unclear whether this was nevertheless limited by the term *legitimate*. What if the employer proffered a totally arbitrary reason or one that ran afoul of some other statute? The Supreme Court's decision in *Hazen Paper Co. v. Biggins*[55] seems to have resolved the issue by necessary implication. There, the Court held that "there is no disparate treatment under the ADEA when the factor motivating the employer is some feature other than the employee's age,"[56] even if that factor made the termination illegal under another federal statute, ERISA in that case. The Court said that the contrary view, although suggested by the language of *McDonnell Douglas*, was "obviously incorrect."[57] The Court went even further in *Raytheon Co. v. Hernandez*,[58] holding that the application of a facially neutral policy would be considered a "legitimate, nondiscriminatory reason" even if it had a disparate impact. The Court indicated that the lower court, in holding to the contrary, "erred by conflating the analytical framework for disparate-impact and disparate-treatment claims." In *Hazen*, the Court also said that even nonsensical explanations—characterized by the Supreme Court as "implausible," "silly," and "fantastic"—may still satisfy the Court's articulation requirement.[59] As one court put it, "Title VII is not violated by the exercise of erroneous or even illogical business judgment."[60]

On the other hand, the *Burdine* Court said the defendant's explanation must be "clear and reasonably specific."[61] While "I did not like his appearance" would not satisfy that test, "I did not like his appearance because his hair was uncombed and he had dandruff all over his shoulders" would qualify, despite its subjective nature.[62]

The Supreme Court described the inferential logic of these first two steps in the proof of discrimination by circumstantial evidence, together with the third and final step which will be discussed next, as follows:

> If the defendant carries this burden of production, the presumption raised by the prima facie case is rebutted, and the factual inquiry proceeds to a new

52. McDonnell Douglas, 411 U.S. at 802.
53. Texas Dep't of Cmty. Affairs v. Burdine, 450 U.S. 248, 255 (1981).
54. *Id.* at 256.
55. 507 U.S. 604 (1993).
56. *Id.* at 609.
57. *Id.* at 612.
58. 540 U.S. 44 (2003).
59. *Cf.* Purkett v. Elem, 514 U.S. 765 (1995) (Court used Title VII analysis in a juror exclusion case in which race bias was alleged).
60. Sanchez v. Philip Morris, 992 F.2d 244 (10th Cir. 1993).
61. Burdine, 450 U.S. at 258.
62. Chapman v. AI Transport, 229 F.3d 1012 (11th Cir. 2000).

> level of specificity. Placing this burden of production on the defendant thus serves simultaneously to meet the plaintiff's prima facie case by presenting a legitimate reason for the action and to frame the factual issue with sufficient clarity so that the plaintiff will have a full and fair opportunity to demonstrate pretext.[63]

In other words, the first two steps of the proof process have narrowed the motivational possibilities to two—one discriminatory and the other not.

The first two steps of the *McDonnell Douglas* method of proof raise, initially, questions of law that guide the judge in deciding whether the case should go to a jury. The plaintiff's failure to adduce any evidence of an essential element of the prima facie case and the defendant's failure to articulate a legitimate, nondiscriminatory reason are both fatal to the respective parties, thus allowing the case to be resolved on motions. But once those hurdles are passed, most courts hold that it is not necessary for the jury to be instructed on these shifting burdens of proof and production.[64]

[C] Plaintiff Proves Pretext

Once defendant articulates a nondiscriminatory reason for the employment decision, the plaintiff's burdens of production and persuasion are fully activated and the plaintiff must complete the proof by demonstrating that the proffered reason was a mere "pretext" for discrimination—specifically, that "the proffered reason was not the true reason for the employment decision. This burden now merges with the ultimate burden of persuading the court that [the plaintiff] has been the victim of intentional discrimination."[65] And this is where the confusion really begins. The critical question relates to the circumstances under which the defendant still prevails on a motion for summary judgment rather than being subjected to a jury trial.

In *McDonnell Douglas*, the employer's articulated reason for refusing to rehire the plaintiff was that he had engaged in an unlawful "stall-in" protesting alleged discrimination. The Supreme Court suggested several ways in which the plaintiff could prove that this reason was pretextual. These included proof that non-minority employees were involved in similar acts of misconduct and were nevertheless retained or rehired—in other words, use of a comparator to prove discrimination. Other possible evidence cited by the Court included the employer's treatment of the plaintiff during his prior term of employment, the employer's reaction to the plaintiff's

63. Burdine, 450 U.S. at 255–56.

64. Loeb v. Textron, Inc., 600 F.2d 1003 (1st Cir. 1979). *But see* Sanders v. N.Y.C. Human Res. Admin., 361 F.3d 749 (2d Cir. 2004) (harmless error to give instructions); Brown v. Packaging Corp. of Am., 338 F.3d 586, 598 (6th Cir. 2003) (suggesting that an explanation of the *McDonnell Douglas* test might be "beneficial in assisting a jury's comprehension of the issues it has been asked to resolve").

65. Burdine, 450 U.S. at 256; *see also* Forrester v. Rauland-Borg Corp., 453 F.3d 416 (7th Cir. 2006) (strongly repudiating a "persistent dictum to the effect that pretext can be shown not only by proof that the employer's stated reason was not the honest reason for his action but also by proof that the stated reason was 'insufficient to motivate' the action").

legitimate civil rights activities, the employer's general practice and policy with respect to minority employment, and the statistical composition of the workforce.[66] In *Patterson v. McLean Credit Union*,[67] the Court provided some additional types of evidence relevant to pretext, including proof of qualifications superior to those of the person who was promoted into the position and the refusal of the defendant to train her for that position.[68] Other evidence that may be relevant to the pretext issue may include the defendant's failure to follow its normal policies in making a promotion[69] and proof that the employer's reasons were constantly changing and inconsistent.[70]

On the other hand, proof that the employer's asserted reason was objectively false, while relevant,[71] is usually found to be insufficient proof of pretext unless the employer knew at the time the decision was made that there was no factual basis for the asserted reason.[72] This includes honest business decisions made on faulty economic data or baseless predictions.[73] Finally, although it may support an after-acquired evidence defense, the fact that the defendant did not know of the alleged misconduct at the time the adverse employment decision was made would be telling evidence that this could not have motivated the employer when making that decision.

The important thing about these various illustrations of proof of pretext is that some of them tend to discredit the articulated reason itself, while others provide additional evidence that discrimination was the real reason. The question that eventually divided the courts was whether both types of evidence were required.

Several views emerged. Some courts held that convincing the finder of fact that the articulated reason did not actually motivate the employer was enough. These were the *pretext only* courts. Within this group, however, some courts held that such proof *required* judgment for the plaintiff as a matter of law, while others said it only *permitted* judgment for the plaintiff. Other courts held that the plaintiff must produce, in addition to the evidence adduced in the prima facie case, additional evidence of discrimination itself. This was the *pretext plus* point of view.

The Supreme Court purported to resolve this issue in *St. Mary's Honor Center v. Hicks*.[74]

Unfortunately, the decision has produced more confusion than clarity. The Court of Appeals in this case had adopted the *pretext only* viewpoint and held that once the plaintiff convinced the trier of fact (the judge, in that case) that the employer's proffered reason was not the real reason for the plaintiff's demotion and discharge, the

---

66. *McDonnell Douglas*, 411 U.S. at 804–05.
67. 491 U.S. 164 (1989).
68. Patterson, 491 U.S. at 187–88.
69. Carter v. Three Springs Residential Treatment, 132 F.3d 635 (11th Cir. 1998).
70. Edwards v. United States Postal Serv., 909 F.2d 320 (8th Cir. 1990).
71. Golomb v. Prudential Ins. Co. of Am., 688 F.2d 547 (7th Cir. 1982).
72. Grohs v. Gold Bond Bldg. Prods., 859 F.2d 1283 (7th Cir. 1988).
73. Kelley v. Airborne Freight Corp., 140 F.3d 335 (1st Cir. 1998).
74. 509 U.S. 502 (1993).

plaintiff was entitled to judgment as a matter of law. The Supreme Court seemed to reject only the *as a matter of law* aspect of this holding. The Court stated:

> The factfinder's disbelief of the reasons put forward by the defendant (particularly if disbelief is accompanied by a suspicion of mendacity) may, together with the elements of the prima facie case, suffice to show intentional discrimination. Thus, rejection of the defendant's proffered reasons will *permit* the trier of fact to infer the ultimate fact of intentional discrimination, and the Court of Appeals was correct when it noted that, upon such rejection, "[n]o additional proof of discrimination is *required*."....[75]

On the other hand, this apparent adoption of the second form of *pretext only* is undermined by other language in the opinion. Specifically, in explaining why the dissent had misconstrued the majority opinion, Justice Scalia said:

> The dissent takes this [referring to some language from *Burdine*] to mean that if the plaintiff proves the asserted reason to be *false*, the plaintiff wins. But a reason cannot be proved to be "a pretext for *discrimination*" unless it is shown both that the reason was false, and that discrimination was the real reason.[76]

Since *show* in legal parlance normally means *to produce evidence of*, this suggests that the Court was adopting the *pretext plus* approach after all.

Following *Hicks*, the lower courts continued to be divided over this issue. Some courts indicated that summary judgment for a defendant would be appropriate in only the rarest of circumstances. Other courts, however, continued to grant summary judgment motions quite freely, often without fully articulating the reasons for doing so under *Hicks*. And a few held that *pretext plus* was still the controlling rule and that anything in *Hicks* to the contrary was simply dicta.

The Supreme Court, thus, found it necessary to revisit the issue in *Reeves v. Sanderson Plumbing Products, Inc.*[77] Applying the *McDonnell Douglas/Hicks* approach in an ADEA case, the Court of Appeals found that the plaintiff had proved the elements of the prima facie case and had presented sufficient evidence from which the jury could have concluded that the employer's articulated reason was pretextual. But the Court of Appeals said this was not enough. Rather, the lower court said it must, as an essential final step, determine "whether Reeves presented sufficient evidence that his age motivated [respondent's] employment decision."[78] The Court of Appeals then evaluated the plaintiff's additional evidence of the discrimination itself, which consisted of some age-based comments that were directed at the plaintiff and some comparative-treatment evidence, and concluded that this was not enough to sustain the jury's finding of age discrimination. The Supreme Court said that "the Court of Ap-

---

75. *Id.* at 511 (quoting Hicks v. St. Mary's Honor Ctr., 970 F.2d 487, 493 (8th Cir. 1992)).
76. *Id.* at 515.
77. 530 U.S. 133 (2000).
78. Reeves, 530 U.S. at 139 (quoting from the Court of Appeals decision, 197 F.3d at 694).

peals proceeded from the assumption that a prima facie case of discrimination, combined with sufficient evidence for the trier of fact to disbelieve the defendant's legitimate, nondiscriminatory reason for its decision, is insufficient as a matter of law to sustain a jury's finding of intentional discrimination."[79]

The Supreme Court held that this was error. Although in this case there was some evidence that went directly to the discrimination itself, the Court apparently felt that the evidence going to the pretext issue alone could be sufficient to sustain a jury verdict. That is, "because a prima facie case and sufficient evidence to reject the employer's explanation may permit a finding of liability, the Court of Appeals erred in proceeding from the premise that a plaintiff must always introduce additional, independent evidence of discrimination."[80]

On the other hand, the Court stopped short of saying that evidence of pretext would always require sending the case to a jury. Rather, the Court indicated that "there will be instances where, although the plaintiff has established a prima facie case and set forth sufficient evidence to reject the defendant's explanation, no rational factfinder could conclude that the action was discriminatory."[81] The Court noted that the employer might be able to show conclusively that although the articulated reason was pretextual, the real reason was still something other than discriminatory, or present other evidence that no discrimination had occurred. Indeed, even in the absence of defendant surrebuttal evidence of that kind, a judge might find that the plaintiff's evidence going to pretext alone was so weak that no rational juror could believe it. In sum, "Whether judgment as a matter of law [or summary judgment] is appropriate in any particular case will depend on a number of factors. Those include the strength of the plaintiff's prima facie case, the probative value of the proof that the employer's explanation is false, and any other evidence that supports the employer's case and that properly may be considered on a motion for judgment as a matter of law."[82]

Another potentially limiting element is the Court's repeated emphasis on the existence of *evidence* to establish pretext. Seizing upon the "suspicion of mendacity" language of *Hicks*, some plaintiffs had argued that a jury's disbelief of the employer's testimony was itself sufficient to establish pretext. Several pre-*Reeves* courts of appeals decisions had implicitly rejected that argument, and it seems not to have survived *Reeves*.

In short, *Reeves* fails to provide a bright-line test for when a plaintiff can survive a motion for summary judgment. It is thus highly likely that in the immediate future the federal district and circuit courts will continue to reach radically different results in factually similar cases.

In addition to the residual uncertainty over the basic question of when summary judgment is appropriate, the issue of *Hicks/Reeves* jury instructions remains to be re-

---

79. Reeves, 530 U.S. at 146.

80. *Id.* at 149.

81. *Id.* at 148; see also Hoffman v. Applicators Sales & Serv., Inc., 439 F.3d 9, 18 (1st Cir. 2006) (quoting Reeves, 530 U.S. at 148).

82. Reeves, 530 U.S. at 148–49.

solved. The question is whether the trial court must, may, or should never tell the jury that *from their disbelief in the employer's asserted reason they may—but need not—infer that the employer's true motive was discriminatory*. The courts are divided over the issue. Although no court has held that such an instruction is improper, some courts have held that the trial court must give this instruction in every case.[83] But other courts have held that it is not reversible error for the trial court to refuse to give the instruction, either because in that particular case the plaintiff could not have been prejudiced by the lack of this instruction[84] or on the broader principle that permissive inferences should be dealt with in the counsel's closing argument.[85]

Thus, while the exact meaning of the three steps in the *McDonnell-Douglas* minuet grows increasingly complex and obscure, the basic framework of proof remains the same. The process has, however, been enormously complicated by the introduction of jury trials. Some courts have held that the jury need not be instructed on the existence and nature of these shifting burdens.[86] Others, however, have found giving instructions to be "harmless error"[87]—assuming, of course, that the reviewing court happens to agree with the substantive content. And, indeed, one court has even said that "while not required, the instruction is often beneficial in assisting a jury's comprehension of the issues it has been asked to resolve."[88]

§ 5.08 Model III.A—Establishing a Bona Fide Occupational Qualification Defense

When discrimination on the basis of membership in a protected class is conclusively proved or readily admitted, the employer will sometimes assert that particular characteristic of that class falls under the bona fide occupational qualification defense.

Section 703(e) provides that it is not illegal for an employer to discriminate "on the basis of ... religion, sex, or national origin in those certain instances where religion, sex, or national origin is a bona fide occupational qualification reasonably necessary to the normal operation of that particular business or enterprise." The Age Discrimination in Employment Act also recognizes a BFOQ for that basis of discrimination.

Most BFOQ law is fairly specific to the basis of discrimination being alleged and is best left to coverage in later chapters. However, a few preliminary generalizations are appropriate at this introductory stage.

The BFOQ defense has been narrowly construed by the courts. The parameters of the defense have been narrowly drawn, and the specific applications reflect this.

---

83. Townsend v. Lumbermens Mut. Cas. Co., 294 F.3d 1232 (10th Cir. 2002); Smith v. Borough of Wilkinsburg, 147 F.3d 272 (3d Cir. 1998); Cabrera v. Jakabovitz, 24 F.3d 372 (2d Cir. 1994).

84. Palmer v. Board of Regents of the Univ. Sys. of Ga., 208 F.3d 969 (11th Cir. 2000).

85. Gehring v. Case Corp., 43 F.3d 340 (7th Cir. 1994).

86. Gordon v. New York City Bd. of Education, 232 F.3d 111 (2d Cir. 2000).

87. Sanders, 361 F.3d 749 (2d Cir. 2004).

88. Brown v. Packaging Corp. of Am., 338 F.3d 586, 598 (6th Cir. 2003) (Clay, J., concurring).

In *United Automobile Workers v. Johnson Controls, Inc.*,[89] the Supreme Court indicated that the characteristic-related qualification in question must "affect an employee's ability to do the job." Not only that, it must also "relate to the 'essence' or to the 'central mission of the employer's business.'" What controls, however, is the court's perception of that "essence" or "central mission," not that of the business entity. This divergence of viewpoints has led to a healthy amount of litigation, which will be discussed later.

Employment action that is predicated on generalizations (even accurate ones) about the characteristics or abilities of members of a protected class is inconsistent with a ruling norm of employment discrimination law—namely, that decisions must be made on an individual rather than a class basis. The BFOQ, however, provides a narrow exception to that.

In *Western Air Lines v. Criswell*,[90] an age discrimination case, the Supreme Court articulated two ways for establishing a BFOQ on the basis of class membership correlated characteristics.

First, a BFOQ may exist if all or substantially all members of a particular class possess a characteristic that prevents them from safely and efficiently performing the duties of their job. In other words, the BFOQ is nothing more than a valid, strong generalization. Thus, in *Dothard v. Rawlinson*,[91] the Supreme Court held that a female guard's presence in an overcrowded prison containing sex offenders within the general population, by her "very womanhood" (possessed by all women) posed a risk of precipitating inmate attacks and endangering other guards.

Second, according to the *Criswell* Court, a BFOQ also may exist if only some members of a particular sex possess the characteristic, but it is impossible or highly impracticable to make this determination on an individual basis. This can be thought of as a slightly weaker but still valid generalization, and one that it would be rational to rely on because of the difficulty of individualizing the decision. This situation also rarely exists, however. For example, while it may be true that women *generally* have weaker upper-torso body strength than *most* men, this is a characteristic that can easily be determined on an individual basis.

The statute does not recognize race as being a potential BFOQ. To deal with situations when, however, race would be relevant to job performance, the courts originally borrowed the "business necessity" defense from the disparate impact model of proof. Thus, one court held that refusing to hire a white person to be an undercover inspector of minority-operated barbershops could be justified as a "business necessity."[92] The Civil Rights Act of 1991 foreclosed that possibility. Section 703(k) provides that a "demonstration than an employment practice is required by business necessity may not be used as a defense against a claim of intentional discrimination."

89. 499 U.S. 187 (1991).
90. 472 U.S. 400 (1985).
91. 433 U.S. 321 (1977).
92. Miller v. Texas State Bd. Barber Exam'rs, 615 F.2d 650 (5th Cir. 1980).

In sum, the courts generally recognize the BFOQ only when one of three things is at stake:

- Authenticity, usually involving national origin discrimination.
- Privacy, usually involving sex discrimination.
- Safety of the public or other employees, usually involving age discrimination.

§ 5.09 Model III.B — Mixed-Motive Employment Decisions

For many years, the assumption of employment discrimination law was that unfavorable employment decisions were *either* motivated by an impermissible factor *or* they were not. This is so-called *single-motive* discrimination. Models I and II operated on this assumption. However, employment decisions based on a mixture of motives, some permissible but some not, had been recognized for many years in both constitutional law (involving the right of public employees to engage in constitutionally protected activity) and labor-management relations law (involving the right of employees to not be discriminated against because of union activities). The courts wrestled mightily with the issue of how to deal with those situations. Eventually, employment discrimination law was also forced to recognize that particular factual paradigm and has done so with an even greater amount of difficulty and anguish. It has caused a fundamental reexamination of the kind of causation that must be proved in an employment discrimination case of any kind.

The Supreme Court first dealt with Title VII mixed-motive employment decisions in *Price Waterhouse v. Hopkins*.[93] Unfortunately, the Court did not issue a majority opinion. Justice Brennan's plurality opinion suggested one model of analysis; Justice O'Conner's concurrence suggested another.

As was discussed earlier, in *Price Waterhouse*, Justice Brennan apparently rejected *but for* or *necessary* condition causation in favor of the more easily established *sufficient* condition causation. Although that establishes a violation of the statute, Justice Brennan would then allow the employer to prove, as a true affirmative defense, that "even if it had not taken gender [or race] into account, it would have come to the same decision regarding a particular person."[94] In other words, the employer can defend by showing that a nondiscriminatory reason was also a sufficient condition of the decision. Since showing that X (a nondiscriminatory reason) is a sufficient condition of A (the job decision) necessarily disproves that Y (the discriminatory reason) is a necessary condition, *but for* causation is still implicitly involved in Justice Brennan's formulation. However, if the plaintiff prevails in proving *sufficient condition* causation and the employer fails in establishing the defense, then the employer's ultimate liability

93. 490 U.S. 228 (1989).

94. Price Waterhouse, 490 U.S. at 242 (plurality).

will be predicated on something less than *but for* causation. If, however, the employer does succeed in proving that the same decision would have been reached regardless of the impermissible bias, then this operates as a complete defense.

Justice O'Connor, on the other hand, adhered to the conventional view that the *because of* requirement of Title VII involves *but for* causation. However, in her scheme of analysis, if a plaintiff could produce "direct evidence that an illegitimate factor played a substantial role in a particular employment decision,"[95] then a true burden of persuasion shifts to the employer to prove that the same decision would have been made anyway, for nondiscriminatory reasons. In other words, although *but for* causation is still the test, this is something that the defendant must disprove rather than something the plaintiff must prove. In her view, what distinguishes this type of case from *McDonnell Douglas v. Green*, where the burden that shifts is merely one of producing evidence, is that the plaintiff's burden is also more strenuous. Rather than the flaccid prima facie case, which is easily proved, to shift a true burden of persuasion the plaintiff must produce *direct evidence* that race or sex was a *substantial factor* in the decision. Again, however, a defendant's failure of proof means that liability has been predicated on something less than *but for* causation. But if the proof is made, it operates as a complete defense.

Congress was apparently not happy with the ambiguity flowing from the Brennan/O'Connor disagreement over causation nor with what the two Justices did agree upon, namely that the *same decision* proof provided a complete defense. Thus, as was indicated earlier, Congress apparently adopted Justice Brennan's *sufficient condition* interpretation of the *because of* language of Title VII, at least in mixed-motive cases. Under Section 706(g)(2)(B), all that is required is that the protected characteristic be "a motivating factor." While Congress did not modify the foregoing analytical discussion about the relationship between motives and results, it modified the remedies that are available. When an impermissible factor is a motivating factor but not the *but for* factor, the employee's remedy is limited to declaratory and injunctive relief, and attorney's fees and costs.

The courts were initially split on the application of the statutory reconciliation, but the Supreme Court resolved it in favor of coverage of all status-based discrimination claims. In *University of Texas Southwestern Medical Center*,[96] the Court ruled that when an employee alleges status-based discrimination, the "but-for causation is not the test."[97] Even if the employer has lawful motives which are substantial factors in the adverse action, it is sufficient to have only one unlawful motivating factor.[98]

---

95. Price Waterhouse, 490 U.S. at 275 (O'Connor, J., concurring).

96. 570 U.S. 338, 343 (2013).

97. For reasons that are not readily apparent, in *Bostock v. Clayton County*, 509 U.S. __ (2020), which involved a form of status-based discrimination (sexual orientation), the Court engaged in an extensive and somewhat confusing discussion of but-for causation and at some points seemed to be suggesting an understanding of what this theory of causation means that differs from the traditional view.

98. *Nassar*, 570 U.S. at 343.

However, in a Title VII case raising retaliation, *but-for* causation is still required. More recently, *EEOC v. Abercrombie & Fitch Stores, Inc.*[99] reaffirmed that a protected characteristic cannot lawfully be a motivating factor in an employment decision. Because *Abercrombie & Fitch* is a "single motive" case, all future disputes should resolve in favor of the conclusion that an employee is entitled to prevail based on the showing that an unlawful factor motivated the adverse action, regardless of whether a single or mixed motive is involved.

Although *Abercrombie & Fitch* resolved the *motivating factor* dispute, another dispute arose among the lower courts based on whether Justice O'Connor's *direct evidence* requirement in *Price Waterhouse* survived Section 706(g)(2)(B). The lower courts disagreed over whether *direct evidence* was the triggering mechanism for shifting the burden of persuasion. Most courts initially held that it does,[100] albeit with widely divergent views as to what constitutes *direct evidence.* The theory was that since Justice O'Connor's opinion represents the narrowest ground on which the result can be based, it represents the "holding" of the case, even though it was a plurality decision. And while Congress did change the effect of proof of the *same* decision defense (from being a complete defense to liability to merely affecting the remedy), the other aspects of the case remain unchanged—including Justice O'Connor's direct evidence requirement. This would thus preserve the *quid pro quo* that was implicit in Justice O'Connor's concurrence. In exchange for agreeing to allow something less than the existence of *but for* causation to shift a true burden of proof onto a defendant (rather than merely a burden of going forward with the evidence), Justice O'Connor nevertheless extracted the requirement that proof of this *motivating factor* be by more probative evidence than is necessary to sustain a mere prima facie case. Hence, the direct evidence requirement.

In *Desert Palace, Inc. v. Costa,*[101] the Supreme Court disagreed, at least with respect to the requirement that something known as *direct evidence* be required, although some remnant of the underlying quid pro quo theory of Justice O'Connor's concurrence may remain. Adopting a *plain meaning* approach to the statutory text, the Court stated that neither Section 2003(m), which defines "demonstrate" in terms of meeting the burdens of production and persuasion, nor Section 2003-2(m), which allows an unlawful practiced to be proved when the plaintiff "demonstrates" that an impermissible criterion was a "motivating factor," both of which were added by the 1991 Act, imposes an express requirement that the proof be by "direct evidence or some other heightened showing." Therefore, none exists under the statute. The Court reinforced this point by pointing out that when Congress has intended to impose heightened evidentiary requirements, it used specific language to that effect. And finally, in a broader sense, the Court noted that the law generally recognizes no difference in the

99. 135 S. Ct. 2028, 2032 (2015).

100. EEOC v. Alton Packaging Corp., 901 F.2d 920 (11th Cir. 1990); Gautier v. Watkins, 747 F. Supp. 82 (D.D.C. 1990), aff'd mem., 948 F.2d 781 (D.C. Cir. 1991).

101. 539 U.S. 90 (2003).

probative value of direct and circumstantial evidence and that there was no reason why either or both should not be sufficient to establish a Title VII violation.

While the Court may have been able to find the *plain meaning* of the statute, others have been unable to find that in the Court's decision. The basic, still unresolved question relates to when a court is required to give the mixed-motive instructions, which in colloquial terms consist of the following:

> If you find from a preponderance of the evidence that race [or some other impermissible criterion] was a motivating factor in the defendant's decision to terminate [or otherwise disadvantage] the plaintiff, then you must find that the defendant committed an unlawful employment practice. Both direct evidence of the defendant's unlawful motivation and circumstantial evidence suggesting its existence may be used in making this determination. But if you further find from a preponderance of the evidence that the defendant would have terminated the plaintiff anyway, for entirely legitimate reasons, then you may only award only the following remedies: ... [basically, declaratory and injunctive relief and attorneys' fees, but no damages or reinstatement].

After *Desert Palace*, is a mixed-motive instruction like this now appropriate in every case where the plaintiff has introduced any evidence, circumstantial or otherwise, of improper motivation? After all, the elements of the prima facie case are themselves "circumstantial evidence" that support an inference of illegal motivation. Is that now enough to qualify for the *motivating factor* standard of causation establishing liability, to shift the burden of proof, and not to merely limit the remedy? If so, the *McDonnell Douglas* approach is relegated to the dust bin. Instead, a unified theory of proof and burden-allocation applies in all cases. Some courts have indeed reached that conclusion, including the Ninth Circuit in the *Desert Palace* case.

On the other hand, although the Supreme Court affirmed the Ninth Circuit decision, it did so on other, narrower grounds. Moreover, although the bulk of the opinion speaks in unqualified terms that could encompass both single- and mixed-motive cases, the concluding paragraph finally limits the holding to mixed-motive cases, and footnote one says, "This case does not require us to decide when, if ever, Sec. 107 applies outside the mixed-motive context."[102]

Beyond that, *Desert Palace* raises an enormous number of practical application questions—or exacerbates those that were already developing under the original *Price Waterhouse* direct/circumstantial-evidence dichotomy. What impact will all of this have on motion practice, especially motions for summary judgment and judgment as a matter of law?[103] How much more evidence, if any, than the mere bare bones of

---

102. Desert Palace, 539 U.S. at 94.

103. Griffith v. City of Des Moines, 387 F.3d 733, 736 (8th Cir. 2004) ("Desert Palace had *no* impact on prior Eighth Circuit summary judgment decisions").

a prima facie case must a plaintiff produce for it to qualify as *circumstantial evidence* of the *Desert Palace* variety?[104] How and when are the parties and the courts expected to be able to decide whether the *McDonnell Douglas* single-motive approach or the *Desert Palace* mixed-motive approach applies? How does *Desert Palace* affect the pleading practice of both the plaintiff and the defendant? How does the uncertainty affect discovery and other pre-trial case preparation practices? Must a defendant now be prepared to not only articulate a *legitimate, nondiscriminatory reason* but also prove it as a *same decision* limited defense? How can all this be made clear to the jury through jury arguments and instructions?[105] And what impact will all of this have on post-trial motion practice and procedure? (And is the Section 107-predicated *Desert Palace* decision limited to what Section 107 literally covers (Title VII substantive discrimination claims), or does it also apply to Title VII retaliation and discrimination claims under other federal statutes?)

The post-*Desert Palace* case law, which is still relatively sparse, will eventually address and resolve these questions, albeit undoubtedly in a variety of ways. Due to the importance of the matter and the likelihood that the circuits will adopt a dizzying array of approaches to the proof of intentional discrimination, one may expect the Supreme Court to eventually revisit the issue.

In a mixed-motive case, if an employer establishes the same decision defense, this merely limits the remedies the plaintiff may receive. A court may still grant "declaratory relief, injunctive relief, ... and attorney's fees and costs," but it cannot "award damages or issue an order requiring any admission, reinstatement, hiring, promotion, or payment." By its terms, Section 706(g) is limited to Title VII mixed-motive discrimination based on race, color, religion, national origin, and sex. Mixed-motive Title VII retaliation cases are not included, and neither are other protected categories. Most courts thus continue to recognize the nondiscriminatory motive as a complete defense in retaliation cases.[106] The Supreme Court has ruled that a nondiscriminatory motive is a complete defense in an ADEA case.[107]

§ 5.10 Model III.C—The After-Acquired Evidence Defense

In a mixed-motive case, the alternative motivation must have been in the employer's mind at the time the decision was made.[108] When an employer terminates an employee

---

104. Diamond v. Colonial Life & Accident Ins. Co., 416 F.3d 310 (4th Cir. 2005) (rejecting the notion that a plaintiff can survive summary judgment by merely presenting a prima facie case).

105. Rowland v. American General Fin., 340 F.3d 187 (4th Cir. 2003) (suggesting that when in doubt, the trial judge should give the mixed motive instruction).

106. *See* Chapter 12, § 12.03.

107. Gross v. FBL Fin. Servs., Inc., 557 U.S. 167, 180 (2009).

108. Sagendorf-Teal v. Rensselaer County, N.Y., 100 F.3d 270 (2d Cir. 1996).

for an impermissible reason but later discovers that the employee had been guilty of misconduct that would have justified a termination for cause anyway, this *after-acquired evidence* will at least provide the employer with a partial defense with respect to the remedy.

In *McKennon v. Nashville Banner Publishing Co.*,[109] the Supreme Court held that to qualify for this limited-liability defense an employer must "establish that the wrongdoing was of such severity that the employee in fact would have been terminated on those grounds alone had the employer known of it at the time of the discharge."[110] But unless the subsequently discovered misconduct was in violation of a fixed rule or other employees have also been disciplined for engaging in it, an employer may have a difficult time satisfying that test. An EEOC *Enforcement Guidance* suggests, however, that the following would usually be adequate:

- Criminal acts;
- Divulging trade secrets, plant security information, or other confidential information;
- And, indeed, "whenever the misconduct is of such a nature that the adverse action appears reasonable and justified."

Often, the after-acquired evidence consists of so-called *resume fraud*, where the plaintiff has included materially false information in his or her resume.[111] Except in refusal to hire cases, the employer usually must prove that it would have terminated the employee anyway at the time it learned of the fraud, not that it would not have hired the individual in the first place.[112]

The relevance of post-termination misconduct is also open to dispute. Most courts hold that such evidence is irrelevant and thus inadmissible.[113] Other courts, however, have held that even if the *McKennon* theory does not apply to post-termination misconduct, if the misconduct was of a nature that would make reinstatement an inappropriate remedy under general equitable principles, the court should not make that a part of the discriminatory termination remedy, nor award its monetary substitute, front pay.[114]

If the employer does prevail on its *McKennon* after-acquired evidence proof, then this merely operates to limit the remedy. The plaintiff is entitled neither to reinstatement nor front-pay, and back-pay is measured from the date of the unlawful termination to the date the new information was acquired and presumably would have been acted upon.

---

109. 513 U.S. 352 (1995).

110. *Id.* at 362–63.

111. Russell v. Microdyne Corp., 65 F.3d 1229 (4th Cir. 1995).

112. Wallace v. Dunn Constr. Co., 62 F.3d 374 (11th Cir. 1995) (en banc).

113. Carr v. Woodbury County Juvenile Detention Center, 905 F. Supp. 619 (N.D. Iowa 1995), aff'd per curiam, 97 F.3d 1456 (8th Cir. 1996).

114. Sellers v. Mineta, 358 F.3d 1058 (8th Cir. 2004); Shick v. Illinois Dep't of Human Services, 307 F.3d 605 (7th Cir. 2002).

Since after-acquired evidence is used as a form of affirmative defense, one court has held that under the FRCP it must be pleaded at the appropriate time and if not, else the defense is waived.[115]

§ 5.11 The Affirmative Action Defense

In a literal sense, when an employer takes race, sex, or any other protected characteristic into account in making employment decisions, this constitutes discrimination on a proscribed basis. However, in *United Steelworkers of America v. Weber*[116] the Supreme Court held that under certain circumstances such differentiations were not *discrimination* in the statutory sense, because "a thing may be within the letter of the statute and yet not within the statute, because not within its spirit, nor within the intention of its makers."[117]

Under *Weber* and the Court's later decision in *Johnson v. Transportation Agency, Santa Clara County*,[118] preferential hiring or promotion policies are permitted if:

- The job in question has been "traditionally closed" to minorities.
- The plan is designed to "eliminate a manifest ... imbalance," measured by a comparison of the percentage of minorities in the job and the percentage in the either the general or the qualified workforce, depending on the nature of the job.
- The plan is temporary and will end when that balance is achieved.
- The plan does not "unnecessarily trammel the interests of [non-minority] employees" by requiring that they be replaced or by creating an absolute bar to advancement.

The extent to which these criteria survive the Supreme Court decision in *Ricci v. DeStefano*[119] is an open question. This is discussed in Chapter 7. Complicating the issue is that the Supreme Court later held in *City of Richmond v. J.A. Croson Co.*[120] that race-based affirmative action plans are subject to strict scrutiny when faced with a constitutional challenge. If the employer is a government contractor, such an employer will necessarily have an affirmative action plan that complies with Executive Order 11246 and the regulations that have been adopted pursuant to it.[121] These regulations require an employer to adopt goal and timetables to correct any "under-utilization" of minorities in various job categories. To the extent that "under-utilization" is different from a "manifest imbalance" and must be corrected regardless of any historical pattern of discrimination, EO 11246 affirmative action plans may go beyond what *Weber* seems to allow and not satisfy strict scrutiny. There is currently a circuit

115. Red Deer v. Cherokee County, 183 F.R.D. 642 (N.D. Iowa 1999).

116. 443 U.S. 193 (1979).

117. Weber, 443 U.S. at 201 (quoting from Holy Trinity Church v. United States, 143 U.S. 457, 459 (1892)).

118. 480 U.S. 616 (1987).

119. 557 U.S. 557 (2009).

120. 488 U.S. 469 (1989).

121. *See* Chapter 29.

split over whether sex-based affirmative action plans must meet strict scrutiny or the lower intermediate scrutiny to survive.

However, Section 713(b) of Title VII provides a defense for any employment practice that would otherwise be illegal if the defendant proves that the action was "in reliance on any written interpretation or opinion" of the EEOC. Pursuant to this section, the EEOC has issued a regulation stating that an affirmative action plan that conforms with the requirements of the Executive Order is deemed also to be in compliance with Title VII.[122] Whether an administrative agency can promulgate an authoritative interpretation of a statute that is inconsistent with the Supreme Court's interpretation is questionable.

§ 5.12 Chapter Highlights

1. Proof of subjective, biased motivation is critical in an individual disparate treatment case. Usually, only the bias of the ultimate decisionmaker is relevant. In some instances, however, the unrevealed bias of a subordinate who was involved in the process will be attributed to the person who actually made the decision. (§ 5.02)

2. The *because of* element in a Title VII cause of action involves proof of some form of causation—that is, showing a connection between an alleged causal event (subjective bias) and the claimed causal consequence (an adverse employment action). Logically, a causal event may be a *necessary condition* of the causal consequence, a *sufficient condition*, or a *necessary and sufficient condition*—and if there is none of those, then no logical causation exists. (§ 5.03[A])

3. The Civil Rights of 1991 codified the mixed-motive standard of causation. Section 703(m) states that "an unlawful employment practice is established when the complaining party demonstrates that race, color, religion, sex, or national origin was a motivating factor for any employment practice, even though other factors also motivated the practice." (§ 5.03[B])

4. The distinction between single-motive and mixed-motive employment decisions is less important today than it was when it was determinative of the kind of evidence a plaintiff had to produce in order to shift a burden of proof onto the defendant. Nevertheless, it still remains a critical analytical point of departure. A single-motive decision is an *either/or* proposition. The adverse employment action was either motivated by impermissible bias or it was motivated by a legitimate concern. In a mixed-motive decision, both legitimate and illegitimate considerations contributed to the decision. The nature of the evidence and whether burdens of some kind shift during the process is still being worked out in litigation. (§ 5.04)

5. There are basically three paradigms of individual disparate treatment proof. The first simply tracks the normal civil case (Model I). The second starts with a set

122. 29 C.F.R. § 1608.1.

of facts proved by the plaintiff that create an inference of discrimination. The defendant is then required to produce evidence of a legitimate reason. This joins the ultimate issue, and the plaintiff must then demonstrate that discrimination rather than the defendant's articulated legitimate reason caused the adverse employment decision in question (Model II). The third model is akin to a *confession and avoidance* type of case, where the plaintiff proves discrimination (or the defendant openly admits it) but the defendant presents an affirmative defense (Model III). (§ 5.05)

6. In a Model I type of case, most of the evidentiary issues relate to the following kinds of proof: statements and documents admitting discriminatory intent; evidence comparing the treatment of specific individuals; epithets, derogatory remarks, demeaning jokes and comments, and expressions of stereotypical views; and evidence relating to the *same actor* defense. (§ 5.06)

7. In a Model II type of case, the evidentiary issues are a bit more complex. Questions still exist, for example, over which facts are necessary to establish a prima facie case. Indeed, rather than being a fixed formula, the prima facie case can be any set of facts that raises an inference of discrimination. But a good bit of litigation still exists over proof or disproof of job qualifications. (§ 5.07[A])

8. If the plaintiff establishes a prima facie case, a burden of production shifts onto the defendant to articulate a "legitimate, nondiscriminatory reason" for the adverse employment action. The operative word, however, is "nondiscriminatory." A reason that would make the decision illegal under another statute, that would be illegal under a Title VII disparate impact theory of discrimination, or that is based on some irrational whim of the employer will still qualify at this point. The articulated reason, however, must be relatively clear and specific. (§ 5.06[B])

9. The first two steps in a Model II case simply operate to frame the issue, and the burden is then on the plaintiff to prove the ultimate issue—an illegally motivated employment decision. This is the so-called *pretext* stage. A wide variety of types of evidence can be used for this purpose, some of it consisting of additional proof of the discrimination itself and some of it consisting of proof that the employer's articulated reason was not the real reason. Although the Supreme Court has visited this issue twice in recent years, a significant amount of disagreement still exists in the lower courts over exactly what kinds of evidence are sufficient and how to instruct a jury on these witty nuances of the law. (§ 5.07[C])

10. The Model III type of case involves situations where the discrimination is admitted or conclusively proved, but the defendant offers an affirmative defense in justification. The statutory BFOQ is less significant today than it was in the early years of Title VII, since it has been narrowly construed and some consensus does exist over what qualified. It is most frequently recognized where a covered characteristic (sex, national origin, or religion) is necessary to establish authenticity, to preserve privacy, and where the safety of others is at stake. (§ 5.08)

11. Of enormously more current significance is the Model III type of case where the plaintiff proves that discrimination was a *motivating factor* in the decision, but

the defendant then proves that the plaintiff would have been terminated anyway, for legitimate reasons—that is, mixed-motive employment decisions. These cases raise the core question of the role of *causation* in Title VII violations. Today, regardless of whether a single or mixed motive was involved, a plaintiff can win by showing discrimination was a motivating factor in the adverse action. In any event, in a mixed-motive case the legitimate motive affirmative defense operates only to limit the relief that is available to a prevailing plaintiff. (§ 5.09)

12. The third type of Model III case involves proof by the plaintiff that the employer was impermissibly motivated at the time the decision was made, but the defendant then proves through the use of *after-acquired evidence* that if this had been known at the time, the plaintiff would have been terminated anyway, for legitimate reasons. Again, this defense only limits the remedies that are available to the plaintiff. (§ 5.10)

13. If the discrimination in question operates in favor of minority individuals and to the corresponding disadvantage of non-minority individuals, then the employer may attempt to justify this by reference to an affirmative action plan. Such a plan, however, must meet the requirements spelled out by the Supreme Court in *Weber*. The employer may also have a defense if the plan, while not meeting the *Weber* requirements, is a part of this employer's affirmative action plan as a federal contractor. If state action is involved, the employer's defense is subject to strict scrutiny, except with sex-based plans, concerning which the circuits are divided. (§ 5.11)

Chapter 6

Systemic Disparate Treatment

Synopsis

§ 6.01 Introduction

An employer's bias against persons on the basis of race, sex, or some other proscribed characteristic usually does not manifest itself only in isolated instances; it affects the class as a whole. In some cases, the systemic discrimination is apparent on the face of a written policy or practice. For example, in *Los Angeles Dep't of Water & Power v. Manhart*,[1] the employer required female employees to make larger contributions to the pension fund than male employees.

Another kind of systemic discrimination case arises when the employer's policies and practices are not overtly discriminatory and, indeed, the employer denies having any discriminatory intent. Yet, a casual examination of the composition of the workforce—showing, for example, few, if any, minorities in the better paying or more desirable jobs—may suggest that something is amiss.

Widespread or systemic discrimination of this kind has been challenged by private defendants, either as named individuals[2] as a true class action or by the EEOC under its enforcement powers. Under Section 707 of the statute, the EEOC is authorized to bring a lawsuit when an employer has "engaged in a pattern or practice of resistance to the enjoyment of any of the rights protected by [the statute]." Establishing this kind of discrimination requires a different model of proof than that used in estab-

1. 435 U.S. 702 (1978).

2. *But see* Lowery v. Circuit City Stores, Inc., 158 F.3d 742 (4th Cir. 1998), vacated on other grounds, 527 U.S. 1031 (1999) (individuals cannot bring pattern or practice suits, and thus benefit from the statistical, systemic discrimination method of proof, except as class actions).

lishing discrimination on an individual basis. It was originally laid out by the Supreme Court in *Teamsters v. United States*.[3]

§ 6.02 The Scheme of Proof

[A] Stage I

The existence of class-wide discrimination is established at the so-called "Stage I" of a *Teamsters* systemic disparate treatment case. The proof consists primarily and sometimes exclusively[4] of statistics, but they are usually bolstered with proof of discrimination in a number of individual situations as well.

Although every imaginable kind of statistic has been proffered as proof of systemic disparate treatment, the prototypical statistic involves a comparison of the percentage of minorities in the defendant employer's workforce (usually focusing on specific job categories) and the percentage of minorities in the so-called *relevant labor market*.[5] The theory is that in the absence of discrimination, the percentage would be roughly the same; and when it is not, this creates an inference of discrimination. For example, if a jar contains 100 marbles, 60 white and 40 black, a blind drawing of 10 marbles on average will yield six white and four black. If the average is eight white and two black, then this suggests the selector is peeking.

The critical issue in nearly every systemic disparate treatment case involves the identification of the relevant labor market, against which to compare the workforce figures. This involves not only competing geographic considerations[6] but also job qualification requirements.[7] Sometimes, the courts will simply look to the area from which the existing workforce is drawn, although that can be distorted if the employer is charged with recruitment discrimination. Generally speaking, the less skilled the job (or the lower the wages), the narrower the relevant geographic area. For minimum wage jobs, this may be the immediate neighborhood of the plant itself, although the precise lines often will take into account public transportation routes. Thus, the map may extend out from the plant five miles in one direction, but 20 miles along a subway or bus route. For highly skilled jobs, the relevant market may be the entire metropolitan area, a region of the country, or even the entire country.

---

3. 431 U.S. 324 (1977). The lower courts have noted that the proof must be "substantial" and that the "burden of establishing a pattern or practice of discrimination is not an easy one to carry." EEOC v. Bloomberg, 778 F. Supp. 2d 458, 468 (S.D.N.Y. 2011) (quoting *In re* W. Dist. Xerox Litig., 850 F. Supp. 1079, 1085 (W.D.N.Y. 1994)).

4. United States v. Sheet Metal Workers, Local 36, 416 F.2d 123 (8th Cir. 1969).

5. Hazelwood School Dist. v. United States, 433 U.S. 299 (1977).

6. Detroit Police Officers' Ass'n v. Young, 608 F.2d 671 (6th Cir. 1979) (City of Detroit rather than the entire metropolitan area found to be the relevant geographic area); United States v. County of Fairfax, 629 F.2d 932 (4th Cir. 1980) (refusing to use the District of Columbia SMSA data because the suburban county rarely hired D.C. residents).

7. EEOC v. United Virginia Bank, 615 F.2d 147 (4th Cir. 1980).

Within the relevant geographic area, the next question is which individuals can be counted as comparators. For unskilled jobs or those that require only minimal training, general population statistics may be used. For skilled jobs, the relevant comparators are obviously only those who possess the qualification for the job. Such data is available from a number of sources.

The narrowest labor market, and the one favored by most employers, is that specific employer's own qualified applicant pool. This accurately reflects the "jar" from which the actual selections are being made, and includes not only those possessing the necessary qualifications but also limits it to individuals who are actually in the job market and are interested in working for this employer. On the other hand, this data base may be self-selecting—if for example, the employer has a reputation for discriminating against minorities, who would thus be deterred from even applying.[8]

Once the proper comparison is established, the next question is whether it is statistically significant—that is, is the disparity substantial enough to raise an inference that it is caused by intentional discrimination rather than by chance? In *Hazelwood*, the Supreme Court approved the use of binomial distribution to make this determination. This statistical model is based on the theory that the actual workforce will mirror the relevant labor market, creating a *null hypothesis* that no discrimination exists. The extent to which the actual workforce distribution differs from what would be expected is measured in terms of *standard deviations*. If the standard deviation is more than two or three, then this is grounds for rejecting the null hypothesis and attributing the result to intentional discrimination.

The formula for determining standard deviations is as follows:

$SD = M - (W \times P)/(W \times P) \times (1 - P)$

SD = standard deviations.

M = number of minorities in workforce.

W = total number of minorities in workforce

P = percentage of minorities in the relevant labor market.

In *Teamsters*, for example, in the defendant's Atlanta terminal, there were 57 employees in the questioned job category. Although minorities comprised 22% of the relevant labor market, there were no minorities in that job category—the so-called "inexorable zero." When those figures are plugged into the formula, it produces a standard deviation of four, which is enough to infer the presence of intentional discrimination.

In addition to binomial distribution, the Supreme Court has also approved the use of the multiple regression technique, which measures the respective influence of several factors or variables.[9]

8. *See* Moore v. Hughes Helicopters, 708 F.2d 475 (9th Cir. 1983).

9. Bazemore v. Friday, 478 U.S. 385 (1986) (involving alleged pay discrimination).

A defendant employer can respond to a plaintiff's statistics in a number of ways. First, an employer may be able to show flaws in the accuracy and reliability of the statistical data, either through cross-examination of the plaintiff's expert or by testimony of other experts. Second, the employer may simply submit counter-statistics. For example, if the plaintiff shows that 25% of the general labor market is Hispanic but only 10% of the employer's unskilled workforce is Hispanic, this reflects a statistically significant disparity. But if the employer shows that only 10% of the applicants for its unskilled jobs are Hispanic, the disparity disappears—raising, however, the legal question of which comparison is most apt. Third, the employer may be able to explain away the disparity by showing that it is caused by neutral factors. For example, in *EEOC v. Chicago Miniature Lamp Works*,[10] the employer's comparatively low percentage of black employees was explained by the fact the jobs in question did not require a fluency in English, which made them especially attractive to non-English speaking Hispanics and Asians living in the immediate area, who applied in disproportionate numbers. On the other hand, if the employer attempts to explain away the statistics by reference to something like an inability to pass a certain test, then this simply sets the employer up for a claim of disparate impact discrimination.

In any event, if the plaintiff prevails with its statistical data (usually, but not always reinforced with proof of illustrative examples of individual discrimination), then this establishes a violation of Title VII that at least warrants declaratory and injunctive relief on behalf of the class. The litigation then moves to the next stage.

[B] Stage II

If the plaintiff prevails at Stage I, this creates a presumption of discrimination against every member of the class who applied for the job or promotion (or would have applied except for the employer's known discriminatory practices) and who possesses the minimal qualifications for the job. This presumption, of course, defies reality. If the discrimination relates to hiring and the employer had only 10 vacancies during the period in question, then not every one of the 100 plaintiffs could possibly have been discriminated against. The next problem is figuring out who would have been hired *but for* the illegal discrimination and who, thus, is entitled to backpay compensation.

Stage II then devolves into a series of mini-trials focusing on each individual member of the class. The burden, however, is on the employer to show that a specific plaintiff would not have been hired for entirely legitimate reasons. In a case involving multiple forms of alleged discrimination (hiring, promotion, transfer), a class of plaintiffs in the 100s, and extending over a period of several years, such proof is virtually impossible; and the cost of litigation nearly always exceeds the benefits to be obtained by either the plaintiffs or the defendant. The common practice, thus, is to achieve a settlement that somehow distributes the compensatory damages among the

10. 947 F.2d 292 (7th Cir. 1991).

members of the class in a manner that at least has the appearance of fairness—although the courts differ over how much individualization of relief is required.

§ 6.03 Chapter Highlights

1. Systemic disparate treatment discrimination is discrimination against the whole class of individuals within the protected category. It may consist of policies or practices that can themselves be proved. When there is no direct evidence of such policies or practices, the necessary intent can be inferred from statistical data. (§ 6.01)

2. Stage I of the proof consists of a comparison of the composition of the *relevant labor market* (which may be defined in a variety of ways) and the composition of the workforce. If a difference exists and it is *statistically significant*, this establishes a violation of Title VII. It also creates a presumption that every member of the class has been a victim of the discrimination. (§ 6.02[A])

3. At Stage II, the burden is on the employer to prove that any specific member of the class was not in fact a victim of the violation. Because of the difficulty of determining which of 10 applicants would have gotten the job *but for* the discrimination, the courts often approve settlements that allocate the damages among the 10 plaintiffs. (§ 6.02[B])

Chapter 7

Disparate Impact

Synopsis

While the disparate impact theory of discrimination has had an enormous impact on the elimination of many of the vestiges of employment discrimination, it is also a classic tale of legal misadventure. It involves the story of a Supreme Court decision that created the theory virtually out of whole cloth, many years of working out the details regarding the proof of and defenses to this kind of discrimination, another Supreme Court decision that radically altered the theory, and then a congressional codification that created a virtually unfathomable scheme of proof.

Unfortunately, knowing the history of the origin and evolution of the disparate impact theory is absolutely essential to an understanding of the meaning and significance of the various stages of the theory—and especially to what its current incarnation might happen to mean. Hence, the prolixity of this Chapter.

§ 7.01 The Origin of the Theory

The seminal case, *Griggs v. Duke Power Co.*,[1] involved a challenge to two employment practices—possession of a high school degree and the ability to pass certain tests in order to qualify for certain jobs. The imposition of these requirements occurred in the context of pre-Act discrimination. Prior to the passage of Title VII, discrimination precluded blacks from being hired into these jobs at all. The issues at the district court and court of appeals levels were whether the *present effects of prior* (pre-Act) *discrimination* on plaintiffs violated Title VII even when the employer presently had no subjective intent to discriminate. Complicating this issue was that Title VII was not to be applied retroactively, and intent to discriminate was generally required. The argumentation over those issues proceeded at a fairly technical and arcane level. The defendant prevailed, and the majority opinion reflected its arguments. But the dissenting opinion of Judge Sobeloff in the Fourth Circuit, rather than espousing the plaintiffs' rather humdrum arguments, instead sowed the seeds of an entirely new theory of discrimination—seeds that fell on fertile ground in the chambers of the United States Supreme Court. It was his theory and language that the Supreme Court adopted in *Griggs*.

The Court's own statement of the issue is significant, however, for technically it limits the scope of the holding. The Court stated:

> We granted the writ in this case to resolve the question whether an employer is prohibited by the Civil Rights Act of 1964, Title VII, from requiring a high school education or passing of a standardized general intelligence test as a condition of employment in or transfer to jobs when (a) neither standard is shown to be significantly related to successful job performance, (b) both requirements operate to disqualify Negroes at a substantially higher rate than white applicants, and (c) the jobs in question formerly had been filled only by white employees as part of a longstanding practice of giving preference to whites.[2]

Although that statement of the issue did not include the intent question, the Supreme Court addressed it anyway. The Supreme indicated that actual, subjective intent was not a necessary element of all Title VII causes of action, noting that "Congress directed the thrust of the Act to the *consequences* of employment practices, not simply the motivation."[3] Significantly, however, in this case the consequences being condemned were clearly rooted in prior intentional discrimination of the company—albeit at a time when such discrimination was not illegal. This is reflected in the third element of the issue statement quoted above. Indeed, the Court implicitly recognized the importance of this nexus with prior intentional discrimination when it stated: "Under the Act, practices, procedures, or tests neutral on their face, and even neutral in terms of intent, cannot be maintained if they operate to 'freeze' the status quo of

1. 401 U.S. 424 (1971).
2. Griggs, 401 U.S. at 425–26.
3. *Id.* at 432.

prior discriminatory employment practices."[4] Although the *Griggs* holding thus seemed to be grounded in the *present effect of prior discrimination* (or *perpetuation*) theory of discrimination (in which intent is one step removed), the Court never used those terms and thus avoided the retroactivity issue altogether.[5] Moreover, this factual component of the *Griggs* case has been largely ignored in subsequent decisions. Rather, the theory has been extended to cover any employment practice that has a disparate impact on a protected class, regardless of whether the cause of this impact was the prior intentional discrimination by the defendant employer, existing or prior societal discrimination, or even the physical characteristics of certain protected classes.

§ 7.02 The *Griggs/Albemarle* Model

As clarified by the Supreme Court decision in *Albemarle Paper Co. v. Moody*,[6] proof of disparate impact discrimination consisted of three steps: proof by the plaintiff of the existence of a statistically significant disparity, proof by the defendant that the challenged practice or policy could be justified by *business necessity*, and rebuttal proof by the plaintiff that the interest asserted by defendant could be served by other practices or policies not having a disparate impact (sometimes called the *pretext* stage).

[A] A Statistically Significant Disparate Impact

In the early days of the Act, when proof theories and labels were still relatively uncertain, a few courts used the term "disparate impact" to refer to cases that were actually of the systemic disparate treatment type and in which the courts used the *Teamsters* type of statistics and method of proof. But from the beginning, in true disparate impact cases, the courts nearly always used so-called *pass/fail* or *gateway* statistics, with the *gate* referring to the employment policy, practice, or requirement at issue that was allegedly screening out the plaintiff class. These statistics compare the percentage of minorities who have actually passed through or who can be predicted to pass through the gate against the percentage of non-minorities who otherwise qualify. For example, in *Griggs*, 34% of white males in North Carolina possessed a high school diploma, while only 12% of black males did. Similarly, 58% of whites passed the standardized tests used by the employer, while only 6% of the blacks did. In both instances, more whites than blacks could be expected to pass through those respective *gates*.

Although statisticians developed various tests for determining when comparative pass/fail rates became statistically significant, the EEOC relied on the so-called *80%*

---

4. Griggs, 401 U.S. at 430.

5. The Supreme Court later rejected the *present effects* theory as an actionable form of Title VII discrimination altogether, first implicitly and then expressly. *See* Chapter 16, § 16.04[A].

6. 422 U.S. 405 (1975).

or *4/5th rule* when making "cause" determinations. Under this rule, if the passage rate for minorities was 80% or less than the passage rate for non-minorities, then a significant disparity was said to exist. Although some courts have demanded more exact proof of disparity, the Supreme Court in *Ricci v. DeStefano* referred to it favorably in reference to the statistics present in that case.[7]

As was seen earlier, systemic disparate treatment discrimination is also proved primarily with the use of statistics.[8] The theory behind *Teamster* statistics is that color-blind hiring will produce a workforce whose racial composition matches the pool of applicants; if it does not, this suggests discrimination.

It is essential, however, to understand this original difference between *Teamster* systemic disparate treatment statistics and *Griggs* disparate impact statistics. The first compares workforce against labor market; the other compares actual or predicted passage rates. A disparity in one set of statistics (impact) will often produce a disparity in the other set (systemic). Assume, for example, in a start-up company, a relevant labor market of 100 (70% non-minority and 30% minority); half of each group within that market apply for a job; the employer has a hiring criterion that disqualifies 25% of the non-minorities and 50% of the minorities. The results are as follows:

Labor Market	Applications	% Disqualified	Pass & Hired
non-M – 70	35	25%	26 = 78% of workforce
M – 30	15	50%	7 = 21% of workforce

Here the disqualification comparison (25% to 50%) establishes a disparate impact under *Griggs*, and the minority workforce/labor market comparison (21% to 30%) establishes systemic disparate treatment under *Teamsters*.

But this will not always be the case. Assume, for example, that a lower percentage of non-minorities and a higher percentage of minorities apply for the job than non-minorities.

Labor Market	Applications	% Disqualified	Pass & Hired
non-M – 70	31	25%	3 = 70% of workforce
M – 30	20	50%	10 = 30% of workforce

Here, the *Teamsters* statistics fail to reveal any evidence of discrimination. The percentage of minorities in the workforce is the same as the percentage in the relevant labor market. The *Griggs* pass/fail statistics, however, remain the same, revealing that the criterion has a disparate impact on minorities.

7. 557 U.S. 557 (2009). *See* §7.06[A].

8. *See* Chapter 6, §6.02[A].

An affirmative action plan that aimed for proportional representation could have the same effect. A question arose over whether good *Teamster* statistics were a defense to bad *Griggs* statistics. The Supreme Court held that they were not. In *Connecticut v. Teal*,[9] the Court rejected the so-called *bottom line defense* in a disparate impact case. There, the employer used a test to determine eligibility for promotion that disqualified a disproportionately large number of minorities. From among those who did qualify, however, the employer gave an affirmative action preference to minorities. The *Teamsters* bottom-line statistics (promotion pool minority percentage compared to the promoted minority percentage) were thus within the norm. But the Supreme Court held that this was no defense to the use of an intermediate criterion that had a disparate impact on who was considered eligible.

Finally, the courts have recognized that for the comparative percentages to be statistically significant, they must be based on a sufficiently large number of samples.[10]

[B] Business Necessity

The fact that a practice or policy has a disparate impact on minorities does not, however, conclusively establish its illegality. The Court in *Griggs* indicated that an unintentional effect of this kind could nevertheless be justified. The Court stated: "The touchstone is business necessity. If an employment practice which operates to exclude Negroes cannot be shown to be related to job performance, the practice is prohibited."[11] In large part, the business necessity defense that the Court recognized came directly out of the statute itself. Insofar as the tests were concerned, the employer relied on Section 703(h), which authorizes the use of "any professionally developed ability test" that is not "designed, intended, or used to discriminate because of race." Although it could have concluded that a test which has a disparate impact is, a fortiori, being "used to discriminate," the Court relied instead on broader considerations of congressional intent and concluded that Congress intended to allow only tests that are "demonstrably a reasonable measure of job performance."[12] On the other hand, to the extent that the business necessity defense applied to the high school degree requirement, this was purely a judicial creation. But regardless of whether the defense was grounded in Section 703(h) or the Court's broader concept, the lower courts consistently agreed that the defendant employer bore a true burden of proof in establishing the existence of a business necessity.

Beyond that, however, the courts construing *Griggs* agreed on very little about the defense. The disagreement revolved around three related variables—the focus of the

9. 457 U.S. 440 (1982).

10. Harper v. Trans World Airlines, 525 F.2d 409 (8th Cir. 1975) (rule prohibiting employment of spouses not subject to disparate impact analysis because only five couples had been affected by the rule).

11. Griggs, 401 U.S. at 431.

12. Griggs, 401 U.S. at 436.

employment requirement being challenged, the relative importance of this requirement to the employer, and the strength of evidence necessary to establish it.

First, the courts disagreed over whether the employment policy, practice, or requirement had to be focused more or less directly on the performance of a specific job or whether the defense also encompassed requirements that focused on the promotion of business interests in a larger sense. Certainly, the focus of the tests and degree requirements in *Griggs* were on suitability for employment in certain classes of jobs. Focus on broader business interests were later found to be insufficient. In rejecting an employer's customer-preference justification for a no-beard policy that had a disparate impact on black males, a court noted that the "existence of a beard on the face of a delivery man does not affect in any manner Domino's ability to make or deliver pizzas to their customers."[13] Other courts, however, allowed the focus to shift from qualifications that relate directly to job tasks to job performance in a broader sense. For example, in one case a court allowed a business necessity defense to a no-spouse rule on the grounds that the rule generally promoted productivity, efficiency, and ease of management.[14] And finally, another court allowed an employer to justify a policy that gave special benefits to employees who qualified as a "head of the household" on the grounds that it tended to benefit the largest number of employees, including those with the greatest need.[15]

Second, regardless of what the appropriate focus is, the post-*Griggs* courts also disagreed over whether the challenged requirement must be essential or can be merely relevant. In one case, a court referred to a need to prove the existence of "an *overriding* legitimate business purpose such that the practice is *necessary* to the safe and efficient operation of the business" and that is "*sufficiently compelling* to override any racial impact."[16] On the other hand, another court stated that *Griggs* "implicitly approves employment practices that significantly serve, but are neither required by nor necessary to, the employer's legitimate business interests."[17]

Third, the courts disagreed over the type of evidence that was sufficient to establish business necessity. In *Griggs*, the Supreme Court held that the testimony of a company official expressing the belief that the challenged requirements would improve the overall quality of the workforce was insufficient. Despite that, a later Tenth Circuit case upheld a college degree requirement solely on the basis of the testimony of a company official that "the possession of a college degree indicated that the applicant had the ability to understand and retain concepts and information given in the atmosphere of a classroom or training program," which were an ongoing part of the job.[18] On the other hand, with respect to employment tests, the courts require hard, empirical evidence establishing the validity of the test by showing that it correlates

13. Bradley v. Pizzaco, 7 F.3d 795, 799 (8th Cir. 1993).
14. Yuhas v. Libbey-Owens-Ford Co., 562 F.2d 496 (7th Cir. 1977).
15. Wambheim v. J.C. Penney Co., 705 F.2d 1492 (9th Cir. 1983).
16. Robinson v. Lorillard Corp., 444 F.2d 791, 798 (4th Cir. 1971) (emphasis added).
17. Contreras v. City of Los Angeles, 656 F.2d 1267, 1280 (9th Cir. 1981).
18. Spurlock v. United Airlines, Inc., 475 F.2d 216, 219 (10th Cir. 1972).

with job performance. The EEOC has promulgated extensive guidelines on how this can be done.[19] This is an expensive and time-consuming endeavor that requires the use of experts.

In short, no consistency has ever existed with respect to the meaning or application of the original *Griggs* business necessity defense. This is significant, because in enacting the Civil Rights Act of 1991, Congress erroneously assumed that such a consensus existed—or could be reasonably derived from the earlier Supreme Court cases.

[C] Pretext

The third step of the traditional disparate impact analysis was stated by the Supreme Court in *Albemarle Paper Co. v. Moody*,[20] as follows:

> If an employer does then meet the burden of proving that its tests are "job related," it remains open to the complaining party to show that other tests or selection devices, without a similarly undesirable racial effect, would also serve the employer's legitimate interest in "efficient and trustworthy workmanship." Such a showing would be evidence that the employer was using its tests merely as a "pretext" for discrimination.

The Court's use of the term "pretext" was unfortunate and confusing. Pretext suggests intentionality, as in the *McDonnell Douglas* individual disparate treatment cases, while disparate impact requires no proof of intent. Of course, if a plaintiff can show that the employer adopted a facially neutral criterion knowing that it would have a disparate impact and intending to accomplish that result, then the criterion would qualify as a proxy for race or sex and the case could proceed on a disparate treatment basis. Short of that, however, all a plaintiff must do is proffer evidence of the existence, feasibility, and efficiency of an alternative device that does not have a disparate impact. Plaintiffs have rarely succeeded on this basis, however.[21]

§ 7.03 The *Wards Cove* Reformulation of the Test

Prior to *Watson v. Fort Worth Bank & Trust*,[22] the Circuits were divided over whether subjective or discretionary employment practices could be subject to disparate impact

19. Uniform Guidelines on Employee Selection Procedures, 29 C.F.R. pt. 1607. *See* § 7.05[A].

20. 422 U.S. 405, 425 (1975).

21. MacPherson v. University of Montevallo, 922 F.2d 766 (11th Cir. 1991) (no proof that paying professors the "market rate" was economically possible); Gillespie v. Wisconsin, 771 F.2d 1035 (7th Cir. 1985) (plaintiff's "bare assertion" that the employer could have developed a multiple-choice test to replace the essay test failed to satisfy the burden on this issue). *But see* United States v. Warren, 759 F. Supp. 355 (E.D. Mich. 1991) (court accepted as a reasonable alternative to a residency requirement at the time of hire a requirement that applicants actually selected for hire move into the city within a reasonable time).

22. 487 U.S. 977 (1988).

analysis. In most instances, the usual focus of disparate impact analysis had been various objective tests and requirements, which were capable of being evaluated prior to being applied. The high school degree requirement in *Griggs* would disqualify a disproportionate number of blacks regardless of who the employer was. And if a particular test was shown to have a disparate impact among employees of one employer, then it would likely have the same impact on the employees of another employer—which, of course, could then be established in litigation. But subjective or discretionary employment practices cannot be identified in a similar fashion. They might produce a disparity when used by one employer, but not another. Thus, rather than trying to shoehorn this form of discrimination into the disparate impact model, some courts concluded that the *Teamsters* scheme of statistical proof was better designed to deal with this phenomenon.

The Supreme Court, however, saw no reason why disparate impact analysis, as it was to construe it, could not be applied to subjective and discretionary employment practices. The Court viewed this as a way of addressing both intentional discrimination that could not be proved and subconscious reliance on stereotypes and prejudices. This suggests that the Court had in mind a merger of the two theories of discrimination, with a "one size fits all" method of proof. But the Court did not agree on what that method of proof was. The portions of Justice O'Connor's plurality opinion dealing with statistical proof and the nature of the business necessity defense did, however, serve as a preview of things to come.

Wards Cove Packing Co. v. Atonio[23] was an atypical type of case, factually, for disparate impact purposes. The plaintiffs were challenging a number of employment practices, including the lack of any objective hiring criteria. Because of the seasonal nature of the operation, all the employees were essentially hired at the same time—rather than incrementally, as in most business operations. This unusual factual pattern allowed the Court to use the statistics that it did, but in doing so the Court radically altered the nature of disparate impact proof in other types of cases as well.

The Court held that in establishing disparate impact discrimination, the "proper comparison [is] between the racial compositions [of the jobs at issue] and the racial composition of the qualified ... population in the relevant labor market."[24] Those, of course, are prototypical *Teamsters*-type statistics used for establishing systemic disparate treatment, not the *Griggs gateway* type of statistics. In this particular case, because of the company's policy of hiring the workforce for each season all at once, if one type of comparison produced a disparity, then the other would as well. A criterion that produces a passage rate for non-minorities that is higher than the rate for minorities will automatically produce a workforce/relevant-labor-market disparity as well. This, however, is not necessarily true of a *Connecticut v. Teal* type of disparate impact claim, where the test had a disparate impact—measured by *gateway* statis-

23. 490 U.S. 642 (1989).

24. *Wards Cove*, 490 U.S. at 650 (quoting Hazelwood School Board v. United States, 433 U.S. 299, 308 (1977)).

tics—while the *bottom line*, *Teamsters*-type statistics were unexceptional.[25] In any event, by virtue of its reliance on these statistics, the Court seems to have fused systemic disparate treatment and disparate impact into a single cause of action.

Having identified the relevant statistical comparison in this fashion, the Court then found it necessary to add another element to the analysis—namely, the requirement that the plaintiff identify "a specific or particular employment practice that has created the disparate impact under attack."[26] In the traditional *gateway* statistics type of disparate impact case, it was unnecessary to list this as a separate requirement. Obviously, one could not measure and compare the pass/fail ratios of minorities/non-minorities unless one knew what the pass/fail criterion was. Essentially, the Court added a proof-of-causation element to the *Teamster*-type statistics. Of course, the whole theory of the *Teamsters* model of proof is that the statistical disparity creates an inference that it was caused by intentional discrimination.

Third, since it would be difficult if not impossible to prove the more rigorous formulations of *business necessity* in reference to subjective or discretionary hiring practices, the Court found it necessary to tinker with that aspect of the test as well. It adopted the most relaxed version of business necessity imaginable.

> [T]he dispositive issue is whether a challenged practice serves, in a significant way, the legitimate employment goals of the employers. The touchstone of this inquiry is a reasoned review of the employer's justification for his use of the challenged practice.... [T]here is no requirement that the challenged practice be "essential" or "indispensable" to the employer's business for it to pass muster....[27]

Moreover, now borrowing from the *McDonnell Douglas* analytical model for establishing individual disparate treatment discrimination, the Court said that the employer's burden in this regard was merely one of producing evidence; the burden of persuasion, that of proving that the practice was not justified, is on the plaintiff.

Finally, with respect to the *pretext* element of the old *Griggs/Albemarle* model, the Court emphasized that the suggested alternative "must be equally effective as [the employer's] chosen hiring procedures in achieving [the employer's] legitimate employment goals," and that the "cost or other burdens" of the proposed alternative is relevant. In sum, "the judiciary should proceed with care before mandating that an

25. Oddly, the Court reiterated the *Connecticut v. Teal* holding, namely that "an employer cannot escape liability under Title VII by demonstrating that, 'at the bottom line,' his workforce is racially balanced," *Wards Cove*, 490 U.S. at 656, even though this is precisely what the Court had said a few pages earlier, namely that "if the percentage of selected applicants who are nonwhite is not significantly less than the percentage of qualified applicants who are nonwhite, the employer's selection mechanism probably does not operate with a disparate impact on minorities," *Wards Cove*, 490 U.S. at 653—an assertion that is true because of the unusual hiring procedures of *Wards Cove*, but which would not necessarily be true in other situations.

26. *Wards Cove*, 490 U.S. at 657.

27. *Wards Cove*, 490 U.S. at 659 (citations omitted).

employer must adopt a plaintiff's alternative selection or hiring practice in response to a Title VII suit."[28]

One can truly *understand* only two things about the *Wards Cove* decision. First, the Court clearly was changing the structure of disparate impact analysis, as it had been established both by its own precedents and the lower court decisions. Second, the Court made disparate impact a far less attractive and much more difficult theory of discrimination for a plaintiff to prove.

§ 7.04 The Civil Rights Act of 1991

The Civil Rights Act of 1991 was the result of congressional dissatisfaction with several late 1980s Supreme Court decisions, not the least of which was *Wards Cove.* In many respects, this Act is a model of legislative incompetence. The studied refusal of Congress to resolve the retroactivity issue cost the country millions of dollars in litigation costs and finally had to be resolved by the Supreme Court.[29] The Act is afflicted with ambiguity and bad drafting. And the legislative debates consisted mainly of political posturing by persons who quite clearly did not understand the corpus of law they were purporting to amend. And nowhere is this more evident than in the new Section 703(k)(1), which purports to codify a disparate impact model of proof. In brief, what it does to *Wards Cove* and the pre-*Wards Cove* body of law is as follows:

First, it says that a party must "demonstrate[] that a respondent uses a particular employment practice that causes a disparate impact," but the Act does not address the question of whether that *demonstration* must be by the old *Griggs gateway* statistics or whether they now must be by the *Wards Cove/Teamsters* statistics. The courts have since taken both approaches.[30]

Second, as just indicated, Congress did retain the *Wards Cove* requirement that a plaintiff identify the employment practice that is alleged to have caused the disparity,[31] "except that if the complaining party can demonstrate to the court that the elements of a respondent's decisionmaking process are not capable of separation for analysis, the decisionmaking process may be analyzed as one employment practice." It is not clear whether this refers to the use of criteria that are functionally integrated and essentially merge into a single criterion, such as the height/weight combinations used in *Dothard v. Rawlinson*,[32] or whether this applies if the plaintiff merely lacks the ev-

28. *Wards Cove*, 490 U.S. at 661.

29. McKnight v. General Motors Corp., 511 U.S. 659 (1994).

30. *Compare* Vitug v. Multistate Tax Commission, 88 F.3d 506 (7th Cir. 1996) (plaintiff failed to make the necessary comparison between hiring/promotion rates and the composition of the relevant labor market), *with* Paige v. California, 291 F.3d 1141 (9th Cir. 2002) (comparing "the group that enters the process with the group that emerges from it"), *and* Bullington v. United Air Lines, 186 F.3d 1301 (10th Cir. 1999) (plaintiff established disparate impact by comparing the interview "pass rates" of women (27.9%) with those of men (46.6%)).

31. *See* EEOC v. Joe's Stone Crab, Inc., 220 F.3d 1263 (11th Cir. 2000).

32. 433 U.S. 321 (1977).

identiary resources to determine which step in a multi-step hiring or promotion process has produced the statistical disparity. That it means the former is strongly suggested by the only authoritative legislative history on the issue, as follows:

> When a decisionmaking process includes particular, functionally-integrated practices which are components of the same criterion, standard, method of administration, or test, such as the height and weight requirements designed to measure strength in *Dothard v. Rawlinson*, ... the particular, functionally-integrated practices may be analyzed as one employment practice.[33]

On the other hand, that it perhaps means the latter is suggested by the further provision that "if the respondent demonstrates that a specific employment practice does not cause the disparate impact, the respondent shall not be required to demonstrate that such practice is required by business necessity." One interpretation posits that this refers to a practice that is a part of a multi-step decisionmaking process that the plaintiff cannot break down, but the defendant employer can. Otherwise, the provision is meaningless, since in a situation involving a single criterion the burden is on the plaintiff to establish impact anyway, and the mere failure of the plaintiff to do that relieves the employer of the burden of proving business necessity; the employer is not required to disprove impact as a condition of avoiding the necessity of proving business necessity.

Third, the Act clearly puts a true burden of proof on the employer to establish the *business necessity* defense, not merely a burden of articulation as under *Wards Cove.*

Fourth, the defense itself is worded in terms of proof that "the challenged practice is job related for the position in question and consistent with business necessity." Although the language used suggests a job focus and some degree of essentiality, actual congressional intent in this regard is unknowable. During the debates, some members of Congress said this means what the Supreme Court in *Wards Cove* said the defense means (essentially, a rational justification); others vigorously insisted that the language imposed a much more rigorous standard than that. The opposing sides decided simply to cancel each other out. A section of the Act provides that

> No statements other than the interpretive memorandum appearing at Vol. 137 Congressional Record S 15276 (daily ed. Oct. 25, 1991) shall be considered legislative history of, or relied upon in any way as legislative history in construing or applying, any provision of this Act that relates to Wards Cove—Business necessity/cumulation/alternative business practice.

What the cited legislative history says in this regard is as follows:

> The terms "business necessity" and "job related" are intended to reflect the concepts enunciated by the Supreme Court in *Griggs v. Duke Power Co....* and the other Supreme Court decisions prior to *Wards Cove Packing Co. v. Atonio.*

---

33. 137 CONG. REC. S15276 (daily ed. Oct. 25, 1991).

Unfortunately, this is not very enlightening.[34] Although some of these decisions, usually involving the Section 703(h) test defense, do focus on job relatedness rather than larger business concerns and speak in terms of *necessity* rather than mere *relevance*, others seem to adopt a much more relaxed approach to the issue. Needless to say, the courts are now in considerable disagreement over what this congressional mandate means.[35]

Fifth, the way the Act structures the three steps of the traditional test is odd, to say the least. In outline form, Section 703(k)(A) says that a plaintiff can prevail in a disparate impact case if—

(i) Plaintiff proves disparate impact

and

Defendant fails to prove business necessity

or

(ii) Plaintiff proves the existence of an alternative practice that the defendant refuses to adopt.

As drafted, element (ii) is divorced from any proof of disparate impact. Obviously, the "alternative" in question is an alternative to a practice that has a disparate impact, but this bad drafting is merely symptomatic of the more fundamental conceptual flaws.

Sixth, the Act provides that the demonstration of an alternative employment practice "shall be in accordance with the law as it existed on June 4, 1989...." That is the day before the *Wards Cove* decision—which certainly suggests a congressional repudiation of *Wards Cove* on that issue. This is odd, however, because the alternative practice discussion was one of the least exceptionable parts of the *Wards Cove* decision. Indeed, the law at that time was that a plaintiff would virtually never be able to recover at this stage of the analysis, and *Wards Cove* did nothing to lessen a plaintiff's chances in that regard.

Seventh, the Act imposes liability only if the plaintiff "demonstrates" the existence of an alternative "and the respondent refuses to adopt such alternative employment practice." Since the Act defines "demonstrates" as meaning "meeting the burdens of production and persuasion," the employer's option of ultimately defeating the cause of action (by adopting the alternative practice) can apparently be exercised at the

---

34. The relevant cases are as follows: Connecticut v. Teal, 457 U.S. 440 (1982); New York City Transit Auth. v. Beazer, 440 U.S. 568 (1979); Dothard v. Rawlinson, 433 U.S. 321 (1977); Washington v. Davis, 426 U.S. 229 (1976) (applying the *Griggs* standard to a federal civil service law that required tests to be job-related); Albemarle Paper Co. v. Moody, 422 U.S. 405 (1975); Griggs v. Duke Power Co., 401 U.S. 424 (1971).

35. *Compare* Lanning v. Southeastern Pa. Transp. Auth., 181 F.3d 478, 489 (3d Cir. 1999) (adopting a strict test and holding that "a discriminatory cutoff score is impermissible unless shown to measure the minimum qualifications necessary for successful performance of the job in question"), *with* Bryant v. City of Chicago, 200 F.3d 1092, 1098 (7th Cir. 2000) (adopting a more relaxed "reasonable measure of job performance" test).

very end of what could be a long and expensive trial—which imparts a certain *Alice in Wonderland* sense of dis-reality to the whole undertaking.

Because of the complexities and uncertainties involved in bringing a disparate impact action under the 1991 Act, some have suggested that the whole theory is dead letter—especially since most of the practices that do create a disparate impact (however measured) already have been identified and are generally avoided by employers.

§ 7.05 The Section 703(h) Exceptions

Although *Griggs* and *Albemarle* were the progenitors of the disparate impact theory of discrimination that applies to all manner of employment practices and policies, both cases technically involved an interpretation and application of the *professionally developed test* exception contained in Section 703(h), which provides that it is not an unlawful employment practice "for an employer to give and to act upon the results of any professionally developed ability test provided that such test, its administration or action upon the results is not designed, intended or used to discriminate because of race, color, religion, sex or national origin." Section 703(h) contains a similarly worded exception for any "bona fide seniority or merit system, or a system which measures earning by quantity or quality of production."

[A] Professionally Developed Tests

Section 703(h) was not contained in the House version of the Act. It was added by the Senate, to dispel the fear of some that the Act would somehow be construed as prohibiting all testing and force employers to hire persons, qualified or not, simply because they had been the subject of prior discrimination. Senator Tower thus introduced an amendment that would have allowed the use of all "professionally developed ability tests." Opponents contended that this would permit an employer to give any test, "whether it was a good test or not, so long as it was professionally designed. Discrimination could actually exist under the guise of compliance with the statute."[36] Senator Tower then introduced a substitute amendment containing the qualifying language, "not designed, intended or used to discriminate because of race. . . ." Although the literal language may suggest that Congress disallowed only those tests that were intentionally constructed and applied for the purpose of achieving a discriminatory result, in its broader articulation of a disparate impact theory the Supreme Court had already said that it was not necessary to prove intent. The Court in *Griggs* then seemed to focus on the statutory term *used* (perhaps thinking that if a test has a disparate impact then it is necessarily being *used* to discriminate), relied on a memorandum from Senators Clark and Case emphasizing that the allowed tests were only those that actually measure job qualification,[37] and afforded "great deference"

36. 110 Cong. Rec. 13504 (remarks of Sen. Case) (quoted in Griggs, 401 U.S. at 435).
37. Griggs, 401 U.S. at 434.

to the EEOC interpretive guidelines that construed the amendment as applying only to "a test which fairly measures the knowledge or skills required by the particular job or class of jobs which the applicant seeks."[38]

The EEOC's Uniform Guidelines on Employee Selection Procedures, which have been modified over the years, contain detailed and highly technical provisions regarding what constitutes a legally sufficient *validation study*—that is, the demonstration of a correlation between test results and actual job requirements and performance. These include criterion-related validation, content validation, and construct validation.

- *Criterion related validation* focuses on whether a correlation exists between how an applicant or employee did on the test and how he or she actually performs the job.
- *Content validation* focuses on whether a correlation exists between the level of knowledge and skills that are reflected by the test and those that are actually necessary for successful job performance.
- *Construct validation* focuses on whether a correlation exists between what the test reveals with respect to the applicant's behavioral characteristics and those that are actually necessary for successful job performance.

In *Griggs*, the Court said the Guidelines were entitled to "great deference." In *Albemarle*, however, the Court did more than just defer to the general philosophy of the interpretive guidelines. It treated their detailed and highly technical *validation* requirements almost as if they had the positive force of law, which they do not. On the other hand, in *Watson v. Fort Worth Bank & Trust*,[39] Justice O'Connor stated, "Our cases make it clear that employers are not required, even when defending standardized or objective tests, to introduce formal 'validation studies' showing that particular criteria predict actual on-the-job performance."[40] The lower courts are also conflicted over how much deference to pay to these Guidelines.

In any event, the stringency of the requirements and the costs of conducting validation studies led many employers to abandon employment testing altogether for a time. That proved unsatisfactory, and employers and employment agencies then began to look for ways to accommodate both hiring needs and the law. Since the test validation requirement applies only to tests that have a disparate impact, many employers and employment agencies avoided that impact by using different cut-off scores for minorities (even sub-categories of minorities) and non-minorities, and thus also

---

38. Griggs, 401 U.S. at 433 n.9. The irony is that Section 703(h) was intended to limit the scope of Title VII and to assuage the fears of certain senators that the Act would be construed as prohibiting employment tests and other qualification requirements that were not overtly discriminatory or even intended to achieve a discriminatory result. But, as construed, that is precisely what Section 703(h) now prohibits. Indeed, the Court in *Griggs* used the legislative history surrounding the Section 703(h) amendment as the springboard and justification for its broader disparate impact theory of discrimination, and but for that legislative history it is possible that Title VII would have been construed as prohibiting intentional, disparate treatment discrimination only.

39. 487 U.S. 977 (1988).

40. *Id.* at 998 (O'Connor, J., joined by Rehnquist, White, and Scalia, JJ.).

avoided the need to validate. This so-called "race norming" was, however, prohibited by Section 703(l) of the Civil Rights Act of 1991.

Although *Albemarle* was a straightforward Section 703(h) testing case, without any broader disparate impact claims like those in *Griggs* (the high school degree requirement), the Court also used the case to introduce the surrebuttal *pretext* stage of the general disparate analysis—namely, the plaintiff's burden of proving the existence of alternative tests or selection devices that also serve the employer's legitimate needs but without any disparate impact. This third step of disparate impact analysis is now a part of the statutory language added by the Civil Rights Act of 1991 and applies to both tests and other selection devices. The Uniform Guidelines, however, require the employer to show the absence of these alternatives as part of the validation study proof. Although a few courts have endorsed this requirement, most continue to put the burden on the plaintiff.[41]

[B] Seniority Systems

One of the earliest uses of the original *Griggs* disparate impact theory was to challenge seniority systems—although this was also conceptualized in terms of the later-to-be-repudiated theories of *perpetuation* or *present effects of prior discrimination*. The facts of *Teamsters v. United States*[42] are illustrative. There, prior to the effective date of the Civil Rights Act of 1964, the employer had discriminated against blacks and Hispanics by putting them in the lower paying city driver positions, and reserving line driver positions for whites. After the effective date of the Act, the employer allowed city drivers to transfer into available line driver positions. But since the seniority in the two job categories was separate, a city driver who transferred lost his seniority and was thus vulnerable to layoffs. Although neutral on its face, the rule disproportionately affected the black and Hispanic employees. The employer relied on Section 703(h) which essentially allows discrimination if it is pursuant to a "bona fide seniority ... system."

Some of the lower courts had held that a seniority system having that effect or impact on minorities simply could not be considered "bona fide." In *Teamsters*, the Supreme Court disagreed. The Court held that this was an inevitable consequence of the operation of a seniority system that bridged both pre-Act discrimination and post-Act compliance, but that Congress did not intend to "destroy or water down the vested seniority rights of employees."[43]

Subsequently, although the logic of *Teamsters* might have suggested otherwise, the Court held that the Section 703(h) defense applied regardless of whether the seniority system being challenged was created before or after the effective date of the Act.[44] The

---

41. *Compare* Ashton v. City of Memphis, 49 F. Supp. 2d 1051 (W.D. Tenn. 1999), *with* Bullington v. United Air Lines, 186 F.3d 1301 (10th Cir. 1999).

42. 431 U.S. 324 (1977).

43. Teamsters v. United States, 431 U.S. at 353.

44. American Tobacco Co. v. Patterson, 456 U.S. 63 (1982).

Court also had to determine exactly what qualified as being a part of a seniority system. In *California Brewers Ass'n v. Bryant*,[45] the Court held that while seniority itself refers only to the measurement of the length of employment, Section 703(h) encompassed "ancillary rules that accomplish certain necessary functions, but which may not themselves be related directly related to length of employment"[46]—such as rules for determining when seniority begins to be counted and how it may be forfeited.

Although the Supreme Court has never defined what makes a seniority system less than "bona fide," most courts have relied on the somewhat cryptic criteria articulated by the Fifth Circuit in *James v. Stockham Valves & Fittings Co.*,[47] as follows:

> (1) whether the seniority system operates to discourage all employees equally from transferring between seniority units; (2) whether the seniority units are in the same or separate bargaining units (if the latter, whether that structure is rational and in conformance with industry practice); (3) whether the seniority system had its genesis in racial discrimination; and (4) whether the system was negotiated and has been maintained free from any illegal purpose.[48]

The Supreme Court, however, has held that the bona fide issue ultimately boils down to a question of discriminatory intent, which is a fact issue to which the "clearly erroneous" standard of appellate review applies.[49] Although this started out as a significant form of intent-based disparate impact discrimination, with many theoretical and factual complexities, seniority-related discrimination is now relatively rare.

[C] Merit and Piecework

These statutory defenses relating to promotions and payment based on merit and piecework have provoked little litigation. To qualify as a merit system, however, the policy must somehow measure and reward the employee's fitness and performance in the job.[50] The quantity/quality of production defense seems to have produced no significant litigation whatsoever.

§ 7.06 The Emergence of a Potential Conflict between Disparate Treatment and Disparate Impact Forms of Discrimination

Legal scholars have long suspected that deep within the complex theoretical contours of the disparate treatment and disparate impact theories of discrimination there

45. 444 U.S. 598 (1980).
46. California Brewers *Ass'n*, 444 U.S. at 607.
47. 559 F.2d 310 (5th Cir. 1977).
48. James, 559 F.2d at 352.
49. Pullman-Standard v. Swint, 456 U.S. 273 (1982).
50. Guardians Ass'n v. Civil Service Comm'n., 633 F.2d 232 (2d Cir. 1980), aff'd on other grounds, 463 U.S. 582 (1983).

lurked the possibility of a fundamental conflict—a situation in which one theory required an employer to do something that the other prohibited it from doing.

[A] *Ricci v. DeStefano*[51]

Such a situation finally arose in the case of *Ricci v. DeStefano,* with the specific issue being whether avoidance of a disparate impact violation constituted a defense to the disparate treatment violation that was a consequence of the avoidance. The reported opinion is 89 pages long, consisting of the opinion of the Court, written by Justice Kennedy, concurring opinions by Justice Scalia[52] and Justice Alito, and a lengthy dissenting opinion by Justice Ginsburg.

From this boiling cauldron of conflicting opinions emerges a broth that has provoked many disputations, questions, and speculation within the legal community—between scholars and the practicing bar alike. For the purposes of this book, however, it will not be necessary or possible to add to that cacophony of detailed commentary and analysis. What follows is a relatively brief but sufficient-for-our-purposes description of the facts of the case. The essence of the majority opinion will then be developed through quotations from the opinion itself. No attempt will be made to summarize the complex point/counter-point debate between Justices Alito and Ginsburg.

Pursuant to its contract with the firefighters union, the City of New Haven retained an outside consultant to develop and administer a test that would be used when considering otherwise eligible firefighters for promotion to lieutenant and captain. The tests were given, and the results showed that the pass rate for white candidates was substantially higher than the pass rate for blacks and Hispanics. When these results became public, the mayor and other local politicians held a public hearing over the use of the test. A "rancorous" debate ensued, accompanied by threats of a lawsuit if the test results *were* used and threats of a lawsuit if the results *were not* used. Eventually, the City decided not to certify the results of the tests or use the results in making promotion decisions.

Consequently, a lawsuit was brought by a group of white and Hispanic firefighters who passed the examinations but were denied a chance at promotions as a result of the City's decision. They claimed that the decision not to promote them was "based on their race" and that this violated the Equal Protection Clause of the Fourteenth Amendment and Title VII of the Civil Rights Act of 1964. The City defended on the grounds that if they used the test results in making the promotions they feared they would face liability under Title VII "for adopting a practice that had a disparate impact

51. 557 U.S. 557 (2009).

52. Justice Scalia's concurring opinion is significant for the fact that it raises a question that he says the Court will have to confront eventually—namely, "Whether, or to what extent, are the disparate-impact provisions of Title VII ... consistent with the Constitution's guarantee of equal protection?" *Id.* at 594 (Scalia, J., concurring).

on minority firefighters." The conflict between the two theories of discrimination was thus starkly presented. After losing in both the district court and the Second Circuit Court of Appeals, the plaintiff firefighters filed a Petition for Certiorari, which was granted.

The Court noted that, "This action presents two provisions of Title VII to be interpreted and reconciled, with few, if any, precedents in the courts of appeals discussing the issue." More specifically, the Court said the issue was "whether the purpose to avoid disparate-impact liability excuses what otherwise would be prohibited disparate-treatment discrimination." Implicitly recognizing the possibility of such an *excuse*, the Court then proceeded to delineate the circumstances under which such an *excuse* could be recognized as a defense. The test that the Court adopted for resolving this issue was borrowed from the Fourteenth Amendment cases that allow remedial discrimination only where there is a "strong basis in evidence" that the remedial actions are necessary, Applying that test to the summary judgment facts of the case, the Court concluded that the City did not have a "strong basis in evidence" that using the test results in making promotion decisions would have an illegal disparate impact on blacks and Hispanics.

"Our analysis begins," the Court said, "with this premise: The City's actions would violate the disparate-treatment prohibition of Title VII absent some valid defense." According to the Court, the violation in question arose out of the fact that the City "rejected the test results solely because the higher scoring candidates were white." With the first component of the conflict thus established, the Court then turned to the second putative component, the existence of sufficient evidence of a disparate impact violation.

Using the usual three-step mode of analysis for disparate impact cases, the Court first concluded that the "racial adverse impact here was significant, and Petitioners [the plaintiff firefighters] do not dispute that the City was faced with a prima facie case of disparate-impact liability." This conclusion was based on the pass-fail statistics and the application of the EEOC's 80% rule.[53] The Court, however, said that these statistics alone did not provide "a strong basis in evidence" that the City would commit a disparate impact violation if it applied the test results. It said: "That is because the City could be liable for disparate-impact discrimination only if the examinations were not job-related and consistent with business necessity, or if there existed an equally valid, less-discriminatory alternative that served the City's needs but that the City refused to adopt."

Turning to the application of this test, the Court said: "There is no genuine dispute that the examinations were job-related and consistent with business necessity. The City's assertions to the contrary are 'blatantly contradicted by the record.'" The City thus failed to establish one of the critical elements of its defense, although it could still prevail if it were successful on the third one.

---

53. *See* § 7.02[A].

With respect to this final step in the analysis—the availability of non-discriminatory alternatives—the Court again concluded that the City "lacked a strong basis in evidence of an equally valid, less-discriminatory testing alternative that the City, by certifying the examination results, would necessarily have refused to adopt." The City had advanced three alternatives.

First, the City contended that using a different composite-score calculation—that is, weighting the written and oral examination scores 30/70 instead of 60/40—would have allowed the City to consider three black candidates for promotion. The Court, however, noted that because the 60/40 weighting "was the result of a union-negotiated collective-bargaining agreement, we presume the parties negotiated that weighting for a rational reason." In addition, the Court noted that changing the weighting formula after the test was given "could well have violated Title VII's prohibition of altering test scores on the basis of race." Thus, the Court rejected this as a legitimate alternative.

Second, the City argued that it could have adopted a different interpretation of the "rule of three" that would have produced less discriminatory results. The rule referred to was one in the City charter that requires the City to promote only from the applicants with the three highest scores on a promotional exam. The Court concluded, again, that altering the results of a test on the basis of race would have violated Title VII. The Court also rejected this alternative.

Third, the City relied on the statements of one witness regarding an alternative to written examinations that would have demonstrated less adverse impact. Later, in addition to matters not directly germane to the issue, he testified that the City should "certify the list as it exists." The Court concluded as follows: "Especially when ... the strong-basis-in-evidence standard applies, respondents cannot create a genuine issue of fact based on a few stray (and contradictory) statements in the record." The City's third proffered alternative was thus rejected. And that sealed the fate of the City's defense.

Thus, because the City lacked sufficient evidence that a disparate impact violation would occur if the test results were used, the potential conflict between that theory of discrimination and the disparate treatment discrimination against the Plaintiff firefighters never materialized. Finally, near the end of the majority opinion, the Court offered this intriguing bit of dicta: "If, after it certifies the test results, the City faces a disparate-impact suit, then in light of our holding today it should be clear that the City would avoid disparate-impact liability based on the strong basis in evidence that, had it not certified the results, it would have been subject to disparate-treatment liability."

[B] Post-*Ricci* Developments

It was not long before the City did indeed face such a lawsuit. In *Briscoe v. City of New Haven*,[54] Michael Briscoe, an African American firefighter in New Haven, filed suit alleging that the City's use of the 60/40 (60 for the written exam and 40 for the oral exam) weighting numbers instead of 30/70 violated Title VII because of the disparate impact it had on minorities, specifically himself. The district court had dismissed, holding that the case was foreclosed by *Ricci*.[55] On Briscoe's appeal to the Second Circuit, the City continued to argue that "an employer may defeat a disparate-impact claim if it had a strong basis in evidence that it would have been subject to disparate-treatment liability [relying on the Court's statement to that effect] ... and that the Court's *Ricci* mandate itself supplied the strong basis in evidence of disparate treatment liability (for not certifying the results)."

The Second Circuit rejected the City's arguments. According to the court, the language in *Ricci* that the City relied on was not only dicta that it was not bound to follow, it was dicta that was contrary to reason, prior precedent, the words of the statute, and even the Equal Protection cases from which *Ricci* borrowed the test. In short, contrary to the express statement in the *Ricci* dicta, the Second Circuit disallowed a defendant from ever claiming "a strong basis in evidence" that a disparate treatment violation would occur as a defense to a claim that doing or failing to do a certain thing would constitute a disparate impact violation.

On remand from the Second Circuit, however, the district court dismissed Briscoe's case on different grounds: "I conclude that the Plaintiff in this case has not pleaded a prima facie Title VII claim. Stripped of conclusory rhetoric and distilled to reveal its essence, Briscoe's complaint is really about the 60/40 weighting's adverse impact upon him personally, not a disparate impact upon African American firefighters."[56]

The Third Circuit addressed another factual variation of disparate treatment/impact conflict in *NAACP v. North Hudson Regional Fire & Rescue*.[57] The plaintiffs (the NAACP and several African American firefighter candidates) brought suit against defendant North Hudson Regional, claiming that the defendant's residency requirement had a disparate impact on African Americans and was illegal under Title VII. Several Hispanic firefighter candidates who were on the existing hiring list intervened, claiming that elimination of the residency requirement and the resulting adverse

---

54. 654 F.3d 200 (2d Cir. 2011), *cert. denied*, 567 U.S. 913 (2012).

55. 2010 U.S. Dist. LEXIS 69018 (D.D.C. 2010).

56. *See also* Maraschiello v. City of Buffalo Police Dep't, 709 F.3d 87, 95–96 (2d Cir. 2013) ("Even if it were determined that the City's choice to adopt a new test was motivated in part by its desire to achieve more racially balanced results ... Maraschiello cannot demonstrate that the generalized overhaul of departmental promotion requirements amounted to the sort of race-based adverse action discussed in *Ricci*.")

57. 665 F.3d 464 (3d Cir. 2011).

effect it would have on them would constitute illegal disparate treatment discrimination. All three parties filed motions for summary judgment. The district court granted the plaintiffs' motion and denied the other two. The Third Circuit affirmed.

The court held that the plaintiffs had established a prima facie statistical case of disparate impact discrimination but rejected the employer-defendant's purported business necessity claims. The court rejected the intervenor-defendant's disparate treatment claim on three grounds. First, since the defendant's elimination of the residency requirement would be a result of the court's mandate, it could not be an intentional or deliberate act of discrimination, which is what Title VII prohibits. Second, the court identified a "legitimate nondiscriminatory reason" for eliminating the requirement. And third, the defendant's reliance on the possibility that it would face a lawsuit by Hispanic residence did not rise to the level required by *Ricci*: "'Fear of litigation alone' does not suffice; a demonstrated potential for liability is required."

Finally, in *United States v. Brennan*,[58] the Second Circuit Court of Appeals laid down some guidelines for the district court in that case to use in applying the "strong basis in evidence" test. After a full and extremely useful discussion of each of these points, the court summarized as follows: "[A] strong basis in evidence of disparate-impact liability is an objectively reasonable basis to fear such liability. It is evaluated at the time an employer takes a race-conscious action. It relies on real evidence, not just subjective fear or speculation. Because it focuses on liability rather than mere litigation it requires both objectively strong evidence of a *prima facie case* (or perhaps actual proof of a *prima facie* case) of disparate impact, and objectively strong evidence of non-job-relatedness or a less discriminatory alternative."

[C] Conclusion

Although the inherent but heretofore theoretical conflict between disparate treatment and disparate impact has finally surfaced, the current but limited caselaw on the subject has not yet produced a coherent and comprehensive resolution. Thus, it is impossible at this point to make generalized assertions of broad legal principles dealing with this subject. Much disagreement exists among scholars as to the meaning, correctness, and future of *Ricci* and its prodigy. Thus, it remains to be seen whether *Ricci* and the caselaw growing out of it will become part of the "misadventure" referred to in the first sentence of this chapter. One can only hope that the law will at least become sufficiently clear and settled so that employers, unions, and employment agencies can make their decisions in a way that does not precipitate the lengthy, costly, and divisive results of the caselaw thus far.

---

58. 650 F.3d 65, 113 (2d Cir. 2011).

§ 7.07 Chapter Highlights

1. Although intentional disparate treatment discrimination seemed to have been the primary evil at which Title VII was directed, in *Griggs* the Supreme Court held that Congress also intended to focus on the consequences of employment practices, not merely the motivation. Since the practices in question operated "to 'freeze' the status quo of prior [openly discriminatory] employment practices," the Court found that the employer had violated the Act. In subsequent cases, however, the nexus between the neutral practices and the employer's prior discrimination was implicitly held not to be an integral element of the disparate impact form of discrimination. (§ 7.01)

2. The original *Griggs/Albemarle* disparate impact formula had three components:

- The plaintiff was required to prove that an employment practice or policy disqualified a higher percentage of minority applicants or employees than non-minority applicants or employees. These are the so-called "gateway" or pass/fail comparative statistics.
- The defendant was then required to prove that the policy or practice was supported by *business necessity*, although the scope and meaning of the defense was subject to enormous disagreement among the courts.
- The plaintiff could then come back in and prevail by showing that this business necessity was a *pretext*, apparently meaning that the employer's asserted business justification could be equally served by another policy or practice that did not have discriminatory effects.

(§ 7.02)

3. In *Wards Cove*, the Supreme Court said that it was merely clarifying its prior decisions, but most people read the case as a significant reformulation of the original test, in several particulars:

- The Court indicated that the relevant statistics for proving disparate impact discrimination were the systemic disparate treatment statistics used in *Teamsters* (involving a comparison of the percentage of minorities in the workforce with the percentage of minorities in the relevant labor market). These, at least, were the statistics the Court said were relevant when evaluating a multi-component, partially subjective "black box" hiring procedure.
- The Court adopted a very relaxed business necessity defense, essentially reducing it to showing a rational relationship to a legitimate business interest, with considerable deference being given to the employer's judgment in this regard.
- Moreover, the Court said that the employer did not have the burden of actually proving business necessity and that a mere articulation was sufficient.
- The Court held that the plaintiff must establish a causal relationship between the disparate statistics and a particular employment policy or practice.

- And the Court adopted a rigorous pretext requirement—namely, proof that the alternative practice be "equally effective" and that the "cost and other burdens" of the alternative could be taken into account.

(§7.03)

4. Congress was not happy over the *Wards Cove* decision and attempted to codify the disparate impact theory in the Civil Rights Act of 1991.

- The Act, however, did not address the question of the kind of statistics that must be used to establish a disparate impact.
- Congress agreed that the plaintiff must identify the practice that causes this disparity but allowed an employer's multi-component hiring procedure to be treated as a single employment practice if the components are not capable of separation.
- The Act puts the true burden of proof and persuasion on the defendant to establish the existence of business necessity.
- Congress, however, could not agree on what the test was, with the legislative history reflecting both a strict and relaxed view. In the words of one judge, "unable to muster a veto-proof majority for either view, Congress 'punted.'"[59] It worded the test in terms of the challenged requirement being "job related for the position in question and consistent with business necessity" and said this means what it meant prior to *Wards Cove.*
- Although the logical structure of the Act is confusing with respect to how the pretext component fits in, Congress nevertheless codified it and said the component means what it meant prior to *Wards Cove*—which is not very enlightening, since it had been scarcely litigated before.
- Whether or not an instance of disparate impact discrimination against one employee or group of employees can be justified by the possibility of otherwise creating an instance of disparate impact discrimination against another group of employees depends on whether the defendant-employer has a "strong basis in evidence" for the existence of disparate impact liability. On the other hand, it is unclear whether the possibility of disparate treatment liability can ever be a defense in a disparate impact lawsuit. Supreme Court dicta suggests that it can, but one court of appeals decision has emphatically held that it cannot. This is as yet an unsettled and still developing area of the law.
- To date, there has been only a limited amount of litigation under the 1991 Act's codified version of disparate impact.

---

59. Lanning, 181 F.3d at 497 (Weis, J., dissenting).

(§ 7.04)

5. Section 703(h) of the original Act contains three defenses that would seem to apply only with respect to practices that have a disparate impact. The professionally developed test defense applies to tests, like those used in *Griggs* and several other Supreme Court cases, that have a disparate impact. Indeed, this defense was the progenitor of the broader business necessity defense. The bona fide seniority system defense was heavily litigated in the early days of the Act, but rarely so today. Unless a seniority system is facially discriminatory, was adopted for a discriminatory reason, or is applied in a discriminatory fashion, it will be considered bona fide even if it does have a disparate impact. The merit and piecework defenses are rarely invoked. (§ 7.05)

6. The conflict between disparate treatment and disparate impact has not yet produced a coherent and comprehensive resolution. Much disagreement exists among scholars as to the meaning, correctness, and future of *Ricci* and its progeny. Thus, it remains to be seen whether *Ricci* and the caselaw growing out of it will become part of the "misadventure" referred to in the first sentence of this chapter. (§ 7.06)

Chapter 8

Special Problems Relating to Race Discrimination

Synopsis

§ 8.01 The Meaning of "Race"

Because Title VII also covers national origin, the courts have not found it necessary to carefully delineate where that category ends and *race* begins—a problem, however, that has confronted the courts in Section 1981 suits.[1] Often, a plaintiff may allege either race or national origin discrimination, or both. It makes a difference, however, with respect to the BFOQ defense, which is available for national origin but not race discrimination. Although the purpose of Title VII was to protect members of historically disadvantaged races, in *McDonald v. Santa Fe Trail Transp. Co.*[2] the Court held that the Act protects Caucasians on the same basis as it does minorities. The inclusion of *color* as a protected characteristic prevents intraracial discrimination, such as a preference for a light-skinned African American over one with darker skin or vice versa.[3]

1. *See* Chapter 22, § 22.03.
2. 427 U.S. 273 (1976).
3. Walker v. Secretary of the Treasury, 713 F. Supp. 403 (N.D. Ga. 1989).

§ 8.02 Forms of Discrimination

Individual disparate treatment claims continue to predominate. Although almost all of the early cases that established the controlling law with respect to systemic disparate treatment claims involved race, claims of this nature are less prevalent today. Similarly, although the original disparate impact case, and most of those that followed, involved facially neutral criteria that disadvantaged blacks at a higher rate than others, this type of litigation has been on the wane for years. In part, this may be due to the fact that the most frequently used criteria having this effect have already been identified and either found to be illegal or justified on terms of business necessity. The litigated criteria include: standardized tests,[4] educational requirements,[5] job experience,[6] arrest records,[7] conviction records,[8] repeated garnishments,[9] less than honorable discharge from the military,[10] drug use,[11] residency requirements,[12] nepotism,[13] and clean shavenness.[14] The confusing dimensions of current disparate impact law may have also deterred plaintiffs from pursuing this cause of action.

§ 8.03 Miscellaneous Race Discrimination Issues

[A] Proxy Analysis

Plaintiffs have not had much success with the proxy analysis in race discrimination cases.[15] For example, in *Rogers v. American Airlines, Inc.*,[16] the plaintiff was prohibited from wearing a *corn row* hairstyle. She alleged that this hairstyle "has been, historically, a fashion and style adopted by Black American women, reflective of cultural, historical essence of the black women in American society." The court, however, held that the Act prohibited discrimination on the basis of immutable characteristics like *race*, not easily changed characteristics, like hairstyle, even if they were associated socioculturally with a particular race.

---

4. Griggs v. Duke Power Co., 401 U.S. 424 (1971).

5. Griggs, 401 U.S. 424.

6. Spurlock v. United Airlines, Inc., 475 F.2d 216 (10th Cir. 1972).

7. Reynolds v. Sheet Metal Workers, Local 102, 498 F. Supp. 952 (D.D.C. 1980), aff'd, 702 F.2d 221 (D.C. Cir. 1981).

8. Green v. Missouri Pacific R.R. Co., 523 F.2d 1290 (8th Cir. 1975).

9. Johnson v. Pike Corp. of America, 332 F. Supp. 490 (C.D. Cal. 1971).

10. Dozier v. Chupka, 395 F. Supp. 836 (S.D. Ohio 1975).

11. Davis v. City of Dallas, 777 F.2d 205 (5th Cir. 1985). The Civil Rights Act of 1991 now makes drug use an impermissible criterion only if the employer uses it with an actual intent to discriminate. 42 U.S.C. § 2000e-2(k)(3).

12. United States v. City of Warren, 759 F. Supp. 355 (E.D. Mich. 1991).

13. Thomas v. Washington County Sch. Bd., 915 F.2d 922 (4th Cir. 1990).

14. Bradley v. Pizzaco, 7 F.3d 795 (8th Cir. 1993).

15. *See* Chapter 4, § 4.02[B].

16. 527 F. Supp. 229 (S.D.N.Y. 1981).

[B] Association

Although there are a few early cases to the contrary, the prevailing view is that "[w]here a plaintiff claims discrimination based upon an interracial marriage or association, he alleges, by definition, that he has been discriminated against because of *his* race."[17] Certainly, *but for* the plaintiff's race, he or she would not have been penalized for associating with a person of a different race.

[C] Race-Plus Discrimination

Race-plus discrimination has occurred in a number of contexts.[18] Perhaps the most common involves the employer who does not discriminate against women or blacks as a class but does discriminate against black women on the supposition that they possess characteristics the employer deems unfavorable. This can be litigated as either sex- or race-plus discrimination.[19] The situation is complicated even further if age is also alleged to be a factor.

[D] Dress and Grooming Codes

As indicated above, plaintiffs have not had much success in challenging facially neutral grooming and dress codes, however ethnically and culturally related they might be to race. Yet, at some point the claim may go beyond mere proxy analysis and rise to the level of direct racial discrimination. For example, an employer's policy prohibiting the "Afro/bush" hairstyle might well violate Title VII.[20]

The greatest amount of litigation, however, has involved no-beard policies. Because of the predisposition of black men to develop pseudofolliculitis barbae (PFB), a condition that is exacerbated by shaving, an employer's no-beard policy may have a disparate impact on the basis of race.[21] The issue then becomes whether the rule can be justified by business necessity. In *Bradley v. Pizzaco of Nebraska, Inc.*,[22] the employers believed that customers preferred clean shaven delivery persons and contended that "the better our people look, the better our sales will be." The court held that this was largely speculative and that the presence or absence of a beard was not job-related.[23] On the other hand, in *Fitzpatrick v. City of Atlanta*,[24] the court held that a fire department's clean shaven rule was justified on the grounds that a beard interfered with a firefighter's ability to wear a respirator.

---

17. Parr v. Woodmen of the World Life Ins. Co., 791 F.2d 888, 892 (11th Cir. 1986) (emphasis added).

18. *See* Chapter 5, §5.03[B].

19. Jefferies v. Harris County Community Action Ass'n, 615 F.2d 1025 (5th Cir. 1980).

20. Rogers, 527 F. Supp. at 232.

21. EEOC v. Greyhound Lines, Inc., 635 F.2d 188 (3d Cir. 1980).

22. 7 F.3d 795 (8th Cir. 1993).

23. Customer preferences are not a defense to race discrimination claims. Chaney v. Plainfield Healthcare Ctr., 612 F.3d 908, 913 (7th Cir. 2010).

24. 2 F.3d 1112 (11th Cir. 1993).

§ 8.04 Justifications and Defenses

Proven intentional racial discrimination is still subject to the mixed-motive[25] and after-acquired-evidence[26] defenses. A valid affirmative action plan is also a defense to intentional reverse racial discrimination,[27] and business necessity is available for disparate impact discrimination. Although some courts once suggested that intentional racial discrimination might be subject to the "business necessity" defense,[28] the Civil Rights Act of 1991 foreclosed that possibility.[29] The statute also does not include *race* or *color* within the BFOQ defense.[30]

§ 8.05 Racial Harassment

Although sexual harassment has received the greatest amount of attention by the courts and commentators, the Supreme Court's original recognition of this as a form of proscribed sex discrimination was based on earlier, lower court racial harassment cases.[31] However, unlike the sexual harassment cases, which recognize both quid pro quo and hostile environment variants, racial harassment is by its very nature limited to hostile environment, and is subject to the same standards of proof as prevail in cases of sexual harassment.[32] The typical racial harassment case involves the use by co-workers and, sometimes, by supervisors of racial epithets, racially offensive jokes and cartoons, sexual innuendoes, nooses and dummies hung over the employee's workstation, graffiti, references to the KKK, and threats of violence.[33] Corporate employer liability is also subject to the same tests as in sexual harassment cases.

§ 8.06 Chapter Highlights

1. For Title VII purposes, *race* seems to be construed in its conventional, contemporary sense—in contrast to the somewhat arcane Section 1981 interpretation. In any event, it covers discrimination against both racial minorities and non-minorities. (§ 8.01)

2. Race discrimination may be of the disparate treatment or disparate impact variety and thus subject to all the complexities of those two forms of discrimination. (§ 8.02)

---

25. *See* Chapter 5, § 5.09.
26. *See* Chapter 5, § 5.10.
27. *See* Chapter 5, § 5.11.
28. Miller v. Texas State Bd. of Barber Exam'rs, 615 F.2d 650 (5th Cir. 1980).
29. 42 U.S.C. § 2000e-2(k)(2).
30. *See* Chapter 5, § 5.08.
31. Meritor Savings Bank v. Vinson, 477 U.S. 57 (1986).
32. Hernandez v. Valley View Hosp. Ass'n, 684 F.3d 950 (2012).
33. Daniels v. Essex Group, Inc., 937 F.2d 1264 (7th Cir. 1991).

3. In rare cases, the nebulous proxy analysis may apply. Discrimination on the basis of interracial associations, race-plus, and grooming code violations frequently arise. (§ 8.03)

4. Once intentional racial discrimination is proved, only the mixed-motive and after-acquired evidence limited defenses are available. Racial discrimination cannot be justified as a *business necessity* or BFOQ. (§ 8.04)

5. Hostile environment harassment against racial minorities is subject to the same elements of proof and establishment of corporate employer liability as in a sexual harassment situation. (§ 8.05)

Chapter 9

Special Problems Relating to Sex Discrimination

Synopsis

§9.01 History

As originally drafted and reported out of Committee, Title VII of the Civil Rights Act of 1964 did not contain a prohibition against discrimination on the basis of sex. Although wage discrimination on the basis of sex had been curtailed to some extent by the earlier Equal Pay Act,[1] a blanket prohibition on sex discrimination in employment was not thought to be a political reality in 1964. An amendment including it was defeated in the Judiciary Committee, but on the last day of the Title VII debate in the House, Representative Howard Smith of Virginia, who was generally opposed to Title VII, offered a floor amendment to include sex. Some have suggested that this was intended as a *poison pill* that, if *swallowed*, would eventually defeat the entire bill. Whether this was the motivation or not, the amendment passed—as did then the entire bill. The significance of this ironic scenario, however, is that unlike other provisions of Title VII, the sex-discrimination provision has no legislative history in the form of Committee findings and reports. Only the floor debates are available as evidence of Congress' original intent, and they are scant.

Straightforward disparate treatment (individual and systemic)[2] and disparate impact[3] discrimination are discussed elsewhere. This chapter will thus only discuss several unique aspects of sex discrimination.

§9.02 Pregnancy Discrimination

[A] Introduction

Although being pregnant could easily be regarded as a proxy for being female and discrimination on the basis of pregnancy obviously has a disparate impact on females, the Supreme Court originally refused to apply either theory of discrimination and thus held that pregnancy was not a protected characteristic under Title VII.[4] Congress responded with the Pregnancy Discrimination Act (PDA), which provides that

> The terms "because of sex" or "on the basis of sex" include, but are not limited to, [1] because of or on the basis of pregnancy, childbirth, or related medical conditions; and [2] women affected by pregnancy, childbirth, or related medical conditions shall be treated the same for all employment-related pur-

1. *See* Part VI, Chapters 25–28.
2. *See* Chapters 5 and 6.
3. *See* Chapter 7. Criteria that have been found to have a disparate impact on the basis of sex include height and weight requirements, *Dothard v. Rawlinson*, 433 U.S. 321 (1977); agility and physical ability tests, *Legault v. Arusso*, 842 F. Supp. 1479 (D.N.H. 1994); a no-spouse hiring rule, *Yuhas v. Libbey-Owens-Ford Co.*, 562 F.2d 496 (7th Cir. 1977); prior experience, *Kilgo v. Bowman Transp., Inc.*, 789 F.2d 859 (11th Cir. 1986); and others.
4. General Electric Co. v. Gilbert, 429 U.S. 125 (1976).

poses, including receipt of benefits under fringe benefit programs, as other persons not so affected but similar in their ability or inability to work....[5]

The Act's [1] *because of* clause and its [2] *equal treatment* clause are not necessarily consistent. For example, an employer who knows that an applicant will need to take a pregnancy leave shortly after being hired and who thus refuses to hire that applicant is guilty of discrimination *because of* pregnancy. But what if the employer also refused to hire a male applicant who indicated that he would need to go on medical leave shortly after being hired? Does this *equal treatment* trump the *because of*?[6]

The Supreme Court has sent mixed signals about the proper resolution of the question. In *Newport News Shipbuilding & Dry Dock Co. v. EEOC*,[7] the Court stated that "[t]he meaning of the first clause is not limited by the specific language in the second clause, which [merely] explains the application of the general principle to women employees."[8] On the other hand, in *International Union, UAW v. Johnson Controls, Inc.*,[9] the Court viewed the second clause as containing its own "BFOQ standard."[10] The Court's reference to a BFOQ is both unfortunate and misleading. What the Court is talking about is not some essential qualification for the job that only non-pregnant individuals possess—which is the focus of a true BFOQ analysis. The Court, rather, is apparently using the term loosely to suggest that *equal treatment* trumps any first clause *because of* discrimination. This is how most of the lower courts have applied the statute,[11] although the courts are divided over who has the burden of proving or disproving the equal treatment.[12] Moreover, unlike the comparator in a normal Title VII case, who some courts have held must be similarly situated "in all respects,"[13] the PDA specifically focuses on the putative comparator's similarity only with respect to the "ability or inability to work." The equal treatment interpretation of the PDA is, however, subject to the following exception.

[B] More Favorable Treatment

Although preferential treatment is not required, it is not illegal for an employer to treat pregnant women more favorably than similarly situated men. In *California*

5. 42 U.S.C. § 2000e(k) (bracketed numbers added).

6. Marafino v. St. Louis Cty. Circuit Court, 707 F.2d 1005 (8th Cir. 1983) (no violation for refusing to hire a pregnant woman under those circumstances).

7. 462 U.S. 669 (1983).

8. Newport News Shipbuilding, 462 U.S. at 678 n.14.

9. 499 U.S. 187 (1991).

10. Johnson Controls, 499 U.S. at 204.

11. Stout v. Baxter Healthcare Corp., 282 F.3d 856 (5th Cir. 2002); EEOC v. Elgin Teachers Assn., 27 F.3d 292 (7th Cir. 1994).

12. *Compare* White v. Frank, 8 F.3d 823 (4th Cir. 1993) (plaintiff must prove that a similarly situated non-pregnant employees were treated differently), *with* Byrd v. Lakeshore Hosp., 30 F.3d 1380 (11th Cir. 1994) (burden on employer to prove someone else was treated the same way).

13. Mitchell v. Toledo Hosp., 964 F.2d 577, 583 (6th Cir. 1992).

Federal Savings & Loan Ass'n v. Guerra,[14] the Court was confronted with a California law that required employers to provide female employees with unpaid pregnancy leave and reinstatement rights. Men were entitled to no equivalent benefits. Although the technical issue was whether the state statute was preempted by the sex-discrimination prohibitions of Title VII, in resolving that issue the Court addressed the broader meaning of pregnancy-related discrimination itself. Using reasoning that is reminiscent of that used in *Weber* to sustain voluntary affirmative action, the Court held that despite the literal *because of* language, Congress intended the Pregnancy Discrimination Act to be "a floor beneath which pregnancy disability benefits may not drop—not a ceiling above which they may not rise."[15] In other words, it is illegal to discriminate *against* pregnant women, but not *in favor* of them. This preferential treatment allowance, however, applies only to benefits granted during the actual pregnancy period, not to post-pregnancy or special child-raising benefits.[16]

[C] Pregnancy Benefits for Spouses

In a decision that essentially declared the Pregnancy Discrimination Act to be redundant of how the basic prohibition against sex discrimination could have been construed in the first place, the Court in *Newport News Shipbuilding & Dry Dock Co. v. EEOC*[17] held that a medical plan that provided greater pregnancy benefits to female employees than to the spouses of male employees was illegal. The illegality, however, was found in the differential treatment the plan made between the spouses of male and female employees. It noted that while "the husbands of female employees receive a specified level of hospitalization coverage for all conditions; the wives of male employees receive such coverage except for pregnancy-related conditions"[18]—thus disadvantaging male employees. This established facial discrimination *because of sex* in the literal sense, and the fact that the benefit related to pregnancy was essentially irrelevant.

[D] The Absence of Any Medical or Leave Benefits

Although an employer who provides medical benefits and leaves cannot discriminate against women because of pregnancy or disabling conditions relating to pregnancy, Title VII does not require an employer to provide any medical or leave benefits in the first place. In spite of that, the claim that the absence of any medical leave policy has a disparate impact on women, whose capacity for becoming pregnant

14. 479 U.S. 272 (1987).

15. Guerra, 479 U.S. at 285 (quoting from the decision below, 758 F.2d at 396).

16. Schafer v. Board of Public Educ. of School Dist. of Pittsburgh, 903 F.2d 243 (3d Cir. 1990). And the requirements of the Family and Medical Leave Act of 1993, 28 U.S.C. §§ 2601 et seq. must also be taken into account.

17. 462 U.S. 669 (1983).

18. Newport News Shipbuilding, 462 U.S. at 684.

makes the availability of leave time a critical job benefit, has received a mixed response from the courts.[19] That particular issue, of course, has been rendered moot by the Family and Medical Leave Act of 1993, which requires employers to grant unpaid leave for the birth of a child.[20]

[E] Fetal Vulnerability

Motivated both by humanitarian and legal liability concerns, many employers in the past refused to allow pregnant or even fertile women to work in certain jobs, usually involving exposure to toxic chemicals. The issue finally came before the Supreme Court in *Automobile Workers, UAW v. Johnson Controls, Inc.*[21] Obviously more concerned with achieving what it regarded as a fair and sensible result than with the niceties of rigorous legal analysis, the Court of Appeals in that case had treated such a policy as only having a disparate impact and then applied a liberal *business necessity* test to exonerate the employer.

The Supreme Court, however, said the policy involved facial discrimination on the basis of sex and that it could be justified, if at all, only under the more rigorous BFOQ analysis. The Court, however, rejected both the safety of the woman and that of the fetus as a basis for the BFOQ defense, noting that safety was a relevant concern only when it was somehow related to the job or business of the employer—as where sex or pregnancy jeopardized the safety of coworkers or customers.[22] With respect to the employer's possible state-law tort liability for injury to the fetus, the Court said that informing the woman of the risks involved would probably absolve an employer from such liability. And even if the employer did incur costs (workers compensation liability, for example), the Court noted that Congress assumed that the practice of nondiscrimination would involve some employer costs and that it was not presented here with "a case in which costs [of compliance] would be so prohibitive as to threaten the survival of the employer's business"—thus leaving that open as a possible basis for the BFOQ defense.

[F] Non-Pregnancy as a BFOQ

As is true of the BFOQ defense in other situations, the non-pregnancy BFOQ has been narrowly construed and has been recognized primarily in situations where a

19. *Compare* Maganuco v. Leyden Cmy. High Sch. Dist. 212, 939 F.2d 440 (7th Cir. 1991) (school district's policy restricting sick leave did not have a disparate impact on pregnant women), *with* EEOC v. Warshawsky & Co., 768 F. Supp. 647 (N.D. Ill. 1991) (no leave during the first year found to have disadvantaged more pregnant than non-pregnant employees).

20. 29 U.S.C. § 2611.

21. 499 U.S. 187 (1991).

22. Just as potential danger to the fetus cannot justify discrimination against pregnant women, a pregnant woman's own fear of causing harm to her fetus does not constitute a Title VII justification for refusing to follow work directives. Armstrong v. Flowers Hosp., Inc., 33 F.3d 1308 (11th Cir. 1994) (pregnant nurse who refused to treat an HIV-positive patient is not protected by Title VII).

pregnant employee would pose a safety risk to third parties. For example, not being pregnant has been found to be a BFOQ for airline cabin attendants, at least at the stage when pregnancy could interfere with the attendant's ability to provide for the safety of passengers—although the courts do not agree on when that is.[23]

A decision that construes the pregnancy BFOQ as encompassing more than mere safety-related concerns is *Chambers v. Omaha Girls* Club,[24] which held that for an unmarried woman, not being pregnant was a role-model based BFOQ for a job in a club whose major constituency was teenage girls and when one of the club's major concerns was unwed pregnancies.[25]

[G] Questions about Marital Status and Child-Bearing Plans

An employer who asks female applicants questions about their marital status and child-bearing plans and does not ask similar questions of male applicants is obviously discriminating on the basis of sex. Some courts treat this as illegal per se,[26] while others require proof that the employer relied on the answers to these questions when making an adverse hiring decision.[27]

§ 9.03 Sexual Harassment

Sexual harassment has been a major topic of employment discrimination law for several years and has received a significant amount of the Supreme Court's attention. It involves some unusual concepts of discrimination and some difficult evidentiary problems.

[A] Quid Pro Quo Harassment

The earliest and still most blatant form of sexual harassment occurs when a supervisor (or someone with power to make employment decisions) demands sexual favors from an employee and, when they are not provided, terminates or otherwise disadvantages that employee. After some initial hesitancy due to doubts that Congress really intended to make this kind of employment misconduct illegal, most courts

---

23. *Compare* Harriss v. Pan Am. World Airways, Inc., 649 F.2d 670 (9th Cir. 1980) (upholding mandatory leave beginning when attendant learns that she is pregnant), *with* In re Pan Am. World Airways, Inc., 905 F.2d 1457 (11th Cir. 1990) (holding that this policy could not be justified under the BFOQ defense).

24. 834 F.2d 697 (8th Cir. 1987).

25. *But see* Cline v. Catholic Diocese of Toledo, 206 F.3d 651 (6th Cir. 1999) (Catholic school cannot discriminate against an unwed pregnant teacher as a means of enforcing its moral code). When dealing with a religious employer, the ministerial exception should be considered post-*Hosanna-Tabor Lutheran Church & Sch. v. EEOC*, 565 U.S. 171 (2012).

26. King v. TWA, 738 F.2d 255 (8th Cir. 1984).

27. Bruno v. Crown Point, Indiana, 950 F.2d 355 (7th Cir. 1991).

quickly recognized that the conduct satisfied the *because of sex* requirement of Title VII. Since, *but for* the employee-victim's sex (status), she would not have been asked to *have sex* or punished when she refused to do so, the necessary causal relationship was said to exist.[28]

[1] Proof

As in other areas of Title VII law, sexual harassment law has recently been complicated by the now fuzzy distinction between the prima facie case form of proof and proof by what was previously called *direct* evidence. Nevertheless, proof of quid pro quo sexual harassment, in its simplest form, usually consists of the following:

- Requests for sexual favors by a heterosexual member of the opposite sex or a homosexual member of the same sex.[29] Whether such a request was made or not often devolves into a *he-said/no-I-didn't* dispute of fact.
- The employee's refusal to honor that request.
- An adverse employment decision or loss of a tangible job benefit.
- Evidence of a causal relation between the refusal and the adverse decision.

This last element is, of course, the critical one. And the strength of that evidence determines whether and what kind of burden shifts to the defendant. If the evidence is *direct* in the most literal and correct evidentiary sense,[30] then this establishes liability—although the employer may still be able to establish a mixed motive or after-acquired evidence partial defense. Circumstantial evidence, on the other hand, may consist of the temporal proximity of the refusal and the adverse employment action,[31] the presence of a comparator,[32] relative power of the alleged harasser to cause or influence the decision,[33] or anything else that would support the inference. Such circumstantial evidence will *at least* establish a prima facie case and shift the burden onto the employer to articulate a legitimate, nondiscriminatory reason for the adverse employment action—with the ultimate burden still residing on the plaintiff to prove that this is pretext. And if the circumstantial or inferential evidence is regarded as being strong enough, this may establish liability, shifting the burden of establishing the limited mixed-motive defense.

If the supervisor's threat is never acted upon, this could constitute part of the proof for a hostile environment claim. If the employee unwillingly acquiesces in the demand for unwelcome sexual favors, this is still an illegal form of quid pro quo sexual harassment.

---

28. Barnes v. Costle, 561 F.2d 983, 990 (D.C. Cir. 1977).

29. Wright v. Methodist Youth Servs., Inc., 511 F. Supp. 307 (N.D. Ill. 1981).

30. Gallagher v. Wilton Enters., 962 F.2d 120 (1st Cir. 1992) (employer demanded that "our [sexual] relationship" improve and, when it apparently did not, later terminated the employee explicitly because of "our relationship").

31. Nichols v. Frank, 42 F.3d 503 (9th Cir. 1994).

32. Heyne v. Caruso, 69 F.3d 1475 (9th Cir. 1995); Henson v. City of Dundee, 682 F.2d 897 (11th Cir. 1982).

33. Sparks v. Pilot Freight Carriers, 830 F.2d 1554 (11th Cir. 1987).

[2] The Quid Pro Quo Implication of Consensual Office Affairs

If a supervisor and an employee have a romantic or sexual relationship that is initially consensual on both sides, quid pro quo problems may still arise for the employer. First, the supervisor may reward his or her paramour with certain job-related benefits—such as shift or vacation-time preferences, easy job assignments, promotions, and the like. Clearly, the favored employee has no complaint—as yet. But co-employees of the opposite sex may well claim that *but for* their sex, they too would at least have had the *opportunity* to have an affair with the supervisor and also enjoy the bestowed benefits. If a heterosexual supervisor does this on a recurring basis, then this may also be construed as implicitly making sexual favors or romantic relationships a general condition of employment, a condition members of the opposite sex cannot satisfy—thus constituting illegal sex discrimination.[34] On the other hand, when the benefits are provided to a single paramour, most courts regard this as a mere incident of romance, not illegal sex discrimination.[35]

Second, if the relationship eventually *goes sour*, the supervisor may discontinue the previously bestowed job benefits—indeed, perhaps conferring them on the current employee-paramour of choice. If the breakup was at the employee's instigation, then this fits very neatly into the normal quid pro quo paradigm—although the *because of* sex as a status is now one step removed. Theory to the contrary notwithstanding, the courts seem reluctant to treat these failed personal relationships as involving illegal sex discrimination under Title VII.[36]

[B] Hostile Environment Sexual Harassment

A sexually hostile work environment, rather than one in which sex must be provided in order to retain the job, has been and continues to be the most common form of sexual harassment—and one that raises the most difficult conceptual and evidentiary problems. Apart from the fact that no required exchange is involved, hostile environment differs from quid pro quo harassment in two respects. First, it covers conduct that is not necessarily of a *sexual* nature. Conduct that is simply disparaging of women, as women, is also covered.[37] Second, the harassing conduct may

---

34. Toscano v. Nimmo, 570 F. Supp. 1197 (D. Del. 1983).

35. DeCintio v. Westchester Cty. Med. Ctr., 807 F.2d 304 (2d Cir. 1986). *But see* King v. Palmer, 598 F. Supp. 65 (D.D.C. 1984), rev'd on other grounds, 778 F.2d 878 (D.C. Cir. 1985).

36. Keppler v. Hinsdale Twp. School District 86, 715 F. Supp. 862 (N.D. Ill. 1989) (suggesting, however, that a different result might be reached if the supervisor had demanded the renewal of sexual relations prior to the termination); Freeman v. Continental Technical Servs., Inc., 710 F. Supp. 328 (N.D. Ga. 1988) (rejecting a claim of sex discrimination when an employee in a consensual affair was terminated after she became pregnant and the affair broke up).

37. Boumehdi v. Plastag Holdings, LLC, 489 F.3d 781 (7th Cir. 2007); Hall v. Gus Constr. Co., 842 F.2d 1010 (8th Cir. 1988). Hostile environment discrimination, thus, may also encompass racial, national origin, and religious workplace harassment.

come not only from supervisors or others in a position of power, but also from third parties, such as customers, vendors, and co-employees.

[1] Satisfying the Literal Language and Requirements of the Statute

Needless to say, hostile environment sexual harassment does not fit neatly within the paradigm of the typical disparate treatment case. The *because of sex* requirement is usually not hard to satisfy. If the plaintiff's sex motivates the conduct in question, then whatever consequences follow from that conduct are causally related to a protected status. The second question, however, is how a hostile environment—which, unlike quid pro quo harassments, may result in no tangible loss of an economic nature—can be discrimination with respect to "compensation, terms, conditions, or privileges" of employment. In other words, how is the fundamental *adverse employment action*[38] requirement met?

The Supreme Court resolved that question in *Meritor Savings Bank v. Vinson*,[39] by essentially holding that the work environment itself is a *condition of employment* that cannot be altered on a discriminatory basis. However, for that alteration to occur and be considered *adverse*, the conduct in question must be *unwelcome* and it must be *severe or pervasive.*

[2] Unwelcomeness

In *Meritor*, the Court said that "[t]he gravamen of any sexual harassment claim is that the alleged sexual advances were 'unwelcome.'"[40] The plaintiff has the burden of establishing unwelcomeness; this burden is usually met by showing a prior or contemporaneous objection to[41] or a prompt subsequent complaint about[42] the conduct. The Defendant, of course, will attempt to present affirmative evidence of welcomeness. The Court in *Harris* held that testimony about the plaintiff's "dress and personal fantasies" was relevant to the welcomeness issue. Some courts have also considered relevant the plaintiff's use of foul language,[43] actively participating in sexual horseplay,[44] telling provocative jokes and stories,[45] and others. The types and nature of conduct that might not suggest welcomeness is huge, does not lend itself to generalization, depends heavily on the specific circumstances of each case, and has been variously treated by the courts. An employee who in the past has willingly participated in or

38. *See* Chapter 4, § 4.05.

39. 477 U.S. 57 (1986).

40. Vinson, 477 U.S. at 68.

41. Showalter v. Allison Reed Group, 767 F. Supp. 1205 (D.R.I. 1991).

42. Stoeckel v. Environmental Mgmt. Sys., Inc., 882 F. Supp. 1106 (D.D.C. 1995).

43. Balletti v. Sun-Sentinel Co., 909 F. Supp. 1539 (S.D. Fla. 1995) (vulgar language and open discussion of her use of a vibrator). *But see* Swentek v. U.S. Air, Inc., 830 F. 2d 552 (4th Cir. 1987) (mere prior use of foul language not sufficient to establish that plaintiff welcomed the specific harassing conduct in question).

44. *Balletti*, 909 F. Supp. 1539 (ripping and attempting to pull down a co-worker's pants).

45. Reed v. Shepard, 939 F.2d 484 (7th Cir. 1991).

contributed to a sexually charged workplace may, of course, change his or her mind. But the employer and co-workers must be put on notice that the conduct is no longer welcome.[46]

The plaintiff's conduct must, however, occur within the context of the workplace. In 1994 the Federal Rule of Evidence 412 was extended to cover both civil and criminal cases involving claims by persons alleging to be the victim of sexual misconduct. The Rule generally excludes:

(1) Evidence offered to prove that any alleged victim engaged in other sexual behavior.

(2) Evidence offered to prove any alleged victim's sexual predisposition.

Such evidence is admissible, however, if "its probative value substantially outweighs the danger of harm to any victim and of unfair prejudice to any party." The courts have consistently construed the new Rule 412 as applying to Title VII sexual harassment claims. But what the Rule means in this context is still in its evolutionary stage. With respect to the welcomeness issue, evidence of non-workplace conduct is generally inadmissible,[47] while the admissibility of workplace related conduct seems to turn on how closely it relates to the alleged harassment in question.[48]

[3] Severe or Pervasive

In *Harris v. Forklift Systems, Inc.*,[49] the Supreme Court established that the *hostile* element had both a subjective and an objective prong. That is, the plaintiff herself must not only "subjectively perceive the environment to be abusive," she must also show that a reasonable person would perceive the environment as hostile or abusive. In most cases, evidence showing that the conduct was unwelcome will also suffice to show that it was subjectively perceived as being sufficiently severe and pervasive to alter the plaintiff's conditions of employment. Conceptually, however, the two issues are distinct since a plaintiff could regard the conduct as unwelcome but trivial.

The more difficult prong of the test is the objective one. In *Harris*, the Court twice used the term "reasonable person" rather than "reasonable woman," which was the term used by the court below. On the other hand, in *Oncale v. Sundowner Offshore Services*,[50] the Court used the phrase, "a reasonable person in the plaintiff's position"—which would seem to include the plaintiff's gender.

In any event, the Court has stated that to sustain a hostile environment claim, a plaintiff must demonstrate that the "workplace is permeated with discriminatory in-

46. Weinsheimer v. Rockwell Int'l Corp., 754 F. Supp. 1559 (M.D. Fla. 1990) *aff'd* 949 F.2d 1162 (11th Cir. 1991).

47. Rodriguez-Hernandez v. Miranda-Velez, 132 F.3d 848 (1st Cir. 1998).

48. Raatts v. Board of Cty. Commr's, 189 F.R.D. 448 (D. Kan. 1999); Sheffield v. Hilltop Sand & Gravel Co., 895 F. Supp. 105 (E.D. Va. 1995).

49. 510 U.S. 17 (1993).

50. 523 U.S. 75 (1998).

timidation, ridicule, and insult"[51] and that the "conduct must be extreme" before it can "amount to a change in the terms and conditions of employment."[52] Conversely, the "'mere utterance of an ... epithet which engenders offensive feelings in an employee' ... does not sufficiently affect the conditions of employment to implicate Title VII."[53] And, the Court has stated that Title VII was not intended to impose "a general civility code for the American workplace."[54] Whether conduct is objectively offensive requires a consideration of "all the circumstances," including "the frequency of the discriminatory conduct; its severity; whether it is physically threatening or humiliating, or a mere offensive utterance; and whether it unreasonably interferes with an employee's work performance."[55] Economic or personal injury and psychological harm are relevant considerations, but an environment may be regarded as hostile even if it does not rise to that level of abuse. The inquiry also "requires careful consideration of the social context in which particular behavior occurs."[56] This is because the "real social impact of workplace behavior often depends on a constellation of surrounding circumstances, expectations, and relationships which are not fully captured by a simple recitation of the words used...."[57] The *pervasiveness* of the harassment may, moreover, be evidenced by conduct that occurred at any time during the employment relationship, as long as at least one harassing act occurred within the statutory filing period.[58]

Although the *severe or pervasive* issue is resolved by the fact finder, summary judgment is still appropriate if the conduct could not satisfy the objective prong as a matter of law. But the trial and appellate courts have different notions about how objectively offensive the conduct must be before the matter can be resolved as a matter of law, one way or the other. The presence of physical contact or physically threatening remarks heavily influences the courts' perception of this issue.[59]

[C] Third-Party Claims

An employee who is not the direct target of sexual harassment, of either the quid pro quo or hostile environment variety, may nevertheless have a cause of action. For example, if a supervisor repeatedly receives sexual (whether coerced or consensual) favors from employees, who in turn receive various employment benefits, this may be construed as making it "generally necessary for women to grant sexual favors to

51. Harris, 510 U.S. at 21.
52. Faragher v. City of Boca Raton, 524 U.S. 775, 788 (1998).
53. Harris, 510 U.S. at 21 (quoting *Meritor*, 477 U.S. at 67).
54. *Oncale*, 523 U.S. at 80.
55. Harris, 510 U.S. at 23.
56. Oncale, 523 U.S. at 81.
57. Oncale, 523 U.S. at 81–82.
58. AMTRAK v. Morgan, 536 U.S. 101 (2002).
59. *Compare* Pryor v. Seyfarth, Shaw, Fairweather & Geraldson, 212 F.3d 976 (7th Cir. 2000), *with* Curde v. Xytel Corp., 912 F. Supp. 335 (N.D. Ill. 1995).

decisionmakers for professional advancement"[60]—in other words, an implied quid pro quo. In that situation, even employees of the opposite sex may claim that *but for* their sex, they too would have been eligible to compete for the benefits in question from the presumably heterosexual supervisor. But when the benefits have been provided to only one consenting paramour, most courts hold that this is an incident or romance, not illegal sex discrimination of any variety with respect to any of the putative claimants.[61]

A third-party female employee may also be able to state a hostile environment claim for employer comments and conduct that seem to be directed at a lone specific female but can be, nevertheless, construed as being targeted at and derogatory of women as a class.[62]

[D] Same-Sex Harassment

Quid pro quo sexual harassment by a homosexual supervisor against an employee of the same sex has long been recognized as an illegal form of sex discrimination. Same-sex hostile environment discrimination has been more problematic. In *Oncale v. Sundowner Offshore Services, Inc.*,[63] the Supreme Court finally held that there was no reason why conduct between members of the same sex could not rise to the level of creating a sexually hostile working environment.

The Court declined to articulate a bright-line test for distinguishing between rough, workplace "horseplay" and illegal sexual harassment. However, the Court did emphasize that the harassment must be *because of sex*, rather than something else. According to the Court, the critical issue is whether members of one sex are exposed to disadvantageous terms or conditions of employment to which members of the other sex are not exposed. The Seventh Circuit has construed *Oncale* as suggesting that same-sex harassment may be considered gender based if the plaintiff can prove either "that the harasser is gay or lesbian—in which case it is reasonable to assume that the harasser would not harass members of the other sex" or "that a plaintiff was harassed in 'such sex specific and derogatory terms' as to reveal an antipathy to persons of plaintiff's gender."[64] The *tangled web* of the law relating to sexual stereotyping, dress and grooming codes, and transsexualism will obviously have an impact on the issue of whether certain forms of harassment are *because of sex* in the *Oncale* sense.

---

60. Piech v. Arthur Andersen & Co., 841 F. Supp. 825 (N.D. Ill. 1994).

61. DeCintio v. Westchester Cty. Med. Ctr., 807 F.2d 304 (2d Cir. 1986); Burgess v. Gateway Communications, Inc., 26 F. Supp. 2d 888 (S.D. W. Va. 1998).

62. Yuknis v. First Student, Inc., 481 F.3d 552 (7th Cir. 2007) (recognizing the "target area" legal concept, but finding the conduct in question did not meet the test); Chambers v. American Trans. Air, Inc., 17 F.3d 998 (7th Cir. 1994). Of course, males in a predominantly female workforce could face the same form of generally anti-male harassment.

63. 523 U.S. 75 (1998).

64. Shepherd v. Slater Steels Corp., 168 F.3d 998, 1009 (7th Cir. 1999).

The *Oncale* decision also leaves open the question of how to deal with the *indiscriminate harasser*—the supervisor who creates a sexually hostile work environment for both men and women.[65]

[E] Employer Liability

Most defendant employers, upon whom monetary liability will ultimately attach, are fictional entities like corporations or partnerships, which are capable of acting only through their human agents.[66] The issue is thus one of identifying the agent-individuals whose misconduct will result in corporate liability. The Supreme Court has recently brought clarity to this area of law in *Vance v. Ball State University*.[67] The key initial question is whether the harasser is a co-worker or a supervisor. If the harasser is a co-worker, the employer is liable only if it is negligent in controlling workplace conditions.

However, if the harasser is a supervisor, the employer is strictly liable. Whether a fellow employee is a supervisor does not turn on a workplace label. Rather, to qualify as a supervisor for harassment liability purposes, the employee must have the authority to take "*tangible employment actions*" against the victim of harassment. A tangible employment action is a significant change in the victim's employment status, such as the authority to hire, fire, demote, promote, transfer, discipline, or cause a significant change in benefits.

If the harasser is a supervisor with the authority to take tangible employment actions but refrains from taking any against the victim, the employer has an available affirmative defense. This defense has two parts. First, the employer must prove that it exercised reasonable care to prevent and correct harassing behavior. Second, the employer must show that the victim unreasonably failed to take advantage of the preventive or corrective opportunities that the employer provided.

The reasonable care element reflects the Court's prior comment in *Burlington Industries, Inc. v. Ellerth*, that the policy of Title VII is "to encourage the creation of anti-harassment policies and effective grievance mechanisms."[68] *Ellerth* explained, "While proof that an employer has promulgated an anti-harassment policy with complaint procedure is not necessary in every instance as a matter of law, the need for a stated policy suitable to the employment circumstances may appropriately be addressed in any case when litigating the first element of the defense."[69] If an employer creates a complaint procedure and the victim fails to take advantage of it, that failure will normally suffice to satisfy the employer's burden under the second element of the defense.[70]

---

65. *Compare* Ray v. Tandem Computers, Inc., 63 F.3d 429 (5th Cir. 1995) (no "discrimination"), *with* Steiner v. Showboat Operating Co., 25 F.3d 1459 (9th Cir. 1994) (suggesting that both men and women could assert viable claims).

66. Whether these agents are independently liable is discussed in Chapter 4, § 4.03[A][1].

67. 570 U.S. 421 (2013).

68. 524 U.S. 742, 764 (1998).

69. Ellerth, 524 U.S. at 765.

70. Ellerth, 524 U.S. at 765.

Is a constructive discharge claim a *tangible employment action* for the purpose of establishing strict liability? The Supreme Court previously discussed this in *Pennsylvania State Police v. Suders.*[71] Here, the Supreme Court addressed the question of whether a constructive discharge was a *tangible employment decision*, which if established would preclude the employer's use of an affirmative defense. The Third Circuit had held that the defense was never available in constructive discharge cases. The Supreme Court disagreed. First, the Court summarized the plaintiff's required proof in the following terms:

> For an atmosphere of sexual harassment or hostility to be actionable, ... the offending behavior "must be sufficiently severe or pervasive to alter the conditions of the victim's employment and create an abusive working condition."... A hostile-environment constructive discharge claim entails something more: A plaintiff who advances such a compound claim must show working conditions so intolerable that a reasonable person would have felt compelled to resign.[72]

The Court, however, noted that unlike an actual termination, a constructive discharge situation could come from three sources: "co-worker conduct, unofficial supervisory conduct, or official company acts."[73] Only *official company acts* precluded the use of the affirmative defense in a constructive discharge situation. The Court cited as an example of "unofficial supervisory conduct" a case where the claim of constructive discharge was based on the supervisor's repeated sexual comments and one instance of sexual assault.[74] And as a counter-example of an "official company act" the Court cited a case where a presiding judge had decided to transfer his clerk to another judge and told her that her first six months with the new judge would be "hell" and that it was thus in her best interests to resign.[75]

[F] The First Amendment Defense

If the harassment for which the employer would otherwise be liable consists of words, pictures, or some form of symbolic speech, then the employer may be able to assert a First Amendment defense. For example, a public employer was found to have violated the First Amendment rights of a public employee when, pursuant to the employer's anti-sexual harassment policy, the employee was prohibited from reading certain magazines in the workplace.[76] There are, however, several exceptions to the broad First Amendment prohibition,[77] and these are sometimes invoked in the

---

71. 542 U.S. 129 (2004).
72. Suders, 542 U.S. at 146–47.
73. Suders, 542 U.S. at 148.
74. Suders, 542 U.S. at 149–50 (citing Reed v. MBNA Marketing Systems, Inc., 333 F.3d 27 (1st Cir. 2003)).
75. Suders, 542 U.S. at 150 (citing Robinson v. Sappington, 351 F.3d 317 (7th Cir. 2003)).
76. Johnson v. Los Angeles Cty. Fire Dep't, 865 F. Supp. 1430 (C.D. Cal. 1994).
77. For example, the courts recognize exceptions when the speech involves "fighting words," are uttered to a "captive audience," or are truly "obscene."

Title VII cases.[78] The greatest limitation on First Amendment speech rights for public employees is the *Pickering/Connick* line[79] of cases which protect only speech dealing with matters of public concern. As a result, courts do not treat workplace-related speech with the same degree of protection against government sanction as the same utterance would enjoy in the broader social context.[80]

§ 9.04 Sexual Orientation and Identity

Cases involving discrimination based on sexual preference or orientation, and cases involving discrimination against transsexuals reached mixed results until the decision of the U.S. Supreme Court in *Bostick v. Clayton Cty.*[81] The Court resolved the conflict in the lower courts by finding that these types of discrimination satisfy the *because of sex* (in its conventional sense) requirement. For example, if he were not male, a male homosexual would not be discriminated against because of his sexual or romantic association with another male; a similarly situated female would not be so treated. If he were not a male, he would not be discriminated against because he dressed like a female; a similarly situated female would not suffer discrimination. The Court determined that this satisfies the *but for* test of causation.

§ 9.05 Compensation Discrimination

Although on average men are paid more than women in most occupations, Title VII's prohibition against compensation discrimination because of sex has been largely unsuccessful in altering the situation.

[A] The Equal Pay Act and the Bennett Amendment

The Equal Pay Act of 1963[82] essentially requires equal pay for equal work. Most sex-based wage discrimination claims are litigated under this statute, rather than Title VII. When Congress enacted Title VII, which also contained a prohibition against wage discrimination on the basis of sex, the overlap between the two statutes

---

78. Baty v. Willamette Indus., 172 F.3d 1232 (10th Cir. 1999); Jenson v. Eveleth Taconite Co., 824 F. Supp. 847 (D. Minn. 1993).

79. Pickering v. Bd. of Educ., 391 U.S. 563 (1968); Connick v. Myers, 461 U.S. 138 (1983).

80. Baty, 172 F.3d 1232; Jenson, 824 F. Supp. 847.

81. 509 U.S. __ (2020).

82. *See* Part VI, Chapters 25–28.

was supposedly resolved by the so-called Bennett Amendment, which provides as follows:

> It shall not be an unlawful employment practice under [Title VII] for an employer to differentiate upon the basis of sex in determining the amount of wage or compensation paid ... if such differentiation is authorized by ... [the Equal Pay Act].

In *County of Washington v. Gunther*,[83] the defendant had argued that the Bennett Amendment meant that wage discrimination could not be considered illegal under Title VII unless it also satisfied the tests for determining illegal unequal pay under the EPA. The Supreme Court, however, held that the term *authorized* referred to and thus incorporated into Title VII the four EPA affirmative defenses—differentiation based on seniority, merit, work quantity or quality, and a "factor other than sex." The defendant had argued against this construction on the ground that the first three EPA affirmative defenses were already expressly included in Title VII and that the "factor other than sex" was simply the logical converse of Title VII's prohibition against discrimination *because of sex*—which would thus make the Bennett Amendment superfluous. The Court, however, explained that this was not so, because the "factor other than sex" defense would preclude a plaintiff from establishing wage disparity liability on the basis of a *Griggs*-type, disparate impact analysis. The prevailing view, thus, is that true disparate impact analysis cannot be used to establish wage discrimination under either the EPA or Title VII.[84]

[B] Proof of Intent

Some courts require direct evidence of intent in a Title VII case.[85] Most courts, however, hold that an EPA-type proof of equal jobs but unequal pay is at least sufficient to create an inference of intentional discrimination under Title VII.[86] Others go further and allow an inference of intent to be drawn from the fact that a higher wage is being paid to a comparator of the opposite sex who is in at least a "similar" job.[87] Once that inference of intent is established, some courts merely require the employer to articulate a legitimate, nondiscriminatory reason—as in the typical *McDonnell Douglas* approach.[88] Others hold that when the proof of intent is in the form of equal work but unequal pay under the EPA standards, the employer must actually prove the existence

83. 452 U.S. 161 (1981).

84. International Union, UAW v. Michigan, 886 F.2d 766 (6th Cir. 1989); AFSCME v. Washington, 770 F.2d 1401 (9th Cir. 1985).

85. EEOC v. Sears, Roebuck & Co., 839 F.2d 302 (7th Cir. 1988).

86. Gunther, 623 F.2d at 1321, aff'd, 452 U.S. 161 (1981).

87. Miranda v. B & B Cash Grocery Store, Inc., 975 F.2d 1518 (11th Cir. 1992).

88. Miranda, 975 F.2d 1518.

of a legitimate, nondiscriminatory reason—which is the functional equivalent of the EPA "factor other than sex" defense.[89]

Fringe benefit packages that facially discriminate on the basis of sex or pregnancy are, of course, illegal per se.

§ 9.06 Dress and Grooming Codes

Prohibiting a female employee from wearing pants and shaving her head or a male employee from wearing a dress and affecting a shoulder-length hair style is *literally* a form of differentiation in the conditions of employment *because of* the sex of the respective employees. The courts, however, have consistently held that it is permissible for an employer to impose "reasonable regulations that require male and female employees to conform to different dress and grooming standards."[90] Some opine that since this is not discrimination on the basis of an immutable characteristic and is something that can easily be complied with, this is not a significant burden and does not, thus, alter the terms of employment.[91] On the other hand, differential grooming and dress codes for men and women must be roughly equivalent with respect to burdensomeness.[92] Moreover, an employer cannot adopt a dress code that is demeaning. In one case, for example, male bank tellers were only required to wear "appropriate business attire," while female tellers were required to wear prescribed uniforms, euphemistically referred to as "career ensembles" by the employer.[93] Moreover, except in rare situations where such attire is integral to the job, an employer cannot require an employee to wear a sexually provocative uniform that would subject the employee to sexual harassment.[94]

Although some have suggested that the Supreme Court's condemnation of sexual stereotyping in *Price Waterhouse v. Hopkins*[95] undermines the existing case law with respect to grooming and dress codes, this argument has been generally rejected.[96] The stereotyping that was present there related to how a female employee ought to act generally, and Hopkins' perceived failure in that regard was cited as evidence that her lack of promotion to partner was *because of* her sex. The Supreme Court's 2020 decision in *Bostick v. Clayton Cty.* protecting transsexuals from discrimination presents stronger arguments for undermining existing law.

---

89. Korte v. Diemer, 909 F.2d 954 (6th Cir. 1990).

90. Nichols v. Azteca Restaurant Enterprises, Inc., 256 F.3d 864, 875 n.7 (9th Cir. 2009).

91. Jespersen v. Harrah's Operating Co., 444 F.3d 1104 (9th Cir. 2006) (en banc); Willingham v. Macon Tel. Publ'g Co., 507 F.2d 1084 (5th Cir. 1975).

92. Laffey v. Northwest Airlines, Inc., 366 F. Supp. 763 (D.D.C. 1973), vacated and remanded in part on other grounds, 567 F.2d 429 (D.C. Cir. 1976) (allowing men to wear glasses or contacts, but requiring women to wear contacts only).

93. Carroll v. Talman Federal Sav. & Loan Ass'n, 604 F.2d 1028 (7th Cir. 1979).

94. EEOC v. Sage Realty Corp., 507 F. Supp. 599 (S.D.N.Y. 1981).

95. 490 U.S. 228 (1989).

96. *Jespersen*, 444 F.3d 1104; Harper v. Blockbuster Entm't Corp., 139 F.3d 1385 (11th Cir. 1998) (employer's grooming policy forbidding men but not women from having long hair did not violate Title VII).

§ 9.07 Discriminatory Advertisements

Section 704(b) prohibits advertisements that indicate a "preference, limitation, specification or discrimination based on race, color, religion, sex, or national origin," unless the BFOQ defense applies. Advertisements indicating a sex preference are the most common offenders. Clearly, job advertisements in columns classified as "male" and "female" are illegal. The EEOC has also faulted individual advertisements seeking an "attractive lady"[97] and "career minded men."[98] Gender-specific job titles, such as "fireman" and "meter maid," are not illegal per se, according to the EEOC, provided the advertisement also expressly states that the employer is seeking applicants from both sexes.[99]

§ 9.08 Chapter Highlights

1. Since the prohibition against discrimination on the basis of sex was added to Title VII as a floor amendment, there is very little legislative history with respect to its intended meaning. (§ 9.01)

2. After the Supreme Court determined that discrimination on the basis of pregnancy was not discrimination on the basis of sex, Congress amended the statute to include pregnancy within the definition of sex. Although the PDA's *because of* clause is arguably inconsistent with its *equal treatment* clause, the courts seem to have resolved the inconsistency in favor of the *equal treatment* clause. (§ 9.02[A]) On the other hand, the equality requirement does not apply when the discrimination is in the form of benefits that favor pregnant women over men. (§ 9.02[B])

3. In a decision that relies more on the underlying prohibition against discrimination on the basis of sex rather than the PDA's specific language, the Supreme Court has held that a medical plan providing greater pregnancy benefits to female employees than to the spouses of male employees was illegal. (§ 9.02[C])

4. The courts have been split over whether the absence of any medical or leave benefits is illegal because of the disparate impact it has on pregnant women. The leave aspect, however, is now taken care of by the FMLA. (§ 9.02[D])

5. An employer cannot exclude fertile or pregnant women from certain jobs out of concern for the well-being of the fetus. (§ 9.02[E]) On the other hand, not being pregnant will qualify as a BFOQ in jobs where being pregnant would pose a safety hazard to third parties and perhaps in some "role model" situations. (§ 9.02[F])

6. An employer cannot ask women questions about their marital status and child-bearing plans if males are not asked similar question. (§ 9.02[G])

---

97. EEOC Dec. YNO-9-082 (1969).

98. EEOC Dec. 72-0066 (1971).

99. EEOC Compl. Man. (BNA) N:915-051 (Apr. 16, 1990).

7. The most literal form of sexual harassment discrimination occurs when an employer or supervisor makes yielding to sexual demands a condition of continued employment or the receipt of certain benefits. This is so-called *quid pro quo* harassment and is generally proved with direct evidence or *McDonnell Douglas* circumstantial evidence. (§ 9.03[A] & [1])

8. Although workplace romances between a supervisor and subordinate may result in the allocation of benefits that are related to the employee's sex, and the breakup of the relationship may involve the withdrawal of those benefits (with both situations theoretically fitting into the quid pro quo paradigm), the courts are reluctant to find sex discrimination in these situations. (§ 9.03[A][2])

So-called *hostile environment* discrimination exists when unwelcome conduct is so severe or pervasive as to alter the conditions under which an employee works—an alteration that arises because of that employee's sex and that does not similarly alter the conditions under which members of the opposite sex work. This is a factual determination that takes a number of considerations into account. (§ 9.03[B])

9. Although harassment by employees and supervisors of one sex against another employee of the same sex may be actionable, the harassment must be *because of* the victim's sex. Despite *Oncale*, how that is to be determined in same-sex harassment cases is as yet unclear. (§ 9.03[C])

10. If the harasser is a co-worker, the employer is liable only if it is negligent in controlling workplace conditions. Employers are strictly liable for hostile environment discrimination created by supervisors. To qualify as a supervisor, the employee must take "*tangible employment actions*" against the victim, such as causing a significant change in the victim's employment status or benefits. If the supervisor does not take a tangible employment action, the employer has an available affirmative defense. First, the employer must prove that it exercised reasonable care to prevent and correct harassing behavior, and, second, that the victim unreasonably failed to take advantage of the opportunities the employer provided. (§ 9.03[E])

11. In 2020 the Supreme Court recognized discrimination on the basis of sexual orientation or transgender status as sex discrimination under Title VII. (§ 9.04)

12. If a plaintiff brings a claim under Title VII alleging sex discrimination in the form of unequal pay for substantially equal work, a claim that could also be brought under the EPA, then the plaintiff can probably use the EPA model of proof, but the four EPA affirmative defenses are also available to the defendant. All this means, however, is that the plaintiff cannot establish a violation through a disparate impact theory of proof. Otherwise, the law with respect to proof of pay disparity discrimination under Title VII is in a state of disarray. (§ 9.05)

13. Provided that an employer has equally onerous dress and grooming codes for male and female employees, the fact that the requirements for the respective sexes are quite different does not convert into a sex discrimination claim. Whether this statement of the law survives the Supreme Court decision protecting transgendered status remains to be seen. (§ 9.06)

14. Employers cannot use classified advertisements that discriminate, directly or by implication, on the basis of sex. (§ 9.07)

Chapter 10

Special Problems Relating to National Origin Discrimination

Synopsis

§ 10.01 Definition of "National Origin"

The legal definition of *national origin* is short and clear: it means the country a person or that person's forebearers came from.[1] Conceivably, however, a person could have more than one national origin. For example, in *Bennun v. Rutgers State University*,[2] the plaintiff, who was born in Argentina, claimed he was of Hispanic national origin, even though his mother was Romanian and his father a Sephardic Jew born in what was then Palestine. Although the court upheld the determination that he had a Hispanic national origin, if the employer had acted out of an anti-Romanian or anti-Palestinian bias, presumably either one of those could also have been claimed as his *national origin*. The courts, moreover, have defined *country* broadly to include ethnic enclaves within a larger political unit[3] and even those lacking a fixed geographic base, as in the case of Gypsies.[4] Native American tribal membership is also a protected

1. Espinoza v. Farah Mfg. Co., 414 U.S. 86, 89 (1973).
2. 941 F.2d 154 (3d Cir. 1991).
3. Pejic v. Hughes Helicopters, Inc., 840 F.2d 667 (9th Cir. 1988) (discrimination against Serbians even when Serbia was part of Yugoslavia); Kovalevsky v. West Publ'g Co., 674 F. Supp. 1379 (D. Minn. 1987) (discrimination against Ukrainians even when it was part of the Soviet Union).
4. Janko v. Illinois State Toll Highway Auth., 704 F. Supp. 1531 (N.D. Ill. 1989).

form of national origin.[5] National origin, however, does not refer to citizenship,[6] and alienage discrimination is not prohibited by Title VII. For public employees, alienage discrimination is protected to some degree based on the Equal Protection clause of the U.S. Constitution.

§ 10.02 Proof of a Violation

National origin discrimination is subject to both the disparate treatment (individual and systemic) and disparate impact methods of proof. For example, the Supreme Court has held that alienage discrimination, though not illegal itself, might be shown to be a pretext or subterfuge for intentional national origin discrimination and that it might also have a disparate impact in some situations.[7] Likewise, many courts have held that height and weight requirements have a disparate impact on Hispanics.[8] National origin harassment is treated in much the same manner as sex discrimination.[9] The BFOQ defense may also be invoked in appropriate situations. According to some of the legislative history, for example, this would allow a French or Italian restaurant to hire only French or Italian chefs.[10]

§ 10.03 Language Discrimination

Plaintiffs have been generally unsuccessful in connecting various forms of language discrimination with illegal national origin discrimination.

[A] Accent Discrimination

Because a person's accent is often the most obvious outer manifestation of that person's national origin, the EEOC and some courts treat the "*linguistic characteristics* of a national origin group" as being synonymous with national origin category itself—or at least sufficient to establish a prima facie case of such discrimination.[11] This is the *proxy by operation of law* theory of discrimination.[12] Assuming the continued validity of this theory, the courts evaluate the employer's asserted justification for

---

5. Dawavendewa v. Salt River Project, 154 F.3d 1117 (9th Cir. 1998).

6. This omission resulted in 8 U.S.C. § 1324b being passed to protect against discrimination based on citizenship.

7. *Espinoza*, 414 U.S. 86.

8. Sondel v. Northwestern Airlines, Inc., 63 FEP Cases 408 (D. Minn. 1993). *See*, Majeske v. City of Chicago, 218 F.3d 816 (7th Cir. Ill. July 10, 2000).

9. Faragher v. City of Boca Raton, 524 U.S. 775, 787 & n.1 (1998); *see* Amirmokri v. Baltimore Gas & Elec. Co., 60 F.3d 1126, 1129 (4th Cir. 1995) (Iranian referred to as "the local terrorist," a "camel jockey," "the ayatollah," and "the Emir of Waldorf").

10. 110 Cong. Rec. 2456 (1964) (remarks of Representative Dent).

11. 29 C.F.R. § 1606.1; Berke v. Ohio Dep't of Pub. Welfare, 628 F.2d 980 (6th Cir. 1980).

12. *See* Chapter 4, § 4.02[B].

making a job decision on this basis by determining whether the plaintiff's heavy accent qualifies as a legitimate, nondiscriminatory reason under the *McDonnell Douglas* rubric, or whether not having an accent is a BFOQ because speaking clearly is reasonably necessary to the normal operation of that particular business or enterprise. The leading case, *Fragante v. City of Honolulu*,[13] utilized a confusing mixed analysis in this regard, but ultimately concluded that the employer did not illegally discriminate when it refused to hire the plaintiff because of his heavy and difficult to understand Filipino accent for a job that required communication with the public. On the other hand, some courts have held that an accent that does not interfere with job duties cannot be the basis of an adverse employment decision.[14]

[B] Fluency Requirements

Although the EEOC regards the language a person speaks like it does accents, namely as an "essential national origin characteristic,"[15] the courts have generally upheld fluency requirements. Some regard English fluency as a necessary job qualification, which thus prevents the plaintiff from establishing an element of the *McDonnell Douglas* prima facie case.[16] Others treat lack of fluency as a legitimate, nondiscriminatory reason, which defeats the prima facie case unless pretext can be proved.[17] English fluency has also been recognized as a BFOQ.[18] Although a fluency requirement may also have a disparate impact on persons with a non-English speaking national origin, the courts generally uphold the requirement as a business necessity.[19]

[C] English-Only Rules

Of the three most common forms of language discrimination, English-only rules have the most tenuous connection with national origin. Although the EEOC views these rules with a jaundiced eye,[20] the courts have generally rejected claims of illegal discrimination on this basis.[21] For example, in *Garcia v. Gloor*,[22] the court refused to equate "national origin with the language that one chooses to speak," although the court did recognize the possibility that an English-only rule could simply be a cover for intentional national origin discrimination. In *Garcia v. Spun Steak Co.*,[23] the court

---

13. 888 F.2d 591 (9th Cir. 1989).
14. Carino v. University of Oklahoma, 750 F.2d 815 (10th Cir. 1984).
15. 29 C.F.R. § 1606.7.
16. Villarreal v. ATC Management Corp., 64 FEP Cases 418 (D. Or. 1994).
17. Mejia v. New York Sheraton Hotel, 459 F. Supp. 375 (S.D.N.Y. 1978).
18. Vasquez v. McAllen Bag & Supply Co., 660 F.2d 686 (5th Cir. 1981).
19. Garcia v. Rush-Presbyterian-St. Luke's Med. Ctr., 660 F.2d 1217 (7th Cir. 1981).
20. 29 C.F.R. § 1606.7.
21. *But see* EEOC v. Synchro-Start Prods., Inc., 29 F. Supp. 2d 911 (N.D. Ill. 1999) (once the existence of an English-only rule is established, the employer has the burden a establishing a legitimate justification for the requirement).
22. 618 F.2d 264, 268 (5th Cir. 1980).
23. 998 F.2d 1480 (9th Cir. 1993).

dealt at some length with the plaintiffs' disparate impact claim, ultimately holding that the plaintiffs failed to show that the rule adversely affected them with respect to a term, condition, or privilege of employment. Specifically, it held that the expression of a cultural heritage (by speaking Spanish) is not itself a privilege of employment, nor is the ability to converse in the language with which one is most comfortable. Finally, specifically rejecting the EEOC position in this regard, the court held that an English-only rule normally does not create "an atmosphere of 'inferiority, isolation, and intimidation' "[24]—although the court recognized that in some situations, English-only rules, especially if they are enforced in a draconian manner, might contribute to the existence of a national origin, hostile work environment. Finally, even when a court does recognize that an English-only rule might have a disparate impact on some national origin group, they generally uphold the requirement as a business necessity.[25]

§ 10.04 Chapter Highlights

1. *National origin* means the nation that you or your forebearers came from. It does not mean alienage or citizenship. (§ 10.01)

2. National origin discrimination is established by the same models of proof that are used with respect to the other protected classes. It is subject to the BFOQ defense. (§ 10.02)

3. Plaintiffs have not had a great deal of success in equating the various forms of language discrimination—accent, fluency, and English-only—with national origin discrimination. This is because the courts frequently either reject the equation altogether or justify it in terms of a legitimate job qualification, a BFOQ, or a business necessity. (§ 10.03)

24. Spun Steak, 998 F.2d at 1489.

25. Vasquez, 660 F.2d 686.

Chapter 11

Special Problems Relating to Religious Discrimination

Synopsis

§ 11.01 The Definition of "Religion"

Although the term *religion*, as used in the Section 703 prohibition against discrimination on this basis, is said to include "all aspects of religious observance and practice, as well as belief," the terms *religion* and *religious* themselves are otherwise left undefined. The courts, thus, have generally borrowed the test that is used in defining *religion* for the purposes of the military-service exemption, as follows:

> A sincere and meaningful belief which occupies in the life of its possessor a place parallel to that filled by the God of those admittedly qualifying for the exemption comes within the statutory definition.[1]

So defined, *religion* includes moral or ethical beliefs that occupy the role of religion in the individual's life.[2] Purely secular beliefs derived from economic, political, and social ideology do not qualify. The line between the two is, however, fuzzy at best. For example, a lack of belief in religion has been protected.[3] The racist and anti-Semitic philosophy of the Ku Klux Klan has been held not to qualify as a *religion*, even though it allegedly derives from Biblical sources.[4] On the other hand, an employee's religiously based opposition to abortion has been found to warrant protection,[5] even though at the time of that decision, opposition to anti-abortion laws on constitutional grounds alone would not qualify. Although protecting the environment is an article of religious faith for many, as is promoting civil rights and protecting the public virtue from things like gambling, it is unclear whether these are *religious* beliefs warranting Title VII protection and whether advocacy in this regard is a *religious practice* requiring accommodation.

Although it is easier to prove an employee's religious belief if it is part of the teaching of an organized religion or is logical and reasonable, this is not required. All that can be required is a sincere belief.[6] Lax beliefs are protected as well as beliefs that are rigidly practiced.[7] Judges are not authorized to act as theologians, although the temptation is great when dealing with eccentric or illogical religious beliefs. Compare two bizarre religious claims: In one case, the employee's "personal religious creed" dictated that he eat a can of a particularly odiferous cat food each day in the company cafeteria, a practice his co-employees and employer apparently found of-

---

1. Welsh v. United States, 398 U.S. 333, 339 (1970).

2. Welsh, 398 U.S. 333. Similarly, the EEOC defines religion to include "moral or ethical beliefs as to what is right and wrong which are sincerely held with the strength of traditional religious views." 29 C.F.R. § 1605.1.

3. Young v. Southwestern Savings & Loan Ass'n, 509 F.2d 140 (5th Cir. 1975).

4. Commonwealth v. Lower, 1989 Pa. Dist. & Cnty. Dec. LEXIS 264 (Pa. C.P. April 12, 1989).

5. EEOC v. University of Detroit, 904 F.2d 331 (6th Cir. 1990). At the time of this decision, a constitutional objection would not suffice. That has now changed. Janus v. AFSCME Council 31, 138 S. Ct. 2448 (2019). One of the authors, Prof. Cameron, was counsel of record for the intervening employee in *University of Detroit* and part of the litigation group in *Janus*.

6. Thomas v. Review Bd. of Ind. Emp't Sec. Div., 450 U.S. 707, 715–16 (1981).

7. Univ. of Great Falls v. NLRB, 278 F.3d 1335, 1342–44 (D.C. Cir. 2002).

fensive. He was afforded no Title VII protection.[8] On the other hand, an employee whose religious belief manifested itself in body modifications was accepted as being sincere.[9]

Two aspects of religious belief are protected. First, employees cannot be treated differently because of their religion. Second, and somewhat inconsistently, they also have the right to request to be treated differently when their religious beliefs require it. In addition, non-religion is also protected in the context of a religious employer, thus making it illegal to discriminate against agnostics and atheists who object to being involved in workplace religious activities.[10]

While the *sincerity* of religious belief is often litigated, it is rarely successfully challenged. Sudden conversions are, of course, suspect, but not fatal to a plaintiff's claim.[11]

§ 11.02 Disparate Treatment

In 2015, the Supreme Court upended decades of caselaw in *EEOC v. Abercrombie & Fitch Stores, Inc.*[12] Previously, every circuit to consider a religious accommodation claim had held that religious accommodation was an independent cause of action. The circuits had also uniformly agreed on a three-part prima facie case: (1) Proof of a sincere religious belief in conflict with a work requirement; (2) notice of that conflict; and (3) adverse action arising from the conflict between the religious belief and the work requirement. *Abercrombie & Fitch* swept all of this away with its holding that religious accommodation was not a freestanding cause of action. Instead, Title VII only created two basic types of religious discrimination claims, disparate treatment and disparate impact.

The Court did not dispense with the right of religious accommodation. Instead, the Court read the definition of religious belief and practice contained in Section 701(j) into the analysis of disparate treatment. The result was this: The protected category was not a *Baptist*; it was *a Baptist who did not work on Sunday*. It was not a *Catholic;* it was *a Catholic who could not pay dues to a union which promoted abortion rights*. As is true with respect to the other protected categories, refusing to hire or otherwise discriminating against a person *because of* that person's religious beliefs or affiliations is illegal. The result, post-*Abercrombie & Fitch*, is that employers and unions can neither fire a Seventh-day Adventist because they have a bias against the religion nor fire an Adventist who would not work on Saturday. Disparate treatment based on bias is illegal, and disparate treatment based on religious practice requires an accommodation absent undue hardship.

---

8. Brown v. Pena, 441 F. Supp. 1382 (S.D. Fla. 1977).

9. Cloutier v. Costco Wholesale, 390 F.3d 126 (1st Cir. 2004)

10. EEOC v. Townley Mfg., 859 F.2d 610 (9th Cir. 1988).

11. *Compare* Hansard v. Johns-Manville Prods. Corp., 5 Fair Empl. Prac. Cas. (BNA) 707 (E.D. Tex. 1973), *with* Cooper v. Oak Rubber Co., 15 F.3d 1375 (6th Cir. 1994).

12. 135 S. Ct. 2028 (2015).

The result is that plaintiffs are entitled to use the *McDonnell Douglas* prima facie case approach—albeit with some modifications from the norm. If the underlying claim is that the employee was treated differently *because of* the employee's religion, the plaintiff would follow the normal *McDonnell Douglas* prima facie approach, with the employer then having a burden to produce evidence of a legitimate, non-discriminatory reason for the adverse action. This non-discriminatory reason cannot be the employee's religious practice because then the employee would have been harmed *because of* his religious practice. Instead, the employer would have to produce evidence of a non-discriminatory reason having no connection to the employee's religious practice, after which the employee would carry the ultimate burden of showing that the defendant's stated non-discriminatory reason was pretextual.

On the other hand, if the underlying claim is that the employee needs to be treated differently because of his religious belief (an accommodation is needed), then the employer's defense can be to attack the elements of the prima facie case, show that the accommodation was made or show that an accommodation would create an undue hardship. The *because of* evidentiary component is, of course, the critical one. In *Abercrombie & Fitch*, the Court dramatically reduced the "notice" requirement created by the circuit courts. Separating knowledge from motive, the Court held that an employer who acts with the motivation of avoiding an accommodation violates Title VII even if it has "no more than an unsubstantiated suspicion that accommodation would be needed."[13]

§ 11.03 Disparate Impact

In *EEOC v. Sambo's of Georgia*,[14] the court held that the disparate impact theory did not apply to religious discrimination claims under Title VII. However, *Sambo's* conclusion that a disparate impact theory of discrimination was not available in religious discrimination cases was overruled in the Civil Rights Act of 1991, which specifically included religion within the ambit of coverage.

The more practical question is why a plaintiff would argue the disparate impact theory when Section 701(j) imposes a duty of reasonable accommodation. In *Sambo's*, a Sikh argued that the company grooming policy barring facial hair violated Title VII because facial hair is required by his religion. He raised both a religious accommodation and a disparate impact claim. The usual reason for bringing a disparate impact claim is to challenge a facially neutral practice that has the effect of discriminating. Intent is not a part of the required proof.[15] However, facial neutrality is also no defense to religious accommodation claims. When it comes to religious accommodation, *Abercrombie & Fitch* determined that Title VII does not require

13. 135 S. Ct. at 2033.

14. 530 F. Supp. 86 (N.D. Ga. 1981).

15. *See* Chapter 7, § 7.01.

"mere neutrality" for religious practice; instead it gives religious practice "favored treatment."[16] An employee entitled to a religious accommodation would have no practical reason to raise the less effective disparate impact claim. This conclusion is supported by the fact that the employer in *Abercrombie & Fitch* tried, unsuccessfully, to force the plaintiff to bring her claim as one of disparate impact rather than of religious accommodation.[17] The employer apparently believed that defending against a disparate impact claim would give it a litigation advantage.

§ 11.04 The Development of Protected Religious Practice

[A] History

Originally, the statute only protected an employee from adverse employment actions based on the employee's religious *beliefs* but provided no protection for religious *practices*. An EEOC Guideline, however, declared that employers had a duty "to accommodate to the reasonable religious needs of employees ... where such accommodation can be made without serious inconvenience to the conduct of the business."[18] Whether this Guideline was a proper interpretation of Title VII law was unsettled after the Supreme Court affirmed by an equally divided Court the Sixth Circuit's equally divided decision in *Dewey v. Reynolds Metal Co.*[19] Congress responded by amending the statute to provide specifically for such a duty. Section 701(j) now provides:

> The term "religion" includes all aspects of religious observance and practice, as well as belief, unless an employer demonstrates that he is unable to reasonably accommodate to an employee's or prospective employee's religious observance or practice without undue hardship on the conduct of the employer's business.

It is significant to note that the undue hardship defense applies to only the duty to accommodate an employee's *religious observance or practice*. One court has thus concluded that an employer cannot rely on the undue hardship defense with respect to discrimination on the basis of an employee's religious *beliefs*.[20] Such discrimination is, however, subject to the BFOQ defense in some cases.

---

16. 135 S. Ct. at 2034.
17. 135 S. Ct. at 2033.
18. 31 Fed. Reg. 8370 (1966).
19. 429 F.2d 324 (6th Cir. 1970), *aff'd per curiam by an equally divided Court, 402 U.S. 689 (1971).*
20. Peterson v. Wilmur Communications, Inc., 205 F. Supp. 2d 1014 (E.D. Wis. 2002). This is consistent with the constitutional interpretation that the freedom to believe is absolute, while the freedom to act is subject to some limitations. Cantwell v. Conn., 310 U.S. 296, 303–04 (1940).

[B] The Analytical Model

The multiple negatives in this statutory provision[21] make it unclear exactly who has the burden of proving what and under what circumstances. The Supreme Court clarified the issue in *Ansonia Board of Education v. Philbrook.*[22] In this case, the employer's collective bargaining agreement with the union allowed an employee to use three days of annual leave for observance of mandatory religious holidays and to use another three days for "necessary personal business," which expressly excluded uses not otherwise covered by the contract. Mr. Philbrook had been taking his three days of religious leave and then leave without pay to attend to his additional religious responsibilities. He became dissatisfied with that arrangement, however, and requested permission to use his "personal business" leave for this purpose. Alternatively, he suggested that he should be allowed to hire a substitute and still receive full pay for these three additional days. The employer declined to follow either suggestion.

On the undue hardship issue, the Court of Appeals assumed that the employer's leave policy (allowing three days of unpaid leave for religious obligations, in addition to the three days of paid leave) was itself a reasonable accommodation, but held that the employer must nevertheless accept the employee's proposal unless that accommodation caused an undue hardship.

The Supreme Court reversed on that issue. It held that once an employer proposes or implements an accommodation that is itself a reasonable one, that is the end of the analysis. An employer has the burden of proving that the employee's suggested accommodations would cause an undue hardship only if the employer has proposed no accommodation at all or has proposed one that is unreasonable. Although proving undue hardship is not difficult, the *Philbrook* decision suggests that employers should take the initiative in resolving conflicts between its work rules and the religious practices of its employees. Indeed, some courts make this a requirement,[23] while others hold that it is not necessary for an employer to suggest or attempt any accommodation if it can show no accommodation would be possible without undue hardship.[24]

[C] The Meaning of *Undue Hardship*

Whether a possible accommodation originates from the employer or from the employee, the employer is obligated to pursue it only if that can be done "without undue hardship to the employer's business." The Supreme Court addressed the question of what this means in *Trans World Airlines, Inc. v. Hardison.*[25] Hardison was a clerk in a TWA department that operated 24 hours a day, 365 days a year. After joining a religion that proscribes work from sunset on Friday until sunset on Saturday, he objected to

---

21. "[u]nless ... unable ... without undue hardship...."
22. 479 U.S. 60 (1986).
23. United States v. City of Albuquerque, 545 F.2d 110 (10th Cir. 1976).
24. United States v. Board of Educ. for the School Dist. of Phila., 911 F.2d 882 (3d Cir. 1990).
25. 432 U.S. 63 (1977).

working on Saturday but had insufficient seniority to bid for a shift having Saturdays off. When he refused to work on that day, he was terminated.

The Court of Appeals held that TWA failed to reasonably accommodate Hardison because the company could have adopted any of Hardison's three proposed alternatives without undue hardship. The Supreme Court disagreed. The first proposal was that TWA allow Hardison to work four days a week, using a supervisor or another employee on duty elsewhere for the Saturday work—despite the fact, according to the Supreme Court, that "this would have caused other shop functions to suffer."[26] The second proposal was that the Saturday position be filled by an employee willing to work overtime. The Court concluded that "both of these alternatives would involve costs to TWA, either in the form of lost efficiency in other jobs or higher wages."[27] Finally, it was suggested that TWA could have arranged a mandatory swap between Hardison and another employee, either for another shift or just for the Sabbath days themselves. The Supreme Court's rejection of this as a reasonable alternative has far-reaching implications. The Court advanced two reasons. First, this would violate the seniority provisions of the collective bargaining agreement. The Court agreed that "neither a collective-bargaining contract nor a seniority system may be employed to violate the statute, but we do not believe that the duty to accommodate requires TWA to take steps inconsistent with the otherwise valid agreement."[28] In addition, arguably even in the absence of a collective bargaining agreement, the Court noted that "to give Hardison Saturdays off, TWA would have had to deprive another employee of his shift preference at least in part because he did not adhere to a religion that observed the Saturday Sabbath. Title VII does not contemplate such unequal treatment."[29] However, it was not merely that a mandatory shift change would disadvantage one employee and benefit another. The Court noted that "while incurring extra costs to secure a replacement for Hardison might remove the necessity of compelling another employee to work involuntarily in Hardison's place, it would not change the fact that the privilege of having Saturdays off would be allocated according to religious beliefs."[30]

Of course, as the dissent pointed out, every accommodation of religious beliefs involves unequal treatment of believers and disbelievers—for example, allowing one employee the day off to go to church but not extending the same privilege to another employee who wished to go fishing. If the Court's *no unequal treatment rational* were carried to its logical extreme, the only accommodation that an employer could be required to make is one that could apply across the board, whether an employee seeks the "accommodation" for religious reasons or secular. Policies of that kind, however, generally would involve considerably more than the *de minimis* cost that the court said constitutes an undue hardship.

---

26. Hardison, 432 U.S. at 76.
27. Hardison, 432 U.S. at 84.
28. Hardison, 432 U.S. at 79.
29. Hardison, 432 U.S. at 81.
30. Hardison, 432 U.S. at 84–85.

Hardison construed the accommodation duty extremely narrowly, but not quite out of existence. The Court noted, for example, that TWA had at least attempted to find a solution to Hardison's problems. It did accommodate his observance of some special religious holidays. It authorized the union to search for someone who would voluntarily swap shifts, "which apparently was normal procedure"[31]—with this perhaps being an example of the neutral, across the board kind of accommodation that is implicit in the Court's equal treatment requirement. And TWA attempted to find Hardison another job. Moreover, the EEOC and the lower courts have not construed *Hardison* as literally as they might and continue to find a duty of accommodation (and the absence of undue hardship) in a number of situations.

The *Hardison* focus on preserving "equal treatment" conflicts with *Abercrombie & Fitch. Abercrombie* determined that Title VII's protection for religious practice "does not demand mere neutrality"; it requires "favored treatment."[32] Later, in a very unusual note attached to a denial of review in *Kennedy v. Bremerton Sch. Dist.*,[33] four justices wrote that the petition in that case had not asked them to revisit *Hardison*. In 2020, the Solicitor General urged the Supreme Court to agree to reconsider *Hardison*. Although the majority declined to follow the Solicitor's urging and denied review, his position did garner the support of three justices.[34]

[D] Recurring Accommodation Situations

[1] Religious Holidays and Work Schedules

Although *Hardison* resolved many of the issues posed by Sabbatarians and others whose beliefs prevent them from working on certain days, cases continue to arise and tend to be very fact specific. Many of the possible or suggested accommodations have been found to fail to satisfy the *de minimus* cost, inconvenience, or unequal treatment test of *Hardison*. Occasionally, however, a court will find that simply allowing an employee to decline Saturday work causes no one any hardship, especially if someone is available as a replacement.[35] Moreover, some courts have held that an employer not only must allow voluntary shift swaps,[36] but the employer also may also be required to facilitate these trades or even arrange them if the employee has scruples against asking another to work on the Sabbath.[37] Likewise, employers have been required to achieve a reasonable accommodation by transferring the employee, even

31. Hardison, 432 U.S. at 77.

32. 135 S. Ct. at 2034.

33. 139 S. Ct. 634, 637 (2019).

34. Concurring opinion denying review in Patterson v. Walgreen Co., 140 S. Ct. 685 (2020).

35. EEOC v. Ilona of Hungary, 108 F.3d 1569 (7th Cir. 1997); Brown v. General Motors Corp., 601 F.2d 956 (8th Cir. 1979).

36. Opuku-Boateng v. California, 95 F.3d 1461 (9th Cir. 1996).

37. Beadle v. Hillsborough County Sheriff's Dep't, 29 F.3d 589 (11th Cir. 1994) (illustrating the various things an employer can do in this regard); Smith v. Pyro Mining Co., 827 F.2d 1081 (6th Cir. 1987).

if it is a demotion.[38] Unpaid leave to attend religious conventions and meetings also may be a necessary reasonable accommodation under some circumstances.[39]

[2] Dress and Grooming Codes

In *Bhatia v. Chevron USA, Inc.*,[40] the employer was not required to accommodate an employee whose religious beliefs forbade the cutting or shaving of body hair—not, at least, by allowing that employee to remain in a job that required wearing a respirator. The employee had been offered four jobs that did not require wearing a respirator and had been promised that he would be returned to his original job if a respirator was developed that could be worn safely with the beard. In another case, a woman who objected to wearing pants for religious reasons was also found to be entitled to an accommodation.[41] Whether an employer must accommodate an employee's desire to wear religious medallions and garb is uncertain.[42]

[3] Union Membership

Employees who, for religious reasons, object to membership in or even compulsory financial support of labor unions have received a considerable amount of attention in the law. In *Janus v. AFSCME*,[43] the Court freed all public employees from being compelled to support a labor union, including but not limited to those objecting for religious reasons. For religious objectors working in the private sector and claiming their rights under Title VII, the courts generally have accepted the *charitable contribution* alternative as a reasonable accommodation.[44] This has not always satisfied either the union or the religious objector.[45] After *Janus*, the future of this accommodation is unclear. *Janus* rejected the "free-rider" theory as an adequate support for compulsory union fees. The theory behind the compelled charity substitute accommodation is also the "free-rider" argument. Whether total exemption for religious objectors is appropriate after *Janus* is presently unresolved. The LMRA contains an

---

38. Mathewson v. Florida Game & Fresh Water Fish Comm'n, 693 F. Supp. 1044 (M.D. Fla. 1988).

39. EEOC v. Universal Mfg. Corp., 914 F.2d 71 (5th Cir. 1990).

40. 734 F.2d 1382 (9th Cir. 1984).

41. Reid v. Kraft Gen. Foods, Inc., 67 Fair Empl. Prac. Cas. (BNA) 1367 (E.D. Pa. 1995) (employer required to provide employee with a dress as a pants-uniform substitute).

42. *Compare* EEOC v. Reads, 759 F. Supp. 1150 (E.D. Pa. 1991) (despite state law prohibiting public school employees from wearing "religious garb," employer required to accommodate employee whose attire, worn for religious reasons, was not facially religious and would not be perceived as religious by many children), *with* United States v. Board of Educ. for the Sch. Dist. of Phila., 911 F.2d 882 (3d Cir. 1990) (undue hardship to require school board to allow substitute teacher to wear traditional Muslim garb).

43. 138 S. Ct. 2448 (2018). The National Right to Work Legal Defense and Education Foundation funded Janus.

44. Tooley v. Martin-Marietta Corp., 648 F.2d 1239 (9th Cir. 1981).

45. Yott v. North American Rockwell Corp., 602 F.2d 904 (9th Cir. 1979) (rejecting employee's demand for a total exemption from the union-security requirement or transfer to another position that would have required extensive retraining); Burns v. Southern Pac. Transp. Co., 589 F.2d 403 (9th Cir. 1978) (rejecting the union's objection and holding that the union's administrative burdens and loss of income would be de minimis).

odd and unconstitutional provision to address religious objections to paying union fees. It requires a union and employer who have a compulsory union fee agreement to allow employees who are members of "bona fide" religions that have "historically held conscientious objections" to union membership to make a nonreligious charitable contribution in lieu of paying union dues.[46] That narrow definition of qualifying religious objectors eliminates coverage for most objectors and discriminates among religions. For that reason, it was held to be unconstitutional.[47]

[4] Mandatory Devotional Services

Employers who require employees to participate in certain religious practices or observances as a condition of employment will generally be required to accommodate employees who object. For example, in *EEOC v. Townley Engineering & Mfg. Co.*,[48] the employer required its employees to attend mandatory devotional services in the workplace. When an employee, who was an atheist, objected to the requirement and asked to be excused, his request was denied. The court required the employer to accommodate the employee's beliefs by excusing him from further attendance.

[5] Mandatory Diversity Statements

Employers who require employees to sign diversity statements or participate in diversity goals have met with mixed results when dealing with employees who have religious objections to supporting homosexuality. In one case, the employer was required to accommodate an employee who refused to sign a diversity agreement,[49] while in another case, the employer was not required to accommodate an employee's request to post his own religious views in response to the employer posting a homosexual diversity banner by his workstation.[50]

[6] Miscellaneous

The list of workplace requirements, prohibitions, or environments that an employee might object to on religious grounds, and for which an employer must consider some accommodation, is virtually endless. The following list is only illustrative: prohibiting the off-the-job use of peyote,[51] prohibiting reading the Bible while on the job,[52] allowing the display of nude women by co-employees,[53] selling sexually oriented mag-

---

46. 29 U.S.C. § 169.

47. Wilson v. NLRB, 920 F.2d 1282 (6th Cir. 1990) (holding this section of the LMRA unconstitutional on the ground that, unlike Title VII, it differentiates among religions). One of the authors, Prof. Cameron, was counsel of record in *Wilson*.

48. 859 F.2d 610 (9th Cir. 1988).

49. Buonanno v. AT&T Broadband, 313 F. Supp. 2d 1069 (D. Colo. 2004).

50. Peterson v. Hewlett-Packard Co., 358 F.3d 599 (9th Cir. 2004).

51. Toledo v. Nobel-Sysco, Inc., 892 F.2d 1481 (10th Cir. 1989).

52. Gillard v. Sears, Roebuck & Co., 32 Fair Empl. Prac. Cas. (BNA) 1274 (E.D. Pa. 1983).

53. Lambert v. Condor Mfg., Inc., 768 F. Supp. 600 (E.D. Mich. 1991).

azines,[54] having on-call medical emergency technicians sleeping in the same room,[55] requiring the employee to distribute draft registration materials,[56] requiring the employee to live within a specific area (which did not contain a synagogue or active Jewish community),[57] prohibiting the wearing of a graphic anti-abortion button,[58] prohibiting workplace prayers,[59] assigning a guard to an abortion clinics,[60] and requiring a pharmacist to sell birth control pills.[61]

§ 11.05 Religious Harassment

Religious harassment often takes the same forms as harassment on the basis of race, national origin, and sex—consisting of disparaging remarks, ridicule, and epithets.[62] As with the other forms of harassment, it must either be of the quid pro quo nature or be sufficiently pervasive and severe to alter the conditions of employment before it rises to the level of a Title VII violation.

Religious harassment, however, also has a unique dimension. What is unwelcome, annoying, distracting, and offensive to one employee may be, from the other employee's perspective, simply the discharge of a religious duty to proselytize. The employer, thus, is caught on the horns of a dilemma. Not restraining the *workplace preacher* may subject the employer to a harassment claim by other employees, while prohibiting the conduct without attempting any form of accommodation may also constitute illegal religious discrimination. The case law provides no bright line test for determining the proper course of conduct. It seems to be a very fact-specific question, and the decisions go both ways. For example, in *Chalmers v. Tulon Co.*,[63] the company terminated an evangelical Christian supervisor who sent letters to co-workers telling them to "get their lives right with God," and explaining the impact of a "God of Love and a God of Wrath" if they did not repent of their sins. The court upheld the termination.[64] On the other hand, in *Tucker v. California Department*

---

54. Stanley v. The Lawson Co., 993 F. Supp. 1084 (N.D. Ohio 1997).

55. Miller v. Drennon, 56 Fair Empl. Prac. Cas. (BNA) 274 (D.S.C. 1991), aff'd mem., 966 F.2d 1443 (4th Cir. 1992).

56. McGinnis v. United States Postal Serv., 512 F. Supp. 517 (N.D. Cal. 1980).

57. Vetter v. Farmland Indus., Inc. 901 F. Supp. 1446 (N.D. Iowa 1995).

58. Wilson v. U.S. West Communications, 58 F.3d 1337 (8th Cir. 1995).

59. Brown v. Polk County, 61 F.3d 650 (8th Cir. 1995).

60. Rodriguez v. City of Chicago, 156 F.3d 771 (7th Cir. 1998).

61. Noesen v. Medical Staffing Network, 232 Fed. Appx. 581 (7th Cir. 2007).

62. Goldberg v. City of Phila., No. Civ. A. 91-7575, 1994 WL 313030 (E.D. Pa. June 29, 1994) (comments consisted of "fucking jew, "the bagel," and "[y]our people killed our lord"). *But see* Kantar v. Baldwin Cooke Co., 69 Fair Empl. Prac. Cas. (BNA) 851 (N.D. Ill. 1995) (supervisor repeatedly referred to plaintiff as a "JAP" (Jewish American Princess), needled her about leaving early on Friday for religious services, and inquired about the cost or price of her religious faith; found not to be sufficiently frequent or pervasive).

63. 101 F.3d 1012 (4th Cir. 1996).

64. Venters v. City of Delphi, 123 F.3d 956 (7th Cir. 1997) (violation found when a police chief imposed his religious views on subordinates in a clearly unwelcome manner).

of Education,[65] an employee wrote "SOTLJC" on his work product and written correspondence, which is an acronym standing for "Servant of the Lord Jesus Christ." Although no co-employees complained about the practice, the employer responded by ordering him to stop using the acronym, initiating religious discussions in the workplace, or displaying any religious symbols, posters, books, or pamphlets in the work area. The court found that the employer's actions were overbroad.[66]

§ 11.06 Religious Employers[67]

[A] Introduction

This chapter examines the religious rights of employees against their employer. What about the reverse situation—religious institutions or employers who have religious beliefs? What are their rights, and are they important? Employer rights in this context raise First Amendment and other potential constitutional rights because it is the government imposing the prohibition on discrimination. Religious beliefs are a guide to what is right and what is wrong, and thus they inherently discriminate. The result is a natural tension between the discrimination required by religious beliefs and the anti-discrimination provisions of Title VII. For example, you would expect that a Baptist seminary would discriminate in favor of Baptists. Title VII, on the other hand, prohibits discrimination between religions and religious views.

Religious freedom, not mere toleration, is a core principle of the First Amendment.[68] By including the religion clauses, "the government of the United States [became] interdicted by the Constitution from intermeddling with religious institutions, their doctrines, discipline, or exercises."[69] As a result, federal courts have generally refused to exercise jurisdiction over the internal affairs of religious organizations. In *Watson v. Jones*, the Supreme Court recognized that civil courts lack jurisdiction over

---

65. 97 F.2d 1204 (9th Cir. 1996).

66. Brown v. Polk Cty., Iowa, 61 F.3d 650 (8th Cir. 1995) (county violated Title VII when it terminated an employee for engaging in group prayer and proselytizing at work).

67. Alexandra L. Overcash, a Regent University law student, provided critical research and writing for this section.

68. The debate of the First Congress resulted in the official adoption of the First Amendment religion clauses; however, the roots of the religion clauses stem from the discussion surrounding the Virginia Bill for Religious Liberty. During that debate, James Madison fought to create the most robust foundation for religious liberty in the United States. He refused to let it appear that the government was the source of religious freedom and defended that it is an unalienable right from the Creator. *See* Heritage Foundation, (Mar. 16, 2001), https://www.heritage.org/political-process/report/james-madison-and-religious-liberty (discussing James Madison's lifelong zeal for religious liberty and his role in drafting the First Amendment); James Madison, *A Memorial and Remonstrance* (circa June 20, 1785), *reprinted in* 8 The Papers of James Madison 298 (R. Rutland & W. Rachal eds. 1973) (illustrating Madison's view on religious liberty).

69. Letter from Thomas Jefferson to Rev. Samuel Miller (Jan. 23, 1808), reprinted in 9 The Writings of Thomas Jefferson 174 (P. Ford. ed. 1898).

purely religious matters governed by an ecclesiastical body.[70] Instead, the Court should accept the decisions of religious tribunals as final.[71] That principle was extended in 1952 when the Court refused to intermeddle with the practice of appointing religious leaders.[72] The Court recognized that religious organizations have independence from "secular control and manipulation" and have the freedom to determine matters of church government, faith, and doctrine.[73] From this line of thinking a number of judicial doctrines and statutory exemptions have arisen.

[B] Statutory Exemptions

[1] Section 702

Section 702[74] of Title VII exempts all "religious" corporations, associations, educational institutions, and societies from the prohibition against religious discrimination. Originally, the exemption was limited to work involving the "religious activities" of the group, but the modifier was eliminated by Congress in 1972. In *Corporation of the Presiding Bishop of the Church of Jesus Christ of Latter-Day Saints v. Amos*,[75] the Supreme Court thus recognized that the exemption applied to a non-profit recreational facility run by the Mormon Church. Although the statute is worded in terms of discrimination "with respect to the employment of individuals of a particular religion," the courts have held that this refers to faithful practice within a particular religious denomination as well as intra-denominational distinctions.[76] Thus, in *Boyd v. Harding Academy of Memphis, Inc.*,[77] a religious school was allowed to terminate an unmarried teacher who became pregnant in violation of the school's code of conduct.

[2] Section 703

Section 703(e)(2)[78] also specifically permits religious discrimination by schools, colleges, universities, and other educational institutions that are operated by a particular religion or if the curriculum is directed toward the propagation of a particular religion. Originally, this was broader than the Section 702 exemption since it was not limited to the "religious activities" of the school. The later deletion of that limitation from Section 702 arguably renders Section 703(e)(2) superfluous.

Regardless of whether a school is seeking an exemption under Section 702 or Section 703, the school nevertheless must establish that it was created to serve a "religious

70. 80 U.S. 679, 727 (1871).

71. 80 U.S. at 727.

72. Kedroff v. St. Nicholas Cathedral, 344 U.S. 94, 119 (1952). The Court reaffirmed the principles of *Watson* and *Kedroff* in 1976. Serbian E. Orthodox Diocese v. Milivojevich, 426 U.S. 696, 714 (1976).

73. *Kedroff*, 344 U.S. at 116.

74. 42 U.S.C. §2000e-1.

75. 483 U.S. 327 (1987).

76. Little v. Wuerl, 929 F.2d 944 (3d Cir. 1991) (teacher who was terminated when she remarried without annulling her first marriage).

77. 88 F.3d 410 (6th Cir. 1996).

78. 42 U.S.C. §2000e-2.

purpose." Although the president of Loyola University of Chicago was a Jesuit priest, as were more than a third of the trustees and many university administrators, the court held that the school did not qualify for the exemption.[79] This was mainly because the Society of Jesus itself did not direct or control the Jesuits within the organization with respect to academic matters. On the other hand, when Samford University claimed that its purpose was to encourage Christianity with a Baptist emphasis, the court said that it "must indulge the presumption ... in favor of what an institution says about itself when it claims status as a religious institution."[80] More recently, the U.S. Court of Appeals for the D.C. Circuit ruled that the idea that the courts can competently judge the religious nature of an institution raises serious constitutional issues. The very process of discriminating based on the institution's approach to indoctrinating religion may violate the Establishment Clause prohibition on preferring some religions over others.[81]

[3] Religion as a BFOQ

In most situations where an employee's religious affiliation or beliefs would be relevant to the job, the employer is also religiously affiliated and thus subject to one of the statutory exceptions. However, even in some secular businesses, religion can be a BFOQ. For example, being a Jesuit was found to be a BFOQ for a teaching position in the philosophy department of a university desiring to maintain a "Jesuit presence."[82] Being of the Islamic faith was found to be a BFOQ for the job of flying over a holy area from which non-Muslims were excluded, upon pain of death.[83] On the other hand, another court held that the risk of danger to a Jewish doctor and his family on being sent to a hospital in Saudi Arabia did not make being non-Jewish a BFOQ.[84] Similarly, although the announcement was for a vacancy in the position of "Protestant chaplain," the court held that being a Protestant was not actually a BFOQ because the responsibilities of the chaplain in a jail were not denominationally related.[85]

[C] Constitutional Protections

[1] Introduction

The Constitution provides protections for religious employers and institutions under both the Free Exercise and Establishment Clauses of the First Amendment.

79. Pime v. Loyola Univ. of Chicago, 585 F. Supp. 435 (N.D. Ill. 1984).

80. Killinger v. Samford Univ., 917 F. Supp. 773, 777 (N.D. Ala. 1996), aff'd, 113 F.3d 196 (11th Cir. 1997).

81. Univ. of Great Falls v. NLRB, 278 F.3d 1335, 1346 (D.C. Cir. 2002).

82. Pime v. Loyola Univ. of Chicago, 585 F. Supp. 435 (N.D. Ill. 1984), aff'd, 803 F.2d 351 (7th Cir. 1986).

83. Kern v. Dynalectron Corp., 577 F. Supp. 1196 (N.D. Tex. 1983), aff'd mem., 746 F.2d 810 (5th Cir. 1984).

84. Abrams v. Baylor Coll. of Med., 805 F.2d 528 (5th Cir. 1986).

85. Rasul v. District of Columbia, 680 F. Supp. 436 (D.D.C. 1988).

The Supreme Court's controversial 1990 decision in *Employment Division, Department of Human Resources v. Smith*[86] has been a problem for both employers and employees who sought to rely on the Free Exercise Clause to protect their beliefs. *Smith* essentially held that any statute that is facially neutral and of general application is not subject to an implied exception merely because it infringes upon the religious practices of some individual. Title VII's prohibition against sex, race, and religious discrimination satisfies that requirement. Congress repudiated the *Smith* decision and restored the *compelling state interest* test of *Sherbert v. Verner* through the Religious Freedom Restoration Act of 1993.[87] In *City of Boerne v. Flores*,[88] the Supreme Court declared the Act unconstitutional to the extent that it extended Free Exercise rights against the states beyond what the Supreme Court itself had declared them to be.

The future of *Smith* is unclear. In *Hosanna-Tabor Evangelical Lutheran Church and School v. EEOC*, 565 U.S. 171 (2012), the Court upheld a church's First Amendment defenses against the ADEA, a statute that is facially neutral and of general application. More recently, in the denial of review in *Kennedy v. Bremerton Sch. Dist.*, 139 S. Ct. 634, 637 (2019), four justices wrote that the petition in that case had not asked them to revisit *Smith*. That signaled that these justices were looking for a case in which to reconsider *Smith*. Just as this book was going to publication, the Supreme Court granted review in *Fulton v. Philadelphia*,[89] which specifically raises the issue of whether *Smith* should be revisited.

[2] The Ministerial Exemption

Although Title VII's two statutory exemptions extend only to discrimination by religious organizations on the basis of religion, the Supreme Court has broadly recognized a constitutional exemption from civil rights claims when the discrimination is on some other proscribed basis against an employee who qualifies as a minister. In *Hosanna-Tabor Evangelical Lutheran Church and School v. EEOC*,[90] Cheryl Perich, a "called" teacher, was determined to be a minister, and therefore the church school was not required to accommodate her disability. The Court determined that both the Free Exercise and Establishment Clauses provide a church with complete authority to be free from state interference regarding its choices of those who propagate its message. Justices Thomas, Alito, and Kagan wrote separately in support of a definition of "minister" that was even broader than that embraced by the majority. In another case, the director of the choir was held to be within the ministerial exception.[91] Likewise, a *mashgiach*, the person who ensures that a Jewish organization's food is prepared

86. 494 U.S. 872 (1990).
87. 42 U.S.C. §§ 2000bb-1 through -4.
88. 521 U.S. 507 (1997).
89. 140 S. Ct. 1104 (2020).
90. 565 U.S. 171 (2012).
91. EEOC v. Roman Catholic Diocese of Raleigh and Sacred Heart Cathedral, 213 F.3d 795, 802 (4th Cir. 2000) ("[a]t the heart of this case is the undeniable fact that music is a vital means of expressing and celebrating those beliefs which a religious community holds most sacred").

in compliance with Jewish dietary law, is subject to the exception.[92] The ministerial exception applies to all Title VII claims.

The unanimity of the *Hosanna-Tabor* decision guarantees all religious institutions protection under the ministerial exception against Title VII claims. However, the lack of consensus in the Court's opinion over who qualifies as a minister has resulted in inconsistency among the circuits. Since the *Hosanna-Tabor* decision in 2012, almost 300 decisions have cited it.[93]

Of these many decisions, the opinions from the Seventh and Ninth Circuits are of particular importance in determining who qualifies as a ministerial employee. The Seventh and Ninth Circuits have taken distinct approaches on how to determine who qualifies as a ministerial employee under the *Hosanna-Tabor* precedent.

The leading Seventh Circuit case post-*Hosanna-Tabor* is *Grussgott v. Milwaukee Jewish Day School, Inc.*[94] In *Grussgott*, Miriam Grussgott sued a private Jewish school devoted to providing non-Orthodox Jewish education to Milwaukee schoolchildren, claiming her termination violated the Americans with Disabilities Act.[95] Miriam Grussgott was a Hebrew and Jewish studies teacher to first and second graders.[96] She had extensive background teaching both subjects, which was relevant to the school's decision to hire her.[97] She taught Hebrew from an integrated Hebrew and Jewish Studies curriculum, attended community prayer sessions, discussed Jewish values with the students, and taught about prayers and Torah portions.[98] Grussgott argued that she voluntarily discussed Jewish values and taught about prayers and the Torah. In contrast, the school maintained that she was employed specifically as a Hebrew and Jewish studies teacher.[99]

On the issue of whether Grussgott qualified as a ministerial employee, the Seventh Circuit applied a fact-intensive analysis.[100] The court borrowed from *Hosanna-Tabor* and addressed four factors: (1) the formal title given by the church; (2) the substance reflected in that title; (3) the teacher's own use of that title; and (4) the important religious functions she performed for the church.[101] In analyzing the four factors, the court found that, at most, two factors weighed in favor of applying the ministerial exception.[102] Even so, the court agreed that the same four considerations need not

---

92. Shaliehsabou v. Hebrew Home of Greater Washington, Inc., 363 F.3d 299 (4th Cir. 2004) (an FLSA case, but one that follows Title VII law).
93. As of November 24, 2019.
94. 882 F.3d 655 (7th Cir. 2018).
95. *Grussgott*, 882 F.3d at 656.
96. *Grussgott*, 882 F.3d at 656.
97. *Grussgott*, 882 F.3d at 656.
98. *Grussgott*, 882 F.3d at 656.
99. *Grussgott*, 882 F.3d at 657.
100. *Grussgott*, 882 F.3d at 657.
101. *Grussgott*, 882 F.3d at 658
102. *Grussgott*, 882 F.3d at 659–60.

be present in every case involving the exception.[103] The court refused to adopt a purely functional approach based on the four factors because it read the Supreme Court's decision to impose, in essence, a totality of the circumstances test.[104] Though only two *Hosanna-Tabor* factors weighed in favor of applying the exception, the court was sufficiently satisfied that under the totality of the circumstances, the importance of Grussgott's role as a teacher of the faith to the next generation outweighed other considerations.[105] The court emphasized that in situations such as this one, it defers to the organization to determine whether something constitutes religious activity.[106]

The Ninth Circuit addressed the ministerial exception post-*Hosanna-Tabor* in *Biel v. St. James School.*[107] Kristin Biel, a fifth-grade teacher at St. James Catholic School, was terminated after telling her employer that she had breast cancer and would need to miss work to undergo chemotherapy.[108] Though Biel taught fifth-graders all academic subjects, she was required to educate and test the students in her religion class about Catholicism. St. James expected Biel to incorporate Catholic teachings into her secular courses.[109] Biel also joined her students in twice-daily prayers led by students and attended a school-wide monthly Mass.[110] Despite her religious duties, Biel's formal title was "Grade 5 Teacher."[111]

Though recognizing that religious organizations enjoy a broad right to select their leaders, the court held that the ministerial exception did not apply in this situation.[112] The court traced the four considerations that the Supreme Court used in *Hosanna-Tabor* and explained that Biel's situation did not present the same significant factors.[113] Finding that only one of the four factors of *Hosanna-Tabor* was present—that Biel taught religion in the classroom—the court refused to apply the ministerial exception.[114]

The dissenting opinion by Judge Fisher found that the ministerial exception should have been applied based on case-specific facts.[115] The dissent emphasized the fear that the majority's opinion undermines the relationship between a church and its ministers[116] and "misses the point of the ministerial exception to shield the religious

---

103. *Grussgott*, 882 F.3d at 659–60; Brief for the Becket Fund for Religious Liberty as Amici Curiae Supporting Defendant-Appellee, Grussgott v. Milwaukee Jewish Day Sch., Inc., 882 F.3d 655 (7th Cir. 2018) (No. 17-2332).

104. *Grussgott*, 882 F.3d at 661.

105. *Grussgott*, 882 F.3d at 661.

106. *Grussgott*, 882 F.3d at 660.

107. Biel v. St. James Sch., 911 F.3d 603 (9th Cir. 2018).

108. *Biel*, 911 F.3d at 605.

109. *Biel*, 911 F.3d at 605.

110. *Biel*, 911 F.3d at 605.

111. *Biel*, 911 F.3d at 608.

112. *Biel*, 911 F.3d at 611.

113. *Biel*, 911 F.3d at 609–11.

114. *Biel*, 911 F.3d at 609–11.

115. *Biel*, 911 F.3d at 621 (Fisher, J., dissenting).

116. *Biel*, 911 F.3d at 621.

organization from the eyes of the court without requiring the church to provide a religious justification for an adverse employment decision."[117] A rehearing en banc was denied, but nine judges dissented.[118] The dissent argued that the majority opinion embraces the narrowest construction of the First Amendment's ministerial exception and splits from the consensus of sister circuits that the employee's ministerial function should be the critical focus.[119]

In 2020, the Supreme Court granted review in *Biel*, consolidated it with another Ninth Circuit decision, *Our Lady of Guadalupe School v. Agnes Morrissey-Berru*, and reversed the Ninth Circuit. Rejecting the Ninth Circuit's "rigid test" using a checklist of factors, the Court concluded that the exception should include "any 'employee' who leads a religious organization, conducts worship services or important religious ceremonies or rituals, or serves as a messenger or teacher of its faith." *Our Lady of Guadalupe Sch. v. Morrissey-Berru.*[120]

[D] Statutory Protections for Secular Employers

[1] Religious Freedom Restoration Act

In *Burwell v. Hobby Lobby Stores,*[121] the Supreme Court protected the religious beliefs of owners of a closely held for-profit corporation under the Religious Freedom Restoration Act of 1993. Rejecting the claim that the corporation's for-profit status forfeited protection for the owners' religious beliefs, the court applied the compelling state interest, least restrictive means test to a federal statute requiring corporations to provide employee health insurance. As a result of that application, the corporation was freed from having to provide employee health insurance for those forms of contraceptives that the owners considered to be abortifacients.

[2] Title VII

In *EEOC v. Townley Engineering & Manufacturing Co.,*[122] the employer terminated an employee who refused to attend the employer's mandatory work time, religiously oriented devotional services. The court rejected the employer's Free Exercise claim on the ground that requiring the employer "to travel the extra mile in adjusting its free exercise rights, if any, to accommodate the employee's Title VII rights ... is consistent with the First Amendment's goal of ensuring religious freedom in a society with many different religions and religious groups."[123] The court attempted to defend this balancing of the employer's *constitutional* right to be free of governmental in-

---

117. *Biel*, 911 F.3d at 621.
118. Biel v. St. James, Sch., 926 F.3d 1238, 1240 (9th Cir. 2019).
119. 911 F.3d at 1239.
120. 2020 U.S. LEXIS 3547 (U.S. July 8, 2020).
121. 573 U.S. 682 (2014).
122. 859 F.2d 610 (9th Cir. 1988).
123. Townley *Eng'g*, 859 F.2d at 621.

terference against the employee's *statutory* right to be accommodated, which it admitted "alters the normal relationship between a statutory right and a constitutional one," by reference to what it termed the "overriding governmental interest" in eradicating religious discrimination.[124]

[E] Testing the Exemptions

The religious discrimination protections of Title VII for both employers and employees have been challenged on both Free Exercise and Establishment grounds under the First Amendment. *Establishment Clause* questions will always arise whenever a religious organization or individual is granted an exemption from a statute that is otherwise of general application. In the last 30 years, most Establishment Clause disputes have been resolved under the test originally articulated in *Lemon v. Kurtzman*,[125] which involved aid to religious schools. The test has three prongs:

> First, the statute must have a secular legislative purpose; second, its principal or primary effect must be one that neither advances nor inhibits religion; finally, the statute must not foster "an excessive government entanglement with religion."[126]

The Supreme Court applied that test to Title VII's Section 702 exemption in *Corporation of the Presiding Bishop of the Church of Jesus Christ of Latter-Day Saints v. Amos*.[127] With respect to the first prong of the test, the Court held that "[i]t is a permissible legislative purpose to alleviate significant governmental interference with the ability of religious organizations to define and carry out their religious missions."[128] To fall afoul of the second prong, the Court noted that "it must be fair to say that the government itself has advanced religion through its own activities and influence."[129] The Court found that lacking. The non-entanglement of church and state requirement was also clearly satisfied. Indeed, "the statute effectuates a more complete separation of the two and avoids the kind of intrusive inquiry into religious belief that the District Court engaged in this case."[130]

Although the *Lemon* test seems to be on the wane and may eventually be replaced with Justice O'Connor's simplified *endorsement* test[131] or Justice Scalia's even more tolerant *traditions* test,[132] the constitutionality of the two Title VII religious exemptions has not been revisited.

---

124. Townley *Eng'g*, 859 F.2d at 621.
125. 403 U.S. 602 (1971).
126. Lemon, 403 U.S. at 612–13 (quoting Walz v. Tax Comm'n, 397 U.S. 664, 674 (1970)).
127. 483 U.S. 327 (1987).
128. Amos, 483 U.S. at 335.
129. Amos, 483 U.S. at 337 (emphasis added).
130. Amos, 483 U.S. at 339.
131. Lynch v. Donnelly, 465 U.S. 668, 681 (1984) (O'Connor, J., concurring).
132. Bd. of Educ. of Kiryas Joel Village Sch. Dist. v. Grumet, 512 U.S. 687, 744 (1994) (Scalia, J., dissenting).

[1] The Accommodation Duty

In *Estate of Thornton v. Caldor, Inc.*,[133] the Supreme Court held that a statute requiring employers to provide employees with an absolute and unqualified right not to work on their chosen Sabbath had the primary effect of promoting a particular religious practice and thus violated the Establishment Clause of the Constitution. In Justice O'Connor's concurring opinion, she distinguished that statute from the Title VII's duty of "reasonable rather than absolute accommodation" and also noted that it applies impartially to all religious beliefs and practices rather than just singling out one for special protection.[134] Moreover, many believe that the Supreme Court was motivated by constitutional concerns when it construed the duty of accommodation so narrowly in *Hardison*. Although the lower courts have not been particularly faithful to the *Hardison* limitations, even in the face of slightly more expansive accommodation obligations, they have nevertheless generally upheld the duty against constitutional attack.[135]

§ 11.07 Chapter Highlights

1. Religion is broadly defined to include not only the commonly recognized religions and faiths, but also individual moral and ethical beliefs that are their equivalent in the minds of those who profess them. Although political and social views do not qualify, it is not clear where the line is crossed. (§ 11.01)

2. Disparate treatment religious discrimination can, like other forms of discrimination, be proved with direct or indirect (inferential) evidence. (§ 11.02)

3. Until 1991, it was generally thought that religious discrimination could not be established through a disparate impact model of analysis. The codified version of disparate impact in the Civil Rights Act of 1991 specifically includes religion. Following the Supreme Court's decision in *Abercrombie & Fitch*, all Title VII religion claims must be pled as disparate treatment. (§ 11.03)

4. Once an employer suspects that an employee needs a religious accommodation, the employer is required to propose a reasonable accommodation. While Title VII requires favored and not merely equal treatment for employees needing an accommodation, the employer is not required to accept the employee's preferred accommodation or show that the employee's favored accommodation would itself cause an undue hardship. (§ 11.04[B])

5. If, however, the employer does not propose a reasonable accommodation, then the employer will be required to adopt one suggested by the employee unless the employer can demonstrate undue hardship. Anything more than a de minimus cost or lost efficiency will qualify, as will violation of the seniority provisions of a collective

133. 472 U.S. 703 (1985).

134. Caldor, 472 U.S. at 712 (O'Connor, J., concurring).

135. EEOC v. Ithaca Indus., Inc., 849 F.2d 116 (4th Cir. 1988) (en banc).

bargaining agreement. A recent Supreme Court decision stating that accommodation "does not demand mere neutrality," but, rather, requires "favored treatment" casts a shadow over prior precedent limiting accommodation requirements. (§ 11.04[C])

6. The most common situations in which an accommodation demand may arise include mandatory work on days of worship and religious holidays, dress and grooming codes, diversity statements, mandatory union fee support, and mandatory attendance at religious or devotional services. (§ 11.04[D])

7. As with sex and race, harassment on the basis of religion is a Title VII violation. On the other hand, what is for one employee a religious practice that the employer must accommodate or allow may be for another employee unwelcome harassment on a religious basis. (§ 11.05)

8. Religious employers and secular employers with religious beliefs can claim protection under a series of statutes and the First Amendment. These exemptions have generally been upheld against constitutional challenge. The most powerful of these exemptions is the ministerial exemption. It provides religious employers with a complete shield against discrimination claims by those determined to be ministers of their faith. (§ 11.06)

Chapter 12

Retaliation

Synopsis

Section 704(a) makes it illegal for an employer "to discriminate against any of his applicants or employees ... because [that person] has opposed a practice made an unlawful employment practice by this [Act], or because he has made a charge, testified, assisted, or participated in any manner in an investigation, proceeding, or hearing under this [Act]." The two clauses of Section 704(a) are known as the *opposition clause* and the *participation clause.*

In recent years, retaliation has become a very popular Title VII cause of action. Employees who engage in these protected activities create an almost inherently antagonist relationship with their employer. The employee will naturally tend to construe any subsequent adverse employment action as being retaliatory. And sometimes it is easy for lower level supervisors to react negatively when confronted with what they regard as a meritless claim of discrimination. Indeed, it is not uncommon for the substantive discrimination claim to be dismissed on a motion for summary judgment, but the employer nevertheless found liable for retaliation.

§ 12.01 Coverage

Unlike the prohibition against substantive discrimination against "any individual," which includes former employees in appropriate cases,[1] the prohibition against employer retaliation literally extends only to "employees or applicants for employment." The courts were initially divided over whether the prohibition against employer retaliation extended to former employees.

The Supreme Court resolved the issue in *Robinson v. Shell Oil Co.*,[2] at least in part. After being terminated, Robinson filed an EEOC charge. Subsequently, the company gave him a negative reference, allegedly in retaliation for filing the charge. The Court indicated that "a primary purpose of anti-retaliation provisions ... [is] maintaining unfettered access to statutory remedial mechanisms."[3] From this, the Court concluded that "it would be destructive of this purpose of the anti-retaliation provision for an employer to be able to retaliate with impunity against an entire class of acts under Title VII—for example, complaints regarding discriminatory termination."[4] What *Robinson* does not specifically resolve is whether the protection also extends to post-termination *opposition* activities. These do not directly implicate the policy of securing "unfettered access" to the EEOC or the courts, which the Court in *Robinson* deemed so important. Moreover, *opposition* activities generally receive less protection than *participation* activities.

§ 12.02 The Nature of the Prohibited Retaliatory Conduct

The *Robinson* decision also left open the question of whether the employer's retaliatory acts must somehow be employment related—a limitation imposed on post-termination retaliation by some courts.[5] The Supreme Court addressed this issue—and the issue of how harmful the retaliatory action must be before it becomes actionable—in *Burlington Northern & Santa Fe Ry. Co. v. White*.[6]

With respect to the employment-relation issue, the Court noted that the language of the substantive prohibition in Title VII refers expressly to employment-related harms: "to fail or refuse to hire or to discharge, or otherwise [disadvantage an individual] with respect to his compensation, terms, conditions, or privileges of employ-

---

1. Hackett v. McGuire Bros., Inc., 445 F.2d 442 (3d Cir. 1971) (pensioners covered).
2. 519 U.S. 337 (1997).
3. *Robinson*, 519 U.S. 337 at 346.
4. *Robinson*, 519 U.S. 337 at 346.
5. Nelson v. Upsala Coll., 51 F.3d 383 (3d Cir. 1995) (prohibiting former employee from entering campus without permission not a form of actionable retaliation because the action "had no impact on any employment relationship Nelson had, or might have had in the future"). *Contra* Veprinsky v. Fluor Daniel, Inc., 87 F.3d 881 (7th Cir. 1996) (post-termination assaults and threats may be an actionable form of retaliation).
6. 548 U.S. 53, 62 (2006).

ment,...." In contrast, the retaliation provision contains no similar terms of limitation with respect to retaliatory discrimination. The Court noted that under the rules of statutory interpretation, courts "normally presume that, where words differ as they differ here, 'Congress acts intentionally and purposely in the disparate inclusion or exclusion.'"[7] The Court also noted that while the objective of the substantive prohibition is to ensure a *workplace* that is free of discrimination, an objective that is satisfied by an employment-related limitation on the prohibited employer conduct, the objective of the anti-retaliation provision is to promote the achievement of such a workplace, an objective that requires a prohibition against any kind of conduct—employment related or not—that would deter an employee from opposing violations of the act or participating in enforcement proceedings.[8]

The *adverse employment action* requirement, which is now recognized as being a threshold issue in every type of Title VII case, had its origin in the retaliation cases. In both the retaliation and substantive discrimination cases the lower courts took a wide range of approaches to the question of how *adverse* the employer's action must be before it becomes actionable. One of those approaches, adopted in several circuits, was the so-called *ultimate employment decision* test, which encompasses only final and definite conduct such as hiring, granting leave, discharging, promoting, and compensating. Falling outside the scope of that test were reprimands, warning notices, and a host of other employer actions that a reasonable employee would find *adverse* in the conventional sense.[9] Other courts construed the requirement more broadly.[10]

With respect to substantive discrimination, the Supreme Court's various broader definitions of an *adverse employment action* implicitly rejected the *ultimate employment decision* test. In *Burlington*, the Court rejected it expressly.[11] The test the Court adopted, rather, was this: "a plaintiff must show that a reasonable employee would have found the challenged action materially adverse, which in this context means it well might have dissuaded a reasonable worker from making or supporting a charge of discrimination."[12] The Court emphasized that this was an objective test of *materiality*. While

7. *Burlington*, 548 U.S. at 63.

8. In *Burlington*, all of the retaliatory acts were indeed employment related. Presumably, the Court addressed this issue only because the court below had adopted the so-called *ultimate employment decision* test for identifying actionable conduct—a test that fuses the severity of the conduct with the context of its occurrence. The Court rejected that test, part and parcel, thus the need to discuss the context component even though it was not directly at issue in the case.

9. Bernard v. Calhoon MEBA Eng'g Sch., 309 F. Supp. 2d 732 (D. Md. 2004) (warnings regarding attendance, insubordination, and poor performance); Munday v. Waste Mgmt., Inc., 126 F.3d 239 (4th Cir. 1997) (management instruction to co-workers to shun sexual harassment complainant held not to be illegal retaliation); Mattern v. Eastman Kodak Co., 104 F.3d 702 (5th Cir. 1997) (co-worker ridicule and hostility that the employer did not stop and verbal threats of termination and reprimand held not to be adverse employment actions).

10. Wideman v. Wal-Mart Stores, 141 F. 3d 1453 (11th Cir. 1998) (reprimand held to be an adverse employment action); Berry v. Stevinson Chevrolet, 74 F.3d. 980 (10th Cir. 1996) (filing criminal charges found to be an adverse employment action).

11. Burlington, 548 U.S. at 67.

12. Burlington, 548 U.S. at 68 (internal quotation marks omitted).

"petty slights, minor annoyances, and simply lack of good manners"[13] would not qualify, "excluding an employee from a weekly training lunch that contributes significantly to the employee's professional advancement might well deter a reasonable employee from complaining about discrimination"[14]—and would thus be actionable retaliation.

Generally speaking, if a transfer results in a reduction in wages or benefits, involves more onerous job responsibilities, or is otherwise so demeaning as to rise to the level of a constructive discharge, then it may qualify as an adverse employment action.[15] On the other hand, in an analogous context, the Supreme Court has indicated that a "demotion without change in pay, benefits, duties, or prestige" was not actionable, nor was a "reassignment to [a] more inconvenient job."[16] In *Burlington*, the Court added, "Whether a particular reassignment is materially adverse depends upon the circumstances of the particular case...."[17]

§ 12.03 Standard of Causation and Mixed-Motive Analysis

Until *Price Waterhouse*, it was virtually beyond dispute that all forms of intentional conduct prohibited by Title VII were subject to the *but for* standard of causation, including the retaliation provision. The Court's mixed-motive decision in *Price Waterhouse* initiated, at least in part, the departure from that standard, with Justice Brennan advocating a *motivating factor* standard and Justice O'Connor retaining *but for* as the analytical point of departure. They both agreed, however, that if the defendant could prove it would have terminated (or engaged in any form of "adverse employment action") *anyway*, for nondiscriminatory reasons, this constituted a complete defense.

In the Civil Rights Act of 1991, in the amendments to Title VII, Section 107 adopted Justice Brennan's *motivating factor* standard of causation[18] but changed the employer's rebuttal from being a complete defense to being one that merely limited the remedy.[19] But the 1991 Act's Section 107 does not refer to retaliation claims. To the contrary, it expressly refers to discrimination on the basis of race, color, religion, sex, and national origin. This produced some degree of confusion in the lower courts until the Supreme Court resolved the question in *Univ. of Tex. Southwestern Med. Ctr. v. Nassar.*[20] Because the 1991 amendment did not refer to retaliation claims, the Court decided

---

13. Burlington, 548 U.S. at 68.
14. Burlington, 548 U.S. at 69.
15. Joiner v. Ohio Dept. of Transp., 949 F. Supp. 562 (S.D. Ohio 1996).
16. Burlington Indus., Inc. v. Ellerth, 524 U.S. 742, 761 (1998).
17. Burlington, 548 U.S. at 71.
18. 105 Stat. 1071, § 107(a) (now § 703(m) of Title VII).
19. 105 Stat. 1071, § 107(b) (now § 706(g)(2)(B) of Title VII).
20. 570 U.S. 338 (2013).

that these claims must be decided in accord with "traditional principles of but-for causation."[21]

§ 12.04 Proof of a Violation

A retaliation claim is proved in much the same manner as are claims of substantive-basis discrimination. In a single-motive case, in the absence of any *smoking gun* or some variety of *direct* evidence, plaintiffs commonly rely on a *McDonnell Douglas* prima facie case type of proof. It usually consists of proof of (1) either *opposition* or *participation* activities, (2) a *materially adverse employment action*, and (3) a causal relation between the two motives.[22] The meaning of the terms *opposition*, *participation*, and *adverse employment action* will be discussed below. Proving a causal relation necessarily involves proof that the employer knew of the opposition or participation.[23] Beyond that, causal relation is established by circumstantial evidence, with the proximity of the employee's conduct to the employer's adverse employment action being especially important.[24] The existence of relevant *comparators* can also be compelling circumstantial evidence.[25]

§ 12.05 The Opposition Clause

[A] What Constitutes "Opposition"

[1] Crossing the Threshold

Opposition usually takes the form of a formal complaint, grievance, in-house criticism, expression of support for another employee's claim, protest meetings, discussions with co-employees, circulating or signing petitions, refusal to engage in an allegedly illegal act, and the like. The courts, however, have also recognized forms of *opposition* that would not be so readily apparent to the average employer. For example, in *EEOC v. St. Anne's Hospital, Inc.*,[26] a supervisor hired a black employee for the hospital's security department, which resulted in bomb threats against the hospital. The court held that the hiring was an act of *opposition* by the supervisor to what he perceived to be the employer's discriminatory policies and that the hospital violated Section 704(a) when it terminated the supervisor for making this hiring decision. Similarly, a supervisor's refusal to prevent subordinates from filing complaints of discrimination was found to be a form of protected *opposition* in *McDonnell v. Cisneros*.[27]

---

21. 570 U.S. at 360.

22. Ross v. Commc'ns Satellite Corp., 759 F.2d 355 (4th Cir. 1985).

23. Johnson v. United States Dep't of Health & Human Services, 30 F.3d 45 (6th Cir. 1994).

24. *Compare* Wyatt v. City of Boston, 35 F.3d 13 (1st Cir. 1994) (almost simultaneous adverse action supports inference of causation), *with* Candelaria v. EG & G Energy Measurements, Inc., 33 F.3d 1259 (10th Cir. 1994) (three years supports no inference of causation).

25. Payne v. McLemore's Wholesale & Retail Stores, 654 F.2d 1130, 1135 n. 3 (5th Cir. 1981).

26. 664 F.2d 128 (7th Cir. 1981).

27. 84 F.3d 256 (7th Cir. 1996).

In *Crawford v. Metro. Gov't of Nashville & Davidson County*,[28] an official of the employer Metro was conducting an internal investigation concerning rumors of sexual harassment by Metro's employee-relations director. During this investigation and in response to questions about the matter, the plaintiff-employee Crawford reported that the director had indeed sexually harassed her. Metro took no action against the director, but fired Crawford, alleging embezzlement. Crawford filed suit under Title VII, alleging a violation of both the *opposition* and the *participation* clauses. The district court granted Metro's motion for summary judgment, and this was affirmed by the Sixth Circuit Court of Appeals, holding that the opposition clause requires "active, consistent" opposition activities and that the participation clause applies only to participation pursuant to a Title VII charge pending with the EEOC.

The Supreme Court reversed and remanded. It held that the term "oppose" goes beyond "active, consistent" behavior and may apply to someone who has taken no action at all to advance a claim of a Title VII violation other than to disclose it. The Court noted that "a person can 'oppose' by responding to someone else's question just as surely as by provoking the discussion and nothing in the statute requires a freakish rule protecting an employee who reports discrimination on her own initiative [which is clearly protected] but not one who reports the same discrimination in the same words when her boss asks a question."[29] The Supreme Court did not address Crawford's claim that the Sixth Circuit had also read the participation clause too narrowly. The reasoning of the Court, however, clearly suggests that the Act's prohibition against retaliation should be liberally construed.

[2] Going Beyond the Pale[30]

Some types of conduct will qualify as *opposition* in the literal sense of the word, yet not be entitled to protection under Section 704. For example, in *McDonnell Douglas Corp. v. Green*,[31] the Supreme Court suggested that Green's automobile *stall-in*, which violated the criminal law and denied employees access to the plant, was not a protected form of conduct. Less egregious forms of opposition have also been denied protection.

In determining what is and is not a protected form of opposition, the courts have generally attempted to balance "the need to protect individuals asserting their rights ... against an employer's legitimate demands for loyalty, cooperation and a generally productive work environment."[32] Direct economic action against an employer, in the form of boycotts and picketing, must at least meet the requirements of similar forms

28. 555 U.S. 271 (2009).

29. 555 U.S. at 277.

30. This fifteenth-century term originally meant being outside the jurisdiction of England, but it has come to mean the place where we assign people who have acted outside the bounds of moral or social decency—i.e., *going too far*. Robert Hendrickson, Encyclopedia of Word and Phrase Origins 53–54 (1987).

31. 411 U.S. 792, 797 n.6 (1973).

32. Rollins v. Florida Dep't of Law Enforcement, 868 F.2d 397, 401 (11th Cir. 1989).

of conduct under the National Labor Relations Act, which require some identification of the labor practice being protested.[33] Employees who spend unreasonable amounts of compensated work time on *opposition* activities may also lose their protected status.[34] Finally, the manner or extent of the employee's opposition efforts may either be so offensive[35] or so disruptive of the work responsibilities of other employees[36] as to deprive it of all protection.

All of these decisions reflect a somewhat jaundiced view of these rather extreme forms of *opposition* behavior. It remains to be seen, however, whether this approach can survive the Supreme Court's expansive reading of the anti-retaliation provisions in *Crawford*.[37]

[B] The Meaning of "An Unlawful Practice"

The courts have consistently rejected the argument that the practice being opposed must actually be an *unlawful* practice. Rather, the law merely requires that the plaintiff have a reasonable and good faith belief that the employer's practice is unlawful.[38] This is normally a fact question which may, thus, defeat an employer's motion for summary judgment.[39] Sometimes, however, it can be resolved as a matter of law. In one case, for example, the court noted that "the plaintiff's subjective feeling that the defendants discriminated against him is clearly insufficient" to provide the basis for a reasonable and good faith belief that such discrimination occurred, with the court thus giving the employer judgment as a matter of law.[40] Similarly, since it is not illegal under Title VII for an employer to fail to have an affirmative action plan, protests over the absence of such a plan are unprotected.[41]

§ 12.06 The Participation Clause

Protected *participation* includes filing a charge with the EEOC, testifying, gathering evidence, providing evidence to EEOC investigators, communicating with the EEOC

---

33. Hochstadt v. Worcester Found. for Experimental Biology, 545 F.2d. 222, 232 & n.6 (1st Cir. 1976) (citing *NLRB v. Electrical Workers, Local 1229 (Jefferson Standard)*, 346 U.S. 464 (1953), for the proposition that product disparagement is not protected concerted labor activity). *But see* EEOC v. Crown Zellerback Corp., 720 F.2d 1008 (9th Cir. 1983) (letter to a primary customer protesting discriminatory practices found not to be unreasonable opposition).

34. Hazel v. U.S. Postmaster Gen., 7 F.3d 1 (1st Cir. 1993).

35. Robbins v. Jefferson County Sch. Dist., 186 F.3d 1253 (10th Cir. 1999) (frequent, loud, and sometimes specious complaints, together with highly antagonistic behavior toward a supervisor, held to be unprotected).

36. Hochstadt, 545 F.2d 222.

37. *See* § 12.05[A][1].

38. Trent v. Valley Elec. Ass'n, 41 F.3d 524 (9th Cir. 1994).

39. Hargens v. USDA, 865 F. Supp. 1314 (N.D. Iowa 1994).

40. Arzate v. City of Topeka, 884 F. Supp. 1494, 1504 (D. Kan. 1995).

41. Holden v. Owens-Illinois, Inc., 793 F.2d 745 (6th Cir. 1986).

concerning a charge, and assisting others in any of the above. These activities have virtually absolute protection, even if the charge is without merit and even defamatory.[42] However, the underlying charge, whether it is factually and legally meritorious or not, must at least allege something that could arguably be a violation of Title VII. For example, a charge claiming that the employer accused the employee of reckless driving in the company parking lot would not be protected.[43] In addition, at least one court has held that people who file EEOC charges "must reasonably believe in good faith that they have suffered discrimination," rather than using the EEOC enforcement mechanisms as "a tactical coercive weapon" in pursuit of other objectives.[44]

Although filing false charges with the EEOC is totally protected under the participation clause, repeating those charges during an employer's internal investigation of the claim is subject only to opposition clause protection, which is less absolute. The courts have thus held that an employee who lies during an internal employment investigation may be terminated.[45]

§ 12.07 Opposition/Participation by Management

Personnel managers, EEO officers, and others directly involved in the employment aspects of an enterprise have presented some special problems in retaliation law. Their primary duty is to prevent these kinds of problems, not cause them. Insofar as opposition activities are concerned, one court has noted that "it is axiomatic that the higher an employee is on the management ladder, the more circumspect that employee should be in expressing opposition to employment practices of which he disapproves."[46] Other courts have rationalized that when an employee is simply doing his or her job in reporting and commenting on certain possibly illegal employment practices, this is not *opposition* in the statutory sense and the employee is entitled to no protection.[47]

On the other hand, influenced by the Supreme Court's expansive reading of Title VII's no-retaliation provision in *Crawford,* several circuits have expressly rejected the so-called "manager rule," which some courts have relied on to *automatically* exclude

42. Womack v. Munson, 619 F.2d 1292 (8th Cir. 1980); Pettway v. American Cast Iron Pipe Co., 411 F.2d 998 (5th Cir. 1969). *But see* Barnes v. Small, 840 F.2d 972 (D.C. Cir. 1988) (plaintiff's letter to agency held found to be unprotected because it contained allegations that were both false and malicious).

43. Balazs v. Liebenthal, 32 F.3d 151 (4th Cir. 1994) (employee claimed he was falsely accused of sexual harassment, which the court analogized to a claim of reckless driving—both quite beyond EEOC's jurisdiction).

44. Mattson v. Caterpillar, Inc., 359 F.3d 885, 890–91 (7th Cir. 2004).

45. Vasconcelos v. Meese, 907 F.2d 111 (9th Cir. 1990).

46. Novotny v. Great Am. Fed. Sav. & Loan Ass'n, 539 F. Supp. 437, 451 (W.D. Pa. 1982).

47. McKenzie v. Renberg's, Inc., 94 F.3d 1478 (10th Cir. 1996).

from the protections of the statute anyone who occupies a managerial position. This rule, which originated under the anti-retaliation provisions of the Fair Labor Standards Act, has been found by some circuit courts to have no place under Title VII, whose provisions are intended to provide broad protection to all employees, regardless of their job title.[48]

Participation activities, though otherwise entitled to virtually absolute protection, have been limited in this context. For example, in *Smith v. Singer*,[49] an EEO director filed complaints against his own employer. The court noted that by doing so, he "placed himself in a position squarely adversary to his company" and "disabled himself from continuing to represent the company's interests. . . ." In other words, since that was the motivation for the termination, it was not a matter of retaliation for the exercise of statutory rights.

§ 12.08 Chapter Highlights

1. The retaliation prohibition protects employees, applicants for employment, and former employees (at least with respect to *participation* activities). (§ 12.01)

2. The employer's conduct in retaliation does not have to affect the terms or conditions of the employee's work, nor does it relate only to *ultimate* employment decisions. Rather, it covers any employer conduct a reasonable employee would find to be *materially adverse.* (§ 12.02)

3. The Supreme Court decided that retaliation claims must be decided in accord with "traditional principles of but-for causation" in *Univ. of Tex. Southwestern Med. Ctr. v. Nassar.* (§ 12.03)

4. Retaliation claims are usually proved by the *McDonnell Douglas* prima face case type of circumstantial evidence. (§ 12.04)

5. Under the opposition clause, the courts balance the need and desirability of employees asserting their statutory rights without resort to litigation against the employer's need to maintain order and efficiency in the workplace. What is or is not protected opposition activity depends very heavily on the facts of each individual situation. The Supreme Court, however, has indicated an inclination to read the *opposition* clause more liberally than the courts have done in the past. (§ 12.05[A])

6. Although the opposition must be to "an unlawful practice" under Title VII, a protestor's reasonable belief about the unlawfulness is generally sufficient. (§ 12.05[B])

---

48. DeMasters v. Carilion Clinic, 796 F.3d 409 (4th Cir. 2015); Littlejohn v. City of New York, 795 F.3d 297 (2d Cir. 2015).

49. 650 F.2d 214, 217 (9th Cir. 1981).

7. Actual participation in EEOC proceedings is subject to almost total protection, even if the charges filed are both false and malicious. (§ 12.06)

8. Opposition and participation activities by EEO officers and other members of management are in some limited circumstances subject to less protection than similar activities by regular employees. (§ 12.07)

Chapter 13

Discrimination by Labor Unions

Synopsis

If a labor union has at least 15 employees, it is subject to the same prohibitions against *employment* discrimination as any other employer. But Title VII also imposes additional nondiscrimination obligations on unions when they are acting in their capacity as a *private association* or *representative* of the employees of an employer. When acting in their representative capacity, unions are also subject to the *duty of fair representation* that is imposed on unions under all collective bargaining statutes. This provides a method for combating discrimination for matters that fall outside Title VII.

§ 13.01 The Nature of the Proscribed Discrimination

Under Section 703(c), the basis of the proscribed discrimination by unions is the same as that applying to employers—that is, on the basis of race, color, religion, sex, and national origin. It is thus illegal, when the union is acting on that basis, (1) to exclude or expel anyone from union membership, (2) to segregate or classify its membership, (3) to refuse to refer for employment, (4) to cause an employer to discriminate, or (4) to otherwise discriminate in any other fashion.

[A] Membership

Although lack of membership in a labor union cannot prevent an individual from getting or retaining a job,[1] such membership is often a prerequisite to participating in contract-ratification and strike votes and obtaining certain work-related union benefits that are not provided for under a collective bargaining agreement. Union membership, thus, continues to have a close nexus with the primary concern of Title VII—discrimination affecting the terms and conditions of employment.

Apart from the occasional overt case of racial or sexual discrimination or the use of different admission criteria,[2] membership discrimination is more commonly effected by policies and procedures that have a disparate impact. For example, in a union with predominantly white membership, a policy of giving membership preference to family members or even requiring that new members be sponsored by an existing member could have a disparate impact on African American and Hispanic employees.[3]

[B] Hiring Halls and Union Referral Arrangements

In the maritime, construction, entertainment, and a few other industries, employers frequently agree to hire employees only through a union hiring hall or other referral mechanism. These arrangements provide a rich potential for discrimination, direct and indirect. Unions, for example, have been found to have violated Title VII by giving minorities misleading information about work opportunities, maintaining an atmosphere that discouraged minorities from applying, and operating a *back-room* referral procedure that was available only to whites.[4]

Claims of individual discrimination are often resolved under the traditional *McDonnell Douglas* tripartite allocation of proof. The plaintiff establishes the prima facie case by reference to the same evidential facts that would be used in a hiring

1. For public employees, all compulsory union support is illegal. Janus v. AFSCME, Council 31, 138 S. Ct. 2448 (2018). Under the two federal labor laws covering private sector employees, the Labor-Management Relations Act and the Railway Labor Act, a union and an employer can only require an employee to pay a pro rata share of the union's collective bargaining and contract administration expenses—in other words, an agency-shop arrangement. Communications Workers of America v. Beck, 487 U.S. 735 (1988); Ellis v. Railway Clerks, 466 U.S. 435 (1984).

2. United States v. Ironworkers Local 86, 443 F.2d 544 (9th Cir. 1971).

3. EEOC v. Steamship Clerks Local 1066, 48 F.3d 594 (1st Cir. 1995).

4. Daniels v. Pipefitters' Ass'n Local Union 597, 945 F.2d 906 (7th Cir. 1991); Ingram v. Madison Square Garden Ctr., Inc., 709 F.2d 807 (2d Cir. 1983); Alexander v. Local 496, Laborers Int'l Union, 778 F. Supp. 1401 (N.D. Ohio 1991).

case. For example, to establish a prima facie case of sex discrimination, the plaintiff would have to prove that (1) she is female, (2) was qualified for referral, (3) despite her qualifications she was not referred, and (4) subsequently, the union referred other applicants with her qualifications.[5] The union then has the burden of articulating a legitimate, nondiscriminatory reason for the failure to refer. And the plaintiff must ultimately prove that this is merely a pretext for discrimination. As is true with employers, the union must be careful that the reason it articulates is not one that has a disparate impact. For example, a union whose prior discriminatory referrals had kept minorities out of the workforce could not use prior employment with the requesting employer as a basis of referral because this would resulted "a vicious circle that perpetuated the hiring and rehiring of whites."[6] And, unfortunately, all the confusing nuances of the prima facie case theory of proof that have arisen in the past several years must also be taken into account in the union-membership context.

[C] Apprenticeship Programs

Completion of a joint employer/union training or apprenticeship program is often required of individuals who are seeking employment in certain industries for the first time. This is particularly true of the building and construction trades.

As is true with other union activities, liability may attach if the program's admission requirements have a disparate impact on a protected group, such as a requirement that applicants already have a job with a participating employer. This was found to have a disparate impact on women and could not be justified as a business necessity, since the requirement did not correlate with success in the program.[7] Claims of individual discrimination in admission to apprenticeship and training programs are also subject to the *McDonnell Douglas* prima facie case method of proof.

[D] Causing an Employer to Discriminate

Although it does not exonerate an employer from its own liability, under the literal words of the statute when a union induces or pressures an employer to engage in discriminatory conduct, the union may also be held liable. Indeed, some courts have found unions liable for merely passively acquiescing in the employer's discriminatory conduct.[8] In some cases the union may be required to pay the entire back-pay award.[9]

---

5. Stair v. Lehigh Valley Carpenters Local 600, 66 Fair Empl. Prac. Cas. (BNA) 1473 (E.D. Pa. 1993), aff'd, 43 F.3d 1463 (3d Cir. 1994).

6. *Alexander*, 778 F. Supp. 1401, 1407 (N.D. Ohio 1991).

7. Eldredge v. Carpenters, 46 N. Cal. Counties Joint Apprenticeship & Training Comm., 833 F.2d 1334 (9th Cir. 1987).

8. Woods v. Graphic Communications, 925 F.2d 1195, 1200 (9th Cir. 1991) (but also suggesting that the courts differ over what constitutes *acquiesce*).

9. Guerra v. Manchester Terminal Corp., 498 F.2d 641 (5th Cir. 1974).

[E] Representational Matters

Under the Labor-Management Relations Act, a union that has been properly designated as the collective bargaining representative of a group of employees has the exclusive right to represent those employees in dealings with the employer concerning the terms and conditions of employment. Individual employees can no longer represent themselves. The union's right in this regard carries with it, however, a corollary duty—that of representing each employee "without hostility or discrimination."[10] Under the labor statutes, this is known as the *duty of fair representation.* A breach of the duty can be litigated as either an unfair labor practice before the National Labor Relations Board or in a suit in federal court. When the breach involves discrimination on the basis of race, color, religion, national origin, or sex, it may also be a Title VII violation. These Title VII claims generally arise in two contexts.

[1] Handling Grievances

Collective bargaining agreements typically require that all disputes under the agreement be resolved through grievance and arbitration procedures. Usually, the union has the exclusive right to determine which disputes will be made the subject of a grievance and ultimately taken to arbitration. And a Title VII violation may occur at any step in the process.

When the underlying complaint is that the employer has discriminated against a particular employee, the union may be liable if it fails to adequately investigate the charge or attempt to correct the situation. In *Goodman v. Lukens Steel Co.*,[11] the Supreme Court held that the union had *otherwise discriminated* under Section 703(c) when it failed to challenge the employer's discriminatory discharge of black probationary employees, failed to assert race discrimination as a ground for various grievances, and tolerated the employer's racial harassment. Similarly, in another case, the union was found guilty of sex discrimination when it refused to challenge the employer's refusal to give a female employee light duty during her pregnancy, even though the contract allowed for such an accommodation for persons with a temporary disability.[12]

On the other hand, the union may also be liable if the underlying complaint does not involve alleged employer discrimination, but the union refuses to do anything because of impermissible bias. Proof in these cases usually consists of comparative evidence—a similar complaint by a nonminority employee that the union handled in a different fashion.[13] The union will defend by attempting to establish a dissimilarity between the two situations or by advancing some other justification for its actions.

---

10. Vaca v. Sipes, 386 U.S. 171 (1967).
11. 482 U.S. 656 (1987).
12. Perugini v. Safeway Stores, 935 F.2d 1083 (9th Cir. 1991).
13. Johnson v. Artim Transp. Sys., Inc., 826 F.2d 538 (7th Cir. 1987).

Finally, a union may incur Title VII liability if it settles a grievance over the objections of the grieving employee. Although a union may sometimes find it necessary to sacrifice the interests of a single employee for the good of the entire group of employees, this decision cannot be predicated on discriminatory reasons.[14]

[2] Collective Bargaining

Collective bargaining is another major area in which a union's discharge of its representational responsibilities may entail potential Title VII liability. Certainly, a union will be liable if it initiates or actively participates in the creation of a contract term that is openly discriminatory or has a disparate impact.[15] But a union may also be liable if it passively acquiesces in the inclusion or continuation of an illegal provision in the collective bargaining agreement.[16] A union generally has an affirmative bargaining duty to attempt to change an existing discriminatory provision or actively oppose the creation of one.[17] On the other hand, if the bargaining history shows that the union opposed or attempted to narrow the scope of the discriminatory provision, the union may not be liable even if it ultimately ratified, as a whole, a contract containing this discriminatory provision.[18]

[F] Religious Accommodation

When an accommodation to an employee's religious belief or practices would entail a violation of the collective bargaining agreement, this constitutes an undue hardship almost as a matter of course.[19] This most often arises with Sabbatarian accommodation requests which conflict with a union seniority system. Seniority systems are afforded special protection under Title VII.[20] Neither the employer nor the union violates Title VII by refusing to acquiesce in a violation of the seniority system. Nor is the union under a duty to negotiate contract terms that provide special treatment for those following certain religious practices or beliefs.[21] However, the Supreme Court has determined that Title VII requires religious practices to be given favored treatment and requires otherwise neutral policies to give way to the need for an accommodation.[22]

---

14. Neloms v. Southwestern Elec. Power Co., 18 Fair Empl. Prac. Cas. (BNA) (W.D. La. 1977).

15. Donnell v. General Motors Corp., 576 F.2d 1292 (8th Cir. 1978)

16. Jackson v. Seaboard C. L. R. Co., 678 F.2d 992, 1016 (11th Cir. 1982); Myers v. Gilman Paper Corp., 544 F.2d 837, 850–51 (5th Cir. 1977).

17. Jackson, 678 F.2d 992; *Myers*, 544 F.2d 837

18. Martinez v. Oakland Scavenger Co., 680 F. Supp. 1377, 1398 (N.D. Cal. 1987).

19. Trans World Airlines, Inc. v. Hardison, 432 U.S. 63 (1977). Note that four justices recently expressed an interest in reconsidering *Hardison*. Kennedy v. Bremerton Sch. Dist., 139 S. Ct. 634, 637 (2019).

20. 42 U.S.C. § 2000e-2(h).

21. A failure to include in the agreement a provision explaining the rights of employees who have religious objections to paying union dues may result in releasing the objector not only from compelled dues, but also compelled payments to charity. 29 U.S.C. § 169. Scandia Log Homes, 258 N.L.R.B. 716 (1984).

22. *Abercrombie & Fitch*, 135 S. Ct. 2028, 2034 (2015).

On the other hand, the courts have been sympathetic when an employee objects, on religious grounds, to associating with or providing money to a labor union. Under the Labor-Management Relations Act, an employee cannot be required to become a member of a union as a condition of employment. Even the *agency fee* obligations of religious objectors are accommodated under Title VII by allowing the employee to pay an equivalent amount to charity. As previously discussed, due to recent changes in the law, Title VII might ultimately require no charity payment.[23]

§ 13.02 Liability Issues

[A] Liability for Acts of Officers

Like corporate employers, labor unions are capable of acting only through individual persons. Under Section 701(d), the union is liable for the conduct of those who are its agents. This includes union officers, representatives, business agents, and even shop stewards.[24] On the other hand, established agency principles suggest a union would not be liable for the acts of individual members unless the conduct was either authorized or ratified by the union.

[B] Liability of Higher Union Organizations

Even though the discrimination may have been committed by a local union or its agents, regional, national, and international unions of which the local is a part may also be liable. This most commonly occurs when the larger union organization participated in negotiating a collective bargaining agreement containing a discriminatory provision or was otherwise actively involved in the discriminatory practice.[25] Alternatively, a few courts have allowed liability to attach under theories of agency and failure to control.[26]

[C] Joint Union-Employer Liability

Generally, a union may be jointly liable with an employer under three situations—each of which involves many fact-specific exceptions and qualifications. Joint liability may exist: (1) when the union and employer agree to a discriminatory contract provision;[27] (2) when the union acquiesces in the employer's discrimination that is not based on a discriminatory collective bargaining agreement;[28] and (3) when the union induces or causes the employer to engage in discrimination.[29]

---

23. *See* Chapter 11, § 11.04[D][3].
24. Woods v. Graphic Commc'ns, 925 F.2d 1195 (9th Cir. 1991).
25. Sagers v. Yellow Freight Sys., 529 F.2d 721 (5th Cir. 1976).
26. *Alexander*, 778 F. Supp. 1401 (N.D. Ohio 1991).
27. EEOC v. Elgin Teachers Ass'n, 780 F. Supp. 1195 (N.D. Ill. 1991).
28. Romero v. Union Pac. R.R., 615 F.2d 1303 (10th Cir. 1980).
29. Johnson v. Goodyear Tire & Rubber Co., 491 F.2d 1364 (5th Cir. 1974).

§ 13.03 Chapter Highlights

1. In addition to prohibiting unions from discriminating in their capacity as employers or by causing other employers to discriminate, Title VII also prohibits union discrimination with respect to membership, job referrals, or any other union function or benefit. (§ 13.01)

2. Membership discrimination may be direct or indirect, through the adoption of membership policies that have a disparate impact on minorities. (§ 13.01[A])

3. Union hiring halls or referral services, which are the primary source of employment opportunities in many industries, must be operated on a nondiscriminatory basis. Discriminatory referrals are often established by the *McDonnell Douglas* method of proof. (§ 13.01[B]) The same is true of discrimination in joint employer/union training or apprenticeship programs. (§ 13.01[C])

4. If a union induces or causes an employer to discriminate, the union may be liable. (§ 13.01[D])

5. As the statutory agent of unit employees, the union has not only the right but also the responsibility to represent these employees fairly and without discrimination. The most common breaches of this duty occur in processing grievances and negotiating terms of the collective bargaining agreement. (§ 13.01[E])

6. Employees who object to union membership or paying union fees on religious grounds are entitled to an accommodation, regardless of whether the union security provision of the collective bargaining agreement provides for this or not. This is usually achieved by allowing dissenting employees to pay an equivalent amount to a charity. (§ 13.01[F])

7. As a fictional entity, a labor union acts through and is thus liable for the discriminatory acts of its officers and agents. National union organizations may be liable for the discriminatory acts of local unions if they participated in the discrimination or under general principles of agency law. A labor union and the employer will be jointly liable for certain kinds of discrimination. (§ 13.02)

Chapter 14

Discrimination by Employment Agencies

Synopsis

§ 14.01 The Prohibited Discrimination

With respect to discrimination against its own employees or prospective employees, an employment agency is subject to the same prohibitions as any other statutory *employer*—requiring, thus, that it be an entity with 15 or more employees engaged in interstate commerce.[1] A person or entity that qualifies as an *employment agency*[2] is, however, subject to additional requirements. Section 703(b) makes it illegal for an employment agency to refer or fail to refer for employment, to classify any individual, or to otherwise discriminate against any individual on the basis of race, color, religion, sex, or national origin. Employment agencies must also be especially aware of the discriminatory advertising prohibitions of section 704(b).

1. Greenlees v. Eidenmuller Enters., 32 F.3d 197 (5th Cir. 1994) (rejecting the EEOC position that such discrimination is covered by the "otherwise ... discriminate" language of section 703(b), which applies to employment agencies regardless of the number of employees).

2. *See* Chapter 5, § 5.02[D].

§ 14.02 Discrimination in Processing and Classification

Almost anything that an employment agency might do in dealing with a job applicant that differentiates on the basis of race, sex, or some other protected characteristic is covered by the statutory prohibition. Discriminatory practices include different interview procedures,[3] separate interview desks for male and female applicants,[4] job counselors that are segregated by sex or race,[5] and offering services exclusively to applicants of one sex.[6] These various forms of traditional disparate treatment discrimination are subject to the usual methods of proof.

In addition, employment agencies risk charges of disparate impact discrimination when they use criteria or standards that disqualify a disproportionate number of minorities.[7] This is a particularly acute problem with respect to the use of employment tests, favored especially by state employment agencies.[8] To avoid the disparate impact of a particular test—and to thus escape the necessity of expensive validation studies—some employment agencies adopted the practice of adjusting test scores on the basis of race. This so-called *race norming* was, however, expressly outlawed by the Civil Rights Act of 1991.[9]

§ 14.03 Accepting Discriminatory Job Orders

It is unlawful for an employment agency to accept a job order that specifically requests applicants of a particular race, color, sex, national origin, or religion. But the EEOC is also sensitive to situations where the employer's preferences are *sotto voce* or simply a tacit understanding and the agency's implementing discrimination is accomplished by means of internal coding systems.[10] Employment agencies should also be particularly careful when dealing with employers who are attempting to satisfy their affirmative action obligations. Unless the employer's plan qualifies, preferring minorities over non-minorities is an illegal form of reverse discrimination.[11]

---

3. https://www.eeoc.gov/pre-employment-inquiries-and-marital-status-or-number-children.

4. Barnes v. Rourke, 8 Fair Empl. Prac. Cas. (BNA) 1112 (M.D. Tenn. 1973).

5. EEOC Dec. 72-0157, 4 Fair Empl. Prac. Cas. (BNA) 254 (1971).

6. 29 C.F.R. § 1604.6(a); *cf.* City Comm'n on Human Rights v. Boll, 8 Fair Empl. Prac. Cas. (BNA) 1139 (N.Y. Sup Ct. 1974) (decision under state law).

7. *See* McBride v. Lawstaf, Inc., 1996 U.S. Dist LEXIS 16190 (N.D. Ga. 1996), *magistrate's recommendation adopted*, 71 Fair Empl. Prac. Cas. (BNA) 1758 (N.D. Ga. 1996) (distinguishing a prohibition against the referral of employees with braided hair from a prohibition the referral of employees with an "Afro/bush" style).

8. Pegues v. Mississippi State Employment Serv., 699 F.2d 760 (5th Cir. 1983).

9. 42 U.S.C. § 2000e-2(l).

10. EEOC v. Recruit U.S.A., Inc., 939 F.2d 746 (9th Cir. 1991).

11. EEOC v. David Gomez & Assocs., 1997 U.S. Dist. LEXIS 3269 (N.D. Ill. 1997).

§ 14.04 The BFOQ Defense

If sex, religion, or national origin is a bona fide occupational qualification for the job for which an applicant is being considered, then referring on this basis is not illegal.[12] An agency receiving a job order that requests only applicants of a particular sex, religion, or national origin cannot, however, simply assume that the employer's preference is based on a valid BFOQ. The employer must affirmatively assert that it is. If the agency has no reason to believe otherwise and maintains a written record of each such job order, then the agency is not liable even if the employer's BFOQ defense ultimately fails.[13]

§ 14.05 Refusing to Refer

Refusing to refer an applicant because of that person's race, sex, or other protected characteristic, or granting a preference to applicants on this basis is illegal. Thus, just as it would be illegal for an employer to prefer to hire unemployed fathers over unemployed mothers, an employment agency placing welfare recipients in a job training program similarly violates Title VII when exercising that preference.[14] It is also illegal for an agency to steer women and minorities into lower-paying or domestic jobs[15] or to steer men and women into "traditionally" male and female jobs.[16]

§ 14.06 Discriminatory Advertising

Although section 704(b), which prohibits job advertisements expressing a preference on the basis of an impermissible characteristic, applies equally to employers, labor unions, and employment agencies, the latter are particularly vulnerable because of the large number of advertisements that they place in the regular course of business.

Most of the Title VII violations have involved sex and age. Placing a *help wanted* advertisement in a sex-segregated format in a newspaper is a violation, unless the proscribed basis is actually a BFOQ for the job in question.[17] Similarly, express references to sex or age within an individual advertisement will be construed as an expression of preference, as in one advertisement that sought a "young man with a college degree."[18] Although the use of job titles ending in *-men* are not illegal per se, the EEOC insists that the advertisement also expressly indicate that applicants of

12. *See* Chapter 5, § 5.08.
13. 29 C.F.R. § 1604.6(b).
14. Thorn v. Richardson, 4 Fair Empl. Prac. Cas. (BNA) 299 (W.D. Wash. 1971).
15. Pegues v. Mississippi State Employment Serv., 699 F.2d 760 (5th Cir. 1983).
16. EEOC Dec. 72-0157, 4 Fair Empl. Prac. Cas. (BNA) 254 (1971).
17. 29 C.F.R. 1604.5.
18. Banks v. Heun-Norwood, 566 F.2d 1073 (8th Cir. 1973).

both sexes are being sought.[19] The better practice is to use totally sex-neutral job titles, such as *firefighters* rather than *firemen*.

§ 14.07 Remedies

An employment agency is subject to the same remedies as a discriminating employer. These include injunctive relief designed to stop the discrimination, affirmative action in the form of priority referrals, and even an award of back pay if the applicant can establish that he or she would have gotten the job but for the discriminatory refusal to refer.[20]

§ 14.08 Chapter Highlights

1. In addition to being subject to the discrimination prohibitions that apply to any employer, employment agencies are also prohibited from discriminating against clients who are seeking employment through the agency. (§ 14.01)

2. Discrimination in processing and classifying is perhaps the most common form of violation and may consist of facially discriminatory practices or the use of standards that have a disparate impact. (§ 14.02)

3. It is also unlawful for an employment agency to have an express or tacit understanding with an employer to refer applicants of only a particular race, sex, or ethnicity. (§ 14.03)

4. Although discriminatory referrals are not illegal if sex, religion, or national origin is a BFOQ for the job, an employment agency must take steps to protect itself if the employer's BFOQ defense ultimately fails. (§§ 14.03 and 14.04)

5. An employment agency may not take a person's race, sex, national origin, or religion into account when deciding whether to refer that person for a job, in allocating training program slots, or when recommending particular jobs. (§ 14.05)

6. In its newspaper advertising, an employment agency needs to be especially careful not to use language suggesting an impermissible preference for persons of a particular race, sex, national origin, or religion. (§ 14.06)

7. Employment agencies are generally subject to the same remedies as a Title VII employer who discriminates. (§ 14.07)

---

19. EEOC Compliance Manual, N:915-051 (Apr. 16, 1990).

20. *Barns*, 8 Fair Empl. Prac. Cas. (BNA) 1112.

Chapter 15

Title VII Procedure—An Overview

Synopsis

§ 15.01 Introduction

When legislating the substantive prohibition against discrimination on the basis of race, color, religion, national origin, and sex, Congress necessarily had to paint with a broad brush. The dimensions of the social problem to be cured were too vast, variegated, and uncertain for Congress to simply legislate a list of specifically prohibited or required conduct. It was left up to the courts to work out the very meaning of the concepts of *discrimination*, *because of*, *BFOQ*, and other statutory creations, utilizing a process much like that of the common law.

Congress attempted to address the procedural issues with a higher degree of precision and specificity. But given the amount of litigation over procedure that ensued in the early years of the statute, it appears that Congress was not altogether successful in articulating clear and unambiguous procedural guidelines. Although by 1964 Congress had acquired vast experience in drafting the enforcement mechanisms for social and labor legislation, Congress chose not to borrow from any of the existing models. Rather, it started from scratch and created an administrative/judicial, public/private enforcement mechanism of enormous complexity that was more the product of political compromises than rational legislative choices. Although the procedural questions posed by the original Act were eventually resolved, subsequent amendments have also raised new procedural problems anew. Title VII procedure, thus, continues to be a dangerous land mine for both plaintiffs and defendants. This chapter will provide a very broad overview of the procedure, with the details being discussed in later chapters.

§ 15.02 The Equal Employment Opportunity Commission

The linchpin of Title VII's enforcement mechanisms is the Equal Employment Opportunity Commission. It consists of five persons appointed by the President. Most of the day-to-day work of the Commission is done under the supervision of the Office of the General Counsel. In addition to its office in Washington, D.C., the EEOC also has regional offices located throughout the country.

The primary functions of the EEOC are:

- To receive, process, investigate, and attempt the voluntary resolution of discrimination charges.
- To litigate certain claims of discrimination, usually involving a large number of employees or legal issues of significance. The EEOC periodically publishes the criteria it uses for determining when to undertake litigation, rather than leaving it in the hands of private plaintiffs.
- To promulgate Guidelines and "policy statements" that provide the agency's interpretation of the law. Although these are not binding, the courts sometimes give them "substantial deference"—but sometimes not.

§ 15.03 Three Procedural/Enforcement Models for Private and State Employees

The timing and nature of the EEOC's procedural involvement in a charge of discrimination depends on what kind of relationship the EEOC has with state agencies, if any, that have authority to deal with employment discrimination under state law.

[A] The Basic Model

If there is no state agency with authority to remedy the discriminatory act being complained of, then the federal/EEOC procedural steps can be summarized as follows:

- The person claiming illegal discrimination must file a charge of discrimination with the appropriate regional office of the EEOC.
- EEOC agents investigate the charge.
- The Regional Office determines whether there is cause to believe a violation has occurred.

- If the EEOC issues a *no cause* letter, that is the end of the agency's involvement.
- If, however, the EEOC has cause to believe that a violation has occurred, then it must attempt to achieve voluntary compliance or a settlement. Due to the growing popularity of alternative dispute resolution procedures generally, the EEOC has put greater emphasis on resolving disputes by this method than it did in prior years—when the effort was sometimes no more than *pro forma*.
- If conciliation or mediation fails, the EEOC then decides whether to sue on behalf of the charging party. The EEOC periodically establishes internal guidelines for the types of cases it considers of particular importance and worthy of EEOC involvement.
- If the EEOC decides not to litigate, it issues the charging party a "right to sue" letter. The charging party, however, may also request that letter earlier.
- The charging party then brings suit in federal district court. Suit may also be brought in a state court of competent jurisdiction, although a suit filed there would be subject to removal.

Each of these procedural steps will be discussed in detail in subsequent chapters.

[B] Procedure in Deferral States

If the state (or municipality) in which the alleged discrimination occurred has an administrative agency with the authority to resolve employment discrimination claims, then the individual must also file with this agency. The procedure before these *deferral agencies* is a matter of state law and will not be covered in this text. Whether the EEOC or the state deferral agency handles the charge is the subject of the worksharing agreements described next.

[C] Worksharing Agreements

To avoid the duplication of effort and delay that occurs under the purely statutory scheme involving state deferral agencies, the EEOC reports (2016) that it has entered into 92 worksharing contracts with state and local deferral agencies. These contracts identify the charge processing, investigation, cause finding, and conciliation responsibilities allocation between the state and federal agency.

Under these agreements, an individual may usually file with either agency, and the agency initially receiving the charge will forward the charge to the other agency, thus satisfying both state and federal filing requirements simultaneously.[1] Generally, the agency that first receives the charge handles it, although this is subject to its worksharing agreement. The state agency may also, in the agreement itself or on a case-by-case basis, waive the exclusive jurisdiction it would otherwise have over a claim during the normal 60-day period. Finally, although agreements typically allow ultimate

1. 29 C.F.R. § 1626.10 (c).

recourse to the EEOC, the statute itself provides that the EEOC must accord "substantial weight" to state agency findings and orders—and this includes those arrived at under a worksharing agreement. Although some of the provisions of a worksharing agreement would seem to significantly alter the purely statutory scheme, they have generally been upheld by the courts.[2]

§ 15.04 Chapter Highlights

1. The Equal Employment Opportunity Commission plays a central role in the enforcement of claims of Title VII discrimination. Its primary functions are to receive and process claims of discrimination, to litigate some of these claims, and to promulgate Guidelines with respect to the agency's interpretation of the law. (§ 15.02)

2. In jurisdictions that lack a state agency for the enforcement of their own anti-discrimination laws, a person with a Title VII claim must file a charge with the EEOC. The EEOC will investigate the charge. If the EEOC determinates that the charge has no merit, it will issue a *no cause* letter and end its involvement in the matter. But if the EEOC finds that the charge has merit, it will attempt to achieve a voluntary settlement. If that fails, the EEOC must then decide whether it will bring a law suit itself. If it decides not to sue, then it will issue the charging party a *right to sue* letter. The charging party may then bring a law suit, usually in federal court. (§ 15.03[A])

3. In jurisdictions that have an anti-discrimination law and a state agency with authority to remedy the discrimination being complained of, then the party making a discrimination claim must also file with that state agency. (§ 15.03[B])

4. To avoid the duplication of effort and delay that often occurs under the statutory scheme described above, the federal EEOC and many of these state agencies have entered into *worksharing agreements.* These agreements allocate between the two agencies the various responsibilities for processing discrimination claims. (§ 15.03[C])

2. EEOC v. Commercial Office Prod. Co., 486 U.S. 107 (1988); Puryear v. County of Roanoke, 214 F.3d 514 (4th Cir. 2000).

Chapter 16

Filing and Processing Charges

Synopsis

The Title VII legal process begins with the filing of a charge with the EEOC or appropriate state agency, alleging that an employer, union, or employment agency has engaged in an unlawful employment practice.

§ 16.01 Content and Formal Requirements

Section 706(b) states that charges "shall be in writing under oath or affirmation and shall contain such information and be in such form as the Commission requires." The Commission, in turn, has adopted essentially a *notice* pleading approach, requiring at a minimum that the parties be identified and that the alleged discrimination be described. Although it also requires certain jurisdictional information, it allows these omissions and other technical defects to be cured by amendment subsequent to the filing period—including the formality of the oath or affirmation. Although the lower courts were initially split over the legality of this procedure, in *Edelman v. Lynchburg College*,[1] a case involving the lack of an oath on the original document filed with the EEOC, the Court upheld the regulation. The EEOC, however, must still notify the employer of the unverified charge within the required period. Ultimately, the Supreme Court in *Federal Exp. Corp. v. Holowecki*,[2] determined that only five elements were required for a charge to be considered valid. They are: (1) name of the charged party; (2) an allegation; (3) date, place, and circumstances of the alleged unlawful practice; (4) request for the agency to take remedial action or settle the dispute; and (5) under oath or affirmation.

Mistakes involving the substantive content of the charge are another matter, particularly the *who* and *what* information. If the charging party later attempts to sue someone who is not named in the charge or allege discrimination that is not identified in the charge, the suit may be disallowed. Filing a proper charge, thus, is not a matter to be taken lightly, although *Holowecki* ruled that a charge should be construed to protect the employee's statutory rights. Ambiguities should not be construed against the employee. *Id.* at 406.

By its terms, the statute requires that the charge be filed with the EEOC. However, the Commission has agreements with several other federal agencies, such as the Office of Contract Compliance Programs, which allow charges filed with those agencies to be referred to the EEOC and thus treated as an EEOC filing. Filing with a state deferral agency that has a worksharing agreement with the EEOC is also sufficient. A failure to file a charge with the EEOC is not jurisdictional.[3]

§ 16.02 Identity of the Charging Party

Under Section 706(b), a charge may be filed "by or on behalf of a person claiming to be aggrieved, or by a member of the Commission."

[A] Person Aggrieved

Title VII charges are most often filed by the person against whom the alleged discrimination has been directed. In most instances, there is no question but that this is a *person aggrieved.* To qualify, a person must satisfy two broad requirements. First, the person must be covered by Title VII generally and not within one of the exclusions—that is, not an independent contractor, within the personal staff exception, or subject to one of the other statutory exclusions.

Second, the person must have a personal stake in the controversy sufficient to satisfy the standing requirements under Article III of the Constitution, broadly con-

1. 535 U.S. 106 (2002).
2. 552 U.S. 389 (2008).
3. Fort Bend Cty. v. Davis, 139 S. Ct. 1843, 1851 (2019).

strued. Thus, the charging party must be able to show "that the challenged action has caused him injury-in-fact, economic or otherwise," and that "the interest sought to be protected by the complainant is arguably within the zone of interests to be protected or regulated by the statute ... in question."[4] A person within the protected group who has been denied a job or promotion, who has been terminated, or who has been subject to sexual or racial harassment clearly satisfies that test.

Problems begin to arise, however, when the charging party is within the protected group (a racial minority, for example), but does not claim to be a direct victim of an allegedly discriminatory practice or policy. The problem here is satisfying the *injury* prong of the test. If an employer has a practice of not promoting women as quickly or readily as males, any woman will be able to satisfy that requirement by showing that she is potentially subject to the policy, thus justifying at least injunctive relief. Some courts will also recognize an injury in the form of the stigma that the discriminatory practice attaches to the group and, thus, also to every member of that group.[5] Arguably, this threshold constitutional standing requirement is somewhat broader than the statutory *adverse employment action* requirement.

An organization may sometimes qualify as a *person aggrieved* if it can establish that the discrimination against individuals deprived it of membership or revenues.[6] Indeed, even absent such injury, at least one court has allowed an organization to file a charge if one of its members would have standing, it is seeking to protect an interest germane to its purposes, and the litigation will not require the participation of any individual members.[7]

Testers pose a unique problem. A tester is an individual who applies for a job, but with no intention of accepting an offer of employment if one is extended. If a minority tester and a non-minority tester with similar (albeit fictional) qualifications apply and only the non-minority tester is offered a job, this is thought to be indicative of a discriminatory hiring policy. The problem, however, is that the minority applicant had no intention of accepting a job offer and thus was not *aggrieved in fact* by not receiving one. Although the Supreme Court has upheld tester standing in the context of fair housing legislation[8] and the EEOC maintains that they also have standing under Title VII, the courts are still divided over the issue in Title VII litigation.[9]

---

4. Ass'n of Data Processing Serv. Orgs. v. Camp, 397 U.S. 150, 152–53 (1970).

5. Gray v. Greyhound Lines, 545 F.2d 169 (D.C. Cir. 1976).

6. Chicano Police Officer's Ass'n v. Stover, 526 F.2d 431 (10th Cir. 1975), vacated and remanded on other grounds, 426 U.S. 944 (1976); NAACP v. United States Postal Serv., 22 Fair Empl. Prac. Cas. (BNA) 502 (N.D. Ga. 1977) (holding that the labor union had standing, because of membership injury, but the NAACP did not).

7. NAACP v. Town of East Haven, 892 F. Supp. 46 (D. Conn. 1995).

8. Havens Realty Corp. v. Coleman, 455 U.S. 363 (1982).

9. *Compare* Fair Emp't Council of Greater Washington, Inc. v. BMC Marketing Corp., 28 F.3d 1268 (D.C. Cir. 1994), *with* Kyles v. J.K. Guardian Security Servs., 222 F.3d 289 (7th Cir. 2000) (allowing testers to file a charge, but limiting the available remedies).

Proving a cognizable injury when the putative charging party is not a member of the discriminated class is even more difficult. Sexual and racial harassment claims brought by non-victims who are not even within the harassed class (a woman or racial minority, for example) will have a particularly difficult time establishing the requisite injury.[10]

Standing, however, not only requires an injury-in-fact, it also requires that this injury flow from the alleged discrimination. The disparate impact cases clearly demonstrate the difference between an injury-in-fact and one that is caused by discrimination. In a disparate impact case, the injured *person* must necessarily be conceptualized in terms of the group upon whom the challenged practice has the disparate impact. The practice is *discriminatory* because of the disparity of adverse treatment between the two groups; an individual person's standing is purely derivative of membership in this group. Although a person who is not a member of the disadvantaged group may also be injured by the practice, this person's disadvantage is not the result of discrimination. In standing terms, the non-minority individual's *interest* or *injury*, though real, is not with the *zone of interests* encompassed by the disparate impact theory of discrimination, which focuses on classes rather than individuals. Thus, a white person who was denied a job because of his arrest record would not have standing to challenge that criterion, even though an African American would, because of membership in the group upon whom the criterion has a disparate impact.[11]

[B] On Behalf of a Person Aggrieved

Even if not personally aggrieved, an individual or organization may file a charge on behalf of someone who is. This anomalous procedure is often used when the aggrieved party wishes to remain anonymous, at least temporarily,[12] and a civil rights organization or labor union thus assumes the responsibility of being the charging party. Filing the charge, however, requires the authorization of the aggrieved party and also pretty well exhausts the charging party's responsibility and authority. From then on, the charge is in the hands of the aggrieved person, who must approve any withdrawal of the charge or settlement, is the proper recipient of the right-to-sue letter, and must also bring the lawsuit, if any.[13]

---

10. Childress v. City of Richmond, 134 F.3d 1205 (4th Cir. 1998) (equally divided en banc court affirming a district court decision holding that white male employees did not have standing to challenge the employer's harassment of female and African American co-employees).

11. Gregory v. Litton Sys., Inc., 472 F.2d 631 (9th Cir. 1972).

12. Although the charge need not identify the aggrieved person, the EEOC must be informed so that it can conduct the necessary investigation and, of course, the identity will be revealed if a suit is ever brought on the charge.

13. In some cases, however, the courts have allowed the organization to bring the suit in its capacity as the representative of its members who were injured. NAACP, Newark Branch v. Town of Harrison, 749 F. Supp. 1327 (D.N.J. 1990).

[C] Commissioner Charges

The statute specifically allows an EEOC Commissioner to file charges. A Commissioner charge, however, has several unique aspects. It is subject to stricter requirements about specificity than are charges by individuals.[14] Unlike *on behalf of* charges, a Commissioner charge does not require the authorization of the aggrieved person. Individuals identified as an *aggrieved person* in the Commissioner charge may later block the withdrawal of the charge. And it is not clear whether an aggrieved person has an absolute or merely a permissive right to intervene in the EEOC litigation that might flow out of a Commissioner charge.[15]

§ 16.03 Time Limits

If the alleged discrimination occurred in a jurisdiction that does not have an agency empowered to enforce its own local laws against discrimination, then the charge must be filed within 180 days of the *discriminatory occurrence.* If a jurisdiction has a local agency which has jurisdiction over the claim, and an individual initially files with the local agency, then the time to file the charge is extended to 300 days. Almost all states have agencies empowered to enforce local laws against discrimination. A list of these "FEP agencies," as designated by the EEOC, can be found in 29 C.F.R § 1601.74.

A *timely* filing with the local agency is not required by federal law, with the result that the 300-day filing period applies whether or not the local agency filing is timely.[16] To simplify matters for those filing a charge, the EEOC enters into worksharing agreements with these FEP agencies that resolve the issue of which agency initially handles the dispute and cures the potential problems for charges filed between 240 and 300 days.

These potential problems arise when a state charge is properly filed and there is no worksharing agreement. The state agency may assert exclusive jurisdiction over the dispute for up to 60 days and an EEOC charge cannot be effectively filed during this period.[17] If the matter has not been resolved by then, the individual may then file a charge with the EEOC. To be timely, however, the EEOC charge must be filed within the *earlier* of two times—300 days after the discriminatory occurrence or 30 days after receipt of notice that the state agency has terminated its jurisdiction. If an individual were to file with the state on the 241st day, and the state agency were to

14. EEOC v. Shell Oil Co., 466 U.S. 54 (1984).

15. Spirt v. Teachers Ins. & Annuity Ass'n, 93 F.R.D. 627 (S.D.N.Y.), *rev'd in part on other grounds*, 691 F.2d 1054 (2d Cir. 1982), vacated on other grounds, 463 U.S. 1223 (1983).

16. EEOC v. Commercial Office Products. Co., 486 U.S. 107 (1988).

17. A charge filed early will, however, be held in "suspended animation" and will be considered effectively filed at the appropriate time, thus obviating the need for refiling. Love v. Pullman, 404 U.S. 522 (1972).

continue to assert its exclusive jurisdiction for the full 60 days, then it would be the 301st day before the individual can file the federal charge, which is too late. This is one reason why the great majority of local agencies have eliminated these difficulties through worksharing agreements with the EEOC.[18]

§ 16.04 Determining When a Discriminatory Act Occurs

[A] The *Perpetuation* or *Present Effects of Prior Discrimination* Theory

In the early days of the Act, plaintiffs frequently argued and some courts recognized something known as *the present effects of prior discrimination* or *perpetuation discrimination.*[19] The theory encompassed both a particular form of statutory discrimination and identified the time when the effect of a prior act was felt as the operative discriminatory occurrence, for statute of limitation purposes. After dancing around the theory for many years, showing at least implicit disapproval, the Supreme Court finally rejected it expressly.

The analysis must begin with a pair of Supreme Court cases decided on the same day in 1977. In *Teamsters v. United States,*[20] prior to the effective date of Title VII job categories or bargaining units had been segregated by race, and an individual's seniority was measured by how long the individual had been in that bargaining unit, not by date of hire. After Title VII became effective, segregated bargaining units were eliminated and employees in one bargaining unit were allowed to bid for and fill vacancies in another bargaining unit. By doing so, however, these employees lost their accumulated unit seniority and were thus vulnerable to layoff. Although this could have been treated as a *present effects of prior discrimination* or *perpetuation* type of violation, the Supreme Court declined to evaluate the facts in those terms. Rather, the Court pointed out that the loss-of-seniority provision inured to the disadvantage of those in the lower paying job categories, who were predominantly black or Hispanic and who were seeking to move into the higher paying job categories. The Court thus concluded that this seniority system, in which seniority was measured by longevity in one's production unit rather than by how long one had actually worked for the employer, had a *Griggs*-type disparate impact. The Court, however, ultimately held that this otherwise illegal discrimination was saved by the Section 703(h) seniority exception.

Implicitly, by fitting the case into the disparate impact category, the Court rejected the *present effects* notion of actionable discrimination. This is apparent when *Teamsters*

---

18. Marlowe v. Bottarelli, 938 F.2d 807 (7th Cir. 1991) (worksharing agreement in which the state agency waived its 60 days of exclusive jurisdiction is "self-executing," and a charge is considered filed with the EEOC when it is filed with the state agency); 29 C.F.R. § 1601.13.

19. Quarles v. Philip Morris, Inc., 279 F. Supp. 505 (E.D. Va. 1968).

20. 431 U.S. 324 (1977).

is compared with the contemporaneous case of *United Air Lines v. Evans*.[21] In this case, individuals whose employment with the company terminated for any reason forfeited their accumulated seniority and, if ever rehired, started anew at the bottom of the seniority list. Pursuant to a policy forbidding female airline attendants to be married, Evans was forced to resign in 1968. She did not challenge the decision at that time. Later, after United's policy was found to have been illegal, Evans applied and was eventually rehired. Now lacking the seniority that she previously had, she was at a disadvantage when bidding for desirable flights. Unlike the plaintiffs in *Teamsters*, she could not conceptualize the violation in terms of disparate impact, because she could not prove that a higher percentage of females than males were disadvantaged by the loss-of-seniority rule. On the other hand, like the plaintiffs in *Teamsters*, she could and did claim that "the seniority system gives present effect to the past illegal act and therefore perpetuates the consequences of forbidden discrimination."[22] Clearly, that was true with respect to her individually. But the Court held that the enforcement of this neutral rule was not a *present* violation. And even if it had been, this seniority system would also have been saved by Section 703(h).

Despite the relatively clear implications of *Evans*, in *Lorance v. AT&T Technologies, Inc.*,[23] the Supreme Court was again confronted with a seniority system that the plaintiffs claimed was not protected by Section 703(h) because it was purposefully structured to discriminate against women by altering the way seniority was computed. The plaintiffs in this case, however, did not feel the disadvantage until some time later, when their now diminished seniority caused them to be demoted. The charge was timely when measured from the date of demotion. But the Supreme Court again held that the *discriminatory occurrence* was the change in the seniority system, not when the effect was finally felt. The plaintiff's challenge to it was thus time barred. The Court emphasized, however, that a facially discriminatory seniority system could be challenged at any time.[24]

Congress overruled *Lorance* in the Civil Rights Act of 1991. Under Section 706(e)(2), a challenge to an allegedly discriminatory seniority system may be brought within 180 (or 300) days (1) after the system is adopted, (2) after an individual becomes subject to it, or (3) after an individual is injured by the application of the system. Outside the seniority system context, the *Evans* and *Lorance* decisions continued to suggest that the *present effects* concept of actionable discrimination was not available as a way of satisfying the statute of limitation.

Although both *Evans* and *Lorance* seemed to signal the death of the *perpetuation* or *present effects* theory, the applicability of its demise to pay cases was thrown into question in *Bazemore v. Friday*.[25] Prior to the effective date of Title VII, an agricultural extension program divided its agents into racially segregated "branches," with the pay

21. 431 U.S. 553 (1977).
22. Evans, 431 U.S. at 557.
23. 490 U.S. 900 (1989).
24. Lorance, 490 U.S. at 912.
25. 478 U.S. 385 (1986).

structure being less for the black agents. After Title VII was made applicable to the states in 1972, the two branches were merged, but salary discrepancies were not entirely eliminated. Although the issue was whether these discrepancies had to be eliminated rather than the timeliness of charge per se, some of the Court's language suggests that the *perpetuation* theory was still quite alive. Specifically, the Court said that "to the extent this discrimination was perpetuated after 1972, liability may still be imposed."[26] This led some to suggest that disparities in pay were not subject to the *Evans* concept of when a discrimination act occurs.

The Supreme Court thought to put the issue to rest in *Ledbetter v. Goodyear Tire & Rubber Co., Inc.*[27] Ledbetter alleged that during the course of her employment she had been given poor evaluations because of her sex, which affected the amount of pay she received at the time. In the Supreme Court, she argued that paychecks dispersed during the 180 days prior to her filing, even though not themselves intentionally discriminatory, were nevertheless illegal because they were "the result of intentionally discriminatory pay decisions that occurred outside the limitations period"[28] and that the denial of a raise that occurred during the 180-day period was similarly "unlawful because it carried forward intentionally discriminatory disparities from prior years"—even though the decision itself had been found not to have been made with discrimination intent. The Court of Appeals held that her claims were not timely.

The Court read *Evans* and several other Supreme Court cases as standing for this proposition:

> The EEOC charging period is triggered when a discrete unlawful practice takes place [here, the discriminatory evaluations]. A new violation does not occur, and a new charging period does not commence, upon the occurrence of subsequent nondiscriminatory acts [the 1998 pay decision and the issuance of checks] that entail adverse effects result from the past discrimination."[29]

At the Supreme Court, Ledbetter cited *Bazemore* as being in opposition to the *Evans* line of cases, thus creating a special rule with respect to pay claims. The Supreme Court rejected the argument on the grounds that *Bazemore* involved a facially discriminatory pay structure and that a separate act of discrimination occurred every time that discriminatory policy was applied.[30] Since Ledbetter merely claimed that she was still feeling the effects of the time-barred discriminatory evaluation and not that she was currently subject to a facially discriminatory pay structure, *Evans* rather than *Bazemore* controlled. The *Ledbetter* case signals the end of the *present effect of prior discrimination* as either a statutory form of *discrimination* or as an occurrence that starts the statute of limitations anew.

---

26. Bazemore, 478 U.S. at 395.

27. 550 U.S. 618 (2007).

28. Ledbetter, 550 U.S. at 623 (quoting from plaintiff's petition for certiorari).

29. Ledbetter, 550 U.S. at 628.

30. Ledbetter, 550 U.S. at 634 ("[a]n employer that adopts and intentionally retains a [racially discriminatory pay structure] can surely be regarded as intending to discriminate on the basis of race as long as the structure is used").

Congress overruled *Ledbetter* in 2009, in an act named after her, which modified the trigger for an unlawful act with respect to discriminatory compensation. Congress established these three points: (1) when the discriminatory decision is made or the practice adopted; (2) when an individual becomes subject to the decision; or (3) when an individual is affected by the decision. An adverse effect occurs with every paycheck reflecting the discriminatory decision. At the same time, Congress limited the maximum recovery period to two years preceding the filing of the EEOC charge.[31]

Congress did not, however, disturb the *Ledbetter* ruling outside the area of discriminatory compensation.

[B] Disparate Impact Claims

Disparate impact claims are not subject to the *Ledbetter/Evans* timeliness rule because they focus on impact (the use of a hiring tool that creates a discriminatory result) rather than intent. In *Lewis v. City of Chicago*,[32] the Supreme Court considered a hiring test that the City stipulated had a disparate impact on minority applicants. The results of this test were used to make hiring decisions for the six following years. When plaintiffs filed EEOC charges nearly two years after taking this test, the City argued their claim was time-barred for failing to file EEOC charges within 300 days of taking the unlawful exam. The Supreme Court rejected the City's argument and held the charges were timely because the City continued to *use* the test results to make hiring decisions. As long as the test results were *used* to make a hiring decision, charges could be filed.

[C] The *Notice of Decision* Rule

When the Title VII statute of limitations begins to run was clarified in another respect in *Delaware State College v. Ricks*,[33] which involved the arcane and complicated employment practices of an educational institution. The sequence of events was basically as follows: (1) the faculty tenure committee recommended that Ricks not be given tenure, but agreed to reconsider the next year; (2) upon reconsideration, the committee again recommended against tenure; (3) the faculty senate voted to support that recommendation; (4) the trustees formally voted to deny tenure; (5) Ricks filed a grievance with the school grievance committee; (6) consistent with school policy with respect to persons denied tenure, Ricks was told he would be given a one-year "terminal" contract; (7) the trustees denied the grievance; and (8) Ricks' contract finally expired and he was terminated.

The parties, the EEOC, and the lower courts advanced a number of dates for when the statute of limitations began to run. Ricks, relying on a theory of continuing vi-

31. 42 U.S.C. § 2000e-5(e)(3)(B).
32. 560 U.S. 205 (2010).
33. 449 U.S. 250 (1980).

olations, argued that it was not until the employment actually ended. The Supreme Court, however, held that the continuing violation theory did not apply here. Although admitting that the alleged discriminatory act occurred earlier, the Court of Appeals also adopted the end-of-employment date, on the grounds that it provided a bright-line test. The Court rejected this on the grounds that it ignored the function of a statute of limitations, which is to prevent the litigation of stale claims. The EEOC argued for the date on which the trustees denied the grievance, but the Court pointed out that the discriminatory decision had already been made by then and that the pendency of a grievance or arbitration procedure does not toll the running of the statute, citing *IUEW v. Robbins & Myers, Inc.*[34] Rather, the Court concluded that "the limitations periods commenced to run when the tenure decision was made and Ricks was notified." The Court then concluded that this had occurred *at least* by the time the trustees informed Ricks that he would be offered a terminal contract. In sum, the date of decision and notice generally marks the beginning of the Title VII statute of limitations.

Despite the apparent simplicity of the *notice of decision* test, in the more common industrial setting, questions still remain over whose *decision* counts and what the employee must be *on notice* of. A termination decision may start with a line supervisor filing a disciplinary report that lists what the employee did as a "termination offense" or where the supervisor checks "termination" as the recommended sanction. This may pass through successive layers of supervisors and managers before it becomes final, in the sense that it is something that can then be internally appealed to higher management or made the subject of a grievance[35]—assuming, of course, there truly are *appeals* or *grievances* of an otherwise final prior decision. Similar problems arise in the context of a *decision* not to hire. The cases are enormously fact-specific but tend to focus on the *decision* that is determinative as a practical matter rather than what the company rules say.

The other open question pertains to what the employee must be on notice of. Most courts focus on notice of the adverse action or its potentiality for adversity in fact.[36] Others, however, require that the individual be on notice of facts suggesting that the adverse action was discriminatorily motivated.[37] When the plaintiff's lack of knowledge of discriminatory motive can be attributed to misleading statements or conduct of the employer, the courts sometimes apply the doctrine of equitable tolling.[38]

34. 429 U.S. 229 (1976).

35. Utilization of a union grievance/arbitration procedure does not toll the running of the limitations period, and neither the ultimate decision of an in-house official to whom a true appeal might be lodged nor the decision of an arbitration board is (absent an additional act of discrimination at this stage) the *discriminatory occurrence* that will trigger the running of the limitations period. IUEW v. Robbins & Myers, Inc., 429 U.S. 229 (1976).

36. Hamilton v. 1st Source Bank, 928 F.2d 86 (4th Cir. 1990) (en banc).

37. Vaught v. R.R. Donnelley & Sons Co., 745 F.2d 407 (7th Cir. 1984).

38. Cada v. Baxter Healthcare Corp., 920 F.2d 446 (7th Cir. 1990). *See* § 16.04[E].

[D] Continuing Violations

Although the statute requires that the charge be filed within either 180 or 300 days of the discriminatory practice, Section 706(g) of the statute also provides that back pay may not accrue from a date more than two years prior to the filing of the charge. This would seem to suggest that some otherwise time-barred violations may nevertheless be litigated and remedied.

The original function of the continuing violations theory was to identify those violations. It was an important concept because linking a current discriminatory act to others that occurred in the past could significantly affect, for example, the amount of back pay a successful plaintiff could recover. Several factually distinct types of continuing violations began to emerge. For example, the Ninth Circuit in *AMTRAK v. Morgan*,[39] held that a plaintiff could establish a continuing violation by showing "a series of related acts one or more of which are within the limitations period."[40] Such a "serial violation is established if the evidence indicates that the alleged acts of discrimination occurring prior to the limitations period are sufficiently related to those occurring within the limitations period."[41] The court found that each type of discrimination alleged by the plaintiff satisfied that test.

The Supreme Court rejected this approach, holding that "[d]iscrete acts such as termination, failure to promote, denial of transfer, or refusal to hire ... [each] constitute[] a separate actionable 'unlawful employment practice'"[42] and a charge must be filed within 180/300 days of each occurrence. Reading the text of the statute literally and narrowly, the Court noted that Congress intentionally imposed short deadlines "to encourage the prompt processing of all charges of employment discrimination."[43]

The Court, however, did not read the continuing violations theory out of the statute altogether. Limiting its holding to "discrete acts," the Court further opined that "[h]ostile environment claims are different in kind from discrete acts."[44] Rather, the hostile environment form of discrimination "occurs over a series of days or perhaps years and, in direct contrast to discrete acts, a single act of harassment may not be actionable on its own."[45]

In sum, the sole remaining function of the continuing violation theory is to allow pre-filing period acts to be connected to filing period acts to establish the existence of conduct that when viewed cumulatively violates the statute, even though any one individual act would not qualify—as in establishing that the hostile environment was severe or pervasive. Beyond hostile environment discrimination, it is not clear what other types of Title VII violation the Court might have had in mind.

39. 232 F.3d 1008 (9th Cir. 2000), aff'd in part and rev'd in part, 536 U.S. 101 (2002).
40. *Morgan*, 232 F.3d at 1015.
41. *Morgan*, 232 F.3d at 1015.
42. *Morgan*, 536 U.S. at 114.
43. *Morgan*, 536 U.S. at 109.
44. *Morgan*, 536 U.S. at 115.
45. Morgan, 536 U.S. at 115.

Although *Morgan* disallows recovery for discrete discriminatory acts that are time-barred, the decision does not preclude using these acts as *background evidence* that is relevant to the question of whether an act within the limitations period was impermissibly motivated. Indeed, in a very early case the Supreme Court had expressly indicated that the time-barred action "may constitute relevant background evidence in a proceeding in which the status of a current practice is at issue."[46] And background evidence is likely to play a more significant role in non-harassment cases, where a continuing violation is unavailable.[47] The issue will be whether the proffered evidence is so remote in time and unrelated to the act being litigated that it lacks probative value and would unduly prejudice the defendant. Pre-*Morgan* cases have frequently ruled this kind of evidence inadmissible on that basis,[48] and this is likely to be a more frequently litigated issue.

[E] Waiver, Estoppel, and Equitable Tolling

In *Zipes v. Trans World Airlines, Inc.*,[49] the Supreme Court held that the 180- or 300-day filing requirement was not jurisdictional and was thus subject to waiver, estoppel, and equitable tolling. As is true with other statutes of limitation, a defendant must plead an untimely filing as an affirmative defense and failure to do so will result in waiver.

Although employment discrimination may violate contractual and other statutory prohibitions, the Title VII claim is not tolled by resort to other forums—such as a grievance/arbitration procedures, administrative agency complaint mechanisms, the National Labor Relations Board, or a federal court in a Section 1981 lawsuit.[50] The courts generally hold, however, that a timely filing of a Title VII charge with the state or federal agency will toll the running of the statute.[51]

The more complicated and controversial uses of tolling and estoppel arise in the context of a charging party's excusable ignorance of the employer's discriminatory acts or of the need to file within a certain period. The easiest cases are where the EEOC has misled the charging party,[52] or the employer has lured the employee into delaying a filing.[53] When the issue is whether the charging party knew or should have

---

46. *Evans*, 431 U.S. at 558.

47. Lyons v. England, 307 F.3d 1092 (9th Cir. 2002) (suggesting an expanded emphasis on background evidence after *Morgan*).

48. Stewart v. Adolph Coors Co., 217 F.3d 1285 (10th Cir. 2000); Kline v. City of Kansas City Fire Dep't, 175 F.3d 660 (8th Cir. 1999).

49. 455 U.S. 385 (1982).

50. IUEW v. Robbins & Myers, Inc., 429 U.S. 229 (1976); Johnson v. Railway Express Agency, Inc., 421 U.S. 454 (1975).

51. Husch v. Szabo Food Serv. Co., 851 F.2d 999 (7th Cir. 1988).

52. Gray v. Phillips Petrol. Co., 858 F.2d 610 (10th Cir. 1988).

53. Leake v. Univ. of Cincinnati, 605 F.2d 255 (6th Cir. 1979).

known of the discriminatory nature of the employer's action, some courts require affirmative misrepresentations by the employer while others do not.[54]

The Supreme Court has held that filing a class action tolls the running of the limitation period for putative class members.[55] Thus, if class certification is denied, persons who would have been class members can still use whatever time remains of the statutory period to file individually.

§ 16.05 EEOC Procedures

Once a charge is filed, it is in the hands of the EEOC. Although the EEOC's failure to follow the correct procedures will generally not bar a lawsuit by the charging party, the EEOC itself may be unable to do so. In abbreviated form, the agency procedures are as follows:

- An EEOC administrative assistant will review the charge and put it into one of three categories: (1) an expedited investigation for certain types of discrimination, where further investigation is likely to result in a finding of discrimination and "irreparable harm will result unless the processing is expedited"; (2) normal investigation to determine if the charges have merit; and (3) further investigation is unlikely to produce a finding of discrimination, such as where the EEOC lacks jurisdiction.
- If the jurisdiction in which the discrimination occurred has a deferral or work-sharing agency, the EEOC will refer the charge to that agency.
- The statute requires that the EEOC notify the charged party within 10 days after receipt of the charge.
- One of the EEOC's primary functions is to fully investigate the charge. This will involve a request for a position statement from the respondent, requests for specific information, issuance of subpoenas if necessary, on-site reviews in some instances, and fact-finding conferences between the parties. The EEOC will also encourage mediation. The charging party's failure to cooperate with the EEOC investigation[56] or refusal to accept a settlement providing full relief may bar a subsequent suit.[57] Under Section 709(a), the EEOC may also issue subpoenas if a party, usually the respondent, refuses to supply requested information. The

54. *Compare* Mack v. Great Atl. & Pac. Tea Co., 871 F.2d 179 (1st Cir. 1989), *with* Chappell v. Emco Machine Works Co., 601 F.2d 1295 (5th Cir. 1979).

55. Crown, Cork & Seal Co. v. Parker, 462 U.S. 345 (1983).

56. *Compare Shikles v. Sprint*/United Mgmt. Co., 426 F.3d 1304 (10th Cir. 2005) (ADEA case), *with* Doe v. Oberweis Dairy, 456 F.3d 704 (7th Cir. 2006).

57. *Compare* Wrenn v. Sec'y, Dep't of Veterans Affairs, 918 F.2d 1073 (2d Cir. 1990), *with* Long v. Ringling Bros. Barnum & Bailey Combined Shows, Inc., 9 F.3d 340 (4th Cir. 1993).

scope of the subpoena is, however, limited by the nature of discrimination contained in the charge.[58]

- Before issuing a determination letter, the EEOC will hold a counseling session with either the charging party or the respondent, depending on whether the EEOC has found that a violation probably exists or not, to advise this person of the probable EEOC decision. This can lead either to further investigation, settlement, withdrawal of the charge, or the issuance of a determination letter.
- If the EEOC believes that a violation has occurred, then it must attempt conciliation efforts, aimed toward a settlement between the charging party, the respondent, and the EEOC.
- If the EEOC determines that no probable violation exists, it will notify the charging party and issue a right-to-sue letter—although the courts are divided over whether the EEOC can issue this letter and a charging party bring suit before the expiration of 180 days.[59] Certainly, after 180 days the charging party may request the right-to-sue letter, regardless of whether the EEOC has completed its investigation.

§ 16.06 EEOC Files and Determination Letters

The statute prohibits *public* access to the EEOC's investigative files during the investigative process and settlement attempts. These confidentiality provisions are specifically incorporated into the Freedom of Information Act. Although the charging party and the respondent are not members of the *public* for the purposes of this prohibition,[60] the EEOC frequently relies on other FOIA exceptions to the general duty of disclosure even when one of the parties is seeking the information. These include exceptions relating to trade secrets and commercial or financial information, inter- or intra-agency memoranda that would otherwise be privileged from discovery, and records collected for law enforcement purposes if disclosure would interfere with enforcement proceedings or reveal confidential sources. Recently, the EEOC created an Internet portal for filing certain documents related to a pending charge. This allows the charging party, for example, to read the position statement of the respondent when it is filed.

---

58. EEOC v. Southern Farm Bureau Casualty Ins. Co., 271 F.3d 209 (5th Cir. 2001) (race discrimination charge will not support a subpoena for information relating to sex discrimination).

59. The EEOC issued a regulation allowing it to issue, upon request, an early right-to-sue letter as long as it determined that it was unable to complete its work within 180 days. 29 C.F.R. § 1601.28(a)(2). The D.C. Circuit requires waiting for 180 days. Martini v. Fannie Mae, 178 F.3d 1336 (D.C. Cir. 1999). Three other circuits have upheld the EEOC regulation. Walker v. UPS, 240 F.3d 1268, 1273–77 (10th Cir. 2001); Sims v. MacMillan, 22 F.3d 1059, 1061–63 (11th Cir. 1994); Brown v. Puget Sound Elec. Apprenticeship & Training Tr., 732 F.2d 726, 729 (9th Cir. 1984). Most district courts in circuits that have not ruled have upheld the regulation.

60. EEOC v. Associated Dry Goods Corp., 449 U.S. 590 (1981).

If a lawsuit is ultimately brought on the basis of the EEOC charge, the party who prevailed before the EEOC will often attempt to have the final EEOC determination letter introduced as evidence. And the other party will attempt to have it excluded under Rule 403 of the Federal Rules of Evidence. A majority of the circuits have held that the decision on whether the EEOC determination letter is more probative than prejudicial under Rule 403 is within the discretion of the trial courts, to be determined on a case-by-case basis.[61] The minority view is that because government records are admissible under Rule 803(8)(C), they are per se admissible under Rule 403.

§ 16.07 Chapter Highlights

1. Title VII enforcement begins with the filing of a charge with the EEOC or an appropriate state agency. The EEOC charge must be verified and identify the alleged discrimination and the party who allegedly committed it. (§ 16.01)

2. A charge may be filed by the person aggrieved by the discrimination, by a person on behalf of the person aggrieved, or by an EEOC Commissioner. The constitutional standing test is generally used in determining whether a person is aggrieved for charge-filing purposes. (§ 16.02)

3. A *person aggrieved* is usually the person directly affected by the discrimination, but it may also include organizations of which this person is a member and even *testers.* (§ 16.02[A])

4. An organization or even another individual may file a charge *on behalf of the person aggrieved*, but after filing the charge this organization or person has almost no role to play in the process. (§ 16.02[B])

5. An EEOC Commissioner may also file a charge. (§ 16.02[C])

6. In a state without a deferral agency, the EEOC charge must be filed within 180 days of the discriminatory occurrence. In a deferral state, the EEOC charge must be filed within 300 days of the discriminatory occurrence or within 30 days after the state agency terminates its proceeding, whichever is earlier. (§ 16.03)

7. Individual acts of discrimination occur, for the purpose of starting the running of the limitations period, when the charged party makes the decision and the charging party has notice of it, not when the decision is implemented or when its effects are finally felt. (§ 16.04[A] & [C])

8. Disparate impact claims are timely if the procedure creating the disparate impact was *used* to make an employment decision during the preceding 300 days. (§ 16.04[B])

9. The once prevalent theory of a *continuing violation* is now limited to situations where the existence of a series of related acts is necessary to establish the violation—as in the hostile environment cases. (§ 16.04[D])

---

61. Coleman v. Home Depot, Inc., 306 F.3d 1333 (3d Cir. 2002) (also the rule in the Second, Fourth, Eighth, and Eleventh Circuits).

10. The time requirements for filing a charge are not jurisdictional and are thus subject to waiver, estoppel, and equitable tolling. (§ 16.04[E])

11. The administrative process begins with the filing of the charge and subsequently involves EEOC investigation, a determination of whether a violation is probable, conciliation, and the final issuance of a right-to-sue letter. (§ 16.05)

12. EEOC files are not open to public scrutiny, and even the parties may not be allowed to see parts of them in some circumstances. The courts are divided over whether the EEOC determination letter is admissible in a subsequent lawsuit. (§ 16.06)

13. After a charge is filed, the EEOC procedures are as follows: classification of the charge, reference to a state agency if necessary, notification of the person charged, mediation, investigation, counseling with the parties, issuance of a *cause* or *no cause* determination, conciliation, and issuance of the right-to-sue letter. (§ 16.05)

14. Public access to EEOC files is limited by the Freedom of Information Act. Other FOIA exemptions are used to deny access to the parties during the course of the investigation. (§ 16.06)

Chapter 17

Litigation

Synopsis

Despite the existence of administrative and private mechanisms for conciliation and settlement of employment discrimination claims, civil litigation is still often necessary to resolve disputed facts and controversial legal questions.

§ 17.01 Exhaustion Requirements

The procedures discussed in Chapter 16, leading ultimately to the issuance of a right-to-sue letter, must be exhausted before a Title VII claim can be litigated. Although the EEOC's failure to discharge its statutory duties may foreclose an agency lawsuit, the charging party is rarely prejudiced in this regard. The charging party, however, does have a duty to participate in the investigation in good faith and the failure to do so may result in the suit being dismissed.[1]

---

1. King v. Marsh, 49 Fair Empl. Prac. Cas. (BNA) 1892 (S.D. Ga. 1989), aff'd mem., 901 F.2d 1115 (11th Cir. 1990).

§ 17.02 Mandatory Arbitration of Claims

In *Alexander v. Gardner-Denver Co.*,[2] the Supreme Court held that resort to the grievance and arbitration provisions of a collective bargaining agreement, the terms of which prohibited discrimination, did not constitute an election of remedies and had limited, if any, preclusive effect on a subsequent Title VII lawsuit.[3] Likewise, a Title VII claimant was not required to resort to the arbitration provisions of a collective bargaining agreement in lieu of bringing suit in federal court. The Court's theory was that the statutory and contractual prohibitions and enforcement mechanisms were independent of each other.

This theory was seriously undermined by the Supreme Court's decision in *Gilmer v. Interstate/Johnson Lane Corp.*[4] The Supreme Court held that an individual who had agreed to arbitrate all disputes with the employer could be compelled to arbitrate a claim of discrimination under the Age Discrimination in Employment Act. Subsequently, in the Civil Rights Act of 1991, Congress seemed to endorse arbitration as a preferred method for resolving discrimination disputes. A provision states, "[w]here appropriate and to the extent authorized by law, the use of alternative means of dispute resolution, including ... arbitration, is encouraged to resolve disputes arising under" Title VII, the ADEA, and Section 1981.

The *Gilmer* decision left a number of issues unresolved, and the meaning of the provision in the 1991 Act was uncertain. For example, the lower courts were initially divided over whether *Gilmer* implicitly overruled *Garner-Denver*, thus allowing unions and employers to agree to require employees to arbitrate all their statutory claims. In *Wright v. Universal Maritime Services Corp.*,[5] which arose under the ADA, the Supreme Court distinguished "an individual's waiver of his own rights," which is subject to the *Gilmer* rule, from "a union's waiver of the rights of represented employees," which the Court said would be valid only if its application to statutory rights is "clear and unmistakable"—which is to say that *Garner-Denver* is overruled to some extent.

Ultimately, in *14 Penn Plaza v. Pyett*,[6] the Supreme Court eliminated the distinction between an individual's waiver and a union's waiver by ruling that extinguishing employees' rights to a federal court forum is no waiver at all. Arbitration is simply an alternative forum for litigating employee statutory civil rights. The plaintiff employees in *14 Penn Plaza* had sued both their employer and their union. The Court did not explain why arbitration was appropriate when the employees' litigation opponents both selected and paid for the arbitrator. The Court noted that arbitration might not

2. 415 U.S. 36 (1974).

3. McDonald v. City of West Branch, 466 U.S. 284 (1984) (arbitration is not a "judicial proceeding" and an arbitration decision has no preclusive effect in federal litigation under 28 U.S.C. § 1738). The Court in *Gardner-Denver* suggested, however, that a federal court could "accord ... great weight" to the factual findings of the arbitrator, if supported by an adequate record. Gardner-Denver, 415 U.S. at 60 n.21.

4. 500 U.S. 20 (1991).

5. 525 U.S. 70, 80–81 (1998).

6. 556 U.S. 247 (2009).

be an appropriate alternative forum where the union was the gatekeeper, controlling whether the matter could be arbitrated.

Similarly, although the lower courts were initially divided over whether arbitration clauses in employment contracts were subject to the Federal Arbitration Act, the Supreme Court held that they were in *Circuit City Stores, Inc. v. Adams.*[7] The applicability of the FAA to employment contracts was an issue because the statute expressly provides that the Act shall not apply "to contracts of employment of seamen, railroad employees, or any other class of workers engaged in foreign or interstate commerce." Since virtually all workers are *engaged in interstate commerce* in the judicially prevailing and virtually unlimited sense of the term, it would appear that almost all employer-employee arbitration agreements would be excluded from the Act.

The Supreme Court rejected such a literal interpretation of the statute. First, the Court reasoned that if the residual phrase, "other workers engaged in ... commerce" covered virtually everyone, that would render superfluous the reference to "seamen" and "railroad employees." Second, construing the Act as excluding all employment contracts would violate the *ejusdem generis* canon of statutory interpretation, to wit: when a provision contains a list of specific entities followed by a catch-all general phrase, the general phrase is limited to those entities possessing the same essential characteristic as the specific entities list. Applying this canon of interpretation, the Court thus concluded that the Act only excludes arbitration provisions found in the employment contracts of transportation workers. Third, while the words "affecting" and "involving" commerce reflect an intent to exercise the full extent of the Commerce Clause power, the words "in" and "engaged in" are intended to have a narrower reach. And fourth, the Court concluded that what limited legislative history there was, it supported the conclusion that Congress only intended to exclude transportation workers, primarily because Congress already had or soon would enact specific work-dispute resolution statutes for this class of employees.

Although the Court recognized that the effect of the decision was to preempt various state laws regulating or limiting employment-related arbitration provisions, this was simply the consequence of an earlier preemption case,[8] which the Court choose not to revisit. And, the Court added, any other result "would call into doubt the efficacy of alternative dispute resolution procedures adopted by many of the Nation's employers, in the process undermining the FAA's pro-arbitration purposes...."[9]

The Supreme Court has also held, in *Epic Systems Corp. v. Lewis,*[10] that the National Labor Relations Act's protection of the employee right to engage in "concerted activities for mutual aid of protection" does not encompass the enforcement of labor agreements through class actions or other collective enforcement proceedings. Thus, a labor

7. 532 U.S. 105 (2001).
8. Southland Corp. v. Keating, 465 U.S. 1 (1984).
9. Circuit City, 532 U.S. at 123.
10. 138 S. Ct. 1612 (2018).

agreement provision allowing only for individualized arbitration proceedings was entitled to be enforced as written.

Lower courts are left to examine carefully the wording of the arbitration agreement to see if it truly contains a "clear and unmistakable waiver of the right to a federal forum."[11] Some have been quick to find certain agreements unconscionable and unenforceable contracts of adhesion[12] and to find other substantive and procedural defects sufficient to preclude enforcement.[13]

§ 17.03 The Preclusive Effect of Prior Adjudications

An unreviewed state administrative order is given no preclusive effect at all, even if it would be treated that way under state law.[14] This is based on specific Title VII legislative history.[15] If, however, a state agency order is appealed by either the employee or the employer, the resulting state court decision will be given the same preclusive effect in federal court as it would enjoy in state court.[16] This applies both to claims that were raised or that could have been raised in the appeal.[17] The courts are divided, however, over whether a plaintiff is precluded from suing in federal court for remedies that were not available under the state statute[18] and whether an employee who has lost at the state agency level must appeal that decision, on pain of being foreclosed from bringing a federal action.[19]

Normal res judicata and collateral estoppel rules apply with respect to prior federal judicial proceedings.

§ 17.04 Time and Filing Requirements

A right-to-sue letter from the EEOC is a condition precedent for a private party suit. A person may request this letter 180 days after filing the charge, and the EEOC

11. Rogers v. New York University, 220 F.3d 73 (2d Cir. 2000).

12. Circuit City Stores, Inc. v. Adams, 279 F.3d 889 (9th Cir. 2002) (limited arbitral relief available; no protection of the employee from unreasonable costs, fees, and expenses; and others).

13. Alexander v. Anthony Int'l, 341 F.3d 256 (3d Cir. 2003) (employees allowed only an inadequate time for submitting a claim to arbitration); Penn v. Ryan's Family Steak Houses, 269 F.3d 753 (7th Cir. 2001) (lack of any clear and definite commitments by the arbitration service with whom the employee had contracted).

14. Univ. of Tennessee v. Elliott, 478 U.S. 788 (1986).

15. *Univ. of Tennessee*, 478 U.S. at 799 n.7.

16. Kremer v. Chemical Constr. Corp., 456 U.S. 461 (1982).

17. Migra v. Warren City School Dist. Bd. of Educ., 465 U.S. 75 (1984).

18. *Compare* Chris v. Tenet, 221 F.3d 648 (4th Cir. 2000), *with* Nestor v. Pratt & Whitney, 466 F.3d 65 (2d Cir. 2006).

19. *Compare* McInnes v. California, 943 F.2d 1088 (9th Cir. 1991), *with* Eilrich v. Remas, 839 F.2d 630 (9th Cir. 1988).

must issue it; but the EEOC is not required to issue a letter in the absence of a request.[20] Unreasonable delay in requesting the letter may, however, result in laches against the charging party. Although the charging party is entitled to allow the EEOC to complete its administrative processes without prejudice,[21] in rare cases courts require the charging party to exercise some degree of diligence in this regard.[22] If, however, the right-to-sue letter is issued and suit is filed before the expiration of 180 days from the filing of the charge, a period in which the EEOC normally has exclusive jurisdiction for the purposes of investigation and conciliation, some courts will still entertain the suit,[23] some courts will dismiss it as being premature,[24] while other courts will simply suspend the action until the expiration of the 180 days.[25]

A plaintiff must file within 90 days after receipt of the right-to-sue letter. The 90-day period is not jurisdictional and is thus subject to waiver, estoppel, and tolling. Merely filing the right-to-sue letter with the court does not toll the running of the statute.[26] On the other hand, the Court suggested that the running of the period may be tolled by the EEOC's failure to adequately inform the plaintiff of the limitation period, by the filing of a motion for the appointment of counsel, by misleading conduct or advice by the defendant that lulls the plaintiff into inaction, and by the court itself leading the plaintiff to believe that what had been filed was adequate.[27]

Determining when the right-to-sue letter has been effectively *received* by the charging party has caused some degree of difficulty. Most courts focus on the date of actual receipt and do not rely on the normal presumption that a document is constructively received three days after mailing.[28] However, receipt by the charging party's attorney or by anyone living at the address most recently given to the EEOC by the charging party usually starts the running of the period.[29]

Although a charging party who is represented by counsel will be expected to file a complaint in compliance with the Federal Rules of Civil Procedure, together with answers to whatever interrogatories are required by rule, pro se litigants have been given considerable leeway insofar as filing requirements are concerned. The Supreme Court has held that mailing a copy of the right-to-sue letter together with a request for ap-

---

20. Zambuto v. AT&T, 544 F.2d 1333 (5th Cir. 1977).
21. Howard v. Roadway Express, Inc., 726 F.2d 1529 (11th Cir. 1984).
22. Cleveland Newspaper Guild v. Plain Dealer Publ'g Co., 839 F.2d 1147 (6th Cir. 1988).
23. Sims v. MacMillan, 22 F.3d 1059 (11th Cir. 1994).
24. Martini v. Fannie Mae, 178 F.3d 1336 (D.C. Cir. 1999).
25. Spencer v. Banco Real, S.A., 87 F.R.D. 739 (S.D.N.Y. 1980). See the discussion in Chapter 16, § 16.05 about early requests.
26. Baldwin County Welcome Ctr. v. Brown, 466 U.S. 147 (1984) (per curiam).
27. Baldwin County, 466 U.S. 147.
28. Sherlock v. Montefiore Med. Ctr., 84 F.3d 522 (2d Cir. 1996).
29. Irwin v. Dep't of Veterans Affairs, 498 U.S. 89 (1990) (receipt by attorney); Scholar v. Pacific Bell, 963 F.2d 264 (9th Cir. 1992) (receipt by daughter held sufficient). *But see* Stallworth v. Wells Fargo Armored Servs. Corp., 936 F.2d 522 (11th Cir. 1991) (notice was received by nephew, but charging party never saw it and EEOC failed to send a copy to counsel, as requested).

pointed counsel was not an effective filing.[30] But, filing the EEOC complaint or the EEOC determination letter (which serve the purpose of notice pleadings) has been found to be sufficient.[31] The Supreme Court has also suggested that a formal motion for the appointment of counsel might toll the running of the limitations period.[32]

The EEOC may not sue until the expiration of 30 days after a charge is filed, but no specific outer time limits apply to when the EEOC must bring a lawsuit. However, laches may apply if the EEOC delay is inexcusable and inures to the prejudice of the employer.[33] This may result in the action being barred in its entirety or in the limitation of back pay liability.

§ 17.05 Private Party Suits

Private party suits are brought under Section 706. Despite whatever liberality the EEOC practices with respect to whose discrimination charges it will entertain, constitutional standing requirements clearly apply at the litigation stage. Thus, charges that are brought on behalf of an aggrieved person can be litigated only by the aggrieved person, not by the charging party. Suits brought by organizations must likewise meet traditional standing requirements.

Courts are split over whether the EEOC can also file suit on a charge after the charging party has brought suit. Some courts hold that the EEOC is limited to permissive intervention in the charging party's lawsuit,[34] while others have held that the EEOC has an unequivocal right to enforce the law through a separate action.[35]

§ 17.06 EEOC and Justice Department Litigation

Until 1972, the EEOC had no enforcement powers whatsoever. Under the 1972 amendments, the Justice Department's Section 707 power to bring pattern-or-practice claims against nongovernmental defendants was transferred to the EEOC, and the agency was also authorized to bring suits under Section 706. But because an EEOC Section 706 lawsuit is not limited to seeking relief on behalf of the charging party, the substantive claims could be about the same, regardless of which section the EEOC chooses to rely on.

30. *Baldwin County*, 466 U.S. 147 (1984) (per curiam).

31. Judkins v. Beech Aircraft Corp., 745 F.2d 1330 (11th Cir. 1984); Mahroom v. Defense Language Inst., 732 F.2d 1439 (9th Cir. 1984).

32. Baldwin County, 466 U.S. at 151–52.

33. EEOC v. Dresser Indus., Inc., 668 F.2d 1199 (11th Cir. 1982); EEOC v. Great Atl. & Pac. Tea Co., 735 F.2d 69 (3d Cir. 1984).

34. EEOC v. Continental Oil Co., 548 F.2d 884 (10th Cir. 1977).

35. EEOC v. North Hills Passavant Hosp., 544 F.2d 664 (3d Cir. 1976).

Two limitations exist on the EEOC's power to sue. First, the EEOC must have satisfied the statutory prerequisites of investigation, determination, and conciliation.[36] In *Mach Mining, LLC v. EEOC*,[37] the Court laid down a bright-line rule to determine the adequacy of the EEOC's conciliation efforts. The EEOC must explain the specific allegation to the charged party and try to engage in a discussion of voluntary compliance.[38] If the attempted conciliation has been found to be inadequate, most courts prefer to stay the action rather than dismiss it.[39]

Second, once the charging party has brought suit, under Section 706(f)(1) the EEOC may intervene only with the permission of the court, upon a showing that the case "is of general public importance." On the other hand, if the EEOC has filed suit first, the charging party may intervene as a matter of right.

The Department of Justice has authority to bring either Section 706 or Section 707 suits against state and local governments. Although the statute is unclear about the procedural prerequisites for a Department of Justice lawsuit, in practice the DOJ essentially follows the same procedures as the EEOC with respect to the need for a charge, investigation, cause determinations, and conciliation.

§ 17.07 Class Actions

Because discrimination is almost inherently class-wide in scope, it naturally lends itself to class actions under Rule 23 of the Federal Rules of Civil Procedure. Indeed, a great deal of class action law was developed in employment discrimination lawsuits.

[A] The Basic Requirements

A named plaintiff must have filed a timely charge with the EEOC and otherwise exhausted the administrative process, although this is not required of other members of the class. To be certified as a class action, the case must then satisfy the requirements of both Rule 23(a) and Rule 23(b).

[1] Rule 23(a)—Numerosity, Commonality, Typicality, and Adequacy

Under Rule 23(a) an individual seeking to maintain a class action must establish the following:

- That the members of the putative class are so numerous as to make their joinder as named plaintiffs impractical.
- That common questions of law and fact exist.

---

36. EEOC v. Sherwood Medical Indus., Inc., 452 F. Supp. 678 (M.D. Fla. 1978).
37. 135 S. Ct. 1645 (2015).
38. *Mach Mining*, 135 S. Ct. at 1652, 1655–56.
39. EEOC v. Die Fliedermaus, LLC, 77 F. Supp. 2d 460 (S.D.N.Y. 1999).

- That the named plaintiff's claims, or the defenses that will be raised against these claims, are typical of the class.
- And that the named plaintiff can fairly and adequately represent the class, has no conflicts of interest with other members of the class, and will use qualified counsel.

Although at one time the courts were extremely liberal in applying the Rule 23(a) requirements, thus allowing so-called *across-the-board* charges of discrimination involving diversely situated members of the class and differing forms and bases of discrimination, the Supreme Court now requires closer scrutiny of the Rule 23 requirements.[40] What the commonality, typicality, and adequacy of representation elements essentially boil down to is the establishment of a nexus between the named plaintiff and the class members, so that a class action is both an efficient and a fair method of resolving the problem. The courts thus often focus on three areas—the nature of the claims, the job classifications involved, and the organizational units or geographic facilities involved.

The claims nexus may be difficult to establish if members of the class are alleging discrimination in a variety of different contexts—such as those relating to recruiting, hiring, job placement, transfer, pay, and promotion. Disparate impact claims lend themselves easily to class action treatment, as do systemic disparate treatment claims. Individual disparate treatment claims often fail the commonality requirement because each individual's case tends to be fact specific. Actions involving a large number of job categories or classifications are often denied class certification unless the named plaintiff can show a common policy of discrimination regardless of job or position. Likewise, absent an alleged centralized policy or practice, a named plaintiff in one organizational unit or geographical facility is generally not allowed to represent individuals in other units or facilities. In *Wal-Mart Stores, Inc. v. Dukes*,[41] a nationwide class of 1.5 million female employees failed because the Court required a common contention that was capable of class-wide resolution. The Court looked for a claim central to the entire class that was either true or false. The common claim in *Wal-Mart* was that promotion authority was held by lower level managers, but the Court ruled that was not a sufficient common claim. Rather, the required common claim is that class members suffered the same injury, and the truth or falsity of that claim must be central to the validity of all the class member's claims.

There is no *magic number* insofar as the numerosity requirement is concerned, although some courts have suggested a rule-of-thumb calling for at least 40 members of the class.[42] But in addition to the actual or estimated number of class members, the courts also consider geographic dispersion, the size of the individual claims, and whether the fear of retaliation might deter individuals from wanting to be a member of the plaintiff class. The *Wal-Mart* decision suggests that some classes are simply

40. General Telephone Co. v. Falcon, 457 U.S. 147 (1982).
41. 564 U.S. 338 (2011).
42. Alvarez v. Keystone Plus Constr. Corp., 303 F.R.D. 152 (D.D.C. April 11, 2014).

too big. "Here, [plaintiffs] wish to sue about literally millions of employment decisions at once. Without some glue holding the alleged *reasons* for all those decisions together, it will be impossible ... to produce a common answer to the crucial question *why was I disfavored.*"[43]

The adequacy of the named plaintiff as a representative of the class turns on both the absence of any conflicts of interest with the members of the class and the competency and experience of counsel.

[2] Rule 23(b)—The Suitability of the Case for Class Action Treatment

In addition, under Rule 23(b) the plaintiff must show either that the employer "has acted or refused to act on grounds generally applicable to the class, thereby making appropriate final injunctive ... or ... declaratory relief," (Rule 23(b)(2)) or that "the questions of law or fact common to the members of the class predominate over any questions affecting only individual members, and ... a class action is superior to other available methods" of adjudication (Rule 23(b)(3)). If the class is certified on the basis of common questions of law and fact under Rule 23(b)(3), then members of the class must be given the opportunity to "opt out" and the court may require that each member be given notice—thus making the first basis of certification the more popular one.

[B] The Effect of the 1991 Amendments

For reasons discussed earlier, before the 1991 amendments, Rule 23(b) certification was often predicated on the employer's conduct toward the class as a whole, thus making declaratory and injunctive relief appropriate. Although back pay claims (which are technically equitable remedies) caused some minor difficulties in class certification, the 1991 amendments' addition of compensatory and punitive damages and the right to a jury trial has had a serious impact on this basis of certification. Plaintiffs suing for those remedies are no longer seeking mere injunctive or declaratory relief. Indeed, the individual determinations that are necessary when awarding true damages may even predominate over the common issues of law and fact, thus making the Rule 23(b)(3) basis of certification also unavailable. *Wal-Mart* resolved at least some of the lower court division over this issue[44] by holding that claims for monetary relief could not be certified under Rule 23(b)(2) unless the monetary issues are "incidental

43. *Wal-Mart*, 564 U.S. at 352.

44. Reeb v. Ohio Dep't of Rehabilitation, 435 F.3d 639 (6th Cir. 2006) (denying Rule 23(b)(2) certification because individual claims would always predominate); Robinson v. Metro-North Commuter R.R. Co., 267 F.3d 147 (2d Cir. 2001); Celestine v. Citgo Petroleum Corp., 165 F.R.D. 463 (W.D. La. 1995) (denying Rule 23(b)(2) certification); Butler v. Home Depot, 70 Fair Empl. Prac. Cas. (BNA) 51 (N.D. Cal. 1996) (granting Rule 23(b)(2) certification); Zapata v. IBP, Inc. 167 F.R.D. 147 (D. Kan. 1996) (denying Rule 23(b)(3) certification); Griffin v. Home Depot, 168 F.R.D. 187 (E.D. La. 1996) (denying Rule 23(b)(2) certification but granting Rule 23(b)(3) certification).

to the injunctive or declaratory relief."[45] More recently, in *Tyson Foods, Inc. v. Bouaphakeo*,[46] the Court explained that "careful scrutiny" must be given to the Rule 23(b)(3) requirement that common questions must predominate over individual questions. Individual questions require proof that varies from member to member of the class, while a common question allows the same evidence for each class member. If each class member's damages must be individually proved, then individual questions predominate. However, if a representative sample can be used to prove individual damages, then common questions predominate.[47]

§ 17.08 Party Defendants

Section 706 provides that a "civil action may be brought against a respondent named in the charge." Being named in the charge does not necessarily mean being specifically identified in the block of the EEOC charge form that requests the name of the person or entity against whom the charge is being made. A defendant may be considered *named*, for statutory purposes, if that person was actually involved in the EEOC investigation of the charge, was on actual notice of the alleged violation, or enjoyed an identity of interest with a name party. Consistent with the statutory policy in favor of conciliation and settlement, a defendant who was not given actual or constructive notice of those procedures, did not participate, and was prejudiced thereby is likely to be dismissed from the lawsuit. But even this principle is subject to exceptions. Further complicating matters is the Federal Rule of Civil Procedure 19, which deals with the necessary and indispensable parties to a lawsuit. The question is whether the failure to name such a person or entity justifies dismissal of the lawsuit, on the one hand, or requires joinder despite not being named, on the other. Whether supervisory personnel, as statutory *agents* of the employer, can be held personally liable for their acts of discrimination is discussed elsewhere.[48]

§ 17.09 Scope of the Suit

A recurring issue is whether a Title VII lawsuit is necessarily limited by the charge. If the charge alleged illegal termination, may the lawsuit also allege illegal promotion policies? Or if the charge alleged discrimination on the basis of race, may the lawsuit also allege discrimination on the basis of sex? And may the lawsuit encompass incidents that occurred after the charge was filed?

---

45. *Wal-Mart*, 564 U.S. at 360. For example, individualized back pay requests would not be subject to 23(b)(2) certification.

46. 136 S. Ct. 1036 (2016).

47. *Tyson Foods*, 136 S. Ct. at 1045–47.

48. *See* Chapter 4, § 4.03[A][1].

In *Sanchez v. Standard Brands, Inc.*,[49] the Fifth Circuit articulated an approach for resolving these issues that has been consistently followed:

> [T]he allegations in a judicial complaint filed pursuant to Title VII "may encompass any kind of discrimination like or related to allegations contained in the charge and growing out of such allegations during the pendency of the case before the Commission."... In other words, the "scope" of the judicial complaint is limited to the "scope" of the EEOC investigation which can reasonably be expected to grow out of the charge of discrimination.[50]

The test is sometimes worded in terms of complaint allegations that are "like or reasonably related to" allegations in the charge.[51] The application of the test is, however, problematic and unpredictable. Although many courts are quite liberal in allowing a plaintiff to expand the *issues* or incidents of discrimination, some are not. In one case, for example, a charge that only alleged segregation by sex was sufficient to support a complaint alleging sex discrimination in hiring, firing, transfer, and promotion.[52] Yet, another court found that where the charge only alleged race discrimination in promotions, the charging party could not litigate a claim of discriminatory failure to provide educational opportunities.[53] Almost all courts, however, are less tolerant of a charging party's attempt to expand the *basis* of discrimination—for example, alleging sex discrimination in the complaint based on a charge that alleged only race discrimination.[54] Considerable diversity also exists among the courts over whether the plaintiff will be allowed to litigate incidents that occurred after the charge was filed,[55] with claims of post-charge retaliation being the most frequently allowed.[56]

When the EEOC brings suit, it is not limited to the claims brought by the charging party. As the Supreme Court has noted, "[a]ny violations that the EEOC ascertains in the course of a reasonable investigation of the charging party's complaint are actionable."[57] This allows the EEOC to not only litigate new issues and bases of discrimination, but to also include other victims of the alleged discrimination.[58]

---

49. 431 F.2d 455 (5th Cir. 1970).
50. Sanchez, 431 F.2d at 466.
51. Carrillo v. Illinois Bell Tel. Co., 538 F. Supp. 793, 797–98 (N.D. Ill. 1982).
52. Babrocky v. Jewel Food Co., 773 F.2d 857 (7th Cir. 1985).
53. Kirk v. Federal Property Mgmt. Corp., 22 F.3d 135 (7th Cir. 1994).
54. Lowe v. City of Monrovia, 775 F.2d 998 (9th Cir. 1985), amended, 784 F.2d 1407 (9th Cir. 1986).
55. Stewart v. United States Immigration & Naturalization Serv., 762 F.2d 193 (2d Cir. 1985) (post-charge discriminatory suspension claim found not to be "reasonably related" to a charge of discrimination in promotions and upgrading); Davidson v. Quash, 11 Fair Empl. Prac. Cas. (BNA) 570 (S.D.N.Y. 1975) (post-charge allegations of discrimination in assignment found to be "substantially the same" as those alleged in the charge).
56. Malhotra v. Cotter & Co., 885 F.2d 1305 (7th Cir. 1989).
57. General Tel. Co. v. EEOC, 446 U.S. 318, 331 (1980).
58. EEOC v. Keco Indus., Inc., 748 F.2d 1097 (6th Cir. 1984).

§ 17.10 Chapter Highlights

1. A person seeking to bring a Title VII lawsuit must first exhaust all administrative remedies, state and federal. (§ 17.01)

2. If a person has, as a part of the employment contract, agreed to submit all disputes to binding arbitration, or if a person is subject to a collective bargaining agreement containing such a provision, then a court, rather than hearing the Title VII claim on the merits, may compel the plaintiff to honor that agreement. The courts have been expanding the role of arbitration for Title VII claims. (§ 17.02)

3. A prior state court adjudication of a discrimination claim will have the same preclusive effect in federal court as it would have in state court. (§ 17.03)

4. An individual has 90 days from receipt of the right-to-sue letter to file an action in federal court. This, however, is not a jurisdictional requirement and is subject to waiver, estoppel, and equitable tolling. (§ 17.04)

5. Private party suits may be brought under Section 706, but only by the person aggrieved, regardless of who the charging party was. (§ 17.05)

6. The EEOC can bring an action against a private employer, employment agency, or labor union on behalf of an individual or a group of individuals under Section 706 or a *pattern or practice* lawsuit under Section 707. The Justice Department may bring Section 706 or Section 707 lawsuits against state and local governments. (§ 17.06)

7. Title VII claims are often brought as class actions. To be certified as a class action, the case must meet the numerosity, commonality, typicality, and adequacy requirements of Rule 23(a) and either be suitable for injunctive and declaratory relief under Rule 23(b)(2) or involve common questions of law and fact under Rule 23(b)(3). If a plaintiff is seeking compensatory and punitive damages under the Civil Rights Act of 1991, this may make class certification more difficult because of the individualized nature of these claims. (§ 17.07)

8. Although the defendants must be persons who are "named in the charge," this has been liberally construed. If a person receives notice during the course of an EEOC investigation that he or she is alleged to have committed the discrimination, then a lawsuit can often be brought against that person. (§ 17.08)

9. Although filing a charge is a procedural prerequisite to filing a lawsuit, what is alleged in the complaint may go somewhat beyond what is alleged in the charge—with respect to both the basis of the discrimination and its factual context. The scope of the lawsuit is limited only by the scope of the EEOC investigation that would reasonably grow out of the charge. (§ 17.09)

Chapter 18

Remedies

Synopsis

§ 18.01 Introduction

Section 706(g) specifies the remedies that a successful plaintiff may recover under Title VII, as follows:

> If the court finds that the respondent has intentionally engaged in or is intentionally engaging in an unlawful employment practice..., the court may

> enjoin the respondent from engaging in such unlawful employment practice, and order such affirmative action as may be appropriate, which may include, but is not limited to, reinstatement or hiring of employees, with or without back pay..., or any other equitable relief as the court deems appropriate.

Originally, some argued that this language implicitly repudiates disparate impact discrimination, since intent is not an element of that cause of action. However, as used in Section 706(g), *intentionally* means that defendant was "acting deliberately, rather than accidentally."[1] Disparate impact discrimination, which is *unintentional* only in the sense that it is not discriminatorily motivated, is thus subject to remediation. On the other hand, the Civil Rights Act of 1991 amended Section 1981 of the Civil Rights Act of 1866 to provide additional remedies, as follows:

> In an action brought under ... the Civil Rights Act of 1964 against a respondent who engaged in unlawful intentional discrimination (not an employment practice that is unlawful because of its disparate impact)..., the complaining party may recover compensatory and punitive damages....

Here, *intentional* means discriminatorily motivated, as in disparate treatment discrimination, with disparate impact discrimination being expressly excluded.

The remedial provisions of Title VII are designed to serve two related purposes: (1) to terminate existing discrimination and prevent its recurrence, and (2), as far as practicable, to *make whole* the victims of this discrimination.[2]

§ 18.02 Injunctive and Affirmative Relief

[A] Ending and Curing the Discrimination

Enjoining the defendant from continuing its discriminatory acts, practices, or policies is the most fundamental form of Title VII relief. This is available even in a mixed motive case, even though the plaintiff may obtain no personal benefit from it.[3] To avoid even negative injunctive relief, employers will sometimes argue at the remedy stage of a Title VII case that the issue has become moot or that injunctive relief is otherwise unnecessary because the discriminatory practice has ceased and is not apt to reoccur. Although the courts have accepted the argument occasionally,[4] that is the exception rather than the rule.

---

1. EEOC v. Accurate Mech. Contractors, Inc., 863 F. Supp. 828, 835 (E.D. Wis. 1994).

2. Albemarle Paper Co. v. Moody, 422 U.S. 405, 417–19 (1975).

3. Thomas v. Washington Cty. Sch. Bd., 915 F.2d 922 (4th Cir. 1990) (employer proved that plaintiff would not have been hired anyway for a nondiscriminatory reason, but plaintiff still entitled to an injunction against nepotism and failure to post vacancies).

4. Walls v. Mississippi State Dep't of Public Welfare, 730 F.2d 306 (5th Cir. 1984) (vacating district court injunction because the selection process had been discontinued); EEOC v. Clayton Residential Home, Inc., 874 F. Supp. 212 (N.D. Ill. 1995) (injunction denied where harassment occurred almost four years earlier, the perpetrators were no longer employed, and the employer had adopted a vigorous anti-harassment policy).

In addition to a negative injunction against doing something, a plaintiff may also be entitled to an affirmative injunction requiring the defendant to do something. This may include an order that the plaintiff be hired, reinstated, promoted, transferred, or otherwise put into the employment position he or she would have been in *but for* the illegal discrimination. In addition, a plaintiff is presumptively entitled to retroactive seniority.[5]

The courts, however, will generally refuse to order such affirmative relief when it comes at the expense of another specific individual. The Supreme Court has noted that "relief for actual victims does not extend to bumping employees previously occupying jobs."[6] On the other hand, although retroactive seniority also results in a pro tanto reduction of everyone else's seniority (when it is used to allocate resources on a competitive basis), the Supreme Court has indicated that this impact is simply an unavoidable cost of the *make whole* objectives of the statute.[7]

Reinstatement may also be denied in other situations—such as where it would produce a dysfunctional work environment because of hostilities growing out of the litigation, when the position in question has been eliminated, or when the plaintiff is approaching retirement. In appropriate cases, front pay may be awarded in lieu of reinstatement.

Other affirmative relief may involve ordering the employer, union, or employment agency to develop and implement particular procedures and policies for recruitment, testing, hiring, promotion, evaluation, training, elimination of harassment, leaves, referrals, or any of the other hundreds of employment practices that occasioned the illegal discrimination. An order that spells these matters out in detail can, however, cause serious problems years later. An injunction, once issued, usually runs in perpetuity—although some do contain built-in time limits—and they are difficult to have modified or rescinded later due to changed circumstances. An injunction that requires an employer to recruit, test, hire, evaluate, or promote in a specific manner may become outdated eventually. Indeed, years later, newly hired managers may not even know that they are subject to the injunction and may inadvertently implement changes that violate the order. Nevertheless, conduct in violation of the injunction can be enforced by civil contempt. To avoid this unfortunate scenario, defendant employers often attempt to have a built-in expiration date for the injunction or to otherwise build in some flexibility for changed circumstances.

[B] Race/Gender-Conscious Affirmative Relief

One of the most controversial issues of Title VII remedy law relates to race- or gender-conscious affirmative relief. The Supreme Court has addressed this issue on several occasions. In *Firefighters Local 1784 v. Stotts*,[8] the Court held that the district court

5. Franks v. Bowman Transp. Co., 424 U.S. 747 (1976).
6. Fire Fighters Local 1784 v. Stotts, 467 U.S. 561, 579 n.11 (1984).
7. Franks, 424 U.S. at 767–68.
8. 467 U.S. 561 (1984).

lacked the authority to modify a consent decree that would have overridden the seniority provision of a collective bargaining agreement and afforded preferential treatment to employees who were not themselves proven victims of the original discrimination.

Subsequently, however, in *Sheet Metal Workers Local 28 v. EEOC*,[9] the Supreme Court approved a remedial order that was designed broadly to eradicate the effects of prior discrimination rather than to provide *make whole* relief to any specifically identified victim of the discrimination. Similarly, in *United States v. Paradise*,[10] the Court upheld, against an Equal Protection challenge, a one-to-one minority/non-minority promotion requirement that was not victim specific. Neither *Sheet Metal Workers* nor *Paradise* produced a majority opinion, thus obscuring the precedential value of the decisions. The plurality in *Paradise*, however, articulated criteria for evaluating the propriety of race-conscious, non-victim specific relief, as follows:

> [T]he necessity for the relief and the efficacy of alternative remedies; the flexibility and duration of the relief, including the availability of waiver provisions; the relationship of the numerical goals to the relevant labor market; and the impact of the relief on the rights of third parties.[11]

Although the lower courts have since applied those criteria in allowing or disallowing race-conscious relief in Title VII cases, it remains unclear whether the Supreme Court's adoption of the strict standard of review in *Adarand Constructors, Inc. v. Pena*,[12] which involved a voluntary affirmative action plan, has altered the law with respect to affirmative action as a part of a Title VII remedial order.

[C] Prospective, Class-Wide Remedies

Although they have the power to do so, courts are reluctant to go beyond stopping the particular form of discrimination against the named plaintiff and providing make-whole relief. Broader injunctions, prohibiting prospectively other forms of discrimination against this plaintiff or discrimination against others in the plaintiff class are rare.[13] They entail a continuing jurisdiction by the court and are enforced through the contempt power. Prospective, broad injunctions prohibiting other forms of, for example, race discrimination against anyone in the class are more common in class actions and EEOC lawsuits.

9. 478 U.S. 421 (1986).
10. 480 U.S. 149 (1987).
11. Paradise, 480 U.S. at 171.
12. 515 U.S. 200 (1995).
13. *But see* Briscoe v. Fred's Dollar Store, Inc., 24 F.3d 1026 (8th Cir. 1994).

§ 18.03 Monetary Compensation

[A] Back Pay and Other Lost Benefits

[1] The Presumption

Although the statute authorizes reinstatement or hiring "with or *without* back pay," the Supreme Court in *Albemarle Paper Co. v. Moody*[14] established a strong presumption in favor of back pay awards to the victims of discrimination. A district court denying back pay must articulate its reasons for doing so and these reasons, if generally applied, cannot be of a nature that would frustrate the purpose of eliminating discrimination and making persons whole.[15]

[2] Calculation

The back pay award includes not only the base salary or hourly wage rate, but also lost overtime, commissions, tips, and wage/salary increases that the plaintiff would have earned but for the discrimination. These are difficult and sometimes speculative determinations. In addition, a successful Title VII plaintiff is entitled to the value of fringe benefits lost, such as vacation pay, employer-funded pension benefits, profit sharing, and even sick pay. Lost coverage under medical and life insurance policies is also compensable, although the courts disagree over the method of computation. The alternatives are (1) saved costs to the employer, (2) the cost of obtaining substitute coverage, and (3) expenses actually incurred that would have been covered by the policy. Prejudgment interest is also authorized[16] and, while it is not automatic, the district court must justify a refusal to award it. Post-judgment interest is always awarded.

[3] Period Covered

Back pay liability begins when the discriminatory act occurred, and the plaintiff was ready, willing, and able to assume the position that was denied for discriminatory reasons. Determining the date of the termination of the back pay period is a bit more complicated. In routine cases, it terminates on the date judgment is rendered. However, it may also terminate earlier under the following circumstances: (1) the employee obtains comparable or better employment elsewhere; (2) the employee fails to mitigate by diligently seeking comparable employment that was available; (3) the employee declines an unconditional offer of reemployment in a comparable job from the defendant employer, even if it does not include retroactive seniority or back pay;[17] (4) the discovery of evidence that would have justified the termination for cause or refusal to hire the plaintiff-employee for nondiscriminatory reasons;[18] and (5) the elimination

14. 422 U.S. 405 (1975).
15. Albemarle Paper, 422 U.S. at 421 n.14.
16. Loeffler v. Frank, 486 U.S. 549 (1988).
17. Ford Motor Co. v. EEOC, 458 U.S. 219 (1982).
18. McKennon v. Nashville Banner Publ'g Co., 513 U.S. 352 (1995).

of the job, a layoff that would have affected the plaintiff-employee, plant closure, the plaintiff-employee's retirement date, and other causes that would have ended the employment even if the discrimination had not occurred.

[B] Front Pay

When, for whatever reason, the court determines that instatement or reinstatement would not be a viable remedy, the court has the discretion to order front pay. This is designed to provide the plaintiff with the monetary equivalent of the wages and benefits the plaintiff would have received if employment or reemployment with the defendant employer had been feasible, limited by the duty to mitigate. It is this limitation that causes the difficulty. If the court orders front pay for a fixed period, based on an estimate of how long it will probably take the plaintiff to find equivalent employment, then the plaintiff may enjoy a windfall if that estimate proves to be wrong. On the other hand, making the front pay order terminable if the plaintiff finds equivalent employment or fails to make reasonable efforts to do so, burdens the court with the task of constantly monitoring its order. The courts have taken both approaches.[19]

[C] Compensatory and Punitive Damages

As originally enacted, Title VII provided only for equitable relief, which included back pay, but not compensatory or punitive damages. The hostile environment sexual harassment cases provided the impetus for change. In those cases, unless the plaintiff had quit and sued for constructive discharge, the only remedy was an injunction against the continuation of the harassment—a remedy many thought to be inadequate, because the primary injury flowing from this form of discrimination is emotional distress. Accordingly, in the Civil Rights Act of 1991, Congress amended Section 1981 to allow compensatory and punitive damages for Title VII claims of intentional discrimination.

[1] Compensatory Damages

Compensatory damages include "future pecuniary losses, emotional pain, suffering, inconvenience, mental anguish, loss of enjoyment of life, and other nonpecuniary losses...." The evidence that is required to prove emotional distress seems to depend in part on the egregiousness of the behavior. In a sexual harassment case, for example, if the case involves conduct by a high-level supervisor that involves physical touching, indecent exposure, threats, and truly pornographic displays that are directed specifically at the plaintiff, then her testimony alone may be sufficient. On the other hand, if the harassment is only marginally pervasive and severe and is more in the form of

19. *Compare* Scarfo v. Cabletron Sys., Inc., 54 F.3d 931 (1st Cir. 1995) (front pay awarded on the basis of expert testimony that plaintiff had only a 10% chance of returning to full employment at an equivalent salary), *with* Suggs v. Servicemaster Educ. Food Mgmt., 72 F.3d 1228 (6th Cir. 1996) (suggesting that the district court consider a continuing court-monitored approach).

simply inappropriate and boorish behavior, then qualified psychological testimony may be required to establish the existence and degree of emotional injury.

Although it is the jury's function to determine the amount of compensatory damages, this is subject to review by both the trial judge and the appellate courts. The standard of review is theoretically very limited, allowing reversal or remittitur only when the award is "so large as to 'shock the judicial conscience,' 'so gross or inordinately large as to be contrary to right reason,' 'so exaggerated as to indicate "bias, passion, prejudice, corruption, or other improper motive,"' or as 'clearly exceed[ing] that amount that *any* reasonable man could feel the claimant is entitled to.'"[20] In practice, however, the courts are guided more by the size of awards in comparable cases and will order a new trial or remittitur if a particular award falls outside the customary range.

The courts are divided over whether pre-judgment interest can be awarded on the compensatory damages portion of the recovery.[21]

[2] Punitive Damages

Punitive damages, which cannot be recovered against a government entity, are available only if the defendant "engaged in a discriminatory practice ... with malice or with reckless indifference to the federally protected rights of an aggrieved individual."

In *Kolstad v. American Dental Ass'n*,[22] the Supreme Court discussed both the standard for determining the availability of punitive damages and the vicarious liability of the employer when the actual discriminatory conduct is committed by an agent. Rejecting the Court of Appeals decision that the requisite state of mind was solely a function of the egregiousness of the conduct, the Court concluded that the focus must be on the actor's subjective intent. The Court noted that "[w]hile egregious misconduct is evidence of the requisite mental state, ... § 1981a does not limit plaintiffs to this form of evidence, and the section does not require a showing of egregious or outrageous discrimination independent of the employer's state of mind."[23] Rather, "[t]he terms 'malice' and 'reckless indifference' pertain to the employer's knowledge that it may be acting in violation of federal law, not its awareness that it is engaging in discrimination"[24]—egregious or otherwise. Clearly, certain knowledge of the illegality of the conduct is not required; rather, it is sufficient that the employer "discriminate in the face of a *perceived risk* that its actions will violate federal law...."[25] The Court then proceeded to give examples of when punitive damages might not be appropriate even in cases of intentional discrimination, namely: (1) when the employer was simply unaware of the relevant federal prohibition; and (2) when the employer

---

20. Caldarera v. Eastern Airlines, Inc., 705 F.2d 778, 784 (5th Cir. 1983).

21. *Compare* Perdue v. City Univ., 13 F. Supp. 2d 326 (E.D.N.Y. 1998), *with* Zerilli v. New York City Transit Auth., 973 F. Supp. 311 (E.D.N.Y. 1997).

22. 527 U.S. 526 (1999).

23. Kolstad, 527 U.S. at 535.

24. Kolstad, 527 U.S. at 535.

25. Kolstad, 527 U.S. at 536 (emphasis added).

believed that the discrimination was lawful, such as when the underlying theory of discrimination is novel or otherwise poorly recognized or excused by the BFOQ defense or some statutory exception to coverage or liability.

Turning then to the basis for imputing liability to the employer, the Court relied on agency principles as its point of analytical departure. Specifically, it quoted from the Restatement (Second) of Agency, § 217 C:

> Punitive damages can properly be awarded against a master or other principal because of an act by an agent if, but only if:
>
> (a) the principal authorized the doing and the manner of the act, or
>
> (b) the agent was unfit and the principal was reckless in employing him, or
>
> (c) the agent was employed in a managerial capacity and was acting in the scope of employment, or
>
> (d) the principal or a managerial agent of the principal ratified or approved the act.

Drawing from the examples provided in the analogous provision of the Restatement of Torts, the Court intimated that an agent could be acting in a managerial capacity if the person's role was merely "important" and that it was not necessary for the person to be "top management, officers, or directors."[26] What gave the Court trouble, however, was the traditional meaning of the "scope of employment" requirement. Quoting again from the Restatement of Agency, the Court noted that "intentional torts are within the scope of an agent's employment if the conduct is 'the kind [the employee] is employed to perform,' 'occurs substantially within the authorized time and space limits,' and 'is actuated, at least in part, by a purpose to serve the' employer."[27] The Court then held that this rather expansive notion of the "scope of employment" requirement was inconsistent with the policy of Title VII of encouraging employers to make good faith efforts to comply with the law. That is, the common law test would provide no incentive for employers to implement policies prohibiting discrimination in the workplace, since the employer could still be liable for punitive damages if supervisors and other agents ignore the policy. Focusing specifically on the context within which most punitive damage claims are like to arise, the Court noted that "[i]n some cases, the existence of a written policy instituted in good faith has operated as a total bar to employer liability for punitive damages" and "the institution of a written sexual harassment policy goes a long way towards dispelling any claim about the employer's 'reckless' or 'malicious' state of mind."[28]

---

26. Kolstad, 527 U.S. at 543.

27. Kolstad, 527 U.S. at 543.

28. Kolstad, 527 U.S. at 544 (quoting Harris v. L & L Wings, Inc, 132 F.3d 978, 983–84 (4th Cir. 1997)).

In sum, under *Kolstad* the plaintiff must first establish that the individual who accomplished the discrimination was acting as the agent of the employer at the time. If this is done by showing that this person was acting in a "managerial capacity" and "within the scope of employment" in the common law sense, then the employer can still escape Title VII punitive damages liability by showing that it engaged in good faith efforts to comply with the law.

[3] Limits on Compensatory and Punitive Damages

The 1991 amendments allowed for compensatory and punitive damage, "provided the complaining party cannot recover under [Section 1981]," which had always included these damages for racial discrimination.[29] Although the proviso was originally subject to a variety of interpretations, the EEOC and most courts now construe it as meaning only that a plaintiff cannot recover double damages—one based on the Title VII violation and the other based on the Section 1981 violation.[30]

Title VII compensatory and punitive damages are also subject to a statutory cap, depending on the number of employees. The damages that are subject to the cap do not include "back pay, interest on back pay, or any other type of relief authorized under section 706(g) of the Civil Rights Act of 1964." Although the statute does expressly contemplate damages for "future pecuniary losses," the Supreme Court has held that since front pay has always been a traditional form of Title VII relief under Section 706(g), it is not subject to the cap.[31]

Finally, Title VII punitive damages may also be subject to the Due Process limits that apply in any kind of case.[32] The courts are divided over this, however. Some hold that even if the award is within the statutory cap, it must meet the three-prong constitutional test, which includes consideration of the ratio between the punitive and compensatory damages.[33] Other courts, however, hold that an award within the statutory cap is per se constitutional.[34]

[4] Jury Trial

The Seventh Amendment to the Constitution guarantees the right to trial by jury in "suits at common law, where the value in controversy ... exceeds twenty dollars." Since the relief originally afforded under Title VII was equitable in nature, a jury trial

---

29. 42 U.S.C. § 1981A(a)(1).

30. EEOC Policy Guide on Compensatory and Punitive Damages Under 1991 Civil Rights Act, July 7, 1992, BNA Fair Employment Manual 405:7091, 7092 (1992); Bradshaw v. Univ. of Maine Sys., 870 F. Supp. 406 (D. Me. 1994).

31. Pollard v. E.I. du Pont de Nemours & Co., 532 U.S. 843 (2001).

32. State Farm Mut. Auto. Ins. Co. v. Campbell, 538 U.S. 408 (2003).

33. Rubinstein v. Administrators of the Tulane Educ. Fund, 218 F.3d 392 (5th Cir. 2000) (reducing the award from a 30:1 to a 10:1 ratio).

34. Lust v. Sealy, Inc., 383 F.3d 580 (7th Cir. 2004) (if award is within the caps the ratio is irrelevant).

was not available. By affording a plaintiff compensatory and punitive damages, the Civil Rights Act of 1991 changed that. This requires the trial judge to conduct a jury trial first; with the jury determining both liability and the amount of damages, but with the judge making the determination with respect to the equitable relief.[35]

§ 18.04 Attorney's Fees and Costs

Section 706(k) provides that a Title VII court "may allow the prevailing party ... a reasonable attorney's fee (including expert fees) as a part of the costs...."

[A] Attorney's Fees

[1] The Test

In *Albemarle Paper Co. v. Moody*,[36] the Supreme Court made it clear that a plaintiff should ordinarily recover an attorney's fee unless "special circumstances would render such an award unjust."[37] The courts have been reluctant to find these circumstances. For example, none of the following has qualified as an "unusual circumstance":

- That a private attorney was unnecessary because the state agency offered to represent the plaintiff.[38]
- That the plaintiff's attorney was employed by a public interest group.[39]
- That the defendant acted in good faith, in reliance on EEOC interpretations, or took quick action to remedy the discrimination.[40]
- That the attorney took the case on a contingency fee basis.[41]
- That the plaintiff failed to engage in meaningful settlement negotiations.[42]

In addition, the attorney who fails to submit detailed, contemporaneous time records[43] or to submit them in a timely fashion[44] may be denied attorney's fees. Although they have been denied in a few other unusual circumstances,[45] the circumstances for denying attorney's fees to prevailing plaintiffs are rare.

---

35. Hetzel v. Prince William County, 523 U.S. 208 (1998); Jefferson v. Ingersoll Int'l, Inc., 195 F.3d 894 (7th Cir. 1999).

36. 422 U.S. 405 (1975).

37. Albemarle Paper, 422 U.S. at 415 (adopting the Title II test articulated in *Newman v. Piggie Park Enterprises, Inc.*, 390 U.S. 400 (1968)).

38. New York Gaslight Club, Inc. v. Carey, 447 U.S. 54 (1980).

39. New York Gaslight Club, 447 U.S. 54.

40. Martin v. Heckler, 773 F.2d 1145 (11th Cir. 1985); Rosenfeld v. Southern Pac. Co., 519 F.2d 527 (9th Cir. 1975); Fields v. City of Tarpon Springs, 721 F.2d 318 (11th Cir. 1983).

41. Cooper v. Singer, 719 F.2d 1496 (10th Cir. 1983).

42. Schofield v. Trustees of the Univ. of Pa., 919 F. Supp. 821 (E.D. Pa. 1996).

43. DiPietro v. Runyon, 914 F. Supp. 714 (D. Mass. 1996) (dicta and limited to egregious cases).

44. Mindler v. Clayton County, Georgia, 864 F. Supp. 1329 (N.D. Ga. 1994), aff'd, 63 F.3d 1113 (11th Cir. 1995).

45. Sprogis v. United Air Lines, 517 F.2d 387 (7th Cir. 1975).

Prevailing defendants are not so generously treated. In *Christiansburg Garment Co. v. EEOC*,[46] the Court noted that private plaintiffs enjoy a presumptive entitlement to attorney's fees because they were the chosen instruments of Congress to vindicate public policy—which is not true of prevailing defendants. On the other hand, the Court also noted that Congress apparently intended for attorney's fees to function as a deterrent to burdensome litigation having no legal or factual basis. Balancing those two considerations, the Court thus concluded that a trial court "may in its discretion award attorney's fees to a prevailing defendant in a Title VII case upon a finding that the plaintiff's action was frivolous, unreasonable, or without foundation, even though not brought in subjective bad faith."[47] The test has been applied, not only with respect to the merits of the claim as pled, but also if discovery shows that it is groundless[48] and where the appeal was unwarranted.[49] A claim is not "frivolous," however, merely because the trier of fact rejects the plaintiff's version of the claim.[50]

[2] The Meaning of "Prevailing"

The Supreme Court has explained the meaning of this term in several cases, not all of them involving Title VII. In *Texas State Teachers Ass'n v. Garland Indep. Sch. Dist.*,[51] the Court rejected a test that required a plaintiff to prevail on what it termed the "central issue" of the litigation. Instead, the Court held that if a plaintiff "has succeeded on 'any significant issue in litigation which achieve[d] some of the benefit the parties sought in bringing suit,' the plaintiff has crossed the threshold to a fee award of some kind."[52] In *Farrar v. Hobby*,[53] the lower court sustained the plaintiffs' Due Process claim on the merits, but denied them any compensatory damages and awarded one dollar in nominal damages. The Court, however, held that the plaintiffs were *prevailing parties* and entitled to some attorney's fees. The Court held that "a plaintiff 'prevails' when actual relief on the merits of his claim materially alters the legal relationship between the parties by modifying the defendant's behavior in a way that directly benefits the plaintiff."[54] The Court further held, however, that the amount of the fee should be limited by the extent of the plaintiff's success. In a case like this one, where the plaintiffs failed to prove an essential element of their claim to monetary relief (lack of proximate cause), "the only reasonable fee is usually no fee at all."[55]

The courts are divided over how to apply the *Farrar* test in mixed motive cases. Even if a plaintiff ultimately prevails, that plaintiff will receive no monetary damages

---

46. 434 U.S. 412 (1978).
47. Christiansburg Garment, 434 U.S. at 421.
48. Morgan v. Union Metal Mfg. Co., 757 F.2d 792 (6th Cir. 1985).
49. Hilmon Co. v. Hyatt Int'l, 899 F.2d 250 (3d Cir. 1990).
50. EEOC v. L.B. Foster Co., 123 F.3d 746 (3d Cir 1997).
51. 489 U.S. 782 (1989).
52. Texas State Teachers, 489 U.S. at 791–92 (quoting *Nadeau v. Helgemoe*, 581 F.2d 275, 278–79 (1st Cir. 1978)).
53. 506 U.S. 103 (1992).
54. Farrar, 506 U.S. at 111–12.
55. Farrar, 506 U.S. at 115.

and is not entitled to instatement or reinstatement. The injunctive relief may benefit other employees, but it hardly alters the legal relationship between the plaintiff and the defendant or modifies the defendant's behavior in a way that benefits the plaintiff. That would suggest that the plaintiff would not be entitled to any attorney's fees.[56] On the other hand, Section 706(g)(2)(B)(I) specifically authorizes "attorney's fees and costs" in these cases. This has led several courts to conclude that this specific statutory language overrides the Supreme Court's determination of what *prevailing party* means generally.[57] Other courts, however, have held that the *Farrar* standards are applicable to mixed motive claims, but have not construed them as totally denying attorney's fees. One court, for example, concluded that the decision requires a trial court to determine "whether the public purpose served by resolving the dispute justifies the recovery of fees."[58] The court thus suggested that it would be appropriate for a trial court to weigh the degree and intolerability of the defendant's discriminatory animus, which establishes the violation, against the unacceptability of the plaintiff's conduct, which establishes the partial defense.

In *Buckhannon Bd. & Care Home v. West Virginia Dept. of Health & Human Resources*,[59] the Court held that when the parties voluntarily settle the case, this does not make the plaintiff a *prevailing party*. Rather, the necessary form of alteration of the legal relationship occurs only when there is a judicial imprimatur on the change.[60]

[3] Calculation

Attorney's fees are determined according to the so-called *Lodestar* formula. This is the number of hours reasonably expended multiplied by a reasonable hourly rate.[61] This includes not only the work of lawyers, but also the work of law clerks and paralegals.[62] This then may be reduced if the plaintiff only achieved a partial success. Although an upward adjustment to compensate for the risk the attorney assumed by taking the case on a contingency fee basis is generally not allowed,[63] the extraordinary performance by an attorney in an extremely difficult case might justify enhancement.[64]

Partially overruling *West Virginia University Hospitals, Inc. v. Casey*,[65] the Civil Rights Act of 1991 now expressly includes "expert fees" as a part of attorney's fees, although it is not clear whether this applies only to expert witnesses or also includes expert consultants.

---

56. Canup v. Chipman-Union, Inc., 123 F.3d 1440 (11th Cir. 1997).
57. Gudenkauf v. Stauffer Commc'ns, 158 F.3d 1074 (10th Cir. 1998); Hall v. City of Brawley, 887 F. Supp. 1333 (S.D. Cal. 1995).
58. Sheppard v. Riverview Nursing Ctr., Inc., 88 F.3d 1332, 1336 (4th Cir. 1996).
59. 532 U.S. 598 (2001).
60. Buckhannon, 532 U.S. at 605.
61. Hensley v. Eckerhart, 461 U.S. 424 (1983).
62. Missouri v. Jenkins, 491 U.S. 274 (1989).
63. City of Burlington v. Dague, 505 U.S. 557 (1992) (decided under the federal Clean Water Act).
64. McKenzie v. Kennickell, 875 F.2d 330 (D.C. Cir. 1989).
65. 499 U.S. 83 (1991).

[B] Costs

The Judicial Code allows the recovery of the following costs: (1) clerk and marshal fees, (2) transcripts necessarily obtained for use in the case, (3) fees and disbursements for printing and witnesses (limited to a $40 per diem) (4) copy costs, (5) docket fees, and (6) compensation of court appointed experts.[66] In addition, some courts have also allowed recovery for out-of-pocket expenses for depositions, photography, investigation, parking, and telephone calls.[67]

§ 18.05 Chapter Highlights

1. Title VII's remedies are designed to stop the discrimination and make the victim whole. (§ 18.01)

2. Enjoining the defendant from engaging in the illegal discrimination is the most fundamental form of relief, but affirmative injunctions requiring the defendant to put the plaintiff in the position he or she would have been in but for the illegal discrimination are also routine. This may involve an order that the plaintiff be employed or reemployed, be promoted or transferred, and be given retroactive seniority. (§ 18.02[A])

3. Gender- and race-conscious affirmative relief that eradicates the effects of prior discrimination have survived both statutory and constitutional challenges, even though they are not victim specific. What is or is not legal in this regard is, however, somewhat obscure. (§ 18.02[B])

4. Back pay is routinely awarded in Title VII cases, as part of the *make whole* aspect of the remedy. (§ 18.03[A])

5. When employment or reemployment is not feasible, the courts may also award front pay—equal to the amount the plaintiff would have received upon employment or reemployment, limited by the duty to seek employment elsewhere. This can either be a lump-sum amount or be paid monthly until the plaintiff finds suitable employment elsewhere or fails to seek it. (§ 18.03[B])

6. Under the Civil Rights Act of 1991, a successful plaintiff in an intentional discrimination case may also recover compensatory and punitive damages, although these are subject to a statutory cap depending on the size of the defendant employer. To recover punitive damages, the plaintiff must show that the defendant acted "with malice or with reckless indifference to the federally protected rights" of the plaintiff. The test for determining if a corporate employer is liable in punitive damages for the conduct of supervisors is essentially the same as the test for determining when an employer is liable for the hostile environment discrimination of these supervisors. (§ 18.03[C])

---

66. 28 U.S.C. § 1920.

67. Deary v. City of Gloucester, 789 F. Supp. 61 (D. Mass. 1992).

7. Prevailing plaintiffs are entitled to attorney's fees in almost every case, and a plaintiff will be found to have *prevailed* simply by succeeding on any significant issue in the litigation that brought some benefit to the plaintiff. Prevailing defendants can recover only if the plaintiff's action was frivolous, unreasonable, or without foundation. (§ 18.04)

Part IV

The Age Discrimination in Employment Act

Chapter 19

Coverage and Jurisdiction

Synopsis

§ 19.01 The Proscribed Basis of Discrimination

Like Title VII, which prohibits discrimination *because of* a person's race, color, sex, religion, or national origin, the ADEA[1] is worded in terms of a prohibition against the adverse treatment of individuals "because of such individual's age." Thus, as long as the employer's reason for the adverse action was something other than age, even if the action is patently illegal under some other statute, then it does not violate the ADEA. The Supreme Court made this clear in *Hazen Paper Co. v. Biggins*.[2] There, the employer had terminated an employee just a few weeks before the employee's pension would have vested, in violation of the federal pension laws. But that was not, the Court held, age discrimination. In addition, the Court held that discrimination on the basis of some characteristic that merely correlates with age was not discrimination *because of age* under the ADEA either—unless the employer chose this correlating factor with the intent of achieving the proscribed age discrimination effect.[3]

At one point the lower courts were in conflict about whether the disparate impact theory also applies to the ADEA, but the Supreme Court resolved the conflict by finding the theory is available but applies more narrowly than under Title VII.[4]

1. 29 U.S.C. §§ 621–634.
2. 507 U.S. 604 (1993).
3. *See* Chapter 4, § 4.02[B].
4. Smith v. City of Jackson, 544 U.S. 228, 240, 243 (2005).

The ADEA has an anti-retaliation provision similar to one contained in Title VII, and it has been construed in much the same fashion.[5]

§ 19.02 Entities Subject to the Prohibition

The substantive prohibitions of the ADEA apply to employers with 20 or more employees, labor unions with 25 or more members or that operate a hiring hall, employment agencies, the federal government,[6] and state agencies and political subdivisions.[7] In 1986, state and local governments were granted a limited exemption, allowing them to impose maximum hiring ages or mandatory retirement policies for firefighters and law enforcement officers. Institutions of higher learning could also force tenured professors to retire at age 70. These provisions expired in 1993, but the firefighter and law enforcement officer exemption was reenacted in 1996.

Other than that, to a large extent, the coverage of the listed entities tracks that of Title VII, using the same mode of analysis. Unlike Title VII, however, the ADEA does not expressly exempt churches and other religious organizations. For age discrimination purposes, they enjoy absolute immunity for their "ministers" under the First Amendment.[8] Finally, the ADEA does not apply to a foreign employer not doing business in the United States or controlled by a United States employer.[9] But it does cover United States citizens employed by a United States employer doing business in a foreign country unless complying with the ADEA would violate the laws of that country.[10]

§ 19.03 The Protected Class

The ADEA protects employees, applicants for employment, and retirees if the alleged discrimination is related to or arises out of the employment relationship. The Title VII tests for distinguishing between an *employee* and an *independent contractor* and for determining whether a putative *partner* is really an *employee* are also generally followed in ADEA litigation. The ADEA does not apply to uniformed personnel in

---

5. O'Rourke v. Continental Cas. Co., 983 F.2d 94 (7th Cir. 1993).

6. Since the United States itself enjoys sovereign immunity, only the head of the employing agency is the proper defendant. *See* Quraishi v. Shalala, 962 F. Supp. 55 (D. Md. 1997).

7. States and state agencies are, however, covered by the Eleventh Amendment, and lawsuits against them are limited accordingly. *See* Chapter 3.

8. Hosanna-Tabor Evangelical Lutheran Church & Sch. v. EEOC, 565 U.S. 171 (2012). The Court broadly construed the "ministerial exception" to cover a church schoolteacher. Concurring opinions suggested even broader applications of the exception.

9. 29 U.S.C. §623(h)(2); Morelli v. Cedel, 141 F.3d 39 (2d Cir. 1998); Denty v. SmithKline Beecham Corp., 109 F.3d 147 (3d Cir. 1997).

10. 29 U.S.C. §623(f)(1).

the armed forces. Certain "bona fide executive[s]" and "high policymaking" employees can also be forced to retire under certain circumstances.

Since everyone has a race, a sex, a national origin, and a religion or lack thereof, everyone has a potential claim on those bases. Although everyone also has an age, the ADEA prohibition against age discrimination does not extend to everyone. By the terms of the statute itself, the protected class is limited to those aged 40 or above. Moreover, even within the protected class, the ADEA has been construed as not prohibiting discrimination against a younger person (even one within the class) in favor of an older one. In *General Dynamics Land Systems, Inc. v. Cline*,[11] Justice Souter, writing for the Court, admitted that the "because of age" language of the statute was not expressly modified by any considerations of "younger/older"—thus suggesting the possibility that within the protected class, the respective ages of the disfavored and favored individuals were irrelevant. But the Court rejected this "expansive" interpretation, noting that the Act's preamble and the legislative history show "the ADEA was concerned to protect a relatively older worker from discriminations that work to the advantage of the relatively young"[12]—not vice versa. The age difference between the advantaged younger worker and the disadvantaged older worker is, however, relevant to the question of whether the disadvantage was motivated by age.[13]

§ 19.04 Chapter Highlights

1. The ADEA prohibits discrimination on the basis of age. It does not apply to other motivations, even if illegal under another statute or if based on a criterion that merely correlates with age. (§ 19.01)

2. The ADEA applies generally to employers, unions, employment agencies, and governments—in much the same way as Title VII. It does, however, contain some exclusions that Title VII does not. (§ 19.02)

3. Despite the literal language of the statute, discrimination *because of age* is not illegal if it operates in favor of older individuals and to the corresponding disadvantage of younger ones. (§ 19.03)

---

11. 540 U.S. 581 (2004).

12. General Dynamics, 540 U.S. 581 at 590–91.

13. *See* Chapter 20, § 20.01[C].

Chapter 20

Types of Violations and Their Proof

Synopsis

Many of the theories of discrimination, how they are proved, and the available defenses discussed earlier in connection with Title VII are also generally applicable to the ADEA. This chapter will thus focus mainly on matters that are unique to the ADEA.

§ 20.01 Individual, Single-Motive Disparate Treatment

Among the various types of age discrimination claims, this one most closely tracks the Title VII model. Since individual disparate treatment involves proof of motive, most of the evidentiary issues relate to what is relevant and probative in that regard. From evidence that is literally *direct*[1] in the technical sense of the word to that which is only weakly inferential, the relevant forms of evidence are as follows.

[A] Open Admission of Age Motivations and Policies Expressly Using an Age Criterion

Open admissions that age at least played a role in making adverse employment decisions is certainly compelling if not conclusive evidence of an anti-age motivation.[2] These admissions often occur, however, when the defendant will contend that age is a BFOQ or that the plaintiff is within one of the statutory exceptions to coverage. For example, in *Usery v. Tamiami Trail Tours, Inc.*,[3] a bus company had an open policy of refusing to hire persons over the age of 40 as intercity bus drivers because of legitimate safety concerns. Age was found to be a BFOQ. On the other hand, most generalizations about older people, even if marginally true, fail to satisfy the rather stringent requirements of the BFOQ and are more properly characterized as stereotypes. For example, in one case the employer had expressed the view that younger employees were easier to deal with than older employees, who were also harder to terminate.[4] Or the employer may successfully claim that a particular individual is a *bona fide executive or high policymaking employee* and thus falls within the statutory exemption.[5]

On the other hand, open reliance on a criterion that has a correlation with age may be proof of age discrimination if there is also proof that the defendant adopted that criterion for the *purpose* of achieving an age discrimination. Otherwise, however, the correlation itself is insufficient. For example, in *Hazen Paper Co. v. Biggins*,[6] there was evidence that the plaintiff was terminated just before his pension would have

1. The direct/circumstantial evidence distinction may still control for determining when the mixed-motive structure of proof and allocation of burdens applies, But, as with the pre-*Desert Palace* Title VII case law, what qualifies as *direct evidence* is a matter of some dispute among the circuits.

2. Febres v. Challenger Caribbean Corp., 214 F.3d 57 (1st Cir. 2000); Curtis v. Elecs. & Space Corp., 113 F.3d 1498 (8th Cir. 1997).

3. 531 F.2d 224 (5th Cir. 1976) (cited with approval by the Supreme Court in *Western Air Lines v. Criswell*, 472 U.S. 400, 412 (1985)).

4. Smith v. Berry Co., 165 F.3d 390 (5th Cir. 1999).

5. Colby v. Graniteville Co., 635 F. Supp. 381 (S.D.N.Y. 1986) (head of legal department held to be a bona fide executive).

6. 507 U.S. 604 (1993).

vested and for the purpose of preventing that. Although a correlation existed between pension vesting and age, the Court held that this, without more, did not constitute age discrimination.

[B] Ageist Comments and *Code Words*

Which comments qualify as evidence of age bias and which do not is impossible to generalize about. The *stray comments* principle has been applied here.[7] Beyond that, some commentators suggest that the courts are more tolerant of derogatory, *joking*, and other age-related comments than they are of analogous sex and race comments. For example, one court recently held that comments critical of the "old management team," the "old business model," and "deadwood" did not rise to the level of constituting age harassment when the longtime head of a money-losing division was terminated because higher management did not believe he could turn it around.[8] The court also noted that other courts had found similar comments insufficient proof of age motivation: negative comments like getting rid of "old timers" because they would not "kiss his ass"; "we don't necessarily like gray hair"; "old boy network"; and conversely positive comments about a comparative employee as a "bright, intelligent, knowledgeable young man."[9] Other courts, however, have reached the opposite conclusion with respect to similar comments. For example, all of the following statements have been found to be relevant evidence of age bias: that the current staff was a bunch of "old fogies";[10] that the company needed some "young blood";[11] and even the backhanded complimentary "you old fuckers make good salesmen because most of the garage owners are old and you relate well together."[12]

A surprising number of courts have had to address the specific question of whether referring to an employee as an "old fart" is sufficient evidence of age discrimination, with mixed results.[13] Another recurring issue is whether calling an older applicant "overqualified" for the job is simply an indirect way of saying that person is too old. The courts have resolved the issue both ways, with the other facts of the case being especially important.[14] The effect of *Hazen Paper Co. v. Biggins*[15] on these cases remains unclear. If the theory of liability is that this is discrimination because being *overqual-*

---

7. *See* Chapter 5, § 5.06[C].

8. Pottenger v. Potlatch Corp., 329 F.3d 740 (9th Cir. 2003).

9. Normand v. Research Inst. of Am., 927 F.2d 857 (5th Cir. 1991) (supervisor referred to the plaintiff and other older salespersons as "old geezers," "the old grandad," and an "old buzzard").

10. Danzer v. Norden Sys., Inc., 151 F.3d 50 (2d Cir. 1998).

11. Fast v. Southern Union Co., Inc., 149 F.3d 885 (8th Cir. 1998).

12. Madel v. FCI Mktg., Inc., 116 F.3d 1247 (8th Cir. 1997).

13. *Compare* Montgomery v. John Deere & Co., 169 F.3d 556 (8th Cir. 1999), *with* Kehoe v. Anheuser-Busch, Inc., 96 F.3d 1095 (8th Cir. 1996).

14. *Compare* Taggart v. Time, Inc., 924 F.2d 43 (2d Cir. 1991), *with* Stein v. National City Bank, 942 F.2d 1062 (6th Cir. 1991).

15. 507 U.S. 604 (1993).

ified correlates with age, then *Biggins* would seem to disallow the suit. But if the evidence shows that the employer is using *overqualification* as a euphemism to mask an anti-age bias, then this would satisfy the *Biggins* requirement for age-related intent.

[C] Use of Comparators

Comparators continue to be an important form of evidence in age discrimination cases. That is, an older person who is subject to an adverse hiring, promotion, or termination decision may attempt to show that it was illegally motivated by showing that a similarly situated younger person was treated differently. As is the case whenever comparators are used to establish motivation on any impermissible basis, the more similarly situated the comparator is with the plaintiff, the more compelling the evidence.

In *O'Connor v. Consolidated Coin Caterers*,[16] the Supreme Court held that the comparator need not be outside the age-40-plus protected class, but that to be probative of age motivation the difference in ages must be "substantial." Many courts have adopted an over-10-years differential as the benchmark for the "substantially" younger/older requirement, but others have allowed a much smaller differential.[17]

[D] Proving Discrimination through the *McDonnell Douglas* Method

As with many of the Title VII bases of discrimination, a plaintiff will often rely on the burden-shifting mechanism of the *McDonnell Douglas v. Green*[18] method of proof. This three-step approach consists of plaintiff's burden of proving a set of facts that are sufficient to establish an inference of discriminatory motive (the prima facie case); the defendant satisfying a burden of producing evidence of a nondiscriminatory reason (articulation); and the plaintiff finally carrying the ultimate burden of proving that the defendant's articulated reason is not the true reason and that age was the motivating consideration (pretext).

As in Title VII cases, the elements of a prima facie case are not a rigid formula but are, rather, adjusted to the circumstances of the discrimination and the particular facts of the case.[19] A typical prima facie case, however, might consist of the following:

- That the plaintiff was within the protected age group.
- That the plaintiff was subject to an adverse employment decision.
- That the plaintiff met at least the minimum qualifications for the job, promotion, or other benefit—with disputes over the sufficiency of a bare minimum and

16. 517 U.S. 308 (1996).

17. Grosjean v. First Energy Corp., 349 F.3d 332, 336 (6th Cir. 2003) (survey of the various circuit decisions, including two which hold that a three-year and one-year difference is sufficient).

18. 411 U.S. 792 (1973).

19. Sanchez v. P.R. Oil Co., 37 F.3d 712 (1st Cir. 1994) ("the prima facie case requirement embodies a concept, not a mechanical exercise").

the relative qualifications of the plaintiff and the comparator usually being deferred to the pretext stage.

- That a similarly situated but substantially younger person received the benefit—with the degree of similarity/dissimilarity also being reserved for the pretext stage.

The defendant employer's articulation of nondiscrimination means essentially the same thing in ADEA law as it does in Title VII. There is, however, one significant difference, flowing from the fact that the ADEA also contains the *reasonable factor other than age* and *good cause* statutory defenses. They would appear to be essentially the same thing as a *legitimate, nondiscriminatory reason*. There is a critical procedural difference, however. While the *McDonnell Douglas* articulation requirement entails only a burden of producing evidence, the two statutory defenses involve a true burden of proof (production and persuasion). Most courts have resolved the conundrum by holding that if the plaintiff opts for a prima facie case method of proof, only the normal production burden falls on the defendant; the statutory defenses apply only if the plaintiff establishes pretext.[20]

The plaintiff's proof of the requisite inferential facts then shifts a burden of production of evidence onto the defendant. The original *McDonnell Douglas* worded this in terms of articulating a "*legitimate*, nondiscriminatory reason"—which gave rise to some speculation that a reason that was not discriminatory on a statutory basis but that was other than "legitimate" did not qualify. The Supreme Court put that speculation to rest in *Hazen Paper Co. v. Biggins.*[21] There, the employer terminated the plaintiff because his pension was about to vest, even though that was a probable violation of the federal pension laws and thus by no means a "legitimate" reason. Nevertheless, the Court held that this did not constitute discrimination on the basis of age. It would, thus, also serve to neutralize the inference of age discrimination created by plaintiff's prima facie case—which is the sole function of the *articulation* step in the proof process.

In individual cases, almost every reason imaginable has been proffered—including employee misconduct that would clearly constitute *cause for discharge*; work-related shortcomings, such as the employee's relative level of performance or skill; the employer's changing business needs, such as the simple elimination of the job; nonwork-related activities or misconduct that the employer finds objectionable; and even totally idiosyncratic, nonsensical employer reasons. Of course, the further down on this list the articulated reason goes the less likely it is that it will be accepted as the real reason by the finder of fact, who will assume that the normal employer acts for rational, business-related reasons.

Once that *articulation* has been made, then the plaintiff must proceed to satisfy its ultimate burden by establishing that the employer's asserted reason is a mere *pretext*

---

20. Neufeld v. Searle Lab., 884 F.2d 335 (8th Cir. 1989); Lockhart v. Westinghouse Credit Corp., 879 F.2d 43 (3d Cir. 1989). *But see* Criswell v. Western Airlines, Inc., 709 F.2d 544, 552–53 (9th Cir. 1983), aff'd, 472 U.S. 400. 408 n.10 (1985) (reserving decision on that specific question).

21. 507 U.S. 604 (1993).

and that the actual reason relates to age. Often, the same kinds of evidence that have been or could be offered to prove the motivation directly is also used to establish pretext. For example, it might consist of ageist comments, statistical evidence, or the use of a comparator. Or it could go beyond that and address directly the employer's articulated reason—for example, by showing that the employer's *not qualified* assertion justification is not true or proof that the employer's counter-comparator is significantly distinguishable. Plaintiffs have had a particularly hard time carrying the ultimate pretext burden when the person who terminated the plaintiff is also the person who did the initial hiring, especially when this person is also older than the plaintiff[22]—the so-called *same actor defense*.[23]

Whether the plaintiff's pre-litigation, discovery evidence is sufficient to survive a motion for summary judgment will now be evaluated under the *Hicks/Reeves* case law—which is to say that it is subject to all of the same complexities and continuing confusion that exists under Title VII.[24]

§ 20.02 After-Acquired Evidence

When the defendant employer's asserted justification for the adverse employment action rests on evidence acquired after the decision was made, this generally becomes relevant only if the discriminatory motive can be proved either directly or inferentially. As under Title VII, this may consist of information about employee's misconduct prior to the adverse employment action in question—resumé fraud, for example—or subsequent misconduct that would have justified the action anyway. The effect of this proof is, however, merely to limit the remedy. And, indeed, the leading Supreme Court case on after-acquired evidence arose under the ADEA, not Title VII.[25]

§ 20.03 Individual, Mixed-Motive Disparate Treatment

Prior to *Price Waterhouse v. Hopkins*,[26] the *but for* standard of causation was deemed to control in both Title VII and ADEA cases. Justice Brennan's opinion, however, opened the possibility of the *motivating factor* standard of causation, at least in Title VII mixed-motive cases. Moreover, under *Price Waterhouse*, once the plaintiff established age discrimination by direct evidence,[27] the burden of persuasion shifted to

22. Brown v. CSC Logic, Inc., 82 F.3d 651 (5th Cir. 1996).

23. *See* Chapter 5, § 5.06[D].

24. *See* Chapter 5, § 5.07.

25. McKennon v. Nashville Banner Publ'g Co., 513 U.S. 352 (1995). *See* Chapter 5, § 5.10.

26. 490 U.S. 228 (1989).

27. This appeared in Justice O'Connor's concurring opinion—which has been construed as stating the holding of the Court. And most courts thus adopted the requirement in mixed-motive cases.

the defendant to prove that the plaintiff would not have been hired or would have been terminated for a reason unrelated to age—and this proof operated as a complete defense. The Civil Rights Act of 1991 apparently adopted Justice Brennan's theory of causation. And rather than constituting a complete defense, under the 1991 Act the defendant's proof of an independent reason for the adverse employment action only limited the Title VII remedy. The Supreme Court in *Desert Palace, Inc. v. Costa*[28] then eliminated the *direct evidence* requirement in mixed-motive cases. As a result, the lower courts were divided over whether the Civil Rights Act of 1991 applied to the ADEA.[29]

In *Gross v. FBL Financial Servs.*,[30] the Supreme Court resolved the issue. It ruled that the *motivating factor* standard is inapplicable because the Civil Rights Act of 1991 does not apply to the ADEA. Plaintiffs must show that age is the *but for* cause of the adverse employment action.

§ 20.04 Systemic Disparate Treatment

As under Title VII, class-wide age discrimination that is not the result of some discoverable policy or employment procedure is established primarily through the use of statistics, reinforced with proof by other means of such discrimination against representative members of the class. But if statistical proof is a difficult and complicated undertaking in a Title VII race or sex discrimination case, it is doubly so under the ADEA. This is because age is a continuum that is not subject to simple either/or classification schemes. As one court put it, "where innumerable groupings of employees are possible according to ages and divisions within the corporate structure, statistics are easily manipulated and may be deceptive."[31] The courts thus tend to scrutinize age-related statistical data very carefully.

§ 20.05 Disparate Impact

For many years, the courts were divided over whether the ADEA recognized a disparate impact form of discrimination and, if so, whether it was determined under the original *Griggs* approach, the *Wards Cove* reformulation, or the standards contained in the Civil Right Act of 1991. The Supreme Court finally resolved this issue in *Smith v. City of Jackson.*[32] In 1998, the City adopted a pay plan granting raises to

---

28. 539 U.S. 90 (2003).

29. *Compare* Baqir v. Principi, 434 F.3d 733, 745 n.13 (4th Cir. 2006) (*Price Waterhouse*, not the 1991 Act, still controls), *and* Hill v. Lockheed Martin Logistics Mgmt., Inc., 354 F.3d 277 (4th Cir. 2004) (en banc) (*Desert Palace* does not apply), *with* Rachid v. Jack in the Box, Inc., 376 F.3d 305 (5th Cir. 2004) (*Desert Palace* applies).

30. 557 U.S. 167 (2009).

31. Walther v. Lone Star Gas Co., 952 F.2d 119, 124 (5th Cir. 1992).

32. 544 U.S. 228 (2005). Justice Stevens delivered the opinion of the Court with respect to Parts I, II, and IV and an opinion in Part III, dealing in some detail with the RFOA defense, in which only

all City employees. It later revised the plan, mainly to make starting salaries of police officers more competitive with other public agencies. Although all police officers were granted a raise, the increase for those with less than five years' seniority was proportionately greater than for those with greater seniority. The older officers sued, claiming both disparate treatment and disparate impact. The Court of Appeals dismissed the disparate impact claim on the grounds that it was "categorically unavailable under the ADEA."[33] The Supreme Court disagreed, holding that a form of disparate impact analysis was available under the ADEA, albeit one that differs somewhat from any of the Title VII versions.

Specifically, the Court stated that "two textual differences between the ADEA and Title VII make it clear that even though both statutes authorize recovery on a disparate-impact theory, the scope of disparate impact liability under the ADEA is narrower than under Title VII."[34] First, since Congress did not include the ADEA in the 1991 amendments, the *Wards Cove* approach still controlled in an ADEA case. In that regard, the Court held that the plaintiffs had not satisfied the *Wards Cove* requirement of "isolating and identifying the *specific* employment practices that are allegedly responsible for any observed statistical disparities."[35] Second, the ADEA form of disparate impact is subject to the "reasonable factor other than age" defense. The Court held that the City's desire to make starting salaries competitive was certainly "reasonable" within the meaning of the RFOA. The Court held that the RFOA defense also differs from the regular disparate impact analysis in that it does not entail a further inquiry into the availability of alternative ways of achieving the goal. The employer bears the burden of proving the RFOA defense, just like any other affirmative defense.[36]

Following *City of Jackson*,[37] two circuits ruled that disparate impact claims under the ADEA could not be filed on behalf of job applicants.[38] The full significance of the *City of Jackson* case, with its multiple opinions and surprising brevity of the critical "opinion of the Court" sections, remains to be determined as the lower courts work through its ramifications on a case-by-case basis. It will be particularly important in the reduction-in-force cases, many of which have previously been litigated on the basis of some form of disparate impact analysis.

Justices Souter, Ginsburg, and Breyer joined. Justice Scalia concurred in part and in the judgment. Justice O'Connor wrote a concurring opinion which Justices Kennedy and Thomas joined. And Chief Justice Roberts took no part in the decision. This lack of conceptual and doctrinal unanimity raises many questions that the lower courts will undoubtedly have to grapple with.

33. City of Jackson, 544 U.S. at 231.

34. City of Jackson, 544 U.S. at 240.

35. City of Jackson, 544 U.S. at 241 (quoting *Wards Cove*).

36. Meacham v. Knolls Atomic Power Lab, 554 U.S. 84 (2008).

37. City of Jackson, 544 U.S. 228 (2005).

38. Villarreal v. R.J. Reynolds Tobacco, Co., 839 F.3d 958 (11th Cir. 2016); Kleber v. CareFusion Corp. 914 F.3d 480 (7th Cir. 2019).

§ 20.06 Defenses and Exceptions

[A] "Reasonable Factors Other than Age" and "Good Cause"

Although the statute lists "reasonable factors other than age" and "good cause" as not "unlawful" reasons for adverse employment actions, these would seem merely to be a partial converse of what the statute affirmatively prohibits—adverse employment actions that are "because of" age. Even if these had not been listed as defenses, what they refer to would normally play a role anyway, as either a part of the proof supporting the employer's general denial that age was the reason or as part of the *articulation* burden under the *McDonnell Douglas* methodology of proof.

[B] BFOQ

Age per se will almost never qualify as a BFOQ. For example, the claim that younger sales staff are needed to attract and relate to younger customers, as in a clothing store catering to teenage shoppers, would undoubtedly be rejected on the grounds that mere customer preference cannot serve as the basis for a BFOQ. Rather, the BFOQ is most often asserted when an employer claims that some job-related characteristic, or the lack thereof, correlates with age. The model for proving this type of BFOQ was established in *Trans World Airlines, Inc. v. Thurston*[39] and *Western Air Lines, Inc. v. Criswell.*[40]

Initially, the employer must prove that the characteristic in question is "reasonably necessary to the essence of [the employer's] business,"[41] with the focus being on "the job from which the protected individual is excluded."[42] Then, the employer must justify relying on age rather than the characteristic itself in making employment decision. It may do this in two ways: (1) by proving that all or substantially all persons over a particular age possess a characteristic that prevents them from safely and efficiently performing the duties of their job; or (2) by proving that some persons over a particular age possess that characteristic, but it is impossible or highly impracticable to make this determination on an individual basis.

Most age BFOQ cases involve the alleged mental and physical deterioration that comes with increased age. When slower reflexes or a higher risk of a cardiovascular attack would pose risks to customers, co-employees, or the public, the consequences of being wrong about the existence of a correlation could be enormous. It was for this reason that the employer in *Criswell* argued that in these cases a BFOQ should be recognized if the employer had "a rational basis in fact" that the correlation exists,

39. 469 U.S. 111 (1985).
40. 472 U.S. 400 (1985).
41. Criswell, 472 U.S. at 413.
42. Thurston, 469 U.S. at 122.

thus precluding judicial second-guessing of an employer's good faith determination. While not insensitive to safety concerns and the desirability of deferring to the employer's judgment, the Court stated that this could be accomplished within the context of the requirement that the characteristic be job-related: "'The greater the safety factor, measured by the likelihood of harm and the probable severity of that harm in case of an accident, the more stringent may be the job qualification designed to insure safe [job performance.]'"[43]

Establishing an age-related BFOQ defense thus requires not only expert testimony about the nature and risks of the job, but also medical evidence and validation studies. The defense has thus been recognized in some cases but not in others—depending on the facts of each case. The fact that federal law imposes an age limitation on certain federal jobs will make it a BFOQ for that class of federal employees. But this does not mean that it automatically becomes a BFOQ for state and private jobs of a similar nature, since the federal limitation may be related to employment policies that have nothing to do with the ability of an individual to actually perform the job.[44]

[C] Foreign Law

The ADEA has always applied to employees who are Unites States citizens employed overseas by a United States corporation or its foreign subsidiary—coverage that was extended to Title VII by the 1991 Civil Rights Act. Both statutes, however, provide a defense when compliance with United States law would cause the employer to violate the law of the country in which the workplace is located.

[D] Bona Fide Seniority System

To qualify as *bona fide*, a seniority system cannot have been adopted or administered with an intent to evade the purposes of the ADEA. Moreover, a seniority system cannot require or permit *involuntary* retirement on the basis of age.[45] Other than that, the seniority system defense is rarely involved in age discrimination cases. This is because seniority systems generally inure to the advantage of older workers.

[E] Bona Fide Employment Benefit Plan

As amended by the Older Workers Benefit Protection Act, this ADEA defense has become enormously complicated.[46] The basic principle is that all age-based reductions in employee benefit plans must be justified by significant cost considerations. Thus,

43. Criswell, 472 U.S. at 413 (quoting *Usery v. Tamiami Trail Tours, Inc.*, 531 F.2d 224, 236 (5th Cir. 1976)).

44. Johnson v. Mayor and City Counsel of Baltimore, 472 U.S. 353 (1985).

45. Trans World Airlines, Inc. v. Thurston, 469 U.S. 111 (1985).

46. 29 U.S.C. § 621 (overruling *Public Employees Retirement System of Ohio v. Betts*, 492 U.S. 158 (1989)).

if $1,000 will purchase $100,000 worth of life insurance for a 39-year-old worker but only $65,000 for a 59-year-old worker, then it is not illegal to provide the older worker the lesser amount of insurance.

[F] Bona Fide Executive Exception

An employer may impose mandatory retirement on an employee who is at least 65 years old and who in the preceding two years was employed in a "bona fide executive or high policymaking position," if the employee's annual retirement benefits will aggregate at least $44,000.

[G] Early Retirement Incentive Plans

Early retirement incentive plans are often offered to older employees as a part of an employer's downsizing program. This has led to two problems. First, younger workers (but still within the 40-plus age group) often sued when they were excluded from eligibility. Second, those who accepted often later sued, claiming that they accepted the retirement only because of the implied threat of layoff if they refused.

The Older Workers Benefit Protection Act purported to resolve these difficulties. First, it allows an employer to establish a minimum age for eligibility.[47] Second, it broadly approves any plan that is "consistent with the relevant purpose or purposes of this Act"—which the courts tend to construe as expressing general approval and creating a safe harbor for these plans. Third, the Act provides for waivers and releases, thus obviating the coercion aspect. The statutory requirements in this regard are discussed below.

§ 20.07 Waiver and Release

Although terminated employees are frequently asked to sign a waiver of all legal claims against the employer, waiver of ADEA claims seems to have caused the most difficulty. In response to a mixture of standards enunciated by the courts and disagreement among the various circuits and the EEOC, Congress established in the OWBPA the minimal requirements for a "knowing and voluntary" waiver of ADEA claims.[48] Such a waiver must contain certain information, be written in a style that the employee can understand, give the employee time to consider and later revoke the waiver if desired, inform the employee of the right to consult with an attorney, and provide consideration in addition to anything the employee would otherwise re-

47. Apart from the express statutory protection, plans limited to employees over a certain age would probably be covered by the *General Dynamics* principle, which allows discrimination in favor of older workers because protection of older workers, rather than the elimination of age differential treatment per se, was the purpose of the ADEA.

48. 29 U.S.C. § 626(f).

ceive upon termination. The OWBPA, however, only establishes a minimum.[49] The courts continue to impose additional requirements, allow plaintiffs to introduce parol evidence of alleged coercion to sign, and otherwise make drafting such a waiver a difficult undertaking.

What sometimes happens, thus, is that a terminated employee will sign the waiver, receive the consideration, sue under the ADEA, and claim that the waiver did not comply with the statutory requirements and was thus ineffective. Although some lower courts held that the ADEA suit could not proceed unless the plaintiff returned the consideration, the Supreme Court held otherwise in *Oubre v. Energy Operations, Inc.*[50] Although return of the money is not a condition precedent to suit, the concurring opinions suggested that a defendant could nevertheless petition for a return of the consideration that was paid in return for the now challenged waiver—subject, of course, to the plaintiff still having the money available.

§ 20.08 Chapter Highlights

1. Individual, single-motive discrimination is proved in much the same way as in Title VII cases of this kind, with the principal kinds of evidence being:

- Admission of age motivation and policies that are facially discriminatory.
- Ageist comments and *code words*.
- Comparators.
- *McDonnell Douglas* inferential facts.

(§ 20.01)

2. The after-acquired evidence defense, which merely serves to limit the remedy, is similar to the same Title VII defense. (§ 20.02)

3. Plaintiffs must show that age is the *but for* cause of the adverse employment action.

4. Systemic disparate treatment, which involves the use of statistics plus proof of individual instances of discrimination, is more difficult to establish because age is a continuum rather than an either/or proposition like race or sex. Courts thus tend to scrutinize the statistics very carefully. (§ 20.04)

5. The ADEA has its own unique form of *disparate impact* analysis, one that incorporates the *reasonable factors other than age* defense. Although the Supreme Court addressed this issue in *Smith v. City of Jackson*, the case still leaves many issues unresolved. (§ 20.05)

---

49. Bennett v. Coors Brewing Co., 189 F.3d 1221 (10th Cir. 1999) (the OWBPA "factors are not exclusive and other circumstances, outside the express statutory requirements, may impact whether a waiver under the OWBPA is knowing and voluntary").

50. 522 U.S. 422 (1998).

6. The ADEA contains several affirmative defenses and exceptions.

- Reasonable factors other than age.
- Good cause.
- Bona fide occupational qualification.
- Foreign law.
- Bona fide seniority system.
- Bona fide employment benefit plan.
- Bona fide executive exception.
- Early retirement incentive plans.

(§ 20.06)

7. An age discrimination waiver or release, often signed upon termination, is valid only if it meets the criteria spelled out in the ADEA, plus those articulated by the courts. The object is to ensure that the waiver or release was signed knowingly and voluntarily. (§ 20.07)

Chapter 21

Procedure and Remedies

Synopsis

The enforcement mechanisms and relief available under the ADEA have become more like those of Title VII under amendments contained in the 1991 Civil Rights Act. And the two statutes have always been construed *in pari materia*.[1] Nevertheless, the ADEA still retains some unique features that flow from its incorporation of certain procedures and remedies from the Fair Labor Standards Act.

§ 21.01 Administrative Prerequisites

A person claiming age discrimination is required to file a charge with the EEOC within the same 180 or 300 days required by Title VII. The contents of the charge and the EEOC duties of investigation and conciliation are also the same as under Title VII. In addition, as under Title VII, if the state has an appropriate deferral agency, an aggrieved party is required to file with it. The ADEA permits simultaneous filing with the state FEP agency, and the state-agency filing requirement is deemed satisfied even if it is not timely under state law.[2] A state agency determination that has not been reviewed by state courts has no preclusive effect in a federal lawsuit.[3] Title VII law is also applied with respect to when the discrimination occurred[4] and possible tolling of the statutory period, which is not jurisdictional.

1. Oscar Mayer & Co. v. Evans, 441 U.S. 750, 755 (1979).
2. Oscar Mayer, 441 U.S. 750, n.1; Woodford v. Ngo, 548 U.S. 81, 98–99 (2006).
3. Astoria Federal Savings & Loan Ass'n v. Solimino, 501 U.S. 104 (1991).
4. The Lilly Ledbetter Fair Pay Act of 2009, 42 U.S.C.S. § 2000e-5(e)(3)(A), specifically intended for the new Title VII compensation accrual rules to also apply to age-related pay discrimination cases.

§ 21.02 Lawsuits

An ADEA claimant may file a lawsuit no sooner than 60 days after filing with the EEOC. After that, the claimant may file with or without a notice of termination or right-to-sue letter from the EEOC. If the EEOC does issue one, however, the claimant must file within 90 days. A private individual's right to initiate a lawsuit terminates if the EEOC files first. Most courts, however, allow a previously commenced private suit to continue even if the EEOC also sues later.

ADEA claims may not be brought as a true class action under Rule 23. Instead, the ADEA generally follows the "representative action" procedures of section 16(b) of the FLSA. Instead of being required to meet the Rule 23 standards for numerosity, commonality, typicality, and representativeness, the putative ADEA plaintiff must be merely "similarly situated." And unlike the Rule 23 class members, who must opt out or be bound, no one becomes a party to an ADEA representative action without first filing a written consent with the court. The district court has the discretion to become involved in the opt-in notice that the putative plaintiffs send out—limiting its geographic scope, time for response, and contents of the notice.[5]

The proof structure of an ADEA representative action remains uncertain; no court has analyzed the issue extensively. Plaintiffs generally contend that the two-stage system of proof used in a *Teamsters* systemic disparate treatment case is appropriate—with liability being established by statistics and representative individual cases in the first stage, and the burden shifting to the employer in the second stage to show that a particular member of the representative group was not in fact a victim of discrimination. Defendants, on the other hand, generally maintain that each member of the representative class still has the burden of proving his or her own individual violation.

§ 21.03 Remedies

As under Title VII, the available remedies to a successful ADEA claimant include affirmative and negative injunctive relief (including instatement or reinstatement), back pay, front pay, liquidated damages, attorney's fees, and costs. Punitive and compensatory damages are not available. An ADEA plaintiff is entitled to a trial by jury with respect to both the ultimate issue liability and backpay awards.[6] Front pay, however, is considered an equitable remedy, with availability and amount being decided by the judge.[7] The courts are divided over whether a plaintiff may recover both front pay and liquidated damages.[8] Attorney's fees are subject to the FLSA provisions, which

5. Hoffman-La Roche, Inc. v. Sperling, 493 U.S. 165 (1989).
6. Young v. Lukens Steel Co., 881 F. Supp. 962 (E.D. Pa. 1994).
7. Cox v. Dubuque Bank & Trust, 163 F.3d 492, 498 (8th Cir. 1998).
8. *Compare* Castle v. Sangamo Weston, Inc., 837 F.2d 1550, 1562 (11th Cir. 1988), *with* Walther v. Lone Star Gas Co., 952 F.2d 119, 127 (5th Cir. 1992).

make them mandatory when the plaintiff prevails but allow for nothing when the defendant prevails.

Punitive damages, however, are not available because the statute specifically authorizes liquidated or double damages, which the courts view as the functional equivalent of punitive damages. ADEA liquidated damages are available only for *willful* violations. In *Trans World Airlines, Inc. v. Thurston*,[9] the Supreme Court said that a willful violation is one in which the employer "knew or showed reckless disregard for the matter of whether its conduct was prohibited by the ADEA,"[10] thus requiring proof of more than mere negligent or unreasonable conduct. In *Hazen Paper Co. v. Biggins*,[11] the Supreme Court reaffirmed that test—rejecting lower court decisions that had required proof that the conduct was outrageous, direct rather than circumstantial evidence of motivation, or proof that age was the predominant rather than the merely determinative motive in the decision.

§ 21.04 Chapter Highlights

1. A person claiming an ADEA violation must file a charge with the EEOC and otherwise exhaust all the administrative procedures that are required under Title VII. (§ 21.01)

2. An ADEA lawsuit may be filed no sooner than 60 days after filing the charge and no later than 90 days after receiving the right-to-sue letter, if the EEOC issues one. A claimant is not required to wait for this letter, however. (§ 21.02)

3. An ADEA claimant is entitled to most of the remedies available under Title VII, except punitive damages. Instead, under the ADEA, a successful plaintiff may recover liquidated or double damages if the violation was *willful*, which means that the defendant knew or showed reckless disregard about whether its conduct violated the law. (§ 21.03)

9. 469 U.S. 111 (1985).
10. *Thurston*, 469 U.S. at 126.
11. 507 U.S. 604 (1993)

Part V

Post-Civil War Civil Rights Acts

Following the adoption of the Fourteenth Amendment, Congress enacted several statutes that were designed to enforce the guarantees of due process and equal protection. Insofar as employment discrimination is concerned, Section 1981 applies to race discrimination in contracts of employment. Section 1983 provides protection against discrimination, on several bases, by state and local employers. And Section 1985(3) covers conspiracies to deprive others of their right to be free of employment discrimination.

Chapter 22

Section 1981

Synopsis

Section 1981(a) provides as follows:

> (a) All persons within the jurisdiction of the United States shall have the same right in every State and Territory to make and enforce contracts, to sue, be parties, give evidence, and to the full and equal benefit of all laws and proceedings for the security of persons and property as is enjoyed by white citizens, and shall be subject to like punishment, pains, penalties, taxes, licenses, and exactions of every kind and to no other.

§ 22.01 Persons Subject to Section 1981

[A] State and Local Governments

In *Jett v. Dallas Independent School District*,[1] the Supreme Court held that Section 1981 does not create a direct or independent cause of action against governmental units. A plaintiff, rather, must pursue remedial relief through a Section 1983 action—and subject, thus, to all the limitations that attach to a Section 1983 cause of action.[2] The Civil Rights Act of 1991 amended Section 1981 to allow suits claiming

---

1. 491 U.S. 701 (1998).
2. *See* Chapter 23.

discrimination "under color of State law." The Ninth Circuit has held that *Jett* was modified by the 1991 amendment. Eight other circuits disagree.[3]

[B] Private Employers

The literal wording and the legislative history of Section 1981 strongly suggest that it was originally intended to strike down the various post-Civil War *Black Codes* in the Southern states that limited the civil rights of newly freed slaves in the exercise of the enumerated civil rights. And since no "white citizen" had the right not to be discriminated against because of race in private employment relationships, one could reasonably conclude that this statute did not create such a right for anyone else either. In other words, Section 1981 was limited to cases involving *state action*—the enforcement of statutes that deprived black citizens of the right to contract and otherwise participate on an equal basis in the civil process enjoyed by white citizens. The United States Supreme Court, however, decided otherwise in *Johnson v. Railway Express Agency, Inc.*[4]

Although Title VII was already available as a remedy at the time of this decision, Section 1981 soon became an important supplemental and sometimes alternative means of redress for certain forms of discrimination in the private sector. For example, Section 1981 is not limited by the 15-employee requirement of Title VII. Moreover, Section 1981 applies to discrimination in all forms of employment-related contracts, including those involving non-employee, independent contractors. Section 1981 claimants are not required to exhaust any state or federal administrative remedies. And uncapped punitive and compensatory damages are available under Section 1981.

§ 22.02 The Protected Class

Since the nondiscrimination *rights* of "white citizens" provided the touchstone or definitional source of the *rights* being granted to others by the statute, one could logically conclude Section 1981 granted white persons no rights in addition to whatever they already had. Again, the Supreme Court decided otherwise. In *McDonald v. Santa Fe Trail Transportation Co.*,[5] the Supreme Court concluded that the statutory reference to rights "enjoyed by white citizens" was not intended to delimit the scope of the statutory right or who it extended to, but was rather designed only to indicate the racial nature of the prohibited discrimination. Thus, an employer who discriminates against white employees or applicants on the basis of race can be liable under Section 1981.

---

3. Buntin v. City of Boston, 857 F.3d 69, 74 (1st Cir. 2017).
4. 421 U.S. 454 (1975).
5. 427 U.S. 273 (1976).

§ 22.03 The Proscribed Basis of Discrimination

Under Section 1981, the proscribed basis of discrimination is that of race. The Supreme Court, moreover, has given Section 1981 *race* a very broad meaning, to include ancestry or membership in any "ethnically and physiognomically distinctive sub-grouping,"[6] a nineteenth-century conception of *race* that thus includes Jews, Arabs, Germans, Greeks, Irish, Basques, Poles, Gypsies, and other ethnic groups. The Supreme Court has held that Section 1981 prohibits alienage discrimination by public entities,[7] but the lower courts are split over whether it also prohibits such discrimination by private actors.[8] The Second Circuit, however, has held that the public/private distinction no longer has any validity, since the Civil Rights Act of 1991 expressly treats governmental and nongovernmental violations the same.[9] And in another case the defendant, relying on the public/private distinction, claimed that it discriminated against an individual because he was an Israeli citizen rather than because he was a Jew and that Section 1981 thus did not apply. The court held, however, that in the case of Israel, where the population is predominately Jewish, discrimination on the basis of alienage is the same as discrimination on the basis of race—in other words, the one is the *proxy* of the other.[10] In other contexts, discrimination on the basis of national origin is not protected.[11]

§ 22.04 Contract-Based Discrimination

Employment is inherently a contractual relationship. Originally, the "make and enforce contracts" language of Section 1981 was construed to cover essentially the same employment decisions and conduct that are covered by Title VII. Moreover, although Section 1981 does not contain a separate anti-retaliation provision, most courts concluded that opposition to racial discrimination had a sufficient racial basis to bring it within the Section 1981 ambit of protection.[12]

The law on this changed in *Patterson v. McLean Credit Union*,[13] where the Supreme Court narrowly construed the "make and enforce contracts" language, finding that it applied only to contract formation itself. The Court thus held that Section 1981 did not cover racial harassment and that a promotion could be challenged only if it

---

6. Saint Francis Coll. v. Al-Khazraji, 481 U.S. 604, 613 (1987).

7. Takahashi v. Fish & Game Comm'n, 334 U.S. 410 (1948).

8. *Compare* Duane v. Geico, 37 F.3d 1036 (4th Cir. 1994), *with* Bhandari v. First Nat'l Bank of Commerce, 829 F.2d 1343 (5th Cir. 1987).

9. Anderson v. Conboy, 156 F.3d 167 (2d Cir. 1998).

10. Sinai v. New Eng. Tel. & Tel. Co., 3 F.3d 471 (1st Cir. 1993).

11. Torgerson v. City of Rochester, 643 F.3d 1031, 1053 (8th Cir. 2011).

12. Setser v. Novack Inv. Co., 638 F.2d 1137 (8th Cir. 1981).

13. 491 U.S. 164 (1989).

rose "to the level of an opportunity for a new and distinct relation between the employee and the employer."[14] The lower courts thus consistently construed *Patterson* as excluding claims of discriminatory discharge.

Congress, however, overruled *Patterson* by amending Section 1981 to provide that "the term 'make and enforce contracts' includes the making, performance, modification, and termination of contracts, and the enjoyment of all benefits, privileges, terms, and conditions of the contractual relationship." The apparent intent was to restore pre-*Patterson* law, thus again making Section 1981 and Title VII co-extensive and, as most courts have held, also covering claims of retaliation.[15]

Although under state law most at-will employment relationships are still regarded as being fundamentally *contractual* in nature (basically, a series of automatically renewing unilateral contracts of unfixed duration), the courts are divided over whether Section 1981 applies to these arrangements.[16] An individual, however, can sue only with respect to contracts under which he or she has rights. In *Domino's Pizza, Inc. v. McDonald*,[17] the Court held that the president and sole shareholder of a corporation could not sue another business that had breached its contract with his corporation because of racial animus toward him. The Court reserved judgment, however, on whether a third-party beneficiary might sue on the basis of a contract between two other entities.

§ 22.05 The Nature and Proof of Discrimination

For the most part, proof of individual and systemic discrimination under Section 1981 is the same as under Title VII[18]—with one major exception and perhaps several minor ones.

First, in *General Building Contractors Association v. Pennsylvania*,[19] the Supreme Court held that Section 1981 reaches only purposeful discrimination. This conclusion was predicated on both the legislative history of the section and the fact that its constitutional predicate, the Fourteenth Amendment, itself only addresses intentional acts. This is an early demonstration of the principle that the substantive provisions of a statute cannot go beyond the substantive provisions of the constitutional text

14. Patterson, 491 U.S. at 185.

15. Humphries v. CBOCS West, 474 F.3d 387, 397 (7th Cir.), cert. granted, 128 S. Ct. 30 (2007).

16. *Compare* Skinner v. Maritz, Inc., 253 F.3d 337 (8th Cir. 2001), *and* Perry v. Woodward, 188 F.3d 1220 (10th Cir. 1999), *with* Gonzalez v. Ingersoll Milling Mach. Co., 133 F.3d 1025 (7th Cir. 1998).

17. 546 U.S. 470 (2006).

18. Crawford v. Western Elec. Co., 614 F.2d 1300 (5th Cir. 1980) (applying *McDonnell Douglas* prima facie case analysis in individual disparate treatment situation); Payne v. Travenol Labs., Inc., 673 F.2d 798 (5th Cir. 1982) (applying *Teamsters* analysis to systemic disparate treatment situation).

19. 458 U.S. 375 (1982).

upon which they are based.[20] In practical application, thus, it means that claims of disparate impact discrimination cannot be brought under Section 1981.

As under Title VII, originally, the courts have generally said that *but for* is the proper standard of causation under Section 1981. In the 1991 Civil Rights Act, Congress changed the causation test for most Title VII actions from *but for* to *a motivating factor.* Congress did not, however, legislate a similar change in Section 1981 actions. Finally, a few courts have read some of the express Title VII exemptions into Section 1981, such as those pertaining to bona fide seniority systems[21] and bona fide membership clubs.[22]

§ 22.06 Procedure

There are no administrative procedures to exhaust before filing a Section 1981 lawsuit. Thus, if a plaintiff has failed to file a timely Title VII charge with the EEOC or a state administrative agency and desires to sue persons not even named in the Title VII charge or wants to expand the scope of the alleged discrimination beyond what would be allowed under Title VII law, then Section 1981 provides the answer.

A Section 1981 action may be brought in federal court without regard to the amount in controversy[23] or in a state court of general jurisdiction. A jury trial is available—an early advantage over Title VII that was, however, eliminated by the Civil Rights Act of 1991 which extended that right to Title VII actions as well.

Since Section 1981 contains no statute of limitations, the Supreme Court originally indicated that the courts should borrow the state's general or residual personal injury statute of limitations for Section 1981 actions,[24] including the state's tolling rules, except where they conflict with federal policy.[25] But in 1990, Congress enacted a four-year statute of limitations for all federal statutes enacted after December 1990 and not containing their own limitation period. The Court has since held that Section 1981 actions that are predicated on anything in the Civil Rights Act of 1991 are subject to this new federal statute of limitations.[26] The standards for determining what marks the running of the Title VII statute of limitations are also used generally in Section 1981 actions.

§ 22.07 Remedies

Prior to the Civil Rights Act of 1991, one of Section 1981's primary advantages over Title VII was that compensatory and punitive damages were available under Sec-

20. General Building Contractors Ass'n, 458 U.S. at 388.

21. NAACP, Detroit Branch v. Detroit Police Officers Ass'n, 900 F.2d 903 (6th Cir. 1990).

22. Kemerer v. Davis, 520 F. Supp. 256 (E.D. Mich. 1981). *Contra* Crawford v. Willow Oaks Country Club, 66 F. Supp. 2d 767 (E.D. Va. 1999).

23. 28 U.S.C. § 1343.

24. Goodman v. Lukens Steel Co., 482 U.S. 656 (1987).

25. Board of Regents v. Tomanio, 446 U.S. 478 (1980).

26. Jones v. R.R. Donnelley & Sons Co., 541 U.S. 369 (2004).

tion 1981. Today, the only vestige of that advantage is that Section 1981 damages are not subject to the statutory cap. Other than that, the various remedies that are available under Title VII are also generally available in a Section 1981 action—including instatement, reinstatement, backpay, injunctive relief, limited affirmative action, and attorney's fees.

§ 22.08 Chapter Highlights

1. Subject to the limits of Section 1983 and the Eleventh Amendment, state and local governments are subject to Section 1981, as are private employers. (§ 22.01)

2. Despite the literal wording of the statute, persons of all races, minority or otherwise, are covered by Section 1981. (§ 22.02)

3. Although Section 1981 literally prohibits discrimination only on the basis of *race*, this has been construed very broadly to include ethnicity and alienage. (§ 22.03)

4. Section 1981 prohibits contract-based discrimination, which in the employment context includes the making, performance, modification, and termination of contracts, and the enjoyment of all benefits, privileges, terms, and conditions of the employment relationship. (§ 22.04)

5. Section 1981 covers intentional discrimination only, not disparate impact. The Title VII methods of proof are generally applicable in Section 1981 actions, although Section 1981 may still require proof of *but for* causation in mixed motive cases. (§ 22.05)

6. There are no administrative procedures to exhaust under Section 1981. An action can be brought directly in federal or state court, and all cases are subject to either the relevant state statute of limitations or the federal four-year statute. (§ 22.06)

7. All the remedies that are available under Title VII are also available under Section 1981. But unlike the Title VII compensatory and punitive damages, these damages in a Section 1981 action are not subject to any upper limit. (§ 22.06)

Chapter 23

Section 1983[1]

Synopsis

§ 23.01 Introduction

In addition to pursuing statutory remedies specifically directed at remedying employment discrimination, a person may seek recovery under Section 1983, which provides a remedy for the deprivation of federally protected rights at a state or local level. Section 1983 provides as follows:

> Every person who, under color of any statute, ordinance, regulation, custom, or usage, of any State or Territory or the District of Columbia, subjects, or causes to be subjected, any citizen of the United States or other person within the jurisdiction thereof to the deprivation of any rights, privileges, or immu-

1. This chapter was written by Tracey C. Green, Shareholder, Willoughby and Hoefer, P.A., Columbia, South Carolina.

> nities secured by the Constitution and laws, shall be liable to the party injured in an action at law, suit in equity, or other proper proceeding for redress.[2]

To state a claim under Section 1983, a plaintiff must allege facts supporting the following main elements:

- A person within the meaning of the statute;
- Acting under color of state law;
- A causal connection ("subjects, or causes to be subjected"); and
- A deprivation of rights secured by the Constitution or by federal law.

A plaintiff who meets the burden of proving these elements may recover damages, including nominal, compensatory, and punitive; may obtain injunctive and other equitable relief if appropriate; and may be able to recover attorney's fees.[3]

However, certain defenses are available under Section 1983 that will preclude recovery. The defense asserted by many government officials sued under Section 1983 is absolute or qualified immunity, depending upon the person's position and the facts of the case. In addition, a defendant may argue that the claim should be barred by the Eleventh Amendment, which creates state sovereign immunity, or by the statute of limitations. An extensive discussion of these latter defenses is beyond the scope of this chapter.

§ 23.02 The Meaning of "Person"

Although a state is never a person under Section 1983,[4] a state official may or may not be a person for purposes of the statute depending upon the nature of the lawsuit and the remedy sought by the plaintiff. As a general rule, state officials sued in their official capacity are not persons under Section 1983 because there is no difference between suing an official's office and suing the state itself.[5] If the remedy sought is injunctive relief, a state official is a Section 1983 person even if sued in an official capacity.[6] A state official also is a person if sued individually.[7] The Supreme Court originally held that the term "person" does not include a local government, such as a municipality,[8] but reversed itself 17 years later and held that a local government is a person for purposes of Section 1983.[9] The Court did, however, impose some limitation on that liability: a local government may not be held liable based on a theory of respondeat superior.[10] Rather, the local government may be held liable only based upon the execution of official policy or custom, either through the enactment of laws or

2. 42 U.S.C. § 1983.
3. 42 U.S.C. § 1988.
4. Will v. Mich. Dep't of State Police, 491 U.S. 58, 65 (1989).
5. Will, 491 U.S. at 71.
6. Will, 491 U.S. at 71 n.10.
7. Kentucky v. Graham, 473 U.S. 159, 165–68 (1985).
8. Monroe v. Pape, 365 U.S. 167 (1961).
9. Monell v. Dep't of Soc. Servs., 436 U.S. 658, 690–91 (1978).
10. *Monell*, 436 U.S. at 691.

ordinances or through the actions of an official whose actions "may fairly be said to represent official policy."[11] This analysis differs from Title VII and other anti-discrimination statutes, which generally permit respondeat superior liability.[12]

Considerable dispute exists over whether a person's actions in a particular situation represent official policy.[13] The plaintiffs in *Monell v. Department of Social Services*[14] carried their burden of proving official policy because the city had a formal policy requiring pregnant employees to take unpaid leaves of absence even though still medically able to work. But in *City of St. Louis v. Praprotnik*,[15] the plaintiff was unable to prove that the city took retaliatory action against him as part of an official policy because there was no policy authorizing the alleged retaliatory acts and because the supervisor who took action against the plaintiff lacked policymaking authority.[16] Because few discriminatory employment decisions result from formal policy or the acts of a "final policymaker,"[17] local governments rarely will be liable for the discriminatory acts of their subordinates.[18]

In addition to liability based on its formal policies, a local government also may be held liable based on its informal policies. In some situations, this may involve not an affirmative act, but a repeated failure to take action despite indications that action is necessary—that is, a deliberate indifference to the need for further action.[19] Thus,

---

11. Monell, 436 U.S. at 694–95.

12. *See, e.g., Naumovski v. Norris*, 934 F.3d 200, 212 (2d Cir. 2019) ("[W]hile an employer may be liable under Title VII for any discriminatory conduct that can properly be attributed to the employer through agency principles, § 1983 does not permit such vicarious liability.") (footnote omitted).

13. *See* Monell, 436 U.S. at 713 ("[t]here are substantial line-drawing problems in determining when execution of a government's policy or custom can be said to inflict constitutional injury such that government as an entity is responsible under [Section] 1983") (internal quotation marks omitted) (Powell, J., concurring).

14. 436 U.S. at 694–95.

15. 485 U.S. 112 (1988).

16. Praprotnik, 485 U.S. at 127–31 (plurality), 133–34, 137–42 (Brennan, J., concurring in the judgment).

17. *See, e.g.*, Lane v. Anderson, 660 Fed. Appx. 185, 198–99 (4th Cir. 2016) (holding that a Baltimore City Sheriff is not the final policymaker for Baltimore City because Maryland law, rather than the local government, establishes the Sheriff's authority for hiring and discipling employees); Robinson v. Balog, 160 F.3d 183, 190 (4th Cir. 1998) (agency director's authority to make personnel decisions did not constitute policymaking authority); Hull v. Cuyahoga Valley Joint Vocational Sch. Dist. Bd. of Educ., 926 F.2d 505, 515–16 (6th Cir. 1991) (although the supervisor who recommended the plaintiff's termination had a discriminatory motive, the school board, which was the final policymaker, was unaware of this motive when it accepted the recommendation and, thus, was not liable under Section 1983).

18. *But see* Martinez v. City of Opa-Locka, 971 F.2d 708 (11th Cir. 1992) (city manager was the "final policymaker" with respect to employment decisions because the city charter prohibited review by the county commissioners); Williams v. Butler, 863 F.2d 1398 (8th Cir. 1988) (en banc) (municipal judge who terminated a court clerk found to be the "final policymaker" because the city had absolutely delegated to the judge the authority to make personnel decisions).

19. City of Canton v. Harris, 489 U.S. 378 (1989); *But see* Bd. of Cty. Comm'rs v. Brown, 520 U.S. 397, 410–11 (1997) (holding that a sheriff's isolated failure to perform adequate screening did not constitute 'deliberate indifference' because it did not establish the requisite proof that city poli-

although Section 1983 has not historically supported vicarious liability, the Supreme Court held that a single act of negligently hiring a supervisor with a criminal record who later commits a sexual assault likely would not give rise to Section 1983 liability unless the hiring was done with a deliberate indifference to the person's criminal record.[20]

However, the extent of supervisor liability under Section 1983 absent direct personal involvement became less clear after *Ashcroft v. Iqbal*.[21] In *Iqbal*, the Court rejected the imposition of *Bivens* liability[22] on Attorney General John Ashcroft and FBI Director Robert Mueller for alleged constitutional violations committed by government actors against post-9/11 detainees, expressly rejecting the argument that "a supervisor's mere knowledge of his subordinate's discriminatory purpose amounts to the supervisor's violating the Constitution."[23] The Court held instead that "[b]ecause vicarious liability is inapplicable to *Bivens* and § 1983 suits, a plaintiff must plead that each Government-official defendant, through the official's own individual actions, has violated the Constitution."[24] Since the Court's ruling in *Iqbal*, lower courts have struggled to determine the parameters of supervisory liability under Section 1983—or if it even exists.[25] Prior to *Iqbal*, several courts held, for example, that the "policy" requirement of *Monell* is satisfied when a supervisor or agency fails to take steps to prevent or remedy recurring instances of sexual harassment of which they are aware.[26] Post-*Iqbal*, however, the application of the deliberate indifference analysis is unclear.[27] Vicarious liability remains in effect for Title VII claims, however.[28]

---

cymakers disregarded the known or obvious consequence that a particular omission in screening applicants' backgrounds would cause city employees to violate citizens' federally protected rights).

20. *Brown*, 520 U.S. at 415–16.

21. Ashcroft v. Iqbal, 556 U.S. 662 (2009).

22. *See* discussion *infra* § 23.07. *Bivens* liability is analogous to Section 1983 liability but applies only to federal officials.

23. *Iqbal*, 556 U.S. at 677.

24. *Iqbal*, 556 U.S. at 676.

25. Peatross v. City of Memphis, 818 F.3d 233, 242 n.3 (6th Cir. 2016) ("Since *Iqbal*, the circuits have grappled with the precise contours of § 1983 supervisory liability, and while the claim of supervisory liability has not been altogether eliminated, the requirements for sustaining such a claim vary by circuit."); *see Iqbal*, 556 U.S. at 687–88 (Souter, J., dissenting) ("The Court … does away with supervisory liability under *Bivens*.").

26. Cross v. Alabama, 49 F.3d 1490 (11th Cir. 1995); Bator v. Hawaii, 39 F.3d 1021 (9th Cir. 1994); Andrews v. City of Philadelphia, 895 F.2d 1469 (3rd Cir. 1990).

27. *Peatross*, 818 F.3d at 242 n.3 (noting uncertainty among the circuits regarding the parameters of supervisory liability post-*Iqbal*); *see* Wilkins v. Montgomery, 751 F.3d 214, 226 (4th Cir. 2014) ("[A] plaintiff may establish deliberate indifference by demonstrating a supervisor's continued inaction in the face of documented widespread abuses.") (internal quotation marks and citation omitted); Elkins v. District of Columbia, 690 F.3d 554, 566 (D.C. Cir. 2012) ("Supervisory liability under § 1983 is triggered only when a supervisor fails to provide more stringent training in the wake of a history of past transgressions by the agency or provides training so clearly deficient that some deprivation of rights will *inevitably* result absent additional instruction.") (internal quotation marks and citation omitted).

28. Vance v. Ball State Univ., 570 U.S. 421, 424 (2013) ("We hold that an employee is a 'supervisor' for purposes of vicarious liability under Title VII if he or she is empowered by the employer to take tangible employment actions against the victim. …"). Because the standards for liability differ under

§ 23.03 The Meaning of "Under Color of State Law"

[A] Public Officials

Public officials are acting under color of state law whenever they are "clothed with the authority of state law," regardless of whether their actions are authorized or whether they simply are abusing their authority.[29] Thus, a government supervisor whose unconstitutional discrimination against an employee violates state law or agency policy against sexual harassment nevertheless acts under color of state law for purposes of Section 1983.[30] Similarly, although state-paid public defenders are not acting under color of state law when acting as adversaries to the state, their status changes when performing administrative duties, such as hiring or firing employees.[31]

A public official acting outside the scope of employment nevertheless may be acting under color of state law if the official possesses "indicia of authority" when the action is taken, such as abuse of authority by off-duty police officers.[32] Thus, a supervisor who engages in after-hours, off-premises sexual harassment might be acting under color of state law if a reasonable person would construe the conduct as being employment-related.[33] However, public employees who sexually harass a co-employee generally are not acting pursuant to any actual or apparent state authority and, thus, are not acting under color of state law.[34]

[B] Private Parties

A private person or corporation rarely will be found to have acted under color of state law for purposes of Section 1983. To determine whether a private party's acts may be attributed to the state, courts focus upon whether those acts constitute state action. But, "state action may be found if, though only if, there is such a 'close nexus between the State and the challenged action' that seemingly private behavior 'may be fairly treated as that of the State itself.' "[35] If a private party's conduct constitutes state action, it also constitutes action under color of state law.[36]

Title VII and Section 1983, there presently is no indication that *Vance* has influenced the analysis for supervisor liability under Section 1983, especially in light of *Iqbal.*

29. *See, e.g.*, Monroe v. Pape, 365 U.S. 167, 184 (1961).

30. Robinson v. City of Pittsburgh, 120 F.3d 1286 (3d Cir. 1997), abrogated on other grounds by Burlington Northern & Santa Fe Ry. Co. v. White, 548 U.S. 53 (2006).

31. Polk Cty. v. Dodson, 454 U.S. 312, 325 (1981) ("[i]t may be ... that a public defender also would act under color of state law while performing certain administrative and possibly investigative functions").

32. Davis v. Murphy, 559 F.2d 1098 (7th Cir. 1977) (off-duty police officers carrying their guns and badges were acting under color of state law when they provoked a fight with five African Americans).

33. David v. City & Cty. of Denver, 101 F.3d 1344 (10th Cir. 1996).

34. Edwards v. Wallace Cmty. Coll., 49 F.3d 1517 (11th Cir. 1995).

35. Brentwood Acad. v. Tenn. Secondary Sch. Athletic Ass'n, 531 U.S. 288, 295 (2001) (quoting Jackson v. Metro. Edison Co., 419 U.S. 345, 351 n.2 (1974)).

36. Brentwood Acad., 531 U.S. at 295–96 (quoting Blum v. Yaretsky, 457 U.S. 991, 1004 (1982)).

The Supreme Court has held that a private actor may be a state actor and, thus, acting under color of state law in the following situations:

- the state has exercised "coercive power" over the private actor or has provided "significant encouragement, either overt or covert";[37]
- the private actor willfully participates in joint activity with a state entity;[38]
- the private actor is controlled by an "agency of the State";[39]
- the private actor has been delegated a public function that is "traditionally the exclusive prerogative of the state";[40] or
- the private actor is " 'entwined with governmental policies' or [the] government is 'entwined in its management or control.' "[41]

These standards often are difficult to establish.[42] Moreover, even if one of these standards generally applies, countervailing considerations may lead a court to reject characterizing the private party's behavior as constituting state action.[43] The state action analysis for private parties is very fact-specific and lacks "rigid simplicity,"[44] making it difficult for plaintiffs and defendants to predict with certainty whether private parties closely involved with the state are state actors.[45] However, as a general rule, it is difficult to establish that a private party is a state actor.[46]

---

37. *Brentwood Acad.*, 531 U.S. at 295–96 (quoting Blum v. Yaretsky, 457 U.S. 991, 1004 (1982)).

38. *Brentwood Acad.*, 531 U.S. at 295–96 (quoting Lugar v. Edmondson Oil, 457 U.S. 922, 941 (1982)).

39. *Brentwood Acad.*, 531 U.S. at 295–96 (internal quotation marks omitted).

40. *Brentwood Acad.*, 531 U.S. at 295–96; *see* Manhattan Cmty. Access Corp. v. Halleck, 139 S. Ct. 1921, 1929 (2019) ("[T]o qualify as a traditional, exclusive public function within the meaning of our state-action precedents, the government must have traditionally *and* exclusively performed the function.").

41. *Brentwood Acad.*, 531 U.S. at 295–96 (quoting Evans v. Newton, 382 U.S. 296, 299 (1966)).

42. *Compare Brentwood Acad.*, 531 U.S. at 297–305 (holding that statewide association regulating athletic competition among state public and private schools is a state actor based on level of state entwinement with the association), *with* Nat'l Coll. Athletic Ass'n v. Tarkanian, 488 U.S. 179, 196 n.16 (1988) (rejecting characterization of NCAA as a state actor based on joint action because it was not under the control of any one state and, in fact, acted in opposition to the interests of a state's public college when it threatened to impose sanctions if the basketball coach was not suspended).

43. *See Brentwood Acad.*, 531 U.S. at 295–96; *see also* Rendell-Baker v. Kohn, 457 U.S. 830 (1982) (although almost 90% of a school's operating budget came from public funds and the state extensively regulated its functions, the Court held that the school was not a state actor).

44. *See Brentwood Acad.*, 531 U.S. at 295.

45. *Compare* Blumel v. Mylander, 919 F. Supp. 423 (M.D. Fla. 1996) (private corporation operating a correctional facility under contract with the state engaged in state action), *with* Lloyd v. Corr. Corp. of Am., 855 F. Supp. 221 (W.D. Tenn. 1994) (employee of private corporation operating a correctional facility not acting under color of state law).

46. Marie v. Am. Red Cross, 771 F.3d 344, 363–64 (6th Cir. 2014) (holding that the American Red Cross is not a state actor).

§ 23.04 The "Deprivation of Rights" Requirement

Section 1983 is directed toward the deprivation of rights protected by the United States Constitution or by federal law. The constitutionally protected rights against employment discrimination that may be vindicated through a Section 1983 action are those discussed in Chapter 2. Although the protection afforded by these rights overlaps with many of the federal employment discrimination laws, the procedures for establishing a violation are different. A plaintiff also must assert the violation of a federally protected *right*, not merely the violation of a federal *law*.[47]

In *Blessing v. Freestone*,[48] the Supreme Court explained when a statute creates a federal right for purposes of Section 1983:

> First, Congress must have intended that the provision in question benefit the plaintiff. Second, the plaintiff must demonstrate that the right assertedly protected by the statute is not so vague and amorphous that its enforcement would strain judicial competence. Third, the statute must unambiguously impose a binding obligation on the States.[49]

There is a rebuttable presumption that a statute meeting these requirements creates a right enforceable under Section 1983.[50] This presumption may be rebutted by showing that Congress foreclosed a remedy under Section 1983 either expressly or impliedly through creation of a comprehensive remedial mechanism.[51]

It sometimes is difficult to determine if a particular statute creates a right enforceable under Section 1983.[52] The federal employment discrimination statutes generally do not create a right enforceable under Section 1983 due to the comprehensive remedial schemes enacted by Congress.[53] However, conduct that violates Title VII or

---

47. Gonzaga Univ. v. Doe, 536 U.S. 273, 283 (2002) ("[I]t is rights, not the broader or vaguer 'benefits' or 'interests,' that may be enforced under the authority of [section 1983]").

48. 520 U.S. 329 (1997).

49. *Blessing*, 520 U.S. at 340–41 (1997) (internal quotation marks and citations omitted).

50. *Blessing*, 520 U.S. at 341.

51. *Blessing*, 520 U.S. at 341; Golden State Transit Corp. v. City of Los Angeles, 493 U.S. 103, 106 (1989).

52. *Compare, e.g.*, Suter v. Artist M., 503 U.S. 347 (1992) (holding that federal adoption act requiring states to develop a plan regarding removal of children from their homes did not clearly confer enforceable rights in favor of private individuals), *with* Wilder v. Va. Hosp. Ass'n, 496 U.S. 498 (1990) (holding that federal statute regarding reimbursements for treating Medicare patients created an enforceable right in favor of private health care providers).

53. *See* Great Am. Fed. Sav. & Loan Ass'n v. Novotny, 442 U.S. 366 (1979) (holding that a violation of Title VII may not be alleged as an independent violation of Section 1985(3), which addresses conspiracies to violate a person's federal constitutional or statutory rights, because of the comprehensive administrative scheme provided by the statute); *see also* Kimel v. Fla. Bd. of Regents, 528 U.S. 62 (2000) (holding that the attempted waiver of state sovereign immunity in the ADEA is invalid because it exceeds the power of Congress under the Fourteenth Amendment); EEOC v. Bd. of Regents of Univ. of Wis., 288 F.3d 296 (7th Cir. 2002) (holding that the EEOC may bring an action for legal and

other federal anti-discrimination statutes also may be alleged as a Section 1983 violation if the conduct violates the Constitution or some other statutory right enforceable under Section 1983.[54]

§ 23.05 Remedies

Section 1983 states that a person who deprives another of a federal right under color of state law is "liable at law or in equity." This liability includes actual and nominal damages. If federal law does not provide a sufficient basis upon which to determine the appropriate amount or type of damages, the federal court may look to state common and statutory law to supplant the deficient federal law.[55] In addition, Section 1983 permits injunctive relief.[56]

Punitive damages are available against officials sued in their individual capacity under Section 1983.[57] States and state agencies are never subject to punitive damages unless they waive Eleventh Amendment immunity.[58] Municipalities also are not subject to punitive damages under Section 1983.[59] And an award of punitive damages must be reviewed for excessiveness and must be related to policies designed to punish wrongdoers or to deter misconduct.[60]

Attorney's fees also are available in a Section 1983 case.[61] This generally benefits only plaintiffs. Defendants may recover fees only if the lawsuit is objectively "frivolous, unreasonable, or groundless."[62] To recover fees, the plaintiff must be a prevailing party, which is defined as one who obtains relief that "materially alters the legal relationship between the parties by modifying the defendants' behavior in a way that directly benefits the plaintiff."[63] This is a simple question if the plaintiff prevails completely and receives a judgment against the defendant or obtains a consent decree or settlement.[64] If the plaintiff prevails only in part, an award of attorney's fees still

---

equitable relief under the ADEA despite the invalid waiver of state sovereign immunity because the EEOC represents the United States).

54. *See, e.g.*, Notari v. Denver Water Dep't, 971 F.2d 585, 587–88 (10th Cir. 1992) (holding that a violation of Section 1983 cannot be based solely on the rights created by Section 1983); *see also* Holbrook v. City of Alpharetta, 112 F.3d 1522 (11th Cir. 1997) (same with respect to the ADA).

55. 42 U.S.C. § 1988(a).

56. *See, e.g.*, Mitchum v. Foster, 407 U.S. 225, 242–43 (1972).

57. Smith v. Wade, 461 U.S. 30 (1983).

58. *Will*, 491 U.S. 58, 66 (1989).

59. City of Newport v. Fact Concerts, 453 U.S. 247, 263–64 (1981).

60. State Farm Mut. Auto. Ins. v. Campbell, 538 U.S. 408, 416–18 (2003); BMW v. Gore, 517 U.S. 559, 574 (1996).

61. 42 U.S.C. § 1988(b).

62. Hughes v. Rowe, 449 U.S. 5, 14–15 (1980).

63. Farrar v. Hobby, 506 U.S. 103, 111 (1992).

64. Farrar, 506 U.S. at 111; see also Lefemine v. Wideman, 568 U.S. 1, 4 (2012) (stating that "an injunction or declaratory judgment, like a damages award, will usually satisfy [the prevailing party] test").

may be available, depending upon the degree of success in relation to the judgment sought.[65] Fees are calculated using the lodestar analysis, which considers the number of hours that reasonable counsel would have expended on the case multiplied by a reasonable hourly rate depending upon nature of the case and the experience of counsel.[66]

Finally, given the differing nature of suits in an official versus individual capacity, the parties must evaluate who will be responsible for any judgment. If an official is sued individually, the judgment is executed against the official's personal assets or against the official personally.[67] In contrast, if the official is sued in an official capacity, the judgment is executed against the governmental entity for which the official works.[68]

§ 23.06 Defenses

[A] Immunity

Public officials sued in their individual capacity may be entitled to immunity from liability, depending upon the allegations of the lawsuit, the defendant's official position, and the nature of the claim. If the lawsuit names the defendant in an official capacity, the immunity defenses are not available with respect to that claim.[69] If, in contrast, the lawsuit seeks damages against a public official individually, the defendant may be entitled to absolute or qualified immunity against Section 1983 liability.[70] The defendant carries the burden of proving a claim of immunity, but resolution of the issue is a question of law for the court.[71]

[1] Absolute Immunity

Legislators, judges, and prosecutors enjoy absolute immunity when engaged in legislative, adjudicative, and prosecutorial functions.[72] Legislators possess complete immunity under Section 1983 from both legal and equitable challenges to state laws or other state action.[73] Prosecutors are immune only from liability for civil damages,

65. Farrar, 506 U.S. at 112–16.

66. Venegas v. Mitchell, 495 U.S. 82, 87 (1990); *see* City of Burlington v. Dague, 505 U.S. 557, 559–60 (1992).

67. *Graham*, 473 U.S. at 166 & n.11 (1985).

68. *Graham*, 473 U.S. at 166.

69. *Graham*, 473 U.S. at 167.

70. *Graham*, 473 U.S. at 166–67.

71. Johnson v. Jones, 515 U.S. 304 (1995); Elder v. Holloway, 510 U.S. 510 (1994).

72. Imbler v. Pachtman, 424 U.S. 409 (1976) (prosecutors); Pierson v. Ray, 386 U.S. 547 (1967) (judges); Tenney v. Brandhove, 341 U.S. 367 (1951) (legislators and others acting in a lawmaking capacity); *see also* Rehberg v. Paulk, 566 U.S. 356, 369 (2012) (holding that a grand jury witness, similar to a witness at trial, is afforded absolute immunity).

73. Supreme Court of Va. v. Consumers Union of United States, Inc., 446 U.S. 719 (1980).

not from injunctive or declaratory relief, and only for acts that are not administrative in nature.[74] Judges also may be subject to injunctive relief if "a declaratory decree was violated or declaratory relief is unavailable,"[75] and may be held liable for administrative acts.[76]

Whether a particular act qualifies as being truly judicial or prosecutorial rather than merely administrative depends on the specific nature of the action. Thus, when a judge terminated a probation officer allegedly for sexually discriminatory reasons, the Supreme Court held that the judge was acting in an administrative and not a judicial capacity and was not absolutely immune under Section 1983.[77] In another case, the Supreme Court held that a mayor and a city council member were absolutely immune from liability resulting from an ordinance eliminating the job of an African American who had complained of racial discrimination, concluding that the officials were absolutely immune from liability because the challenged act was legislative in nature.[78] And although a prosecutor had absolute immunity with respect to filing an information and a motion for arrest warrant—because those documents pertain to the prosecutor's role as an advocate—that absolute immunity did not extend to a required certification executed under penalty of perjury.[79]

[2] Qualified Immunity

A public official who may not claim absolute immunity nevertheless may be entitled to qualified immunity. Qualified immunity shields public officials "from liability for civil damages insofar as their conduct does not violate clearly established constitutional or statutory rights of which a reasonable person would have known."[80] The asserted rights cannot be considered "clearly established" unless there existed at the time of the alleged violation some authoritative precedent closely on point with respect to the facts so that a reasonable official would understand that his actions violated that right.[81]

---

74. Burns v. Reed, 500 U.S. 478 (1991); *Consumers Union*, 446 U.S. 719 (1980); see also Van de Kamp v. Goldstein, 555 U.S. 335, 342–45 (2009) (holding that a prosecutor's conduct involving "such supervision or training or information-system management enjoy absolute immunity," if it is "directly connected with the conduct of a trial").

75. 42 U.S.C. § 1983.

76. Forrester v. White, 484 U.S. 219, 228 (1988).

77. *Forrester*, 484 U.S. 219.

78. Bogan v. Scott-Harris, 523 U.S. 44 (1998).

79. Kalina v. Fletcher, 522 U.S. 118 (1997).

80. Harlow v. Fitzgerald, 457 U.S. 800, 818 (1982); see also Ashcroft v. al-Kidd, 563 U.S. 731, 743 (2011) ("Qualified immunity gives government officials breathing room to make reasonable but mistaken judgments about open legal questions").

81. *See* District of Columbia v. Wesby, 138 S. Ct. 577, 589–90 (2018) (quoting Anderson v. Creighton, 483 U.S. 635, 641 (1987) (officers were entitled to qualified immunity because they "reasonably but mistakenly conclude[d] that probable cause [wa]s present")).

Private actors are not entitled to qualified immunity.[82] Their status is inconsistent with the purpose of qualified immunity, which is to enable public officials to exercise some degree of discretion without excessive fear of civil liability.[83]

[3] Interlocutory Appeal

Because the purpose of the Section 1983 immunity is to free a public official from even being required to "answer for his conduct in a civil damages action,"[84] the denial of a motion asserting immunity is subject to immediate interlocutory appeal.[85] Thus, if immunity is raised by a defendant in a Section 1983 action, the case almost certainly will not be tried on the merits unless the immunity issue is resolved against the defendant by an appellate court.[86]

[B] Statute of Limitations

The Supreme Court has stated that the "statute of limitations for a Section 1983 claim is generally the applicable state-law period for personal injury torts."[87] Because this limitation period likely is longer than the applicable period for the federal discrimination statute at issue, plaintiffs generally favor a Section 1983 action when it is available. However, the federal four-year statute of limitations period set forth in 28 U.S.C. § 1658 applies if the Section 1983 action seeks to enforce a federal statute that was enacted after December 1, 1990, and that lacks its own applicable limitations period.[88] Thus, both plaintiffs and defendants must be diligent when evaluating the

---

82. Wyatt v. Cole, 504 U.S. 158, 167–69 (1992) (rejecting claim of qualified immunity by private parties but leaving open the possibility that private parties might assert common law defenses against a Section 1983 claim); *but cf.* Filarsky v. Delia, 566 U.S. 377, 387–91 (2012) (affording qualified immunity to an attorney temporarily retained by a local municipality to assist in conducting an official investigation based on the lack of distinction in the common law "between public servants and private individuals engaged in public service").

83. Wyatt, 504 U.S. at 167–69.

84. Pearson v. Callahan, 555 U.S. 223, 231 (2009) ("[Q]ualified immunity is 'an immunity from suit rather than a mere defense to liability'" (*quoting* Mitchell v. Forsyth, 472 U.S. 511, 526 (1985)).

85. Nixon v. Fitzgerald, 457 U.S. 731 (1982).

86. *See* Plumhoff v. Rickard, 572 U.S. 765, 771–72 (2014) (stating that pretrial orders denying qualified immunity "conclusively determine whether the defendant is entitled to immunity from suit; this immunity issue is both important and completely separate from the merits of the action, and this question could not be effectively reviewed on appeal from final judgment because by that time the immunity from standing trial will have been irretrievably lost").

87. City of Rancho Palos Verdes v. Abrams, 544 U.S. 113, 124 n.5 (2005); Wilson v. Garcia, 471 U.S. 261, 280 (1985) (holding that Section 1983 cases are governed by the forum state's statute of limitations for personal injury suits).

88. *See City of Rancho Palos Verdes*, 544 U.S. at 124 n.5 (stating in a footnote that Section 1658 would seem to apply to a Sectino 1983 claim seeking to enforce provisions of the federal Telecommunications Act of 1996); *cf.* Jones v. R.R. Donnelley & Sons Co., 541 U.S. 369, 383 (2004) (holding that four-year period of Section 1658 applied to lawsuit seeking to enforce provisions of 42 U.S.C. § 1981 enacted by the Civil Rights Act of 1991).

timeliness of Section 1983 claims. The statute of limitations is an affirmative defense that may be waived if it is not pleaded and proved by the party raising the defense.[89]

[C] Sovereign Immunity

When a plaintiff sues a government employee in his or her official capacity, this is the equivalent of suing the governing body itself,[90] which means that the limitations of the Eleventh Amendment apply. Thus, if the suit is for damages rather than prospective injunctive relief, the suit is precluded altogether.[91]

§ 23.07 The Liability of Federal Officials

Because Section 1983 is directed toward violations of federal rights under color of state law, a plaintiff may not state a claim against federal officials under this statute because federal officials act pursuant to federal law. However, in *Bivens v. Six Unknown Federal Narcotics Agents*,[92] the Supreme Court first authorized an analogous but more limited judicial remedy for plaintiffs with a claim against federal officials individually for a violation of the Fourth Amendment.[93] Although lower courts have recognized *Bivens* as a potential remedy for violations of several Constitutional provisions,[94] the Supreme Court has recognized it only as a remedy for claims under the Fourth, Fifth, and the Eighth Amendments.[95]

Thus, a *Bivens* claim is much more limited than a claim arising under Section 1983. Since *Bivens* was decided, the Supreme Court has warned lower courts against readily extending the *Bivens* remedy "into any new context."[96] Thus, a *Bivens* remedy is unavailable if there are "special factors counselling hesitation in the absence of affirmative action by Congress."[97] It also is unavailable if Congress has enacted a remedial

89. *See* Fed. R. Civ. P. 8(c)(1).

90. Hafer v. Melo, 502 U.S. 21, 26 (1991); *Graham*, 473 U.S. 159, 167 (1985).

91. *See* Chapter 3.

92. 403 U.S. 388 (1971).

93. *See, e.g.*, Randall v. United States, 95 F.3d 339, 345 (4th Cir. 1996) (*Bivens* actions are against federal officials in their individual capacity).

94. *See* 2 Federal Civil Rights Acts (3d ed.) § 14:157 (citing cases in which lower courts have recognized *Bivens* as a remedy for violations of the First, Fifth, Eighth, Ninth, and Fourteenth Amendments).

95. Davis v. Passman, 442 U.S. 228 (1979) (Fifth Amendment's Equal Protection Clause); Carlson v. Green, 446 U.S. 14 (1980) (Eighth Amendment). The Court has assumed without holding that *Bivens* extends to First Amendment claims. Wood v. Moss, 572 U.S. 744 (2014).

96. Corr. Servs. Corp. v. Malesko, 534 U.S. 61, 74 (2001) (holding *Bivens* remedy not available against private actors).

97. *Bivens*, 403 U.S. at 396. The Supreme Court has recently stated that the phrase "special factors counselling hesitation ... focuses on whether the Judiciary is well suited, absent congressional action or instruction, to consider and weigh the costs and benefits of allowing a damages action to proceed." Ziglar v. Abbasi, 137 S. Ct. 1843, 1857–58 (2017) (holding that *Bivens* did not extend to allowing aliens unlawfully present in the United States after September 11, 2001, to challenge their detention, though it remanded for further proceedings the question of whether they could challenge their conditions of confinement).

scheme regarding the alleged right at issue.[98] Based on the Supreme Court's recent precedent in this area, it is unlikely that the *Bivens* remedy will be expanded much beyond its already-developed core.[99]

Because it applies only to violations by federal officials and does not apply to private entities, the *Bivens* remedy will be available only to federal employees for certain deprivations of rights by federal officials, such as violations of the Fifth Amendment's Equal Protection Clause.[100] Given the availability of other remedial schemes regarding employment and the Supreme Court's restriction on expanding the *Bivens* remedy, federal employees will in most situations need to look elsewhere to vindicate their rights.

§ 23.08 Chapter Highlights

1. A person for purposes of Section 1983 does not include a state or state officials acting in their official capacity if monetary relief is sought. State officials are persons if the remedy sought is injunctive in nature or if the officials are sued in their individual capacity. Local governments are persons under Section 1983 but are only liable based on the execution or official custom or policy. (§ 23.02)

2. Public officials act under color of state law for purposes of Section 1983 if they have actual or apparent authority to act on behalf of the state. A private person rarely is acting under color of state law even if acting in conjunction with a state or local government. (§ 23.03)

3. Section 1983 remedies the deprivation of rights protected by the United State Constitution or by federal law. This includes both constitutional rights and rights conferred by statute, provided that the statute was intended to benefit the plaintiff. (§ 23.04)

4. Plaintiffs may recover actual and nominal damages under Section 1983, as well as punitive damages in certain situations. Plaintiffs also may obtain injunctive relief if appropriate. A prevailing party may recover attorney's fees in whole or in part under Section 1988. (§ 23.05)

5. A government official sued under Section 1983 in his or her individual capacity may be entitled to absolute or qualified immunity from liability. A statute of limitations

98. *Bivens*, 403 U.S. at 396.

99. *See generally Ziglar*, 137 S. Ct. at 1857–58 (noting Court's instructions to limit expansion of *Bivens* remedy in context of holding that detention policy claims could not proceed under *Bivens* and also rejecting the Court of Appeals' "modest extension" of *Bivens* regarding the a Fifth Amendment claim before the lower court first performed a "special factors" analysis). There are other differences between a Section 1983 action and a *Bivens* action due to the latter's nature as a judicially created remedy. For example, attorney's fees likely may not be recovered in actions against federal officials in their individual capacities because there is no statute authorizing the award of fees in that context. *See* Kreines v. United States, 33 F.3d 1105, 1107–09 (9th Cir. 1994).

100. *Davis*, 442 U.S. at 249 (holding that female employee of Congressman alleging that she was terminated on account of her sex could bring *Bivens* claim for damages on the basis that her Fifth Amendment equal protection rights were violated).

defense also may be available, although the limitations period typically is longer under Section 1983 than under the applicable anti-discrimination statute. Public officials also may have a defense of sovereign immunity if sued in their official capacity. (§ 23.06)

6. Federal officials may be subject to personal liability for violating a person's constitutional rights under *Bivens v. Six Unknown Federal Narcotics Agents.* However, because it is judicially crafted, the *Bivens* remedy is much more circumscribed than Section 1983 and, in most instances, a federal employee will need to look elsewhere for a remedial scheme. (§ 23.07)

Chapter 24

Section 1985(3)

Synopsis

§ 24.01 Nature of the Offense

The Supreme Court has indicated that a typical Section 1985(3) claim consists of proof of four elements:

> (1) a conspiracy; (2) for the purpose of depriving, either directly or indirectly, any person or class of persons of the equal protection of the law, or of equal privileges and immunities under the laws; and (3) an act in furtherance of the conspiracy; (4) whereby a person is either injured in his person or property or deprived of any right or privilege of a citizen of the United States.[1]

Section 1986 further provides that any person, with knowledge of a Section 1985(3) conspiracy and the ability to prevent it, who fails to do so can be held liable for all resulting damages. The interpretive labyrinth that the courts have created for this statute render it a weak tool for challenging employment discrimination. Indeed, what it does cover is more easily dealt with under Section 1981, Section 1983, Title VII, and specific state laws.

1. Carpenters Local 610 v. Scott, 463 U.S. 825, 828–29 (1983).

§ 24.02 Party Defendants

In *Griffin v. Breckenridge*,[2] the Supreme Court held that Section 1985(3) reaches private conspiracies. Although this seems contrary to the literal wording of the statute, this interpretation makes sense because otherwise Section 1985(3) would be duplicative of Section 1983. State action, however, has not been read out of Section 1985(3) altogether, as will be discussed below.

Section 1985(3) does not apply to federal employers. Whatever Eleventh Amendment immunity that states enjoy with respect to Section 1983 also applies in Section 1985(3) actions.

§ 24.03 The Conspiracy Requirement

The requirement that two or more persons conspire to deprive an individual of his or her rights creates a considerable obstacle in most employment discrimination contexts, since a corporate employer and its officers, employees, and agents are considered a single entity that is incapable of conspiring with itself.[3] On the other hand, a conspiracy may be said to exist if the alleged conspirators were acting outside the scope of their employment[4] or if the activity did not otherwise further the company's business interests.[5] A corporate employer may also be found guilty of conspiring with a former employee, a labor union, or another employer.

§ 24.04 The Protected Class

Standing to sue under Section 1985(3) requires proof that the plaintiffs are members of a class that "require[s] and warrant[s] special federal assistance in protecting their civil rights."[6] In the words of the Supreme Court, this "means that there must be some racial, or perhaps otherwise class-based, invidiously discriminatory animus behind the conspirators' action."[7] Racial minorities were, of course, primarily what Congress had in mind. But the protected class has also been construed as covering non-minorities discriminated against on a racial basis,[8] persons of a particular national origin,[9] women,[10] and members of religious groups.[11] The courts are split over whether political

---

2. 403 U.S. 88 (1971).
3. Dombrowski v. Dowling, 459 F.2d 190 (7th Cir. 1972).
4. Garza v. City of Omaha, 814 F.2d 553 (8th Cir. 1987); Alder v. Columbia Historical Soc'y, 690 F. Supp. 9 (D.D.C. 1988).
5. Volk v. Coler, 845 F.2d 1422 (7th Cir. 1988).
6. Maynard v. City of San Jose, 37 F.3d 1396, 1403 (9th Cir. 1994) (quoting Sever v. Alaska Pulp Corp., 978 F.2d 1529, 1536–37 (9th Cir. 1992)).
7. Griffin, 403 U.S. at 102.
8. Triad Assocs., Inc. v. Chicago Hous. Auth., 892 F.2d 583 (7th Cir. 1989).
9. Garza, 814 F.2d 553.
10. N.Y. State Nat'l Org. for Women v. Terry, 886 F.2d 1339 (2d Cir. 1989).
11. Diem v. City & County of San Francisco, 686 F. Supp. 806 (N.D. Cal. 1988).

affiliation constitutes a protected class.[12] On the other hand, nonunion members,[13] gays,[14] abortion opponents,[15] and disabled persons[16] do not qualify as a protected class.

§ 24.05 The Nature of the Protected Rights

The rights that Section 1985(3) protects derive principally from the Fourteenth Amendment but also include the Thirteenth Amendment rights to be free from the badges of slavery and the implied right of interstate travel. Although denial of a person's Section 1981 rights can form the basis of a Section 1985(3) conspiracy, the Supreme Court has held that a Section 1985(3) claim cannot be predicated on facts that have been or could be brought as a Title VII violation.[17]

§ 24.06 The State Action Requirement

Although Section 1985(3) does reach conspiracies among or involving private parties, the prohibited object of the conspiracy must be to deprive another person of his or her constitutional rights—which, except for Thirteenth Amendment and travel rights, can be violated only by state action. Thus, in *Carpenters Local 610 v. Scott*,[18] the Supreme Court held "that an alleged conspiracy to infringe First Amendment rights is not a violation of Section 1985(3) unless it is proved that the state is involved in the conspiracy or that the aim of the conspiracy is to influence the activity of the State."[19]

---

12. *Compare* McLean v. Int'l Harvester Co., 817 F.2d 1214 (5th Cir. 1987), *with* Rodriguez v. Nazario, 719 F. Supp. 52 (D.P.R. 1989).

13. *Carpenters Local 610*, 463 U.S. 825.

14. DeSantis v. Pacific Tel. & Tel. Co., 608 F.2d 327 (9th Cir. 1979).

15. Bray v. Alexandria Women's Health Clinic, 506 U.S. 263 (1993).

16. Compare People of New York v. 11 Cornwell Co., 695 F.2d 34 (2d Cir. 1982), *with* D'Amato v. Wis. Gas Co., 760 F.2d 1474 (7th Cir. 1985), *and* Wilhelm v. Cont'l Title Co., 720 F.2d 1173 (10th Cir. 1983).

17. Great American Sav. & Loan Ass'n v. Novotny, 442 U.S. 366 (1979); *see also* Alexander v. Chicago Park Dist., 773 F.2d 850 (7th Cir. 1985); Richards v. New York State Dep't of Corr. Servs., 572 F. Supp. 1168 (S.D.N.Y. 1983).

18. 463 U.S. 825 (1983); *see also* Great American Federal Sav., 442 U.S. at 380, 383–85 (1979) (Stevens, J., concurring).

19. *Carpenters* Local 610, 463 U.S. at 830.

§ 24.07 Chapter Highlights

1. Section 1985(3) requires proof of a conspiracy to deprive another person of equal treatment under the law, plus an act pursuant to that conspiracy that injures this other person. (§ 24.01)

2. In the employment context, the alleged conspiracy is usually between the corporate employer and either another employer, a labor union, or a former employee. Supervisors acting outside the scope of their employment may also form an actionable conspiracy. (§ 24.03)

3. Section 1985(3) protection extends only to persons who are members of a class who require special federal assistance in protecting their civil rights. This pertains primarily to racial minorities, but other historically discriminated against classes have also been afforded Section 1985(3) protection. (§ 24.04)

5. The rights protected by Section 1985(3) derive principally from the Equal Protection Clause of the Fourteenth Amendment. While Section 1985(3) may be used to vindicate Section 1981 rights, it does not cover the employment rights that are created by Title VII or the other federal discrimination statutes. (§ 24.05)

6. Although Section 1985(3) extends to private employers, either the state must be involved or the purpose of the conspiracy must at least be to affect state action. (§ 24.06)

Part VI

Equal Pay Act

Chapter 25

Equal Pay Act—Introduction

Synopsis

§25.01 History

The Equal Pay Act, which was enacted in 1963, is the first of the modern federal anti-discrimination statutes. It is limited to *sex* discrimination in the payment of *wages*. The factual paradigm that it was designed primarily to address involved sex-segregated job categories, differing only in job title and, more importantly, *wages*. Because employment opportunities for women were limited, however, an employer could offer lower wages in the female-only job category and still obtain a sufficient number of willing workers. This, in turn, tended to provide a competitive ceiling on the wages in the male-only job category. The EPA solution was not to integrate the workforce, but simply to equalize the wages. The early cases dealt primarily with that factual situation, with the central issue being whether the work in the segregated categories was truly *equal* in the statutory sense.

Sex-segregated job categories and discriminatory wages, of course, became illegal under Title VII of the Civil Rights Act of 1964. But rather than repealing the EPA, Congress simply added another layer of statutory protection. However, with the gradual disappearance of the EPA factual paradigm, the EPA itself has become something of an anomaly. Its application in a sex-integrated work unit can lead to bizarre results—suggesting, perhaps, that the defendant employer's wage policies are irrational, but not that they are necessarily dictated by sex.

§ 25.02 Covered Employers

As part of the Fair Labor Standards Act, the EPA applies generally to the same employers who are subject to the FLSA's minimum wage, maximum hours, and child-labor provisions. Under the FLSA, coverage can be established on two bases. First, an employer is covered if the particular employee alleging an EPA violation is "engaged in commerce" or engaged "in the production of goods for commerce." Second, an employer is covered with respect to all its employees if it is engaged in interstate commerce, has two or more employees so engaged, and except for certain industries grosses at least $325,000. Essentially the same *employees* that are covered by the FLSA are, thus, also covered by the EPA. In one respect, however, the employee coverage of the EPA is broader. For minimum wage and maximum hours purposes, the FLSA recognizes an exception for bona fide executive, administrative, and executive employees. These employees are, however, covered by the EPA.

The EPA was amended in 1974 to apply to federal, state, and local government employees; and the courts have consistently held that the EPA waives the state's sovereign immunity under the Eleventh Amendment.[1]

The EPA also prohibits labor unions from causing or attempting to cause an employer to violate the Act.

§ 25.03 An Overview

[A] The Elements of a Violation

To establish a violation of the EPA, a plaintiff must prove that the employer is:

- paying different *wages*;
- to employees of *opposite sexes*;
- who work within the same *establishment*;
- and who are performing *equal* work on jobs that require *equal*
    - *skill*,
    - *effort*,
    - and *responsibility*,
    - and which are performed under *similar working conditions*.

The meaning of these statutory terms will be discussed in Chapter 26.

1. Siler-Khodr v. Univ. of Texas Science Ctr., 261 F.3d 542 (5th Cir. 2002); Hundertmark v. Florida Dep't of Transp., 205 F.3d 1272 (11th Cir. 2000).

[B] Defenses

If the plaintiff carries that burden of proof, which establishes a violation regardless of whether the employer subjectively intended to discriminate or not,[2] then the employer may still defend by showing that the wage differential is caused by:

- a seniority system;
- a merit system;
- a system that measures earnings by quantity or quality of production' or
- a differential based on any other factor other than sex.

These defenses will be discussed in more detail in Chapter 27.

§ 25.04 Relationship with Title VII

Recognizing that the EPA and Title VII overlapped in some respects but potentially conflicted in others, Congress attempted to resolve the matter with the so-called *Bennett Amendment* to Title VII, which provides as follows:

> It shall not be an unlawful employment practice under this subchapter [Title VII] for any employer to differentiate upon the basis of sex in determining the amount of the wages or compensation paid or to be paid to employees of such employer if such differentiation is authorized by the provisions of [the Equal Pay Act].

The Supreme Court determined the meaning of the Bennett Amendment in *County of Washington v. Gunther*.[3] The case involved a pay differential between male and female guards in the county jail, brought under Title VII. Plaintiffs argued (1) that because the facts showed an EPA violation, this was also a Title VII violation, and even if not an EPA violation, (2) that the pay differential was a result of intentional discrimination. The District Court, however, held that the respective jobs were not substantially equal and that, under the Bennett Amendment, even a claim of intentional wage discrimination claim could not be brought under Title VII unless it would satisfy the equal work standard of the EPA. The Court of Appeals affirmed the District Court's finding that the work was not substantially equal but reversed on the Bennett Amendment interpretation.

In the Supreme Court, the employer defended the District Court's interpretation of the Bennett Amendment, arguing that a wage differential could not violate Title VII unless it also violated the EPA. The plaintiff, on the other hand, argued that the Bennett Amendment merely incorporated the four EPA affirmative defenses into Title

---

2. In contrast, the identical Title VII disparate treatment wage discrimination claim would require some form of intent.

3. 452 U.S. 161 (1981).

VII in wage-sex discrimination cases. The employer countered by claiming that this made the Bennett Amendment superfluous, since Title VII already contained the seniority, merit, and quantity/quality of work defenses, and with the *factor other than sex* defense simply being implicit in the requirement that the wage differential in question be *because of* sex, rather than something else.

The Supreme Court disagreed. It read the *factor other than sex* defense as being something more than merely the logical converse of the Title VII requirement that the discrimination be based on sex, rather than something else. The Court said:

> Title VII's prohibition of discriminatory employment practices was intended to be broadly inclusive, proscribing "not only overt discrimination but also practices that are fair in form, but discriminatory in operation."... The fourth affirmative defense of the Equal Pay Act, however, was designed differently, to confine the application of the Act to wage differential attributable to sex discrimination.[4]

In other words, a Title VII sex/wage discrimination claim cannot be established under the disparate impact model of proof. The Court thus concluded that "incorporation of the fourth affirmative defense could have significant consequences for Title VII litigation,"[5] and, so construed, the Bennett Amendment was "not rendered superfluous."[6] The Court declined to speculate on how the *factor other than sex* defense might affect the structure of either Title VII or, by necessary implication, EPA litigation.

§ 25.05 Chapter Highlights

1. The EPA was designed to equalize wages of employees working in sex-segregated job categories but who were performing substantially the same work. Since, because of Title VII, that situation no longer exists to any degree, the EPA has become something of an anomaly. (§ 25.01)

2. The EPA, which is part of the Fair Labor Standards Act, covers all employees who are engaged in interstate commerce, are engaged in the production of goods for interstate commerce, or who work for an employer with two or more employees so engaged. In sum, virtually all employees are covered by the EPA. (§ 25.02)

3. A plaintiff establishes a violation by showing that the employer pays different wages to employees of opposite sexes who work in the same establishment and who are performing equal work with respect to skill, effort, responsibility, and working conditions. If those facts exist, then the employer may defend the wage differential by showing that it is the result of a seniority system, a merit system, a system that measures earning by quantity or quality of production, or any other factor other than sex. (§ 25.03)

4. *Gunther*, 452 U.S. at 170 (quoting Griggs v. Duke Power Co., 401 U.S. 424, 431 (1971)).
5. *Gunther*, 452 U.S. at 170.
6. *Gunther*, 452 U.S. at 171.

4. Under the Bennett Amendment, the four EPA defenses are incorporated into Title VII. As a practical matter, all this really means is that in a Title VII wage discrimination case the plaintiff must prove intent and cannot establish a violation under the disparate impact theory. (§ 25.04)

Chapter 26

The Elements of a Violation

Synopsis

Unlike the Title VII prima facie case, which consists of a set of facts from which an inference of intentional discrimination may be drawn, the EPA merely posits a set of facts that establish a violation, whether the employer subjectively *intended* to discriminate or not. These elements are as follows.

§ 26.01 Different Wages

The plaintiff's *wages* must be unequal in relation to someone else's wages. Under the EPA the relevant figure relates to the bottom-line, total compensation package. At a minimum, this includes everything that would be considered "wages" for FLSA minimum wage purposes. The EEOC, however, construes EPA wages more broadly, covering all forms of remuneration for employment, including wages, salary, commissions, profit sharing, expense accounts, monthly minimum payments to sales personnel, bonuses, uniform allowances, hotel accommodations, use of company car, gasoline allowances, and all other fringe benefits.[1]

The courts, however, have generally rejected an expansive *proportionate inequality of wages* theory of recovery under the EPA. For example, in *Berry v. Board of Supervisors of L.S.U.*,[2] a female professor did the work of two male professors, but at the

1. 29 C.F.R. § 1620.10.
2. 715 F.2d 971 (5th Cir. 1983).

same salary. Although her wages were, in proportion to the work performed, lower than those of the male professors, the majority held that mere workload discrimination, while arguably a Title VII violation, did not fall within the prohibitions of the EPA.

§ 26.02 Employees of the Opposite Sex

Although Title VII admits to the possibility of a plaintiff proving discrimination *because of* sex directly and without the use of an opposite sex comparator[3]—as in an all-female workforce where the employer admits that it pays women less than it would pay men for equivalent work—this is not true of the EPA. Here, a mythical or hypothetical person of the opposite sex will not suffice.[4] Ideally, this comparator is a current employee. However, the comparator may also be the person who previously occupied the position[5] or, according to some courts, the plaintiff's successor in the job.[6] And in one case the comparator was an individual who was no longer employed at the time of the lawsuit but who had allegedly performed equal work for higher wages. Although the employer argued that this individual's departure ended the violation, due to the absence of a relevant comparator, the court held that the violation would continue until the plaintiff received the same pay the comparator had received prior to his departure.[7]

There is some authority for the proposition that the comparator must be a composite of persons of the opposite sex. Representative Goodell, for example, explained that the use of the plural *employees* was intentional, reflecting the congressional view "that there should be established a pattern of discrimination, that there should be something here that is more than an isolated single case, before a violation is held"[8]—a view that would presumably prevent a plaintiff from focusing on a single comparator. In *Houck v. Virginia Polytechnic Inst.*,[9] the court stated that "isolated incidents or random comparisons demonstrating disparities in treatment may be insufficient to draw a prima facie inference of discrimination without additional evidence that the alleged phenomenon of inequality also exists with respect to the entire relevant group of employees." Similarly, in *Hein v. Oregon College of Education*,[10] the court stated that

---

3. In scientific circles, a *comparator* refers to an instrument used for making comparisons, as between distances or colors. The law adopted the term but changed its meaning to refer to the person with whom the plaintiff is being compared rather than the thing that is making the comparison—which, presumably, would be the judge.

4. Gallagher v. Kleinwort Benson Gov't Sec., Inc., 698 F. Supp. 1401 (N.D. Ill. 1988).

5. Clymore v. Far-Mar-Co., 709 F.2d 499 (8th Cir. 1983).

6. *Compare* Brinkley-Obu v. Hughes Training, Inc., 36 F.3d 336 (4th Cir. 1994) (allowing comparison to predecessors, co-workers, and successors), *with* Bielawski v. AMI, Inc., 870 F. Supp. 771 (N.D. Ohio 1994) (rejecting a successor comparator whose higher salary was due to inflation and also because the present-tense language of the EPA precluded after-the-fact comparisons).

7. Jehle v. Heckler, 603 F. Supp. 124 (D.D.C. 1985).

8. 109 Cong. Rec. 9208 (1963).

9. 10 F.3d 204, 206–07 (4th Cir. 1993).

10. 718 F.2d 910 (9th Cir. 1983).

"the proper test for establishing a prima facie case in a professional setting such as that of a college is whether the plaintiff is receiving lower wages than the *average of wages* paid to all employees of the opposite sex...."[11]

Nevertheless, the prevailing view is that an EPA plaintiff needs only to establish that a single person of the opposite sex doing equal work is receiving more pay.[12] This, however, gives rise to what is known as *the EPA paradox*. Assume a work unit of four employees, two male and two female, performing identical work but paid as follows:

Anna, $8.00 per hour.

Andrew, $8.00 per hour.

Betty, $7.00 per hour.

Bill, $7.00 per hour.

Theoretically, Betty can establish unequal wages and an EPA violation by reference to Andrew, and Bill can establish unequal wages and an EPA by reference to Anna. While this may demonstrate that the employer's wage scheme is arbitrary and irrational (and assuming that the employer cannot justify the disparities on the basis of a factor other than sex), it hardly proves any form of sex-related discrimination and is a far cry from the class-wide, segregated-unit discrimination that the EPA was designed to remedy.

Nevertheless, establishing the identity of a specific opposite-sex comparator is important for the plaintiff because it is on this basis that the *equality* of work is established.

§ 26.03 Within the Same Establishment

The plaintiff and the comparator must work within the same "establishment," which generally refers to a physically distinct place of business.[13] If an employer has multiple facilities, each plant, store, or office will ordinarily be treated as a separate establishment. On the other hand, plaintiffs have sometimes been successful in establishing multiple facilities as a single establishment where the employer uses a centralized personnel system and employees frequently move among the units or where there is otherwise a "significant functional interrelationship between the work of the employees in the various locations."[14] Although employers have sometimes argued

---

11. Hein, 718 F.2d at 916 (emphasis added); *see also* Heymann v. Tetra Plastics Corp., 640 F.2d 115 (8th Cir. 1981) (same result, but allowing the plaintiff to use a single comparator to raise an inference that the differential was *on the basis of sex* and then shifting the burden on to the employer to show with statistical data that the plaintiff was not paid less than the class of all male employees performing similar work).

12. Goodrich v. Electrical Workers, 815 F.2d 1519 (D.C. Cir. 1987).

13. Gerlach v. Michigan Bell Tel. Co., 448 F. Supp. 1168 (E.D. Mich. 1978).

14. State, County, & Municipal Emps. v. County of Nassau, 609 F. Supp. 695, 706 (E.D.N.Y. 1985) (leaving open the possibility that all county offices might be a single establishment); EEOC v.

that each department within a single facility should be recognized as the relevant establishment, the courts have generally not accepted the idea in the commercial context,[15] although one court held that comparisons among college faculty members should be confined to the same or at least closely comparable academic departments.[16]

§ 26.04 Equal Work

The equality of the work that the plaintiff and the comparator perform is determined by comparing the skill, effort, responsibility, and working conditions involved in the two jobs. The test, however, is one of *substantial* equality.[17] As one court explained, the standard is higher than mere comparability and lower than absolute identity.[18]

Moreover, it is the actual content of the job, not the job title or description that is determinative. Thus, mere similarity in job titles or descriptions is not sufficient to establish equality,[19] nor are dissimilarities sufficient to disprove it.[20]

Finally, when comparing the content of the two jobs, the courts customarily focus on the "core" functions of the two jobs.[21] An oft-litigated issue is whether the existence of additional duties in one of the two jobs is sufficient to destroy their equality. Typically, the courts consider the amount of time the additional duties require, whether everyone in the higher paid job performs those duties, and whether performance of these has an economic value that is commensurate with the pay differential.[22]

In addition, some courts have held that "[h]igher pay is not related to extra duties when ... [q]ualified females are not given the opportunity to do the extra work."[23] That observation, however, flies in the face of the factual paradigm that the EPA was designed to attack—segregated job categories—and is better resolved under Title VII analysis.

Although the conjunctive *and* between the four criteria of comparison requires a plaintiff to prove that the jobs are substantially equal in all four respects, the courts tend to focus on overall job content, rather than the criteria individually, which makes the equal work component of an EPA case enormously fact driven and context specific. Nevertheless, the four criteria have been construed generally as follows.

Altmeyer's Home Stores, Inc., 672 F. Supp. 201 (W.D. Pa. 1987) (separate stores of a retail chain treated as a single establishment).

15. Hodgson v. City Stores, Inc., 332 F. Supp. 942 (M.D. Ala. 1971).

16. Monroe-Lord v. Hytche, 668 F. Supp. 979, 995 (D. Md. 1987), *aff'd* 854 F.2d 1317 (4th Cir. 1988).

17. Shultz v. Wheaton Glass Co., 421 F.2d 259, 265 (3d Cir. 1970).

18. Brennan v. City Stores, Inc., 479 F.2d 235, 238 (5th Cir. 1973).

19. Epstein v. Secretary of Treasury, 739 F.2d 274 (7th Cir. 1984).

20. Katz v. School Dist., 557 F.2d 153 (8th Cir. 1977).

21. Fallon v. Illinois, 882 F.2d 1206 (7th Cir. 1989).

22. Hodgson v. Brookhaven General Hosp., 436 F.2d 719, 725 (5th Cir. 1970); Shultz v. Wheaton Glass Co., 421 F.2d 259 (3d Cir. 1970).

23. Brennan v. Prince William Hosp. Corp., 503 F.2d 282, 286 (4th Cir. 1974).

[A] Skill

The focus here is on whether the two jobs *require* the same skills, not whether the plaintiff and the comparator *possess* the same skills.[24] It is thus irrelevant that the comparator possesses greater skills, if those skills are not actually used on the job. The *skills* component refers generally to the experience, training, education, and ability that are necessary to perform the job.[25]

[B] Effort

The *effort* component refers to the physical or mental exertion needed for the performance of the job.[26] However, the extra effort required in the comparator's job must be substantial in order for this to establish the dis-equality of the work.[27] Moreover, the greater effort the comparator expends in performing one task may be offset by the greater effort the plaintiff expends performing another task[28]—even if one involves physical effort and the other mental effort.[29]

[C] Responsibility

The *responsibility* aspect of a job refers generally to the accountability the employee is subject to[30] or, more specifically, the significance of the employee's failure to discharge a particular job function. For example, one court found that the responsibilities of two classes of bank tellers was not the same because errors committed by one class were easily corrected within the bank while the errors of the other class were more complicated and difficult to detect.[31]

[D] Similar Working Conditions

On its face, this is the most nebulous of the four criteria. The Supreme Court, however, provided the benchmarks of further definition in *Corning Glass Works v. Brennan*.[32] There the Court stated that

> the element of working conditions encompasses two subfactors: "surroundings" and "hazards." "Surroundings" measures the elements, such as toxic chemicals or fumes, regularly encountered by a worker, their intensity, and

---

24. *Hein*, 718 F.2d 910 (9th Cir. 1983).
25. 29 C.F.R. § 1620.15.
26. 29 C.F.R. § 1620.16(a).
27. Shultz v. American Can Co.-Dixie Prods., 424 F.2d 356 (8th Cir. 1970).
28. Brennan v. Bd. of Educ., 374 F. Supp. 817 (D.N.J. 1974).
29. Hodgson v. Daisy Mfg. Co., 317 F. Supp. 538 (W.D. Ark. 1970), aff'd *in part,* rev'd in part, 445 F.2d 823 (8th Cir. 1971).
30. 29 C.F.R. § 1620.17(a).
31. Brennan v. Victoria Bank & Trust Co., 493 F.2d 896, 899 (5th Cir. 1974).
32. 417 U.S. 188 (1974).

> their frequency. "Hazards" takes into account the physical hazards regularly encountered, their frequency, and the severity of injury they can cause.[33]

The Court thus held that merely working on different shifts did not involve dissimilar working conditions, although shift differentials could probably qualify as a *factor other than sex.*

§ 26.05 Chapter Highlights

1. For EPA purposes, almost every form of remuneration is taken into account. As long as the bottom-line amount is the same, it is irrelevant that one employee performs more work than another of the opposite sex. (§ 26.01)

2. When the EPA was applied in the context of sex-segregated job categories, all females were often paid at one rate and males paid at a higher rate. In this context, the comparison was, in statutory terms, between the lower paid "employees [as a group] ... and employees of the opposite sex [as a group]." Even today, some courts tend to require proof of that sort. More commonly, however, the courts allow a plaintiff to use a single comparator of the opposite sex. (§ 26.02)

3. The plaintiff and the comparator, however, must work in the same "establishment," which is defined in terms of a physically distinct place of business. (§ 26.03)

4. In determining whether the work the plaintiff and the comparator perform is substantially equal, the courts focus on four elements. *Skill* refers to the experience, training, education, and ability that are necessary to perform the job. *Effort* refers to physical or mental exertion. *Responsibility* refers to the amount of accountability that a job entails. And *working conditions* refers to the physical surroundings and hazards of the job. (§ 26.04)

33. Corning Glass, 417 U.S. at 202.

Chapter 27

Defenses

Synopsis

Although it is not expressed on the face of the statute, the Supreme Court has held that once a plaintiff has proved that "the employer pays workers of one sex more than workers of the opposite sex for equal work, the burden shifts to the employer to show that the differential is justified under one of the Equal Pay Act's four exceptions"[1]— a seniority system, a merit system, a system that measures earnings by quantity or quality of production, or a differential based on any other factor other than sex. Since these are affirmative defenses, they will be waived unless pled in the answer or otherwise raised in an appropriate fashion prior to trial.[2]

Three of the four defenses require the existence of a *system*. This means that the criteria in question cannot be applied in an episodic, ad hoc fashion. Rather, to qualify as a system an employer must have in place "an organized and structured procedure whereby employees are evaluated systematically according to predetermined criteria."[3] Although a formal, written policy may not be absolutely required, the prudent employer would have one and would insure that employees are informed of it.

Most of the litigation has arisen under the *factor other than sex* defense.

---

1. Corning Glass Works v. Brennan, 417 U.S. 188, 196 (1974).
2. EEOC v. White & Son Enters, 881 F.2d 1006 (11th Cir. 1989).
3. Maxwell v. City of Tucson, 803 F.2d 444, 447 (9th Cir. 1986) (quoting EEOC v. Aetna Ins. Co., 616 F.2d 719, 725 (4th Cir. 1980)).

§ 27.01 Seniority

Women breaking into new occupations and job classifications as a result of the broader Title VII prohibition against sex discrimination still face a disadvantage if the pay system is based in whole or in part on longevity of employment. But just as a seniority system is not rendered other than bona fide under Title VII merely because it has a disproportionate impact on racial minorities,[4] a seniority-predicated pay system that pays a woman less than a man for doing the same work is still subject to the EPA seniority system defense. Indeed, the courts generally apply the same analysis to seniority systems under the EPA as they do under Title VII.[5] A seniority system, thus, will generally fail as a defense only if it is facially discriminatory or is being applied in a discriminatory fashion. In one case, for example, after creating a new, sex-integrated *cabin attendant* job category, the employer refused to include as a part of the new seniority in this job a female's prior service as a *stewardess,* while crediting a male employee's prior time as a *flight service attendant.*[6]

§ 27.02 Merit Systems

Under a merit system, pay is determined by performance. Ideally, this will consist of a "systematic, formal system guided by objective, written standards."[7] Evaluation systems that rely heavily on the subjective impressions of supervisors have not faired well in the courts.[8] And, indeed, because of the inherent difficulty of ever fully quantifying *performance* or *merit,* one court has suggested that the merit exception should be "strictly construed" against the employer.[9]

§ 27.03 Quantity or Quality of Production

Although two jobs may be equal in the sense that each job requires the same minimal degree of *effort* and *skill,* the actual effort and skill expended by two employees may be radically different, thus affecting either the quantity or quality of goods produced. When each employee's pay is determined on this basis, the resulting differential between employees of the opposite sex is not a violation of the EPA, as long as the unit or piece rate for the two jobs is the same.[10]

---

4. International Bhd. of Teamsters v. United States, 431 U.S. 324 (1977).
5. Mitchell v. Jefferson County Bd. of Educ., 936 F.2d 539 (11th Cir. 1991).
6. Laffey v. Northwest Airlines, Inc., 366 F. Supp. 763 (D.D.C. 1973), *vacated in part on other grounds*, 567 F.2d 429 (D.C. Cir. 1974).
7. Brennan v. Victoria Bank & Trust Co., 493 F.2d 896, 901 (5th Cir. 1974).
8. Marshall v. Security Bank & Trust Co., 572 F.2d 276 (10th Cir. 1978).
9. Hodgson v. Brookhaven Gen. Hosp., 436 F.2d 719, 725 (5th Cir. 1970).
10. Bence v. Detroit Health Corp., 712 F.2d 1024 (6th Cir. 1983).

§ 27.04 A Factor Other than Sex

At first blush, this defense appears to be nothing more than the logical converse of the existence of a violation itself. This would be a harmless redundancy but for the fact that the plaintiff must prove the violation while the employer must prove the defense—thus creating a logical and legal contradiction. The answer lies in the language of the statute itself. It prohibits discrimination "on the basis of sex," but then provides specific benchmarks for how that "basis" is to be established. In a very loose sense, thus, the plaintiff's evidence might be called—and often is—*prima facie* or merely inferential proof of the requisite sex-based causation of the pay discrepancy. This then leaves it open for the employer to prove that a non-sex factor was the actual causal element.[11]

In determining what qualifies as a factor other than sex, most courts are willing to accept almost anything, as long as it is something other than the claimant's sex and is truly the motivating element.[12] Early on, however, the Secretary of Labor opined that "any other factor does not mean any other factor. Instead ... it means any other factor than sex which 'is related to job performance or is typically used in setting wage scales.'" The court quoted this language in *Hodgson v. Robert Hall Clothes, Inc.*,[13] but specifically rejected it as being inconsistent with both the language and legislative history of the EPA. Although a variety of factors have been considered in individual cases, several specific factors have received the most attention and litigation.

[A] Training Programs

Individuals being trained for management positions are often required to work for short periods of time in one or more of the jobs over which they will eventually have managerial authority. They are also frequently paid more than the regular employees in these jobs. To qualify as a factor other than sex, more is required than the employer's subjective, good faith intent to differentiate on that basis. Like the various *system* defenses, a training program must meet certain objective requirements. Broadly speaking, the courts have identified them as follows:[14]

- The job rotation must be regular or based on training rather than personnel needs.

---

11. This model of causation-proof thus differs from both the *McDonnell Douglas* and the Title VII mixed motive models discussed earlier in connection with Title VII. It is like *McDonnell Douglas* in the sense that the plaintiff's proof is subject to rebuttal; but it is different in the sense that it is a true burden of persuasion, not merely a burden of production. It is like the Title VII mixed motive model in the sense that it involves a true burden of persuasion; but it is different in the sense that it refutes the plaintiff's evidence of causation, thus avoiding all liability, rather than merely limiting the available remedies.

12. Deli v. University of Minnesota, 863 F. Supp. 958 (D. Minn. 1994) (sex of the student-athletes being coached).

13. 473 F.2d 589, 593 (3d Cir. 1973) (emphasis added).

14. Hodgson v. Behrens Drug Co., 475 F.2d 1041 (5th Cir. 1973); Schultz v. First Victoria Nat'l Bank, 420 F.2d 648 (5th Cir. 1969).

- The program must be formal, definite, and clearly understood to be a training program.
- More must be involved than the mere acquisition of skills and experience.
- In addition to actually performing the various jobs, individuals should participate in other training activities, such as classroom instruction not available to other employees.
- Ultimate promotion into a management position should have a fixed date and not be subject to the availability of that position.
- The program must be open to persons of both sexes, which introduces a Title VII-like, nondiscrimination in other than pay element into the defense.

[B] *Red Circle* Rates

For a variety of legitimate reasons, an employer may find it necessary to temporarily transfer employees into lower paying jobs, but will not want to reduce that their pay so that they will be available when they are again needed for their old jobs[15]—a so-called *red circle rate.* As long as the higher rate is paid to all similarly situated persons without regard to gender, it will usually qualify as a factor other than sex.

[C] Economic Benefit

Although two jobs may be equal under the four EPA criteria, one may produce more economic benefits for the employer than the other. An employer, however, must be able to demonstrate that benefit. In *Schultz v. Wheaton Glass Co.*,[16] the court discounted the employer's argument that the availability of males on the predominantly male shift to perform work done by "snap-up boys" was an economic benefit that justified paying these employees more than females on the predominantly female shift. The court noted that there was no evidentiary support for that claim and that, indeed, males were paid over 21 cents more than females, although the regular "snap-up boys" were paid only two cents more than the females. Moreover, there was no proof that all males were available to perform the additional work or that no females were—thus undermining the economic justification for paying all males more. On the other hand, if the requisite proof can be made, then this may qualify as a factor other than sex. For example, in *Hodgson v. Robert Hall Clothes, Inc.*,[17] the men's department was shown to be more profitable than the women's department, thus justifying the higher pay of the male sales personnel.

The case is significant in two respects. First, the lower court had found that the exclusion of women from the more profitable department was justified by valid business reasons, something akin to the privacy component of the Title VII BFOQ defense.

15. 29 C.F.R. § 1620.26(b).
16. 421 F.2d 259 (3d Cir. 1970).
17. 473 F.2d 589 (3d Cir. 1973).

By analogy to the training cases, an unjustified exclusion of women from this department would probably have defeated profitability as a factor other than sex.

Second, despite a contrary indication by the same court in *Wheaton Glass Co.*, which seemed to suggest that actual economic benefits from *some* male members did not justify higher pay for *all* male members within the job category, the court in *Robert Hall* looked only at the higher profitability of the department and justified the higher pay for everyone, rather than individualizing the profit determination.

[D] Market Forces

Since the EPA was designed expressly to override the market forces that depressed wages in the traditionally female job classifications (that were, however, the substantial equivalent of the jobs in male classifications),[18] it is odd that this would even be considered as a legitimate factor other than sex. Clearly, an employer cannot pay women as a class less than it pays men, merely because women are generally willing to work at that rate while men are not. On the other hand, in individual cases an employer may justify paying one person more than another person of the opposite sex doing equal work if the higher paid person demands it as a condition of accepting employment.[19]

[E] Prior Salary

Can an employer rely on an employee's prior salary as a factor other than sex? Yes, according to the Tenth and Eleventh Circuits and the EEOC, if it is part of a mix of other factors. This would include a prior salary reflecting the employee's experience or qualifications.[20] The Seventh Circuit always considers prior salary as a factor other than sex.[21] However, the Ninth Circuit in 2020 reversed its long-standing position, and determined *en banc* that prior pay can not be considered a factor other than sex.[22]

§ 27.05 Chapter Highlights

1. Pay discrepancies can be justified if they are pursuant to a *bona fide seniority system*, which is virtually any system that was not adopted for a discriminatory purpose, is not discriminatory on its face, and is not applied in a discriminatory fashion. (§ 27.01)

---

18. *Corning Glass Works*, 417 U.S. 188; Beall v. Curtis, 603 F. Supp. 1563 (M.D. Ga.), *aff'd mem.*, 778 F.2d 791 (11th Cir. 1985).

19. Dey v. Colt Constr. & Dev. Co., 28 F.3d 1446 (7th Cir. 1994).

20. Riser v. QEP Energy, 776 F.3d 1191, 1199 (10th Cir. 2015); Irby v. Bittick, 44 F.3d 949, 955 (11th Cir. 1995); Compliance Manual, Section 10-IV(F)(g).

21. Wernsing v. Dep't of Human Servs., 427 F.3d 466, 468–70 (7th Cir. 2005).

22. Rizo v. Yovino, 950 F.3d 1217 (9th Cir. 2020).

2. The *merit system* defense, which focuses on the job performance of the plaintiff and the comparator, needs to be based on objective, clearly defined standards. (§ 27.02)

3. When employees are paid at a unit or piece rate, one employee may produce more or better products and thus earn more than another. This, however, is a result of a difference in the *quantity or quality of production*, and this provides an EPA defense even though each employee is occupying the job in the statutory sense. (§ 27.03)

4. The most commonly used defense is the *any factor other than sex* defense. Factors that the courts have recognized include training programs, "red circle" rates, economic benefit to the employer, and market forces in some situations. Something cannot qualify as a factor other than sex if it has a disparate impact on persons of one sex, unless the employer has an acceptable business reason for relying on this factor. (§ 27.04)

Chapter 28

Enforcement

Synopsis

§ 28.01 Voluntary Compliance

Once an employer is aware that its pay structure violates the EPA, it may seek to avoid judicial enforcement altogether by voluntarily bringing itself into compliance. The employer's actions, however, are limited by the *no wage reduction* clause of the EPA, which states that "an employer who is paying a wage rate differential in violation of this subsection shall not, in order to comply with the provisions of this subsection, reduce the wage rate of any employee."[1] Thus, an employer can cure a violation only by an upward adjustment or equalization. In the early days of the Act, when the pay disparity was linked to sex-segregated job categories, employers tried to cure both the Title VII segregation and EPA pay discrepancies by elaborate job restructuring schemes. The courts, however, were willing to cut through the complexities and determine if, in fact, the prior discrepancy had been cured or if, worse yet, a wage reduction had somehow occurred in the process.[2]

Employers must also be careful not to create another violation in the process of curing a prior one. For example, in *Board of Regents of the University of Nebraska v. Dawes*,[3] the University created a formula for evaluating the salaries of female employees that was based on a "hypothetical average male salary based ... on education, spe-

1. 29 U.S.C. § 206(d)(1).

2. Corning Glass Works v. Brennan, 417 U.S. 188 (1974); Hodgson v. Miller Brewing Co., 457 F.2d 221 (7th Cir. 1972).

3. 522 F.2d 380 (8th Cir. 1975).

cialization, experience, and merit."[4] When it determined that 33 female employees were being paid less than what the formula suggested they should be paid, the salary of these employees was raised to the formula level. In other words, an average male salary became the minimum female salary. But this left 92 males receiving less than the average. This was found to be an EPA violation. Other courts, however, have been more tolerant of employer attempts to cure EPA violations, even if it involves giving preferential treatment to the previously disfavored sex.[5]

§ 28.02 Government Enforcement

The Department of Labor originally had the authority to sue on behalf of individuals claiming an EPA violation. The EEOC now has that authority. The EEOC is not required to engage in any prelitigation conciliation efforts, wait any certain amount of time before bringing suit, or otherwise follow the normal Title VII procedures.

§ 28.03 Private Enforcement

A private party may, but is not required to, file a charge with the EEOC before bringing an action for enforcement of the EPA. Indeed, the only reason for doing so is that the EEOC might undertake the litigation. Individual plaintiffs may sue on behalf of themselves and other similarly situated employees who consent in writing to become a party to the lawsuit. In a suit against a private employer, the plaintiff is entitled to a jury trial.

A suit by the EEOC terminates a private party's entitlement to bring an individual action.

§ 28.04 Limitations Period

An EPA lawsuit must be commenced within two years after the cause of action accrues, or three years for *willful* violations. In *McLaughlin v. Richland Shoe Co.*,[6] the Supreme Court said that a violation was willful if the defendant "knew or showed reckless disregard for the matter of whether its conduct was prohibited by the statute."[7]

Although a few courts have treated Equal Pay Act violations as *continuing violations* for accrual purposes,[8] the prevailing and better view treats every violation as a *discrete*

4. Dawes, 522 F.2d at 382.
5. Ende v. Bd. of Regents, 757 F.2d 176 (7th Cir. 1985).
6. McLaughlin v. Richland Shoe Co., 486 U.S. 128 (1988).
7. *McLaughlin*, 486 U.S. at 133.
8. Jenkins v. Home Ins. Co., 635 F.2d 310 (4th Cir. 1980).

act.[9] That is, every time an employer issues a paycheck to the member of one sex that is less than the paycheck issued to a member of another sex who is doing equal work, a separate and discrete event occurs. The limitations period is reset with each discriminatory paycheck, thus enabling an employee to sue at any time during his or her term of employment.[10] The amount the plaintiff may recover, however, is limited to the relevant time period—namely, the difference between what the plaintiff was actually paid and what he or she should have been paid for each pay period within the two (or three) year period; a plaintiff cannot recover the differential for prior pay periods.

§ 28.05 Remedies

A successful EPA plaintiff can recover the wages wrongfully withheld during the relevant limitations period. In addition, the employer will be liable for liquidated damages in an amount equal to the unpaid wages award unless the employer can establish that its action was "in good faith" and had "reasonable grounds for believing" that its act or omission was not a violation.[11]

The courts differ over both the meaning of *good faith* and how it compares with the *willfulness* statute of limitations test. With respect to the former issue, courts have denied liquidated damages when the employer relied on a legal opinion, EEOC advice, or a plausible wage comparison. With respect to the latter issue, some courts hold that if the violation is *willful* for the purpose of the limitations period, by definition it cannot be in *good faith*,[12] and that a lack of *willfulness* does not necessarily establish *good faith*.[13] Other courts, however, have held that an employer can act *willfully* and be in *good faith* at the same time.[14] A private claimant can also recover attorney's fees and costs.

§ 28.06 Chapter Highlights

1. An employer may voluntarily cure an EPA violation only by raising the pay of the lower paid employee. In curing class-wide pay discrepancies, an employer must be careful not to do anything that would give rise to another EPA lawsuit by the previously favored class of employees. (§ 28.01)

2. The EPA can be enforced either through a lawsuit brought by the EEOC or by private individuals on behalf of themselves and other similarly situated individuals who consent in writing to join the lawsuit. (§§ 28.02 & 28.03)

---

9. The Supreme Court's decision in *AMTRAK v. Morgan*, 536 U.S. 101 (2002) strongly supports this view. *See* Chapter 16, § 16.04[D].

10. Pollis v. New Sch. for Soc. Research, 132 F.3d 115 (2d Cir. 1997).

11. 29 U.S.C. § 260.

12. EEOC v. City of Detroit Health Dep't, 920 F.2d 355 (6th Cir. 1990).

13. EEOC v. Cherry-Burrell Corp., 35 F.3d 356, 364 (8th Cir. 1994).

14. Herman v. Roosevelt Fed. Sav. & Loan Ass'n, 432 F. Supp. 843 (E.D. Mo. 1977).

3. A lawsuit must be brought within two years after the cause of action accrues, or three years in the case of willful violations. Each paycheck that is less than the paycheck issued to a member of another sex who is doing equal work is a new violation. A violation is willful if the employer knew about or showed reckless disregard over the question of whether its conduct violated the Act. (§ 28.04)

4. A successful plaintiff is entitled to recover the wages that were wrongfully withheld, plus liquidated damages (an amount equal to the wages wrongfully withheld) unless the employer can show that its actions were in good faith and that it had reasonable grounds for believing that it was not violating the Act. Considerable confusion exists over the meaning of *good faith* in this context. (§ 28.05)

Part VII

Obligations of Government Contractors

Chapter 29

Executive Order 11246[1]

Synopsis

Most federal government contractors are already subject to the statutory non-discrimination obligations discussed elsewhere in this text. However, these same obligations are also imposed on them under the contracts they have with the government, albeit with different enforcement mechanisms and the prospect of additional remedies. More significantly, however, government contractors are also subject to non-discrimination obligations that go beyond those imposed by statute. These are the obligations that exist under the presidential Executive Order 11246 (EO)[2] and the Department of Labor regulations implementing it.[3]

§ 29.01 Contractors Subject to the EO

The EO generally[4] applies to any person who is a party to one or more contracts with the executive branch of the federal government in excess of $10,000 for the fur-

---

1. This chapter was written by Leigh Nason, Shareholder, Ogletree, Deakins, Nash, Smoak & Stewart, PC, Columbia, South Carolina.

2. Nondiscrimination provisions in federal contracts date back to 1941. A detailed history of the succeeding Executive Orders can be found in *Contractors Ass'n of Eastern Pa. v. Secretary of Labor*, 442 F.2d 159 (3d Cir. 1971).

3. The Department of Labor Regulations are found in 41 C.F.R. Chapter 60, Parts 1, 2, 300, and 741.

4. This chapter and the next will cover the EO only at the highest level of generality. All the rules, requirements, and obligations discussed herein are subject to numerous qualifications and exceptions.

nishing of supplies or services, or for the use of real or personal property including leases. This includes contracts in which the government is the seller or lessor, as well as the more common contract in which the government is the purchaser or lessee.[5] The EO also applies to anyone who is a subcontractor of a prime contractor with the government in excess of $10,000 and whose subcontract is "reasonably necessary" to the performance of the prime contract[6] or who is performing any portion of the prime contractor's obligations.[7] Finally, although their obligations are different, the EO also applies to persons who contract to perform construction work in excess of $10,000 that is paid for in whole or in part with funds obtained from the government, or borrowed on the credit of the government. Contractors with higher contract amounts may be subject to additional obligations.

A recurring issue is whether corporate affiliates of a covered contractor are also covered. Some courts have held that if one corporation controls another, both are a single entity for EO purposes.[8] But other courts have held that all corporations or entities that are subject to the same "ultimate authority" are covered if any corporation or entity is covered.[9]

§ 29.02 The Protected Bases

The obligations imposed by the EO, which include nondiscrimination and affirmative action, apply to employees on the basis of race, color, religion, sex, sexual orientation, gender identity, and national origin. These classifications are construed in much the same manner as under Title VII.[10]

---

5. The EO applies to financial institutions without regard to a contract dollar amount if the financial institution serves as a depository of government funds or is an issuing and paying agent for U.S. savings bonds and savings notes. 41 C.F.R. § 60-1.7(a). Note that, as of January 1, 2012, financial institutions can no longer issue U.S. savings bonds.

6. OFCCP v. Bridgeport Hospital, 1997-OFC-1 (ARB Jan. 31, 2003); *see also* OFCCP Directive Number 2018-02 (May 18, 2018) (continuing moratorium on enforcement of affirmative action obligations of hospitals, pharmacies, or other medical care providers based on the existence of subcontracts with TRICARE and Veterans Affairs Health Benefits Program Providers); Liberty Mut. Ins. Co. v. Friedman, 639 F.2d 164 (4th Cir. 1981) (company providing workers' compensation insurance to a government contract found to be covered).

7. The OFCCP construes this as meaning that it must be able to trace the subcontractor's goods or services through the contractor and show that they were eventually used by the government. OFCCP v. Monongahela R.R. Co., 1985-OFC-2, 1986 WL 802025 (ALJ Apr. 2, 1986); OFCCP v. Lofland Bros., OEO 75-1, 1984 WL 72747 (Sec'y Apr. 16, 1984).

8. Liberty Mut. Ins. Co. v. Friedman, 485 F. Supp. 695 (D. Md. 1979), rev'd on other grounds, 639 F.2d 164 (4th Cir. 1981).

9. Bd. of Governors of Univ. of North Carolina v. United States Dep't of Labor, 917 F.2d 812 (4th Cir. 1990).

10. The U.S. Supreme Court decided that Title VII covers discrimination based on sexual orientation and gender identity in Bostock v. Clayton, Cty., 509 U.S. __ (2020).

§ 29.03 The Contractor's Obligations

[A] Nondiscrimination

The contractor's obligation not to discriminate is fairly straightforward on its face. Title VII standards and precedents for both disparate treatment and disparate impact are used to determine if a contractor is noncompliant.[11]

[B] Affirmative Action

Each non-construction contractor and subcontractor that has at least 50 employees and a federal contract or subcontract of $50,000 or more must develop and adopt a written Affirmative Action Program (AAP) for minorities and females and file an annual EEO-1 compliance report.[12] All construction contractors must also develop an AAP, although the requirements for these AAPs are somewhat different.

A non-construction AAP is a complex document involving substantial data collection and analysis and must be available for inspection within 120 days of the commencement of the contract.[13] It must contain the following information:

- An organizational profile depicting the staffing pattern of an establishment, utilizing either an organizational display or workforce analysis. The organizational display, if used, identifies each organizational unit in the establishment and shows the relationship of each organizational unit to the organizational units in the establishment. In contrast, the workforce analysis lists each job title ranked from the lowest paid to the highest paid within each department or other similar organizational unit and includes departmental or unit supervision. Both the organizational display and the workforce analysis must reflect the total number of male and female incumbents and the total number of male and female incumbents in certain ethnic groups.[14]
- A job group analysis, putting together in groups all jobs with similar content, wage rates, and opportunities, and stating the percentage of minorities and of women in each job group.[15]
- Availability data for minorities and women within each job group, based on the percentage of minorities and women with the requisite skills in a reasonable re-

11. See, for example, *OFCCP v. Analogic Corp.*, 2017-OFC-00001 (ALJ Mar. 22, 2019), for a discussion of the appropriate legal framework in OFCCP cases.

12. 41 C.F.R. §§ 60-1.7(a), -1.40(a); *see also* § 60-741.40(a) (AAP for qualified disabled individuals). Contractors with 50 employees and a federal contract or subcontract of $150,000 or more must develop and adopt an AAP for protected veterans. 41 C.F.R. § 60-300.40.

13. 41 C.F.R. § 60-2.1(a).

14. 41 C.F.R. § 60-2.11.

15. 41 C.F.R. § 60-2.12.

cruitment area, and the percentage of minorities and women among those promotable, transferable, and trainable within the organization.[16]

- A comparison of the percentage of minorities and women within each job group against the percentage of minorities and women who are available for these job groups.[17]
- Placement goals, if the percentage of minorities and women in each job group is less than what would be expected given their availability.[18] Since these placement goals are predicated on data that would not necessarily satisfy the *Weber* requirements for permissible reverse discrimination under Title VII[19] and clearly do not satisfy the remedial justification required under the Constitution,[20] the Department of Labor Regulations[21] vigorously insist on the following principles:
  - That "[p]lacement goals may not be rigid and inflexible quotas";
  - That all selections decisions be made "in a nondiscriminatory manner";
  - That placement goals do not justify "preference[s]" or "set asides"; and
  - That placement goals cannot be used to supersede "merit selection principles" or to require a contractor "to hire a person who lacks qualifications to perform the job successfully."
- The designation of persons within the organization who will have responsibility for implementing the AAP.[22]
- An identification of problem areas, including an evaluation of:
  - units and job groups to determine the overall utilization of minorities and women and their distribution,
  - applicant flow, hires, terminations, promotions, and other personnel actions to determine if there are selection disparities,
  - compensation systems to determine if there are disparities, and
  - selection, recruitment, referral, and other personnel procedures to determine if they result in disparities.[23]
- Action-oriented programs designed to correct problem areas and attain established goals and objectives, including a demonstration that the contractor has

16. 41 C.F.R. §60-2.14.
17. 41 C.F.R. §60-2.15.
18. 41 C.F.R. §60-2.16.
19. *See* Chapter 5, §5.11.
20. *See* Chapter 2, §2.02[B].
21. 41 C.F.R. §60-2.16(e).
22. 41 C.F.R. §60-2.17(a).
23. 41 C.F.R. §60-2.17(b).

at least "made good faith efforts to remove identified barriers, expand employment opportunities, and produce measurable results."[24]

- An internal audit and reporting system.[25]

[C] Other Requirements

Various other requirements attach to covered contracts and subcontracts:

- Contractors must include the equal opportunity clause in all subcontracts and purchase orders of $10,000 or more related to the government contract.[26]
- Contractors cannot maintain segregated facilities.[27]
- Contractors must preserve all personnel or employment records made or kept by the contractor for at least two years from the date each record is made or of the personnel action, whichever is later.[28]
- Contractors must include an equal opportunity statement in all solicitations and advertisements for employment.[29]
- Contractors must comply with pay transparency regulations prohibiting them from discharging or otherwise discriminating against their employees and job applicants for discussing, disclosing, or inquiring about compensation.[30]
- Contractors must advise each labor union with which they deal of their equal employment opportunity and affirmative action policies.[31]
- Contractors will post appropriate anti-discrimination notices in the workplace.[32]
- Contractors will permit access to their premises during normal business hours for the purpose of conducting compliance evaluations and compliance investigations.[33]

§ 29.04 Enforcement

Within the Department of Labor, the Office of Federal Contract Compliance Programs (OFCCP) is charged with the administrative enforcement of the EO and the government contractor obligations under the Rehabilitation Act and the Veterans

24. 41 C.F.R. § 60-2.17(c).
25. 41 C.F.R. § 60-2.17(d).
26. 41 C.F.R. § 60-1.4(a).
27. 41 C.F.R. § 60-1.8.
28. 41 C.F.R. § 60-1.12. Contractors with fewer than 150 employees and a government contract of less than $150,000 need only retain such records for one year.
29. 41 C.F.R. § 60-1.41.
30. 41 C.F.R. § 60-1.4(a)(3).
31. 41 C.F.R. § 60-1.9.
32. 41 C.F.R. § 60-1.42.
33. 41 C.F.R. § 60-1.43.

Acts. The process, which may be triggered by a specific complaint or initiated by the OFCCP itself, may involve off-site record reviews, on-site investigation, a conciliation agreement with the contractor to correct any violations, and, if necessary, the issuance of a "show cause" notice. Unless otherwise resolved, this will lead to an administrative hearing and decision by an administrative law judge, followed by an appeal to the Administrative Review Board, and, ultimately, to the Secretary of Labor, who will issue a final decision. Sanctions include withholding payment under the contract, suspending the contract, terminating the contract, preferential hiring or promotion requirements, or, in extreme cases, ordering the "debarment" of the contractor from any further government contracts.[34] A contractor may appeal this decision to a federal district court under the Administrative Procedure Act.[35]

§ 29.05 Chapter Highlights

1. The EO generally applies to any person who has federal government contracts in excess of $10,000 for the furnishing of supplies or services or the government's use of real or personal property. Most subcontractors of the primary contractor are also covered. Contractors doing construction work in excess of $10,000 that is paid for by or obtained on the credit of the government are subject to slightly different obligations. (§ 29.01)

2. The special obligations that government contractors are subject to include nondiscrimination on the basis of race, color, religion, sex, sexual orientation, gender identity, and national origin. (§ 29.02)

3. In addition to the duty of non-discrimination, a covered contractor also has a duty to take affirmative action to achieve the equal employment goals of the EO, based on extensive information that the contractor must compile and make available. To avoid going beyond what Title VII and the Constitution allow with respect to affirmative action, the Department of Labor has promulgated regulations that limit or qualify the affirmative action obligations of government contractors. (§ 29.03)

4. The EO is enforced by the Labor Department's Office of Federal Contract Compliance Programs. Contract violations are subject to a range of remedies, from the mere withholding of payments due the contractor to the disbarment of the contractor from future government contracts. (§ 29.04)

---

34. 41 C.F.R. § 60-1.27.

35. 5 U.S.C. § 500, et seq.

Part VIII
Disability Discrimination

Chapter 30

An Overview of the Coverage and Enforcement of Federal Statutes[1]

Synopsis

On January 1, 2009, Congress made sweeping changes to the primary federal statutes prohibiting discrimination against persons with disabilities. The changed statutes were the Rehabilitation Act of 1973[2] and the Americans with Disabilities Act.[3] The Americans with Disabilities Act Amendments Act of 2008[4] not only modified the ADA, it amended the Rehabilitation Act so that it would conform to the new changes. The coverage and enforcement mechanisms of these two statutes differ, but the complex substance of the prohibition is very similar and will be discussed together in the remaining chapters.

In addition, all 50 states prohibit employment discrimination on the basis of disability. In some states, the prohibition is limited to public employment. Some states have separate statutes dealing with the unique aspects of disability discrimination.

1. We thank Leigh M. Nason, Shareholder, Ogletree, Deakins, Nash, Smoak & Stewart, PC, Columbia, South Carolina, for an earlier version of this chapter.

2. 29 U.S.C. § 791, et seq. (2008).

3. 42 U.S.C. §§ 12101–13 (2008). The Veterans' Readjustment Assistance Act of 1974, as amended, 38 U.S.C. §§ 4211–14, also prohibits discrimination against certain disabled veterans. Although government contractors need to be aware of its existence and requirements, it has not played a major role in combating disability discrimination.

4. 42 U.S.C. § 12101, et seq.

Other states have simply included it as an additional basis of proscribed discrimination under their general anti-discrimination statute. These state statutes are beyond the scope of this book.

§ 30.01 The Rehabilitation Act of 1973

[A] Covered Employers

Section 501 covers employment by the federal government.[5] It generally requires the government to take affirmative action to recruit disabled individuals for employment and to make reasonable accommodations for an applicant's or employee's limitations.

Section 503 applies to government contractors and subcontractors with contracts in excess of $10,000.[6] It, too, requires the employer to take affirmative action, and the implementing regulations further prohibit any employment discrimination on the basis of disability.

Section 504 applies to the recipients of federal financial assistance and provides that no "otherwise qualified individual with a disability in the United States" shall, "solely by reason of her or his disability, be excluded from the participation in, be denied the benefits of, or be subjected to discrimination" by a covered entity.[7] The 2008 amendment provided for broad coverage in the definition of disability consistent with the change to the ADA. The Act does not define "federal financial assistance." The term has been construed, however, as including Medicare and Medicaid payments to doctors and hospitals,[8] government guarantees that certain loans will be repaid,[9] and funds funneled through a state to a remote recipient.[10] On the other hand, it does not apply to payments to a bank for its administration of a student loan program,[11] investment tax credits for airlines,[12] or mere certification of an apprenticeship program.[13] Overruling several lower court decisions on the point, the Supreme Court in *Consolidated Rail Corp. v. Darrone*[14] held that Section 504 covered employment discrimination even if employment was not the primary objective of the federal assistance.

---

5. 29 U.S.C. § 791.

6. 29 U.S.C. § 793.

7. 29 U.S.C. § 794.

8. United States v. Cabrini Med. Ctr., 639 F.2d 908 (2d Cir. 1981); New York by Vacco v. Mid Hudson Med. Group, P.C., 877 F. Supp. 143 (S.D.N.Y. 1995).

9. Moore v. Sun Bank of North Fla., 923 F.2d 1423 (11th Cir. 1991), vacated and reh'g en banc granted, 953 F.2d 1274 (11th Cir. Fla.), reinstated, 963 F.2d 1448 (11th Cir. 1992).

10. Moreno v. Consol. Rail Corp., 99 F.3d 782 (6th Cir. 1996).

11. Gallagher v. Croghan Colonial Bank, 89 F.3d 275 (6th Cir. 1996).

12. Paralyzed Veterans of Am. v. Civil Aeronautics Bd., 752 F.2d 694 (D.C. Cir. 1985), *rev'd on other grounds sub nom.* United States Dep't of Transp. v. Paralyzed Veterans of Am., 477 U.S. 597 (1986).

13. Lemmo v. Willson, 583 F. Supp. 557 (D. Colo. 1984).

14. 465 U.S. 624 (1984); *see also* Moreno v. Consolidated Rail Corp., 99 F.3d 782 (6th Cir. 1996) (federal funds received indirectly subjected CONRAIL to suit under Section 504).

Section 508 requires that federal agencies, absent undue burden, provide access to their electronic and information technology to everyone. This includes both disabled employees and members of the public.

[B] Enforcement

Under Section 505, a federal employee is entitled to the same "remedies, procedures, and rights" as federal employees with Title VII claims.[15] This means that after exhausting the necessary procedures, a federal employee may bring a de novo suit in federal court. In contrast, an employee claiming disability discrimination by a federal contractor must seek relief through the Labor Department's Office of Federal Contract Compliance Programs and its administrative enforcement arms, with judicial review limited to a determination of whether the decision was arbitrary, capricious, an abuse of discretion, or otherwise not in accordance with the law.

The most liberal enforcement procedures are those available to persons claiming discrimination by the recipients of federal financial aid. Such a person may file a suit directly in federal court, without the need to first complain to the agency that funded the program or anyone else.[16]

§ 30.02 The Americans with Disabilities Act

[A] Covered Employers

Title I of the ADA prohibits discrimination in employment and requires reasonable accommodation. It applies to all private, state,[17] and local government employers with "15 or more employees for each working day in each of 20 or more calendar weeks in the current or preceding calendar year."[18] It does not apply to the federal government, corporations wholly owned by the United States government, Indian tribes, or bona fide private membership clubs.

[B] Enforcement

The ADA is enforced through the same procedures available to persons claiming discrimination under Title VII. The same remedies are also available.[19]

---

15. 29 U.S.C. § 794a(a)(1).

16. 29 U.S.C. § 794a(a)(2).

17. Damage suits against states are, however, subject to the limitations of the Eleventh Amendment. Bd. of Trs. of the Univ. of Ala. v. Garrett, 531 U.S. 356 (2001). *See* Chapter 3.

18. 42 U.S.C. § 12111(5)(A).

19. The Lilly Ledbetter Fair Pay Act of 2009, 42 U.S.C.S. § 2000e-5(e)(3)(A), specifically intended for the new Title VII compensation accrual rules to also apply to ADA cases.

§ 30.03 Chapter Highlights

1. In addition to the various state laws, disability discrimination is dealt with primarily through the Rehabilitation Act of 1973 and the Americans with Disabilities Act.

2. The Rehabilitation Act applies to the federal government, government contractors and subcontractors, and the recipients of federal financial assistance. (§ 30.01[A])

3. The Act is enforced against the federal government in the same manner as Title VII claims, against federal contractors through Labor Department procedures, and against recipients of federal financial aid in a direct suit in federal court. (§ 30.01[B])

4. The Americans with Disabilities Act covers private and state employees but not the federal government. It is enforced through the same procedures available under Title VII. (§ 30.02)

Chapter 31

The Protected Class[1]

Synopsis

§ 31.01 The Base Definitions

The ADA Amendments Act of 2008 (ADAAA) changed the focus of the inquiry from whether an individual meets the definition of disability to whether discrimination occurred.[2] However, definition is still important to disability law. The disability statutes are *definitional onions.* These *onions* are definitions that contain terms that are themselves defined elsewhere in the statute or that require and generate definitions by the courts; and these definitions, in turn, often contain other terms with a fixed

1. We thank Leigh M. Nason, Shareholder, Ogletree, Deakins, Nash, Smoak & Stewart, PC, Columbia, SC, for an earlier version of this chapter.
2. 29 C.F.R. § 1630.1(c)(4).

statutory or judicial definition—thus creating multiple definitional layers, as in an onion. If one fails to pass all these definitional tests, the matter is at an end. But if one does establish membership in the protected class, proof of the substantive element, *discrimination*, is almost a foregone conclusion. The law not only prohibits discrimination, it requires reasonable accommodation of the disabled.

One must begin with the statutory language. The Rehabilitation Act applies to "individuals with disabilities" regarding federal employment; "qualified individuals with disabilities" regarding employment with federal contractors; and "otherwise qualified individual[s] with a disability" regarding employment with federal fund recipients.[3]

The ADA, using a more consistent terminology, covers "qualified individual[s] with a disability," which is defined to mean "an individual who, with or without reasonable accommodation, can perform the essential functions of the employment position that such individual holds or desires."[4] Both the Rehabilitation Act and the ADA further define the term "disability" to mean:

- a physical or mental impairment that substantially limits one or more of the major life activities of such individual;
- a record of such impairment; or
- being regarded as having such an impairment.[5]

Excluded as disabilities under both Acts are homosexuality, bisexuality, transvestism, transsexualism, pedophilia, exhibitionism, voyeurism, gender identity disorders not resulting from physical impairments, other sexual behavior disorders, compulsive gambling, kleptomania, pyromania, and psychoactive substance use disorders resulting from current illegal use of drugs. In addition, both Acts also exclude persons who are, at the time of the employment action, engaged in the illegal use of drugs.

The Rehabilitation Act's definition of *individual with a disability* excludes persons who are alcoholic and "whose current use of alcohol prevents them from performing the duties of the job in question or whose employment, by reason of such current abuse, would constitute a direct threat to property or the safety of others."[6] Instead of dealing with it in terms of defining the members of the protected class, the ADA simply enables the employer to hold an alcoholic employee "to the same qualification standards for employment or job performance and behavior that such entity holds other employees, even if any unsatisfactory performance or behavior is related to the ... alcoholism of such employee."[7]

The Rehabilitation Act excludes from its definition of the protected class any person "who has a currently contagious disease or infection and who, by reason of such dis-

---

3. The original Rehabilitation Act spoke in terms of individuals with "handicaps." The terminology was later changed to "disability."

4. 42 U.S.C. § 12111(8).

5. *See* 29 U.S.C. § 705(20)(B); 42 U.S.C. § 12102(2).

6. 29 U.S.C. § 705(20)(C)(v).

7. 42 U.S.C. § 12114(c)(4).

ease or infection, would constitute a direct threat to the health or safety of other individuals or who, by reason of the currently contagious disease or infection, is unable to perform the duties of the job."[8] In contrast, the ADA allows an employer to impose as a "qualification standard" a requirement that employees not pose a "direct threat to the health or safety of other individuals in the workplace."[9] The ADA deals with infectious or communicable diseases directly only in the context of food handling jobs, by allowing the employer to refuse to assign such a person to that kind of job if the risk cannot be eliminated by reasonable accommodation.[10]

These loosely worded definitions of the protected class have been the subject of extensive litigation and legal analysis—initially under the Rehabilitation Act. But many of the definitions in the more recent statute, the ADA, were taken directly from the Rehabilitation Act. Since Congress expressly approved the standards applied by the courts under that Act and its regulatory interpretations,[11] the ADA terms came with some already established meanings. With the passage of the ADAAA, some established meanings changed, but the definition of disability discussed above did not change. Instead, Congress indicated its disapproval of Supreme Court decisions narrowly construing the ADA and instead indicated its approval of broad coverage. This is discussed in more detail below.

§ 31.02 The Meaning of "Mental or Physical Impairment"

In traversing the definitional maze that will lead ultimately to a determination of whether a particular individual is within the protected class, one must begin with the meaning of *mental or physical impairment*. The ADA regulations define it broadly, to include "[a]ny physiological disorder, or condition, cosmetic disfigurement, or anatomical loss affecting one or more [body systems]; or [a]ny mental or psychological disorder, such as intellectual disability (formerly termed "mental retardation"), organic brain syndrome, emotional or mental illness, and specific learning disabilities."[12] If a person actually has a current or prior impairment, that person is within the protected class. But even if a person does not have an actual impairment, the person may be protected if he or she is *regarded as* having an impairment.

[A] Actual Physical Impairments

Physical impairments have been found to include the obvious ones of loss or significant deterioration of vision, hearing, and speech; loss of limbs; disfiguring skin

8. 29 U.S.C. § 705(20)(D).
9. 42 U.S.C. § 12113(b).
10. 42 U.S.C. § 12113(e)(2).
11. 42 U.S.C. § 12201(a).
12. 29 C.F.R. § 1630.2(h)(1) & (2).

problems; stroke or injury caused paralysis; multiple sclerosis; cerebral palsy; epilepsy; muscular dystrophy; carpal tunnel, Parkinson's disease; cancer; heart disease; diabetes; chronic back problems; cardiac problems; hypertension; leukemia; and others. The ADAAA intended that the definition of disability "be construed broadly in favor of expansive coverage."[13]

In *School Board of Nassau County v. Arline*,[14] the Supreme Court held that a contagious disease, tuberculosis in that case, was a physical impairment under the Rehabilitation Act. *Arline* crossed what was essentially a conceptual or psychological barrier: could Congress have possibly intended to protect infectious or contagious diseases? The Court held that it could have and did.[15] This decision opened the way for lower courts to resolve the even more emotionally charged questions about HIV, or "AIDS" infection, in favor of coverage under both the Rehabilitation Act and the ADA. In *Bragdon v. Abbott*,[16] the Supreme Court confirmed this reading of the statute by holding that even an asymptomatic infection of the immunodeficiency virus, because of its immediate damage to the white blood cells of the infected person, was a *physical impairment* under the ADA.

In contrast, environmental, cultural, and economic disadvantages are not *impairments*, nor are personality traits such as a quick temper or mere physical characteristics such as eye color, left-handedness, height, weight, or muscle tone that is within the "normal" range and is not the result of a physiological disorder.[17] Pregnancy, by itself, does not constitute a disability.[18] On the other hand, complications arising from pregnancy can rise to the level of a statutory impairment if they are not a normal part of pregnancy.[19] The courts generally agree that extreme obesity is an impairment "only if it is the result of a 'physiological disorder or condition.'"[20]

The EEOC Interpretative Guidance recognize that temporary impairments lasting less than six months can constitute a disability if they are sufficiently severe.[21]

[B] Actual Mental Impairments

Almost any recognized mental or psychological disorder, except those that are expressly excluded, will qualify as an *impairment*. The EEOC's Rehabilitation Act regulations indicate that it includes "mental retardation, organic brain syndrome,

13. 29 C.F.R. § 1630.1(c)(4).

14. 480 U.S. 273 (1987).

15. Section 706(8)(D), which implicitly recognizes contagious diseases as a disability, was added in 1988 and was intended to codify the *Arline* decision.

16. 524 U.S. 624 (1998).

17. 29 C.F.R. § 1630.2(h) app.

18. Richards v. City of Topeka, 173 F.3d 1247 (10th Cir. 1999).

19. Spees v. James Marine, Inc., 617 F.3d 380, 397 (6th Cir. 2010).

20. Richardson v. Chi. Transit Auth., 926 F.3d 881, 887 (7th Cir. 2019).

21. 29 C.F.R. app. § 1630.2(j)(1)(ix); *see also* Summers v. Altarum Inst. Corp., 740 F.3d 325, 330 (4th Cir. 2014).

emotional or mental illness, and specific learning disabilities."[22] The usual issues in these cases are whether the disorder significantly limits a major life activity (often involving the employee's inability to perform the specific job for which he or she was hired) and whether the disorder poses a direct threat to the safety of others. These matters will be discussed in more detail below.

[C] Having a Record of Impairment

A person who has previously had certain kinds of impairments, such as mental illness or cancer, but who has overcome them may still face prejudice and discrimination in the workplace. This category was designed to deal with that situation. In establishing coverage on this basis, however, the plaintiff must show that the prior condition qualified as an impairment at the time—including proof that it substantially limited a major life activity.

[D] Regarded as Impairments

A *regarded as* impairment is the most mysterious of the various definitions of *impairments.* Obviously, it has something to do with the employer's or some third party's perceptions, rather than the actual mental or physical condition of the applicant or employee. Moreover, at least with respect to the employer, the perception must necessarily be an erroneous one. This erroneous perception may then relate to one of two things. First, the employer may erroneously perceive the employee as having some kind of mental or physical impairment. For example, an employer might terminate an employee on the basis of the rumor that the employee has AIDS.[23] The employee would be *regarded as* having a qualifying impairment and thus be within the protected class.

Alternatively, an employer might correctly know that the employee has a particular mental or physical impairment that is not substantially limiting in fact, but the employer erroneously believes it to be so. An employee with high blood pressure who is given non-strenuous work because of the employer's erroneous belief that the employee might have a heart attack would thus be within the protected class because of a *regarded as* impairment.[24]

In *Sutton v. United Air Lines, Inc.*[25] the Supreme Court created a high bar for proving an employer discriminated based on an erroneous perception. The airline regarded low vision as an impairment for the job of airline pilot. That was an erroneous perception for pilots who have corrected their vision with eyeglasses. However, did this erroneous perception substantially limit these pilots in the major life activity of working? The Supreme Court answered that question by requiring pilots with

22. 29 C.F.R. § 33.3(a)(2).
23. *See* 29 C.F.R. § 1630.2(l).
24. *See* 29 C.F.R. § 1630.2(l).
25. 527 U.S. 471 (1999).

corrected vision to show they were barred from holding a broad class of jobs, not merely the specific job of an airline pilot. They must show that corrected vision barred them from working not simply as airline pilots, but from any related jobs such as co-pilot, pilot instructor, or any such related job. *Sutton* was disapproved by name in the ADAAA in favor of the earlier *School Board of Nassau County* decision.[26] *Nassau County* focused on whether the individual was viewed as impaired by the employer in question. The Court wrote that "society's accumulated myths and fears about disability and disease are as handicapping as the physical limitations that flow from actual impairment."[27] The ADAAA regulations followed this up by providing that an employee may qualify as being regarded as having a disability without consideration of whether the perception involved the impairment of a major life activity.[28]

§ 31.03 The Meaning of "Substantially Limits" a "Major Life Activity"

Assuming that one possesses a mental or physical characteristic that qualifies as an *impairment* in the medical sense, it still must qualify as an *impairment* in a functional sense. This is a two-step analysis. First, the court must determine whether the impairment inhibits the plaintiff from performing a *major life activity*. Second, the court must determine if the impairment *substantially limits* the plaintiff from engaging in that activity. This is not a demanding standard. Congress stressed in the ADAAA that the focus must be on compliance with the ADA, and not whether the individual is disabled. The determination of disability "should not demand extensive analysis."[29]

[A] The Meaning of "Major Life Activity"

In *Toyota Motor Manufacturing, Kentucky, Inc. v. Williams*,[30] the Supreme Court limited the definition of *major life activity* to those activities that are of central importance to daily life. However, the ADAAA specifically rejected that standard.[31] Instead, the current regulations provide that the term *major life activities* "shall not be interpreted strictly."[32] The EEOC ADA Interpretive Guidance describes *major life activities* as those that the average person in the general population can perform with little or no difficulty. This includes, but is not limited to, eating, seeing, hearing, speaking, breathing, caring for oneself, performing manual tasks, standing, sitting,

26. 122 Stat. 3553, 3554 (2008).
27. 480 U.S. at 284.
28. 29 C.F.R. § 1630.2(j)(2).
29. 122 Stat. 3553, 3554 (2008).
30. 543 U.S. 184 (2002).
31. 122 Stat. 3553, 3554 (2008).
32. 29 C.F.R. § 1630.2(i)(2).

reaching, lifting, bending, walking, concentrating, learning, and working.[33] In addition, *major life activities* include major bodily functions. This includes, but is not limited to, functions of the immune system, normal cell growth, digestive, bowel, bladder, neurological, brain, respiratory, circulatory, endocrine, hemic, lymphatic, musculoskeletal, and reproductive functions.[34]

[B] The Meaning of "Substantially Limits"

[1] The Baseline for Measurement

In the previously mentioned *Sutton* decision, the Supreme Court also held that "if a person is taking measures to correct for, or mitigate, a physical or mental impairment, the effects of those measures—both positive and negative—must be taken into account when judging whether that person is 'substantially limited' in a major life activity and thus 'disabled' under the Act."[35] This meant that if individuals were able to mitigate their disability, they did not qualify as being impaired. Just as Congress specifically rejected *Sutton's* holding on perception of impairment, it rejected its holding on mitigating measures. Determining whether an impairment substantially limits a major life activity must be made without consideration of "the ameliorative effects of mitigating measures." These mitigating measures include things like hearing aids and low-vision devices, but not ordinary glasses or contact lenses.[36]

Court decisions handed down before the ADAAA should not be relied upon in determining disability. In *Cannon v. Jacobs Field Srvs. N. Am.*[37] an employee was unable to lift his right arm above his shoulder. The district court held that the employee was not disabled because the inability to raise his right arm higher did not impair his daily functioning. The Fifth Circuit disagreed by noting that both lifting and reaching are *major life activities* and an inability to lift one arm above the shoulder qualifies as an impairment. A later district court decision within the Fifth Circuit considered *Cannon* and the ADAAA, and then rejected arguments that relied on "outdated authority for determining what constitutes a substantial limitation under the ADA."[38] This is consistent with the guidelines statement calling for a "lower" standard than that applied by the Courts prior to the passage of the ADAAA.[39]

[2] The Meaning of "Substantial"

In *Toyota Motor Manufacturing Kentucky, Inc* case, the Supreme Court indicated that the "substantial limitations on major life activities" must be "interpreted strictly

33. 29 C.F.R. § 1630.2(h)(2)(i)(1)(i).
34. 29 C.F.R. § 1630.2(h)(2)(i)(1)(ii).
35. *Sutton*, 527 U.S. at 482.
36. 42 U.S.C. § 12102(4)(E)(i)-(l).
37. 813 F.3d 586 (5th Cir. 2016).
38. Cruz v. R2Sonic, LLC, 405 F. Supp. 3d 676 (W.D. Tex. 2019).
39. 29 CFR § 1603.2(j)(1)(iv).

to create a demanding standard" that "prevents or severely restricts the individual from doing activities that are of central importance." The impairment must be "permanent or long-term."[40] Once again, in the ADAAA Congress specifically rejected both this standard and this case by name.[41] Instead, the EEOC guidelines state that "substantially limits is not meant to be a demanding standard." Rather, it is to be "construed broadly in favor of expansive coverage."[42] The guidelines go on to instruct courts that the focus should be on compliance with the ADAAA obligations, and not whether the employee's impairment substantially limits a major life activity.[43]

In addition, an "episodic" impairment or one that is in remission can qualify as a disability if it substantially limits a major life activity when active.[44]

§ 31.04 The Meaning of "Qualified Individual"

The final set of definitional hurdles one must cross to qualify as a member of the ADA protected class is that of being a *qualified individual* with a disability. The Act defines a *qualified individual* as one "who, with or without *reasonable accommodation*, can perform the *essential functions* of the employment position that such individual holds or desires."[45] In contrast, Section 504 of the Rehabilitation Act refers to persons who are *otherwise qualified.* Read literally, this would mean that a person is protected against discrimination if, but for that person's disability, he or she could perform the job. This is nonsensical, because *but for* a blind person's inability to see, he or she would otherwise qualify to be a copy reader, and therefore come within the protected class. The courts, thus, have read this as meaning *nonetheless* qualified[46] or qualified *in spite of* the disability.[47]

[A] Establishing "Qualification"

The burden of proving qualification is part of the plaintiff's proof of a prima facie case.[48]

---

40. 534 U.S. at 197–98.
41. 122 Stat. 3553, 3554.
42. 29 CFR § 1603.2(j)(1)(i).
43. 29 CFR § 1603.2(j)(1)(iii).
44. 29 CFR § 1603.2(j)(1)(vii).
45. 42 U.S.C. § 12111(8).
46. Ward v. Skinner, 943 F.2d 157, 161 (1st Cir. 1991).
47. Southeastern Cmty. Coll. v. Davis, 442 U.S. 397 (1979).
48. Dreschsel v. Liberty Mut. Ins. Co., 695 Fed. Appx. 793, 798 (5th Cir. 2017); Jarvela v. Crete Carrier Corp. 776 F.3d 822, 828 (11th Cir. 2015); Vandenbroek v. PSEG Power Ct LLC, 356 Fed. Appx. 457, 459 (2nd Cir. 2009). *But cf.* Doe v. N.Y. Univ., 666 F.2d 761 (2d Cir. 1981) (employer bears burden of producing evidence of lack of qualification, shifting a burden of persuasion onto the plaintiff to prove otherwise).

[B] The Meaning of "Essential Functions of the Job"

Determining the *essential* functions of any job is a fact specific inquiry, requiring an individual assessment in most cases. In making that assessment, the ADA requires the courts to *consider* the employer's judgment in that regard, and the EEOC guidelines expand that by stating that an employer will not be "second-guessed on production standards, setting the quality or quantity of work that must be performed by a person holding a job, or be required to set lower standards for the job."[49] In addition, the ADA expressly provides that a written description prepared before the employer advertised for or interviewed applicants for the job is evidence of the essential functions of the job. On the other hand, a job description that is prepared after the individual has developed a disability may itself be proof of discriminatory intent.[50]

The ADA regulations also identify other indicia of essentiality.[51] For example:

- Do employees actually perform the listed function?
- Would removing the function fundamentally alter the position? Specifically:
  - Is this the only function of the job?
  - Is it necessary that every employee in that job category perform that particular function?
  - Does performing the function require particular expertise or skill?
- The amount of time devoted to performing that function.
- The consequences of not requiring the individual to perform that particular function, such as where the health or safety of others would be at risk.
- The terms of a collective bargaining agreement.

Even if an individual has been successful in establishing, for workers' compensation or other statutory purposes, that a particular disability has rendered that person totally unable to perform the job, this does not necessarily bar an ADA claim. In *Cleveland v. Policy Management Systems Corp.*,[52] the Supreme Court held that the purposes of the two kinds of statutes are sufficiently different, so that claiming an inability to do the job in one context does not estop a person from claiming the ability to do it in another.

[C] The "Direct Threat" Limitation

By definition, it would seem that if a person's physical or mental impairment poses a direct threat to the health or safety of others, this person would not be *qualified* for the job. Indeed, Section 103(b) of the ADA expressly allows employers to make

49. 29 CFR Appendix to Part 1630, Section 1630.2(n).
50. Muller v. Hotsy Corp., 917 F. Supp. 1389 (N.D. Iowa 1996).
51. 29 C.F.R. § 1630.2(n).
52. 526 U.S. 795 (1999).

the absence of such a threat a job qualification.[53] This is a rather odd way to provide a limit on the *qualified* element in the definition of the protected class and it poses two questions. First, who has the burden of proving this direct threat? And what constitutes a direct threat?

The courts are split over the burden of proof issue. Since not being a direct threat is a part of the qualification proof, some courts make it part of the plaintiff's case.[54] On the other hand, since the authorization of safety standards appears in a section of the statute entitled "Defenses," some courts have held that once a plaintiff shows that a particular safety requirement tends to screen out the disabled, the employer's burden is to justify it under the direct threat standard.[55]

With respect to the direct threat itself, in *School Board of Nassau County v. Arline*,[56] the Supreme Court identified the relevant factors when the impairment consists of a contagious disease. Quoting from the *amicus* brief of the American Medical Association, the court said the inquiry should include:

> findings of fact, based on reasonable medical judgments given the state of medical knowledge, about (a) the nature of the risk (e.g., how the disease is transmitted), (b) the duration of the risk (how long is the carrier infectious), (c) the severity of the risk (what is the potential harm to third parties) and (d) the probabilities the disease will be transmitted and will cause varying degrees of harm.[57]

On the question of whether employees who are HIV-infected pose a direct threat, the courts have generally allowed a conservative approach, especially in the health care sector.[58] Finally, the Supreme Court has unanimously held that the ADA does not require an employer to hire a person with a disability if the job would endanger the person's health. In *Chevron, USA, Inc. v. Echazabal*,[59] the employer refused to hire an otherwise-qualified applicant with a serious liver condition whose illness would be aggravated by exposure to workplace chemicals. Reversing the Ninth Circuit Court of Appeals' decision that the employer violated the ADA, the Supreme Court upheld an EEOC regulation allowing an employer to assert a direct threat defense to dis-

---

53. 42 U.S.C. § 12113(b); *see also* 29 C.F.R. § 1630.2(r).

54. Osborne v. Baxter Healthcare Corp., 798 F.3d 1260, 1268 (10th Cir. 2015); Moses v. American Nonwovens, Inc., 97 F.3d 446 (11th Cir. 1996).

55. EEOC v. Wal-Mart Stores, Inc., 477 F.3d 561 (8th Cir. 2007); Rizzo v. Children's World Learning Ctrs., Inc., 173 F.3d 254 (5th Cir. 1999); *see also* Branham v. Snow, 392 F.3d 896, 906 n.5 (7th Cir. 2004) (identifying circuit split on burden of proof).

56. 480 U.S. 273 (1987).

57. *Arline*, 480 U.S. at 274.

58. *See, e.g.*, Waddell v. Valley Forge Dental Assoc., Inc., 276 F.3d 1275 (11th Cir. 2001) (HIV-positive dental hygienist posed direct threat), *cert. denied*, 535 U.S. 1096 (2002); Doe v. University of Md. Med. Sys. Corp., 50 F.3d 1261 (4th Cir. 1995) (HIV-positive surgical resident was not qualified to perform surgery due to the risk of infecting patients); *see also* EEOC v. Prevo's Family Mkt, 135 F.3d 1089 (6th Cir. 1998) (grocery clerk who claimed to be HIV-positive was properly terminated when he refused to undergo medical testing to document the condition).

59. 536 U.S. 73 (2002).

crimination even when the threat is posed only to the health or safety of the individual claiming discrimination.[60]

Pointing to the EEOC requirement that an employer make a "particularized inquiry into the harms the employee would probably face," the Court dismissed Echazabal's contention that the regulation smacked of workplace paternalism that the ADA was designed to outlaw. Rather, the Court cautioned, "[t]he direct threat defense must be 'based on a reasonable medical judgment that relies on the most current medical knowledge and/or the best available objective evidence,' and upon an expressly 'individualized assessment of the individual's present ability to safely perform the essential functions of the job,' reached after considering, among other things, the imminence of the risk and the severity of the harm portended."[61] In so stating, the Court emphasized the significant burden an employer confronts in utilizing this affirmative defense. Direct threat determinations based on assumptions or generalized fears will not be sufficient to prevail.[62]

[D] The Meaning of "Reasonable Accommodation"

A person with a disability who is unable to perform the essential functions of the job may still be a *qualified* individual if performance of those functions could be made possible by a *reasonable accommodation.* While *reasonable accommodation* is the final link in the definitional chain bringing one within the protected class, an employer's failure to make that accommodation is also a proscribed form of discrimination. An enormous amount of disability law is devoted to determining what constitutes a *reasonable accommodation*—which, if made, would render an individual *qualified* to perform the essential functions of the job, and which, if not made, would be an illegal form of *discrimination.* The topic will thus be discussed in the next chapter, on the meaning of ADA *discrimination.*

§ 31.05 Chapter Highlights

1. The Rehabilitation Act applies to "individuals with disabilities" in federal employment, "qualified individuals with disabilities" in federal contractor cases, and "otherwise qualified individual[s] with a disability" in federal fund recipient cases. The ADA identifies the class of individuals protected by the statute as "qualified individual[s] with a disability." Disability means a physical or mental impairment that substantially limits a major life activity, a record of such impairment, or being regarded as having such an impairment. The ADAAA changed the focus of the inquiry from whether an individual meets the definition of disability to whether discrimination occurred. (§ 31.01)

---

60. 29 C.F.R. § 1630.15(b)(2).

61. *Echazabal,* 536 U.S. at 93 (quoting 29 C.F.R. § 1630.2(r)).

62. *See, e.g.,* EEOC v. E.I. du Pont de Nemours & Co., 406 F. Supp. 2d 645 (E.D. La. 2005) (slightly increased, remote, or speculative risk is not sufficient to constitute direct threat).

2. Actual mental and physical impairments include almost anything that would, in normal discourse, be regarded as a handicap, illness, or disability. (§ 31.02[A] & [B])

3. The *record of impairment* category refers to a person who has had a qualifying impairment in the past, but who no longer does. A plaintiff, however, must establish that the condition qualified as an *impairment* at the time. (§ 31.02[C])

4. The *regarded as having an impairment* category includes persons who do not have a qualifying impairment but the employer thinks they do, and persons who have a qualifying impairment that the employer thinks is substantially limiting when it really is not. (§ 31.02[D])

5. The impairment in question, however, must also substantially limit a major life activity of the person possessing it. The term *major life activity* includes all activities that are of central importance to daily life and it includes major bodily functions. (§ 31.03[A])

6. In determining whether an impairment *substantially limits*, the courts must not consider any corrective measures that have been taken with respect to the impairment. (§ 31.03[B][1])

7. Substantially limits is not meant to be a demanding standard. Rather, it is to be construed broadly in favor of expansive coverage. (§ 31.03[B][2])

8. The burden of proving qualification is part of the plaintiff's proof of a prima facie case. (§ 31.04[A])

9. *Qualification* is defined in terms of being able to perform the essential functions of the job. What those functions consist of is determined by reference to a variety of factors, although it is essentially resolved on a case-by-case basis. (§ 31.04[B])

10. Integral to the qualification element is that the person with the impairment does not pose a risk to the health or safety of either that person or others. The courts are divided over who has the burden of proof in that regard. (§ 31.04[C])

Chapter 32

The Proscribed Forms of Discrimination and Other Prohibited Conduct[1]

Synopsis

Section 102(a) of the ADA broadly prohibits discrimination against a member of the protected class "because of the disability of such individual in regard to job application procedures, the hiring, advancement, or discharge of employees, employee compensation, job training, and other terms, conditions, and privileges of employment."[2]

The most obvious form of violation involves an employer who, without any statutory justification, simply refuses to hire, promote, reassign, or continue to employ an individual who has or develops a disability, or treats disabled persons unfavorably as a class. But the ADA also provides a definition of the term *discrimination* that takes it beyond that most obvious of forms.

---

1. We thank Leigh Nason, Shareholder, Ogletree, Deakins, Nash, Smoak & Stewart, PC, Columbia, SC, for an earlier version of this chapter.
2. 42 U.S.C. § 12112(a).

§ 32.01 Adverse Limitations, Segregation, or Classifications

Section 102(b)(1) includes within the meaning of *discrimination* "limiting, segregating, or classifying a job applicant or employee in a way that adversely affects the opportunities or status of such applicant or employee because of the disability of such applicant or employee."[3] The EEOC's ADA Interpretative Guidance provides several examples[4] of what this means:

- Limiting job duties in the perceived "best interests" of the employee.
- Assigning disabled employees to one particular office or facility that more easily accommodates their disability.
- Classifying persons with disabilities as being more prone to absenteeism.

The EEOC guidelines do not address the meaning of the qualifying phrase, "in a way that adversely affects the opportunities or status of such applicant or employee." At least one court construed this language to suggest that segregation is not a per se violation; one must also show adverse effects.[5]

§ 32.02 Illegal Contractual Arrangements

Section 102(b)(2) prohibits all contractual arrangements that have the effect of subjecting persons to the discrimination that is otherwise prohibited by the Act: "an employer or other covered entity may not do through a contractual or other relationship what it is prohibited from doing directly."[6] The statute provides specific examples of *who* the other contracting party might be, including, "an employment or referral agency, labor union, an organization providing fringe benefits to an employee of the covered entity, or an organization providing training and apprenticeship programs."[7]

There is an enormous amount of uncertainty about what this provision means. Clearly, an express agreement with an employment agency requiring that the agency not refer any disabled applicants would render the contracting employer liable. Whether the employer would be vicariously liable for the unknown, and un-contracted for, discrimination of the referral agency is doubtful.[8]

---

3. 42 U.S.C. § 12112(b)(1).
4. 29 C.F.R. § 1630.5.
5. Hill v. Branch Banking & Trust Co, 264 F. Supp. 3d 1247, 1260 (N.D. Ala. 2017).
6. 42 U.S.C. § 12112(b)(2).
7. 42 U.S.C. § 12112(b)(2).
8. In two cases in which liability was found, the courts focused on the fact that the employer did have knowledge of the discrimination. Holiday v. City of Chattanooga, 206 F.3d 637 (6th Cir. 2000); EEOC v. Texas Bus Lines, 923 F. Supp. 965, 973 (S.D. Tex. 1996).

At the very least, the EEOC guidelines suggest that an employer has an affirmative duty to insure that services provided by a subcontractor be rendered on a nondiscriminatory basis.[9] It gives the example of an employer who uses a subcontractor to provide employment-related training at a remote location. The employer has a duty to insure that disabled employees can be accommodated. But it is not clear whether, despite the employer's best efforts, the employer is vicariously liable for every act of discrimination committed by a subcontractor, such as a referral agency. The guidelines suggest that if the effect occurs, then the employer's lack of intent is irrelevant; however, no court has yet construed the provision in that fashion.

§ 32.03 Discriminatory Tests, Standards, and Selection Criteria

Section 102(b)(3) includes within the definition of *discrimination* "utilizing standards, criteria, or method of administration—(A) that have the effect of discrimination on the basis of disability; or (B) that perpetuate the discrimination of others who are subject to common administrative control."[10]

This provision interestingly suggests that Congress may have recognized the difference between disparate impact discrimination and conduct that merely perpetuates prior discrimination. The Supreme Court has rejected the perpetuation theory under Title VII, on the grounds that most of these claims are time-barred.[11] It remains to be seen whether the Court will reach the same statute of limitations conclusion under the ADA, in face of this express authorization for this type of claim.

Section 102(b)(3) overlaps to some extent with Section 102(b)(6), which includes within the definition of discrimination the use of standards, tests, or other selection criteria "that screen out or tend to screen out an individual with a disability or a class of individuals with disabilities unless the standard, test or other selection criteria ... is shown to be job-related for the position in question and is consistent with business necessity."[12] Section 103 adds the further requirement that the "performance cannot be accomplished by reasonable accommodation."[13] A number of courts have construed these sections of the ADA to incorporate the Title VII disparate impact discrimination approach, including the *Griggs/Wards Cove* analysis.[14]

9. 29 C.F.R. § 1630.6.
10. 42 U.S.C. § 12112(b)(3).
11. Ledbetter v. Goodyear Tire & Rubber, 550 U.S. 618 (2007). *See* § 16.04[A].
12. *See* 42 U.S.C. § 12112(b)(3), (6).
13. *See* 42 U.S.C. § 12113.
14. B.C. v. Mount Vernon School District, 838 F.3d 152, 158 (2d Cir. 2016); Anderson v. Duncan, 20 F.Supp. 3d 42, 54–55 (D.C. 2103) (application of Griggs/Wards Cove).

In an early case arising under the Rehabilitation Act,[15] *Alexander v. Choate*,[16] the State of Tennessee reduced the number of inpatient hospital care days covered by its Medicaid program from 20 to 14. Plaintiffs sued alleging that the change had a disparate impact on handicapped persons. Specifically, they showed that 27.4% of handicapped hospital users required more than 14 days of care, while only 7.8% of non-handicapped hospital users required the same. The Court held that section 504 was not limited to instances of intentional discrimination, but there was also "reason to question whether Congress intended section 504 to embrace all claims of disparate-impact discrimination."[17] Holding that section 504 reaches some, but not all, actions having a disparate impact on the handicapped, the Court further held that the disparate impact in this case was not actionable because the law provided "meaningful access" to the benefit in question.

Section 102(b)(7) also casts a unique spin on disparate impact theory in the disability context, by legislating a particular form of non-impact alternative or accommodation. Basically, it imposes a duty on an employer to select and administer tests in a manner that most effectively measures the applicant's knowledge or abilities, rather than reflect the applicant's impaired sensory, manual, or speaking skills.[18] For example, an employer may be required to provide a reader or tape recorded version of the test for a visually impaired applicant.[19] Still, an applicant must give the employer advance notice of the need for an accommodation.[20]

§ 32.04 Relationship or Association with a Disabled Person

Section 102(b)(4) makes it illegal to discriminate against anyone because of that person's association or relationship with an individual with a known disability.[21] Hence, an employer may not refuse to hire an applicant that has a spouse or child with a disability on the supposition that the applicant would miss work frequently to care for the disabled person. Of course, if that turns out to be true, then the employer may later terminate the person for cause. The duty of reasonable accommodation does not apply, pertaining only to applicants or employees with disabilities.[22]

15. 29 U.S.C. § 794.
16. 469 U.S. 287 (1985).
17. *Alexander*, 469 U.S. at 299.
18. 42 U.S.C. § 12112(b)(7).
19. Fink v. New York City Dep't of Personnel, 53 F.3d 565 (2d Cir. 1995).
20. Morisky v. Broward County, 80 F.3d 445, 448–49 (11th Cir. 1996).
21. 42 U.S.C. § 12112(b)(4).
22. *See, e.g.*, Overley v. Covenant Transport, Inc., 2006 U.S. App. LEXIS 10618 (6th Cir. 2006) (unpublished opinion) (truck driver fired after telling employer she could not drive on certain days due to obligations to disabled daughter was entitled to no accommodation).

However, if it appears that the employer is holding the employee to higher attendance standards due to the disability of a relative, the employer may be liable.[23]

§ 32.05 Failure to Make Reasonable Accommodation

As noted earlier, the concept of reasonable accommodation factors into the analysis twice. First, a person may be regarded as qualified to perform the essential functions of the job if this can be accomplished through a reasonable accommodation. Second, under section 102(b)(5), failing to make "reasonable accommodations to the known physical or mental limitations of an otherwise qualified individual with a disability" is itself a proscribed form of discrimination, unless the employer "can demonstrate that the accommodation would impose an undue hardship on the operation of the business...." In addition, an employer cannot refuse to hire the person on the grounds that doing so would require it to make an accommodation.

Although the grammatical and logical structure of the statute suggest that *reasonable accommodation* and *undue hardship* are distinct concepts, *undue hardship* becomes relevant only after an accommodation has been found to be *reasonable*, and as such, courts tend to treat them as two sides of the same coin. In most cases, if an accommodation would create an *undue hardship*, it is by definition not *reasonable*.[24] On the other hand, in *Vande Zande v. Wisconsin Dep't of Admin.*,[25] the court treated the *cost* factor as having one meaning under the *reasonableness* prong, and another meaning under the *undue hardship* prong. The cost of the requested accommodation was less than $150, which certainly would not have imposed an undue hardship on the state. But the court held that even this cost was not proportionate to the benefit and found that the requested accommodation was thus not *reasonable*.

Unlike the Rehabilitation Act, the ADA provides some specific examples of what might constitute a *reasonable accommodation* and also identifies relevant criteria for determining an *undue hardship*.

There are two categories of reasonable accommodation:[26]

1. Accommodations that ensure equal access to the application process.
2. Accommodations that enable employees with disabilities to perform the essential functions of a job.

---

23. Kelleher v. Fred A. Cook, Inc., 939 F.3d 465 (2d Cir. 2019).

24. This is in contrast to the Title VII analytical model for religious accommodation/undue hardship, which treats them as distinct issues. *See* Chapter 11, § 11.04[B].

25. 44 F.3d 538 (7th Cir. 1995).

26. *See* 42 U.S.C. § 12111(9).

Under section 101(9), examples of *reasonable accommodations* may include the following:

- Altering facilities to make them more accessible and usable;[27]
- Part-time or modified work schedules;[28]
- Job restructuring or altering non-essential duties;[29]
- Reassignment to a vacant position;[30]
- Acquisition or modification of equipment or devices;[31]
- Adjustments or modifications of examinations, training materials, or policies;[32]
- Providing qualified readers or interpreters;[33] and
- Work at home or teleworking.[34]

Although those may be reasonable in a general or abstract sense, the analysis must also take into account whether the action will require significant difficulty or expense in the specific employment context. In assessing this *undue hardship* com-

---

27. Trotter v. B & S Aircraft Parts & Accessories, Inc., 5 AD Cases 1584 (D. Kan. 1996) (suggesting that an employer might be required to provide a higher work table to accommodate employee's bending restrictions).

28. Pattison v. Meijer, Inc., 897 F. Supp. 1002 (W.D. Mich. 1995) (putting employee on a part-time, flexible schedule that enabled him to use public transportation when his seizure disorder preventing him from driving). *But see* Lamb v. Qualex, Inc., 33 Fed. Appx. 49 (4th Cir. 2002) (when employer has no part-time positions available, request for part-time employment is not reasonable).

29. Note that an employer is not required to eliminate or reallocate essential job functions. Dropinski v. Douglas County, 298 F.3d 704 (8th Cir. 2002); Frazier v. Simmons, 254 F.3d 1247 (10th Cir. 2001); Mathews v. Denver Post, 263 F.3d 1164 (8th Cir. 2001); *see also* Hoffman v. Caterpillar, Inc., 256 F.3d 568 (7th Cir. 2001) (employer not required to train employee missing lower left arm on high speed scanner when operation of high speed scanner was not an essential function of her position).

30. In a 5–4 opinion, the Supreme Court has found that reassignment in contravention of an established seniority policy is ordinarily not required. US Airways v. Barnett, 535 U.S. 391 (2002); *see also* Burchett v. Target Corp., 340 F.3d 510 (8th Cir. 2003) (reassignment is an accommodation of last resort).

31. Wernick v. F.R.B., 91 F.3d 379 (2d Cir. 1996) (providing ergonomic furniture for employee with a back problem).

32. *Compare* Christou v. Hyatt Regency-O'Hare, 996 F. Supp. 811, 815–16 (N.D. Ill. 1998) (implying that employer may be required to accommodate a sight disability by enlarging the size of the print or having documents read to the disabled employee); Fernbach v. Dominick's Finer Foods, 936 F. Supp. 467, 473 (N.D. Ill. 1996) (suggesting that employer might be required to specifically explain employment rules to mentally disabled employees), *with* Aquinas v. Federal Express Corp., 940 F. Supp. 73 (S.D.N.Y. 1996) (employer not required to modify attendance or leave policies to accommodate a disability that caused sporadic attendance).

33. Nelson v. Thornburgh, 567 F. Supp. 369 (E.D. Pa. 1983). *But see* Henry v. Unified Sch. Dist., 328 F. Supp. 2d. 1130, 1158 (D. Kan. 2004) (finding that hiring a full-time new employee to aid disabled employees was not a reasonable accommodation).

34. *See* EEOC Fact Sheet, *Work at Home/Telework as a Reasonable Accommodation* (December 20, 2017). *But see* Mason v. Avaya Comms. Inc., 357 F.3d 1114 (10th Cir. 2004); Rauen v. United States Tobacco Mfg., 319 F.3d 891 (7th Cir. 2003) (work at home may not be reasonable accommodation; issue is highly fact-specific).

ponent, the courts are required to consider the factors listed in section 101(10), as follows:

- The nature and cost of the accommodation, which (unlike the religious accommodation duty under Title VII) must be more than de minimus.[35]
- With respect to the facility directly involved in the accommodation:
    - Its overall financial resources;
    - The number of persons employed;
    - The effect the accommodation will have on the operation, expenses, and resources of that facility; and
    - Its geographic separateness and administrative or fiscal relationship to the covered entity.
- With respect to the covered entity itself:
    - Its overall financial resources;
    - The number of persons employed;
    - The number, type, and location of its facilities;
    - The type of operations it performs, including the composition, structure, and functions of the workforce;
    - The nature and net cost of the accommodation needed; and
    - The impact of the accommodation upon the operation of the site, including the impact on the other employees.[36]

In sum, determining whether a particular accommodation is reasonable or imposes an undue hardship is a very fact-specific inquiry, and the law in this area does not lend itself to easy generalization. Ideally, satisfying this statutory duty involves a cooperative process between the employee and the employer. The first step in that process usually begins with the employee's notification to the employer that the employee suffers from a disability, followed by a request that the disability be accommodated.[37] Second, the employer is entitled to have the existence of that disability verified. Third, the parties should pinpoint what barriers the disability imposes on the employee's ability to do the job. Fourth, the parties should identify the various possible forms of accommodation. Fifth, the parties should assess the reasonableness and hardship aspects of each alternative. And finally, the employer must select the accommodation

---

35. H.R. Rep. No. 485, pt. 2, at 68 (rejecting, for ADA purposes, the test of undue hardship adopted by the Supreme Court in Trans World Airlines v. Hardison, 432 U.S. 63 (1977).

36. 42 U.S.C. § 12111(10)(B); 29 C.F.R. § 1630.2(p)(2).

37. It is the employee's burden to request reasonable accommodation. Jones v. United Parcel Serv., 214 F.3d 402 (3d Cir. 2000); Seaman v. CSPH, Inc., 179 F.3d 297 (5th Cir. 1999); Gaston v. Bellingrath Gardens & Homes, Inc., 167 F.3d 1361 (11th Cir. 1999).

to be pursued, if any. Although an employer is not required to accept the accommodation requested by the employee, the legislative history states that the "expressed choice of the applicant or employee shall be given primary consideration."[38]

§ 32.06 Discriminatory Benefit Plans

Many life and health insurance plans facially discriminate on the basis of disability. However, section 501(c) broadly exempts from the prohibitions of the Act any "bona fide benefit plan that [is] based on underwriting risks, classifying risks, or administering such risks that are based on or not inconsistent with State law," provided the plan is not being used as a "subterfuge to evade the purposes" of the Act.[39] This is an enormously complex area of the law—several other statutes also impact the legality of these plans—and its discussion is substantially beyond the scope of this book.

§ 32.07 Medical Examinations and Inquiries

Several statutory provisions address medical examinations and inquiries, serving as a source of considerable confusion and frustration to employers.

First, section 102(d)(2)(A) prohibits an employer from conducting a medical examination or making inquiries of a job applicant "as to whether such applicant is an individual with a disability or as to the nature or severity of such disability."[40] Thus, pre-offer of employment medical examinations are prohibited.

Under section 102(d)(3), however, an employer may require post-offer, pre-employment medical examinations and make actual employment contingent on the results, provided these tests are required of everyone applying for the job.[41] The employer must also record this medical information on separate forms, in separate medical files, and treat it as confidential. The employer has the right to withdraw the offer of employment based on the results of the medical examination and the answers to the disability-related questions. Nevertheless, the employer must show that any examination result or answer, which serves as the basis for withdrawing the offer of employment, is job related and consistent with business necessity.[42]

38. S. Rep. No. 116, at 35; H.R. Rep. No. 485, pt 2, at 67.
39. 42 U.S.C. § 12201(c)(2).
40. 42 U.S.C. § 12112(d)(2)(A).
41. 42 U.S.C. § 12112(d)(3).
42. 42 U.S.C. § 12112(b)(6); 29 C.F.R. § 1630.10.

Third, under section 102(d)(2)(B) an employer may also "make preemployment inquiries into the ability of an applicant to perform job-related functions."[43] The line between an inquiry about a disability and an inquiry about an applicant's ability to perform the job is by no means clear, although the EEOC has issued guidelines on the matter.

Fourth, an employer cannot require a medical examination or make disability-related inquires of existing employees "unless such examination or inquiry is shown to be job-related and consistent with business necessity."[44]

§ 32.08 Retaliation

Section 503 prohibits discrimination against anyone who opposes practices the ADA makes illegal or who participates in enforcement procedures.[45] Going beyond Title VII and other standard provisions prohibiting retaliation against members of the protected class, the ADA also makes it illegal to coerce, intimidate, threaten, or interfere with *any* individual on account of his or her having aided or encouraged any other individual in the exercise of ADA rights.[46] This was apparently directed at providing protection to disability advocacy groups.

§ 32.09 Chapter Highlights

1. Unlike Title VII, in which Congress more or less left the definition of *discrimination* up to the courts, the ADA identifies the specific types of conduct that it intended to prohibit as follows:

- Limiting, segregating, or classifying a disabled person in a disadvantageous way. (§ 32.01)
- Entering into contracts that have the effect of subjecting a disabled person to discrimination. (§ 32.02)
- Using discriminatory tests, standards, and selection criteria. (§ 32.03)
- Disadvantaging a person because of that person's association with a disabled person. (§ 32.04)
- Failing to make reasonable accommodations, unless making them would cause undue hardship. (§ 32.05)

43. 42 U.S.C. § 12112(d)(2)(B).
44. 42 U.S.C. § 12112(d)(4)(A).
45. 42 U.S.C. § 12203(a).
46. 42 U.S.C. § 12203(b).

2. The ADA exempts bona fide benefit plans, even if they do discriminate against disabled persons, provided they are based on legitimate cost considerations and are not a subterfuge to evade the purposes of the Act. (§ 32.06)

3. Mandatory pre-employment offer medical examinations are illegal. Mandatory post-employment offer medical examinations, which make actual employment contingent on the results, are legal if they required of everyone. An employer may not make pre-employment offer inquiries with respect to whether an individual is disabled, but an employer may make pre-employment offer inquiries about the individual's ability to do the job. An employer cannot require a medical examination or make disability-related inquiries of existing employees unless the inquiry is job-related and consistent with business necessity. (§ 32.07)

4. The ADA prohibits retaliation against persons who oppose illegal practices or participate in enforcement procedures. It also prohibits retaliation against third parties who assist disabled person in the exercise of ADA rights. (§ 32.08)

Chapter 33

Proof and Defenses[1]

Synopsis

The ADA and the Rehabilitation Act are similar in purpose; therefore, the patterns of proof and defenses are much the same. There is one difference, however, that may end up being significant. The Rehabilitation Act requires a plaintiff to prove that handicapped status was the *sole* reason for the employment decision, while the ADA Amendments Act of 2008 (ADAAA) prohibits discrimination *on the basis of* a disability. While the legislative history of the ADA suggests that Congress generally intended for the courts to follow the patterns of proof previously established under the Rehabilitation Act, the ADAAA signaled that Congress wanted the focus to be on compliance and not whether the individual is disabled.[2] This difference is discussed in more detail below.

§ 33.01 Individual Disparate Treatment

The plaintiff in an ADA case must prove: (1) disability; (2) ability to perform the essential functions of the job with or without reasonable accommodation; and (3) that the disability was the cause of the adverse employment action by the employer.[3] Proof of disability requires proof of a physical or mental impairment that substantially limits one or more major life activities, a record of such impairment, or being regarded as having an impairment.[4]

---

1. We thank Leigh Nason, Shareholder, Ogletree, Deakins, Nash, Smoak & Stewart, PC, Columbia, South Carolina, for an earlier version of this chapter.
2. 122 Stat. 3553, 3554 (2008).
3. Richardson v. Chi. Transit Auth., 926 F.3d 881, 886 (7th Cir. 2019).
4. 42 U.S.C. § 12102(1).

In *Lewis v. Humboldt Acquisition Corp.*,[5] the Sixth Circuit determined that the ADA plaintiff must prove that disability was the *but for* cause of the adverse action. While this is similar to the "sole reason" proof under the Rehabilitation Act, it is much different than the *motivating factor* proof used under Title VII.[6] In *Silk v. Board of Trustees*,[7] the Seventh Circuit noted that the ADAAA amended the *because of* a disability language and replaced it with language prohibiting discrimination *on the basis of* a disability.[8] *Silk* did not decide whether this new language resolved the conflict with the required proof under Title VII or was simply another way to require *but for* proof. That issue remains unresolved in the Seventh Circuit;[9] however, the Second and Fourth Circuits have decided that the new ADAAA language still requires *but for* proof.[10]

Perhaps this issue remains unresolved because in a large number of cases the employer readily admits making an employment decision based on the plaintiff's mental or physical condition. The issues and proof in these cases, therefore, revolve around whether the condition is an *impairment* that *substantially limits a major life activity*[11] and whether the individual is *qualified*, with or without a *reasonable accommodation*.[12]

Although the employee clearly bears the burden of proving that he or she has a *substantially limiting impairment*[13] and is *qualified*,[14] the courts are split over who has the burden of proof in a case where the employee's alleged disability poses a direct threat to others.[15]

The burden of proving a *reasonable accommodation* is complicated by the fact that this phrase is used in two interconnected ways in the ADA. First, reasonable accommodation is part of the definition of an *otherwise qualified individual*. An employee will be found to be *qualified* for a job if a reasonable accommodation allows the employee to perform the essential functions of the job. Second, employers are required to attempt a reasonable accommodation when requested. If an employer fails to provide a reasonable accommodation, it has discriminated against the employee unless the employer can show the accommodation would create an undue hardship.[16]

---

5. 681 F.3d 312, 318 (6th Cir. 2012).
6. *See* Chapter 5, § 5.03[B].
7. 795 F.3d 698, 705–06 (7th Cir. 2015).
8. 42 U.S.C. § 12112(a).
9. This is also true for the Eighth Circuit. Oehmke v. Medtronic, Inc., 844 F.3d 748, 757 n.6 (8th Cir. 2016).
10. Natofsky v. City of New York, 921 F.3d 337, 348 (2d Cir. 2019); Gentry v. E.W. Partners Club Mgmt. Co., 816 F.3d 228, 235–36 (4th Cir. 2016).
11. 42 U.S.C. § 12102(2).
12. 42 U.S.C. § 12111(8).
13. Tesone v. Empire Mktg. Strategies, 942 F.3d 979, 997 (10th Cir. 2019).
14. Lewis v. City of Union City, 934 F.3d 1169, 1179 (11th Cir. 2019).
15. *See* Chapter 31, § 31.04[C].
16. Boyle v. City of Pell City, 866 F.3d 1280, 1289 (11th Cir. 2017.)

In *Gilbert v. Frank*,[17] the court held that since *reasonable accommodation* is a component of the *otherwise qualified* element on which the plaintiff generally has the burden of proof, the plaintiff must at least "present evidence as to her or his individual capabilities and suggestions for some reasonable assistance or job modification by the employer."[18] Once the plaintiff has done that, "the burden shifts to the employer to show that no reasonable accommodation is possible."[19] The employer carries the burden of proving that the accommodation would create an undue hardship.[20] This shift of the burden of proof is consistent with many other civil rights claims.[21]

Another form of admitted discrimination involves blanket policies or prohibitions against hiring any person with a particular type of disability. An employer might determine, for example, that being sighted is an absolute requirement for the job and that no blind persons will be hired into that position, or that being an insulin-dependent diabetic automatically disqualifies one from operating a commercial motor vehicle. Although the legality of these policies has arisen under both the employment and the non-employment Titles of the ADA,[22] the analysis seems to be relatively the same—focusing on both the validity of the generalization and the possibility of making individualized assessments, similar to the BFOQ analysis under Title VII.[23]

§ 33.02 Indirect Proof

The methods of proving individual disparate treatment are essentially the same under the ADA as under Title VII. This includes where direct evidence is lacking, using some version of the *McDonnell Douglas* prima facie case approach to the allocation of proof in an individual disparate treatment case. One court described the approach as follows:

> [T]he plaintiff has the ultimate burden of proving by a fair preponderance of the evidence that the defendant discriminated against him on the basis of an impermissible factor. [H]e may establish a prima facie case by proving that he applied for a position for which he was qualified and was rejected *under circumstances indicating discrimination on the basis of an impermissible factor.* The burden then shifts to the defendant to rebut the presumption of discrimination by coming forward with evidence that the plaintiff was rejected

---

17. 949 F.2d 637 (2d Cir. 1991).

18. *Gilbert*, 949 F.2d at 642. *Accord*, *Boyle*, 866 F.3d. at 1289.

19. *Gilbert*, 949 F.2d at 642.

20. US Airways, Inc. v. Barnett, 535 U.S. 391, 402 (2002).

21. Snapp v. United Transp. Union, 889 F.3d 1088, 1101 (9th Cir. 2018).

22. Daugherty v. City of El Paso, 56 F.3d 695 (5th Cir. 1995) (upholding a blanket prohibition against insulin-dependent diabetics from driving city buses); Galloway v. Superior Court of the District of Columbia, 816 F. Supp. 12 (D.D.C. 1993) (striking down a blanket prohibition against the use of blind jurors).

23. The Ninth Circuit Court of Appeals has recently found that the ADA does not provide a BFOQ defense. Bates v. UPS, 511 F.3d 974, 996 (9th Cir. 2007).

for a legitimate reason, whereupon the plaintiff must prove that the reason was not true but a pretext for impermissible discrimination.[24]

The italicized language is, of course, the wild card in the analysis; those *circumstances* will inevitably vary from case to case. The Supreme Court's decision on how pretext can be proved in a Title VII case will also be applied in the disability discrimination context.[25]

Federal employees complaining about an adverse action based on age have a different proof standard. The Supreme Court, in *Babb v. Wilkie*,[26] determined that federal employees need only prove that any part of the adverse action was based on age. An employee recovering on the lesser standard of proof is, however, likely to face a limitation on the remedies available.

Both the courts and the EEOC have found that after-acquired evidence merely limits the remedy, as under Title VII, and does not bar the plaintiff from all relief.[27]

§ 33.03 Systemic Disparate Treatment

Although there seems to be no theoretical reason for disallowing a plaintiff to establish systemic discrimination against an entire class of disabled persons using *Teamsters*-type Title VII statistics, the practical problems of proof would seem to be enormous. Given the highly individualized nature of disability and reasonable accommodation, it would probably be impossible to create classes of sufficient numbers to make any comparison statistically significant.

§ 33.04 Disparate Impact

In Raytheon Co. v. Hernandez,[28] the Supreme Court recognized that disparate impact claims can be brought under the ADA. The statute prohibits the use of "qualification standards, employment tests or other selection criteria that screen out" the disabled.[29] To prove a prima facie case the plaintiff must: (1) identify the challenged employment practice or policy; (2) demonstrate that the practice or policy has an adverse impact on the plaintiff; and (3) demonstrate a causal relationship between the identified practice and the disparate impact.[30]

---

24. Norcross v. Sneed, 755 F.2d 113, 117 (8th Cir. 1985) (emphasis added); Flaherty v. Entergy Nuclear Operations, Inc., 946 F.3d 41 (1st Cir. 2019) (detailing the burden-shifting framework in an ADA disparate treatment case).

25. Winarto v. Toshiba Am. Elecs. Components, Inc., 274 F.3d 1276 (9th Cir. 2001); Hooven-Lewis v. Caldera, 249 F.3d 259 (4th Cir. 2001); Shaner v. Synthes (USA), 204 F.3d 494 (3d Cir. 2000).

26. 140 S. Ct. 1168, 1174 (2020).

27. *See, e.g.*, Rooney v. Koch Air, LLC, 410 F.3d 376 (7th Cir. 2005); EEOC *Guidance on After-Acquired Evidence*, Notice No. 915.002.

28. 540 U.S. 44 (2003).

29. 42 U.S.C. § 12112(b)(6).

30. Williams v. ABM Parking Servs., 296 F. Supp. 3d 779, 789 (E.D. Va. 2017).

§ 33.05 Chapter Highlights

1. The ADA and the Rehabilitation Act use essentially the same forms of proof and defenses. These also mirror Title VII law in some, but not all, respects.

2. When purported disability discrimination is admitted or apparent on the face of a company policy, the issues are whether it is a *disability* in the statutory sense and whether the plaintiff falls within the protected class. (§ 33.01)

3. Individual disparate treatment claims may be proved by either *direct* or *inferential* evidence, in a manner similar to those used under Title VII. (§ 33.02)

4. Systemic disparate treatment claims are more a theoretical than actual form of disability proof. (§ 33.03)

5. Disparate impact discrimination is a recognized cause of action under the ADA. (§ 33.04)

About the Authors

Thomas R. Haggard is a Distinguished Professor of Law, Emeritus, at the University of South Carolina School Law. A 1967 Honors graduate of the University of Texas School of Law, he practiced two years as an Associate with Covington & Burling in Washington, D.C. From 1969–74 he taught at the Rutgers-Camden School of Law and then moved to the University of South Carolina School of Law. At USC, he held the David W. Robinson Chair, served briefly as Associate Dean for Academic Affairs, and was the interim Director of Legal Writing for two years. He taught labor and employment law, legal writing/drafting, contracts, constitutional law, and a few other courses. He is the author of 35 articles and 12 books. Professor Haggard retired in 2002 and has since spent his time gardening, doing photography, playing correspondence chess, working on his model railroad layout, reading all manner of interesting books, enjoying his family, and working with his Church.

Bruce N. Cameron is the Reed Larson Professor of Labor Law at Regent University School of Law where he teaches labor law, employment discrimination, and administers the right to work practicum. He recently finished a five-year term as a Member of the Virginia Advisory Committee to the U.S. Commission on Civil Rights. He graduated from Emory University School of Law, where he interned with the U.S. Department of Justice, United States Attorney's Office his during his third year. After graduating, he spent 44 years as a litigator with the National Right to Work Legal Defense and Education Foundation where he focused on religious liberty and compelled speech cases. He is the author of numerous articles and monographs on religion, law, and the intersection between the two. His hobbies are promoting the understanding of the Bible, high-performance cars, and fast sailboats.

Our two contributors, Tracey Green and Leigh Nason, continue to be happy and prosperous in their practice of law.

Table of Cases

Index

[References are to pages.]